New Earth Politics

Earth System Governance

Frank Biermann and Oran R. Young, series editors

Related Books from Institutional Dimensions of Global Environmental Change: A Core Research Project of the International Human Dimensions Programme on Global Environmental Change

New Earth Politics

Essays from the Anthropocene

Edited by Simon Nicholson and Sikina Jinnah

The MIT Press
Cambridge, Massachusetts
London, England

This book was set in Stone Sans and Stone Serif by Toppan Best-set Premedia Limited. Printed and bound in the United States of America.

Library of Congress Cataloging-in-Publication Data

Names: Nicholson, Simon (Simon James), editor. | Jinnah, Sikina, 1977– editor.
Title: New earth politics : essays from the Anthropocene / Simon Nicholson and Sikina Jinnah, editors.
Description: Cambridge, MA : The MIT Press, 2016. | Series: Earth system governance | Includes bibliographical references and index.
Identifiers: LCCN 2015038403 | ISBN 9780262034364 (hardcover : alk. paper)
Subjects: LCSH: Environmentalism—Political aspects. | Environmentalism—Social aspects. | Human ecology—Political aspects. | Human ecology—Social aspects. | Environmental protection—Political aspects. | Environmental protection—Social aspects.
Classification: LCC GE195 .N478 2016 | DDC 363.7—dc23 LC record available at http://lccn.loc.gov/2015038403

10 9 8 7 6 5 4 3 2 1

For our boys: Liam, Lyosha, Julien, Zia, and Ash.

For you shall inherit the New Earth.

Contents

Epilogue

Series Foreword

Humans now influence all biological and physical systems of the planet. Almost no species, land area, or part of the oceans has remained unaffected by the expansion of the human species. Recent scientific findings suggest that the entire earth system now operates outside the normal state exhibited over at least the past 500,000 years. Yet at the same time, it is apparent that the institutions, organizations, and mechanisms by which humans govern their relationship with the natural environment and global biogeochemical systems are utterly insufficient—and poorly understood. More fundamental and applied research is needed.

Such research is no easy undertaking. It must span the entire globe because only integrated global solutions can ensure a sustainable coevolution of biophysical and socioeconomic systems. But it must also draw on local experiences and insights. Research on earth system governance must be about places in all their diversity, yet seek to integrate place-based research within a global understanding of the myriad human interactions with the earth system. Eventually, the task is to develop integrated systems of governance, from the local to the global level, that ensure the sustainable development of the coupled socioecological system that the Earth has become.

The series Earth System Governance is designed to address this research challenge. Books in this series will pursue this challenge from a variety of disciplinary perspectives, at different levels of governance, and with a range of methods. Yet all will further one common aim: analyzing current systems of earth system governance with a view to increased understanding and possible improvements and reform. Books in this series will be of interest to the academic community but will also inform practitioners and at times contribute to policy debates.

This series is related to the long-term international research program "Earth System Governance Project."

Frank Biermann, *Utrecht University*
Oran R. Young, *Bren School, University of California, Santa Barbara*
Earth System Governance Series Editors

Acknowledgments

This book was a joy to write and edit. Not only does it reinforce our conviction that a better world is possible for our children (and yours), but it was a joyous project because we had the great pleasure to work with so many wonderful people along the way.

This book would not have come to be without the intellectual inspiration of our mentor, colleague, and friend Paul Wapner. Thank you, Paul, for helping us conceptualize this project and see it to fruition. Kate Goodwin Reese was also instrumental in organizing the International Studies Association (ISA) workshop where we began testing these ideas with our colleagues. We are heartily grateful for her sweat, the workshop participants' ideas, and ISA's funding in this regard.

Thanks are due, as always, to our colleagues in American University's Global Environmental Politics program, especially Ken Conca and Judith (Judy) Shapiro, who are also contributors to this book. We are so very lucky to have such a wonderfully supportive and engaging community within which to explore New Earth politics.

We owe deep gratitude to our editors at MIT Press: Clay Morgan for seeing the spark, Beth Clevenger for fanning the flames, and Miranda Martin for keeping the fire burning. Thank you also to the Earth System Governance editors, Frank Biermann and Oran Young, for including us in their series, and to all of the *New Earth Politics* contributors for their extraordinary work (and quick revisions!). Three anonymous reviewers provided helpful feedback, and we benefited immeasurably from the support of our research assistants: Kat Diersen, Sharad Ghimire, Abby Lindsay, Elizabeth Moore, and Carolyn Turkaly. We should also note here that we presented several of the draft chapters at the 2014 Annual Meeting of the International Studies Association in Toronto, Canada.

Finally, we take great pleasure in recognizing our families. We offer our heartfelt thanks for their support, insight, and affection. Special recognition is due to our spouses, Anne-Claire Hervy and Doug Bushey. We don't (and could never) thank you enough for all that you do to support us on this journey.

Introduction

Living on a New Earth

Simon Nicholson and Sikina Jinnah

Today the Earth's population exceeds 7 billion people. An ever-increasing number of us are plugged into globalized technologies, patterns of consumption, and systems of commerce such that the ecological foundations of the planet are being pressured like never before. The collective impact of our species is vast. One need only point to climate change, widespread environmental toxification, the destruction of global biodiversity, and a host of other ills to appreciate that humanity is stretching the world to and beyond ecological limits. Humanity is, through the production of widespread environmental harm, in the act of producing what author Bill McKibben has called a new "Eaarth"—an Earth 2.0 on which the human signature is everywhere and in desperate need of humane and insightful guidance.[1]

This book assembles prominent scholars and practitioners in the field of global environmental politics to consider the ecological and political realities of life on the *New Earth*. We asked contributors to give particular thought to the relationship between traditional scholarly activities and the practical work of generating social and political change. The resulting chapters range from meditations on the social and political drivers of environmental harm to musings on the state of environmental pedagogy, from analysis of the links between the environment and geopolitics to cutting-edge thinking about the future of environmental social movements, and from insights on the struggle to build more appropriate international environmental institutions to examinations of the imperative to craft more compelling narratives in the service of global environmental action.

The result is a book designed for students, scholars, and citizens concerned with the productive role that an engaged academy can play in the face of environmental decline. Individual chapters offer a review and interrogation of the most important themes in the study of global environmental politics. Each can be read as a distinct contribution to our collective understanding of the worsening environmental condition and the development of effective forms of analysis and response.

The book is much more, though, than a collection of stand-alone essays. At the heart of the project is an exercise in collective stock taking and a hard-headed assessment of the field of global environmental politics—of its worth and promise—by some of its most respected figures. The authors assembled here were asked to consider what our individual and collective scholarly work ultimately means in the face of rapid and large-scale environmental decline. Are we, as a community of students and scholars, doing the right things in the right ways? Is the field keeping pace with the environmental, social, political, and economic challenges presented by a rapidly changing world? Are we collectively up to the challenges presented by a New Earth?

These are hardly straightforward questions. They can, in fact, be downright uncomfortable notions with which to wrestle. The chapter authors are all motivated by a desire to improve the state of the global environment. Their efforts have been highly valued, as evidenced by numerous book awards; countless academic and popular publications; millions of dollars in grant money; service on government committees, delegations, and expert groups; and many other signifiers of scholarly and intellectual achievement and contribution. Yet the question remains and demands a response: Are we making the best and most important use of our individual and combined energies, given the great tragedy of a worsening environmental condition?

The book is rooted in the belief that the challenges associated with living on a New Earth are immediate, pressing, and unprecedented. So too must be humanity's collective response. Tackling environmental decline requires concentrated scholarly effort and engagement based on a clear understanding of the stakes, the state of knowledge, and the questions that are as of yet unanswered and even unasked. As the global environmental condition shows increasing signs of stress and as the forces driving environmental change become ever more deeply entrenched, it is incumbent on students and scholars of global environmental politics to continually question the nature of our shared enterprise. A business-as-usual mentality is no longer viable. This is as true of scholarly efforts to comprehend, analyze, and craft responses to environmental challenges as it is of the work of the policymakers, business executives, and citizens who so often are the targets of the field's analytic efforts.

The Physical and Political Features of the New Earth

Around the dawn of the new millennium, biologist Eugene F. Stoermer and Nobel laureate chemist Paul Crutzen coined a distinctive term to describe a rapidly changing earth. The term was *Anthropocene*, and it has caught on as an expression of a geologic and climatic epoch characterized by human dominance of the Earth's major processes.[2]

As with all prior geologic epochs, the Anthropocene has its markers. If future generations of archaeologists and geologists ever care to look back on the present moment from some distant time, they will discover indications of the activities of industrial age humans etched indelibly into the planetary record. Our creations of copper and plastics will have found their way into layers of rock; the post–Industrial Revolution explosion in the production of carbon dioxide and other greenhouse gases will be visible in tree rings and ice cores; the mass extinction of species driven by our collective activities will be evident in the fossilized remains of creatures vanished from the land and seas.[3]

The Anthropocene is also a marker of a changed social condition. Recently Clive Hamilton, François Gemenne, and Christophe Bonneuil suggested that what they call the "Anthropocene thesis" rests on two powerful claims that have radical implications for established worldviews, and hence for work in the social sciences and humanities. First, to accept the arrival of the Anthropocene is to claim that "humans have become a telluric force"—that is, a force of nature, with extraordinary power to alter the functioning of earth systems. Second, the onset of the Anthropocene heralds a coming period of "global environmental shifts of an unprecedented scale and speed."[4] Many questions follow from these claims, among them: What does the Anthropocene mean for our individual and collective lives, livelihoods, and politics? Is the planet to become more fully the product of human intervention and engineering? Are our institutions sufficient to the challenges ahead? What are the prospects for human lives of worth and meaning?

A robust body of writing has recently emerged that begins to consider such questions and the myriad social scientific, cultural, historical, and political aspects of the Anthropocene. In the specific realm of global environmental politics, a notable intervention is Frank Biermann's 2014 book positing "earth system" governance as a new paradigm for planet-wide environmental political activity.[5] Other books grappling with the governance implications of the Anthropocene or with the need for evolution in the field of global environmental politics have recently been released or are forthcoming, authored or edited by an international group of scholars, including Simon Dalby, Carl Death, Victor Galaz, Philipp Pattberg and Fariborz Zelli, and others.[6] This book is in conversation with these other works as we invite the global environmental politics community to pause for careful and deep reflection on the nature and meaning of effective work at a time of planetary upheaval.

Our intention in introducing the "New Earth" metaphor as an organizing tool for this book was to provide our contributors the freedom to connect their prior work to the emerging Anthropocene literature and explore the changing nature of global environmental politics without being tethered to the terminological debates that currently characterize Anthropocene studies. Throughout the book, readers will encounter concepts like "planetary stewardship," "emergent planetary Earth-centered civilization," "overarching narrative frames," "ecospace," and many others. We are all struggling for an appropriate language to help us analyze the changing human and environmental condition. The New Earth frame is not meant in any way to supersede or challenge the analytical power of the Anthropocene concept, but rather to complement it and provide additional space for a new analytical language to emerge.

One thing is clear: the shadow cast by the Anthropocene has the potential to be long and dark. What does it mean, though, right now, to live on a human-dominated New Earth? To speak of a New Earth is at once to situate the current period in the 4.5-billion-year-long span of planetary history and also to denote a set of human-induced changes taking place on the planet today. There is mounting evidence that human activities are remaking the planet in profound and sometimes deeply troubling ways. Recent research on what have been called planetary boundaries, for instance, suggests that human activities now threaten the integrity of some of the Earth's most basic ecological functions.[7] A key indicator of the New Earth, this is to say, is extreme and growing levels of human-caused environmental stress. With this in mind, section 1 of this book begins with essays by Ken Conca (chapter 1) and the author team of Daniel Deudney and Elizabeth Mendenhall (chapter 2), who look at the social and political drivers that are producing the New Earth, before our authors move, in the remainder of the book, to consider the most important aspects of humanity's collective response.

Among a litany of contemporary global environmental harms that characterize the New Earth, three, in our view, are particularly egregious. First, let us consider *biodiversity loss*. The planet is now, say a growing chorus of biologists, either on the cusp or already in the throes of a sixth great extinction event, such that the Earth's great web of life is being unraveled at an extraordinary and accelerating pace.[8] At five prior points in the planet's history, upward of 70 percent of species then alive were rendered extinct in a short (by geologic standards) window of time by some cataclysmic event. The last and, to scientists and the public at large, best known of these extinction events happened some 66 million years ago at the end of the Cretaceous period. This was the geologic moment that marked the end of the dinosaurs.

The best evidence available today suggests that a gigantic asteroid hitting the earth was to blame for the Cretaceous-Paleogene extinction. Now, though, as life is being extinguished at rates that rival prior great extinction events, there is no outside agent to blame. We are the asteroid. Humanity has become the force determining each species' chances for survival and flourishing.

In the years ahead, well-established trends are likely to force an acceleration of life's diminishment. Some estimates suggest that upward of 50 percent of the Earth's species will be rendered extinct by the end of this century.[9] The trends are anthropogenic in nature—that is, human caused. Human communities have overfished oceans and river systems, hunted particular land species until few or none remain, wiped out or repurposed essential habitat, spread invasive and nonnative species across the planet, and toxified environments to the extent that particular species are sickened or rendered unable to reproduce, all to the detriment of the diversity of life. Welcome to the Anthropocene.

The significant and varied damage caused by the *proliferation of human-made chemicals* and other toxic substances is a second form of human-induced change that warrants its own special attention. Since World War II, an increasing array of never-before-seen chemicals have found their way into widespread use. Certain of these chemicals have come to be known as persistent organic pollutants (POPs), for their tendency to bioaccumulate in food chains, posing risks to human health and environmental well-being.[10] The spread of such chemicals is dramatic. If one were to travel to the Arctic region and tranquilize a polar bear that had never before encountered human beings, chances are high that damaging levels of POPs would be found in the animal's blood and fat.[11] Similarly, mercury from coal-fired power plants far removed in geographic (but not, clearly, in ecological) terms from the Arctic Circle has found its way through oceanic food chains into the breast milk of some Inuit mothers, adding a level of toxicity to this most precious of foods.[12]

To be sure, POPs are also put to many worthy industrial uses, including, most notably, food production. Yet hazardous chemicals are disruptive of environmental processes and damaging to human health, with the worst effects of global chemical production, trade, and disposal felt indelibly by those with the least political power and voice.[13] Environmental toxification, in this respect, points to one of the defining elements of the New Earth: the manifold benefits that come from technological innovation and economic wealth are paired with devastating environmental and social consequences, with risks and rewards unequally distributed.

A third, and arguably the most pressing, environmental challenge on the New Earth is *climate change*. The basic contours of the climate change challenge are well known and the basic science well understood. A number of human activities, including the burning of fossil fuels and changes to land use patterns, are increasing the concentrations of so-called greenhouse gases in the atmosphere. The most important of these gases is carbon dioxide (CO_2). As concentrations of CO_2 and other greenhouse gases have risen, so too has the atmosphere's ability to hold the sun's heat. Global average surface temperatures have already, due to this layer of heat-trapping gases, risen some 0.85°C over preindustrial averages. This seems, on its face, like a small figure. However, looking back over the planet's long history, scientists have learned that small changes in average temperatures can correspond to massive changes in rainfall patterns, storm activity, sea levels, and even the kinds of species that can make a life on Earth.[14]

Climate scientists work in the realm of probabilities. They tell us that that some of the potential impacts associated with a warming world may be relatively benign from a human standpoint. Others may be merely troubling, while still others could be catastrophic. Further, climate change exacerbates a host of other environmental challenges, including the two discussed above. Climate change is a critical driver of biodiversity loss as, for example, warming and acidifying oceans kill off coral reefs and fisheries, and as changing climatic conditions alter the ranges of land-based plants and animals. Similarly, shifting rainfall patterns in agricultural areas increase dependency on chemicals to sustain agricultural production in increasingly harsh environments. Climate change therefore is such an important expression and consequence of the Anthropocene that it is a recurring subject across this book, and all of section 7 of the book is devoted exclusively to climate and energy politics.

Biodiversity loss, environmental toxification, and climate change are but three signifiers of a world under siege. Others abound. We might just as well have pointed as markers of the New Earth to global freshwater pollution and overuse, acidification of the world's oceans, and massive challenges associated with feeding a human population set to rise to 9 billion or more by midcentury, among many others. It takes little effort on the New Earth to produce a laundry list of local, transboundary, and global environmental harms.

The New Earth, then, is defined by a critical set of environmental changes. At the heart of these changes is a fundamental shift in humanity's role on the planet. Geographers Erle Ellis and Navin Ramankutty have suggested that the dawn of the Anthropocene is best understood as signifying a complex alteration in humanity's relationship to the other-than-human world. For as long as there have been people, there has been human-induced environmental harm. Now, though, our species has moved beyond activities that merely disturb and disrupt ecosystems to the wholesale production of "human systems with natural ecosystems embedded within them."[15] The New Earth is a world in the throes of massive and violent transformation, with humanity, unsteadily, at the helm.

The Challenges Facing Students and Scholars

What roles exist for scholarly communities and communities of practice in the face of the New Earth's environmental challenges? This book brings together scholars working particularly within the field of global environmental politics to take on this fundamental question. It bears noting that the field of global environmental politics is relatively new. It has emerged in just the last few decades to investigate the large-scale social processes that give rise to environmental change and to examine the character of effective forms of response. Said differently, global environmental politics is a still nascent field concerned, at its core, with unpacking and considering the social production of sustainability and unsustainability.[16]

To suggest that global environmental politics is a young field is not to ignore important precursors. Environmental awareness and concern have a long and global history.[17] So, too, have scholarly attempts to understand human-environment interactions. That said, the study of global environmental politics has emerged out of a recent recognition, with its clearest origins in the late 1960s and early 1970s, that the environmental challenges of the emerging New Earth are of a kind, scope, and severity never before seen.

The study of global environmental politics has been innovative and boundary crossing since its inception. This makes sense, given that the subject matter of global environmental politics spans all aspects of the biological, physical, and social sciences. The field is also an evolving one. As with other areas of academic endeavor, there have been waxing and waning trends, and some early preoccupations have gradually been set aside in favor of new lines of investigation.[18] At the same time, there are certain strands of scholarly investigation that have shaped the field of global environmental politics since its inception and that remain crucially important today. Notably, for instance, the study of institutions and regimes, as well as civil society, as mechanisms of international cooperation and social action have been strong points of focus in the field, hence our dedication of two sections of the book to these topics.

Remember, though, that the book is more than simply a review of some loosely connected strands of academic inquiry. Instead, the book should be read as a sustained interrogation of the very purpose of global environmental politics scholarship in an age in which the rate and scale of human-driven environmental destruction is quickly outstripping our political and social capacities for managing environmental challenges. The truth is that while working on environmental questions is enlivening and intellectually stimulating, it can also be desperately bleak. As Donella Meadows famously articulated, the work sometimes feels a little like rearranging deck chairs on the *Titanic*.[19] That said, this book's animating questions, it should be clear, do not come from a place of ambivalence or cynicism about the worth of the academic enterprise. Rather, they are questions that stem from a deep desire to ensure that collective scholarly efforts have real value in the face of the most pressing issues of our time.

Two major themes course through the book and appear to a greater or lesser extent in all of its chapters. The first theme has to do with the split between academic research in the ivory tower and the practical work of taking political action and instigating political and social change. To play out Meadows's *Titanic* analogy a little further, one of the challenges academics routinely face is that much of the audience that would benefit the most from scholarly efforts seems out of the earshot of the work that we produce—as though the students and professors who spend their time examining global environmental politics are standing on the foredecks while the real action is taking place on the bridge. Much academic work speaks about the activities of those in positions of real power, about the various actors who have their hands on the metaphoric steering wheel and other accoutrements of authority rather than to those actors in ways that prompt change.

A related question has to do with engagement by scholars of global environmental politics with the public at large. Here, the *Titanic* analogy starts to break down. The major, chronic environmental challenges we face, at least in the rich, privileged regions of the world, are not at all like a sinking ship. There is no great crash, no sudden tilting of the deck, no immediate engulfment by icy water associated with the bulk of environmental decline. Consider climate change. It is a diffuse set of effects that derive from a set of invisible gases being emitted into an invisible atmosphere, with the worst current impacts being felt by the world's poorest and most politically disenfranchised populations, and with the worst likely impacts still to be felt in the distant future. Former Vice President Al Gore, in his book *Earth in the Balance*, described the environmental situation as akin to a slow-motion nuclear war.[20] How, if Gore's is a fair representation of environmental decline, can scholarship reach a public largely inured against anything but the dramatic and the immediate?

We asked the book's authors to consider whether it is enough, given the mounting severity of the global environmental situation, to continue to work in academic publications and classroom exchanges to illuminate the contours of current challenges and, perhaps, the opportunities that exist for appropriate response. Or, in the face of an ever more desperate environmental situation, are other forms of action required?

Some of the chapter authors demonstrate the great value still to be found in the traditional academic enterprises of developing and propagating new insights about social and political life, creating theoretical hooks on which to hang analysis and rationales for social action, and formulating new visions for a better world. Joyeeta Gupta (chapter 11), for instance, introduces and unpacks the concept of ecospace to offer a new view of how resource and other scarcities will shape future geopolitics; Paul Wapner (chapter 15) looks at environmentalism as a counternarrative, opposed to, and perennially in the shadow of, the dominant social order; and Kate O'Neill (chapter 7) offers a fresh account of the successes and shortcomings of global environmental institutions and explains how they must adapt (fast!) to better engage New Earth problems.

Such work builds from the idea that on the New Earth, established ways of being and thinking must be critically examined, and perhaps reimagined and recast. Even the most comfortable of ideas require constant interrogation. Elsewhere in the book, various chapter authors articulate critical positions in relation to, for example, forms of social mobilization (Peter Jacques, chapter 9, and Erik Assadourian, chapter 10, in particular), dominant institutions (Navroz Dubash, chapter 13, and Ken Conca, chapter 1, among others), and central concepts like sustainability (Peter Dauvergne, chapter 16). The implications of critical social theorizing for the work of students and scholars of global environmental politics are summarized well by Peter Dauvergne, who argues that "those in the academy have a duty to expose the lies and tricks of business and politics." These and other chapters make the implicit case that scholars of New Earth politics must look deeply to understand how the world is put together, how environmental harm comes to be, and what makes for effective response. One role for scholarship, it follows, is to provide those working more directly for social change with the knowledge and tools required for their efforts.

Other chapter authors, by contrast, argue for different, more direct forms of engagement by the scholarly community. Maria Ivanova (chapter 8) calls for a transformation of academia, based in part on a rethinking of the relationships between academic work and the people and institutions they study. Richard Falk (chapter 4) goes further, making the case that academics spend too much time bowing to what he calls "horizons of feasibility" rather than reaching for "horizons of necessity." Falk calls for radical criticism and engagement in direct political action by the academic community. Oran Young (chapter 3) takes a different tack, noting that the divide we, the editors, draw between the academic endeavor and engaged practice is too stark. His personal account of life on what he calls the "policy/science interface" provides still another pathway to a merging of analysis and praxis.

A second connective strand that courses through the book concerns the maintenance of hope in the face of environmental harm. Aldo Leopold once wrote:

One of the penalties of an ecological education is that one lives alone in a world of wounds. ... An ecologist must either harden his shell and make believe that the consequences of science are none of his business, or he must be the doctor who sees the marks of death in a community that believes itself well and does not want to be told otherwise.[21]

Thankfully, those of us working in the field of global environmental politics are not engaged in a solo endeavor. The field is marked by strong collegiality, such that the "world of wounds" we inhabit is a shared one. Still, it can be hard to keep up one's energy when surrounded by what Leopold described as the "marks of death"—the great environmental harms that characterize life on the New Earth.

Hope is a necessary but transitory commodity. Environmental scholar David Orr has remarked that those who consider the environmental situation and remain optimistic don't know enough.[22] Producing and disseminating crucial information about the state of the planet and about the social, economic, political, and cultural forces driving environmental harm are critically important activities to puncture a blind optimism. Orr has gone on to suggest, though, that pessimism is equally ineffectual. There can be no retreat into cynicism or indifference. Where, then, lies an effectual belief in the possibilities for a better future?

Collectively, the chapters that follow provide important clues as to where this better future might be found. As Karen Litfin (chapter 5) and Michael Maniates (chapter 6) explain in their paired chapters on this topic, this is nowhere more evident than in the classroom, where professors struggle to encourage hope among students (and vice versa), while simultaneously teaching them about the world of wounds they have inherited. Several other contributors echo these calls for hope in other ways. Wil Burns and Simon Nicholson (chapter 14), for example, argue that despite imperfections, established institutions hold some promise for governing radical technological interventions designed to respond to climate change. Navroz Dubash (chapter 13) similarly rejects fatalism in the face of New Earth challenges and sees reframing narratives surrounding energy transformation as a pathway for crafting solutions to previously intractable debates on this issue, while Judith Shapiro (chapter 12) imagines a time when China becomes "a champion of norms of justice and sustainability." Hope seeps from the pages of this book.

On the New Earth, hope is certainly a much-needed commodity. James Gustave Speth once noted that nothing particularly dramatic need occur to bring about environmental ruin. All that is required is that we—humanity—continue on our present path.[23] That may be too bleak a forecast. A doomsday scenario is not guaranteed on the New Earth, of course. Perhaps the scientific community has been too pessimistic in its reading of environmental stress. Perhaps some set of technological innovations rests just over the horizon that will pull the world back from the brink. Or perhaps a sharper focus on effective, legitimate, and socially just governance responses, paired with a healthy dose of luck, will pave the way to a future in which humanity can thrive. Whatever awaits, students and scholars of global environmental politics will have a critical hand to play in bringing about the world to come. This book helps to chart that path.

Plan of the Book and a Guide for Readers

The book has eight sections, each representing an important foundational challenge or focus of scholarly enterprise in the field of global environmental politics. The section topics were selected because they reflect a sustained central focus of scholarly attention (i.e., institutions, civil society, climate change), help us understand global environmental politics in the broader landscape of international politics (i.e., geopolitics), and help chart a course forward more broadly in research and teaching on the New Earth (i.e., pedagogies of hope, narrative frames, and scholarship as engagement). We could not, of course, cover all topics that deserve attention here, and so have invited Frank Biermann to reflect on some important additional directions for scholarly enterprise in his concluding chapter.

One of the distinguishing features of the book is that in each section, we invited two different authors occupying differing intellectual positions to prepare paired chapters. Importantly, the goal for each section has not been for one author to write a lead essay with the other author offering a response. Rather, authors were encouraged to coordinate and collaborate during the planning and writing of their chapters, but to then produce essays that offer their unique takes on the questions under examination. Our aim, using this format, has been for the chapters to showcase some of the productive tensions as well as the points of constructive overlap that exist within contemporary global environmental politics scholarship, and to help readers see multiple ways into the field's most important conversations.

The authors were also invited to write in a conversational style, drawing as much from their personal experience as from a lengthy list of citations. The goal was to free the authors to write truly fresh, focused essays that speak to the truth of the academic challenge on the New Earth. As a result, you will see that many of the chapters are as much a biographical account as they are a more traditional academic interrogation.

One way to read the book is, obviously, from front to back. The organizational map that follows will serve as a guide to those who tackle the entire book. Other readers will dip into the sections that cover subjects of specific interest to them. In those cases, we encourage readers to look at entire sections rather than individual essays. This is because each section of the book has been constructed so that chapters are in explicit conversation with one another. There is much to be learned from the distinct ways in which different authors have approached similar subject matters. We trust that this feature of the book will help spark deep reflection and debate among those interested in the future of global environmental politics on a New Earth.

Each section opens with a short statement from us, the coeditors, elaborating a set of specific questions that we posed to section authors in advance of their chapter writing and providing context for the authors' statements.

Section 1 offers two chapters, by Ken Conca (chapter 1) and by Daniel Deudney and Elizabeth Mendenhall (chapter 2), that explore the causes of environmental harm. We begin with causes to set the stage for the book. These chapters present explanations for the emergence of the New Earth and help us to imagine a path forward. We then, in sections 2 and 3, respectively, turn to the central traditional pursuits of our field: scholarship and teaching. The pair of chapters by Oran Young (chapter 3) and Richard Falk (chapter 4) provides reflection on the demands of New Earth scholarship and the relationship between scholarly enterprise and political engagement. On the latter, chapter 5 by Karen Litfin and chapter 6 by Michael Maniates reflect on the challenge of New Earth environmental education, in particular the struggles and rewards that accompany developing mindfulness, compassion, and hopefulness.

Sections 4 and 5 turn the focus to political responses to New Earth challenges through the lens of institutions and social movements, which have both long been central foci of global environmental politics scholarship. In section 4, Kate O'Neill (chapter 7) and Maria Ivanova (chapter 8) explain how institutions have successfully addressed environmental problems in the past yet need reform to maintain relevance on the New Earth. Peter Jacques and Erik Assadourian pick up this discussion in, respectively, chapters 9 and 10, each asking if the energies of environmental activists and those who study them are being properly directed.

Sections 6 and 7 turn to two of the most pressing empirical challenges of New Earth politics: a rapidly shifting geopolitics and climate change. Against the backdrop of a fast industrializing global South, Joyeeta Gupta (chapter 11) and Judith Shapiro (chapter 12) reflect on how we can all live together on a resource constrained planet. In section 7, Navroz Dubash (chapter 13), alongside Wil Burns and Simon Nicholson (chapter 14), sharply examine humanity's response to the most pressing and profound expression of the New Earth: climate change.

Finally, in section 8, Paul Wapner (chapter 15) and Peter Dauvergne (chapter 16) build on Dubash's discussion of the power of narrative shifts in energy transformation to reflect on how narrative frames—the worldviews and broadly shared understandings—can both produce environmental harm and prompt effective response.

Frank Biermann concludes the book with a discussion of where the field of global environmental politics *is* and *ought* to be going, based on his reading of the preceding chapters. In keeping with the rest of the book, this concluding chapter points to important new lines of inquiry and offers ideas about more effective forms of scholarly engagement as we collectively continue to chart our way on a changing planet.

Notes

1. McKibben, *Eaarth*. The additional "a" in McKibben's rendering of "Eaarth" is used to signify that although the planet today looks at first glance much the same as it always has, human activities have so changed the ecological condition that in fact the Earth's most basic features and functions have been radically transformed.

2. Crutzen and Stoermer, "The 'Anthropocene,'" 17–18; Biermann, "The Anthropocene: A Governance Perspective."

3. Kolbert, "Enter the Anthropocene."

4. Hamilton, Bonneuil, and Gemenne, "Thinking the Anthropocene," 3–5.

5. Biermann, *Earth System Governance*.

6. Death, ed., *Critical Environmental Politics*; Galaz, *Global Environmental Governance, Technology and Politics*; Pattberg and Zelli, eds., *Environmental Politics and Governance in the Anthropocene*.

7. Rockström et al., "Planetary Boundaries."

8. Dirzo et al., "Defaunation in the Anthropocene,"; Kolbert, *The Sixth Extinction*.

9. Meyer, *The End of the Wild*.

10. Stockholm Convention on Persistent Organic Pollutants.

11. See, for instance, Tenenbaum, "POPs in Polar Bears."

12. Williams, "Toxic Breast Milk?"

13. Shapiro, "Equity and Information."

14. Intergovernmental Panel on Climate Change, "Climate Change 2013."

15. Quoted in Crutzen and Schwägerl, "Living in the Anthropocene."

16. Paterson, *Understanding Global Environmental Politics*, 15.

17. See, for instance, Guha, *Environmentalism*.

18. See, for a useful account of trends through time in the study of global environmental politics, Dauvergne, "Research Trends in Global Environmental Politics."

19. Meadows, "Leverage Points," 6.

20. Gore, *Earth in the Balance*, 206.

21. Aldo Leopold, *Round River*, 165.

22. Quoted in Nicholas, "The New Abnormal?"

23. Speth, *The Bridge at the End of the World*, x.

Bibliography

Biermann, Frank. "The Anthropocene: A Governance Perspective." *Anthropocene Review* 1, no. 1 (2014): 57–61.

Biermann, Frank. *Earth System Governance: World Politics in the Anthropocene.* Cambridge, MA: MIT Press, 2014.

Crutzen, Paul, and Christian Schwägerl. "Living in the Anthropocene: Toward a New Global Ethos." *Yale e360*, January 24, 2011. http://e360.yale.edu/feature/living_in_the_anthropocene_toward_a_new_global_ethos/2363/.

Crutzen, Paul, and Eugene Stoermer. "The 'Anthropocene.'" *International Geosphere-Biosphere Program Newsletter*, no. 41 (May 2000), http://www.igbp.net/download/18 .316f18321323470177580001401/NL41.pdf.

Dalby, Simon. *Security and Environmental Change*. Cambridge: Polity Press, 2009.

Dauvergne, Peter. "Research Trends in Global Environmental Politics." In *Handbook of Global Environmental Politics*, 2nd ed., edited by Peter Dauvergne, 3–25. Cheltenham: Elgar, 2012.

Death, C., ed. *Critical Environmental Politics*. New York: Routledge, 2013.

Dirzo, Rodolfo, "Defaunation in the Anthropocene." *Science* 345 (2014): 401–406.

Galaz, Victor. *Global Environmental Governance, Technology and Politics: The Anthropocene Gap*. Cheltenham: Elgar, 2014.

Gore, Al. *Earth in the Balance*. Boston: Houghton Mifflin, 1992.

Guha, Ramchandra. *Environmentalism: A Global History*. Oxford: Oxford University Press, 2000.

Hamilton, Clive, Christophe Bonneuil, and François Gemenne. "Thinking the Anthropocene." In *The Anthropocene and the Global Environmental Crisis*, ed. Clive Hamilton, François Gemenne, and Christophe Bonneuil. 1–14. New York: Routledge, 2015.

Intergovernmental Panel on Climate Change. *Climate Change 2013: The Physical Science Basis Contribution of Working Group I to the Fifth Assessment Report of the Intergovernmental Panel on Climate Change*. Cambridge: Cambridge University Press, 2013.

Kolbert, Elizabeth. "Enter the Anthropocene: Age of Man." *National Geographic* (March 2011), http://ngm.nationalgeographic.com/2011/03/age-of-man/kolbert-text.

Kolbert, Elizabeth. *The Sixth Extinction: An Unnatural History*. New York: Holt, 2014.

Leopold, Aldo. *Round River*. Oxford: Oxford University Press, 1953.

McKibben, Bill. *Eaarth: Making a Life on a Tough New Planet*. New York: Times Books, 2010.

Meadows, Donella. "Leverage Points: Places to Intervene in a System." Sustainability Institute, 1999, http://www.donellameadows.org/wp-content/userfiles/Leverage _Points.pdf

Meyer, John. *The End of the Wild*. Cambridge, MA: MIT Press, 1993.

Nicholas, Elizabeth. "The New Abnormal? Adaptation, Optimism, and Why We Can't Wait." *Aspen Idea Blog*, June 23, 2012, http://www.aspeninstitute.org/about/ blog/new-abnormal-adaptation-optimism-why-we-can-t-wait.

Paterson, Matthew. *Understanding Global Environmental Politics: Domination, Accumulation and Resistance*. Basingstoke: Macmillan, 2000.

Pattberg, P., and F. Zelli, eds. *Environmental Politics and Governance in the Anthropocene: Institutions and Legitimacy in a Complex World*. New York: Routledge, 2016.

Rockström, Johan, "Planetary Boundaries: Exploring the Safe Operating Space for Humanity." *Ecology and Society* 14, no. 2 (2009): 32.

Shapiro, Marc. "Equity and Information: Information Regulation, Environmental Justice, and Risks from Toxic Chemicals." *Journal of Policy Analysis and Management* 24 (2005): 373–98.

Speth, James Gustave. *The Bridge at the End of the World: Capitalism, the Environment, and Crossing from Crisis to Sustainability*. New Haven, CT: Yale University Press, 2009.

"Stockholm Convention on Persistent Organic Pollutants," Treaty Series 22, May 22, 2005.

Tenenbaum, John. "POPs in Polar Bears: Organochlorines Affect Bone Density." *Environmental Health Perspectives* 112, no. 17 (2004): A1011.

Williams, Florence. "Toxic Breast Milk?" *New York Times Magazine*, January 9, 2005.

Section 1   *Causes of the New Earth*

In the introductory chapter, we, the coeditors, characterized environmental challenges on the New Earth. We explained that today's environmental problems, such as climate change, biodiversity loss, challenges associated with food production, and chemicals management, are vastly different in scope and scale from those faced by previous generations. The two chapters in this section use those insights as a point of departure to explore how the world landed in this historical moment and how the contemporary narratives surrounding these problems themselves further characterize life and politics on the New Earth.

Note that one of the distinctive features of this book is the arrangement of the individual sections. Each section features a pair of essays, written in direct conversation with one another. The authors were given a set of framing questions (which are listed at the end of each section introduction) and were encouraged to converse and share drafts throughout the writing process. As a result, you will find two standalone and distinct perspectives in each of the book's sections, but also interplay and direct discussion around points of commonality and contention. The book is designed with the hope that readers will engage both essays in each section.

Ken Conca, in chapter 1, begins by asserting that assessments of environmental challenges on the New Earth based on simplistic growth-related trajectories are incomplete. He argues that an identifiable suite of political, economic, social, and technological conditions have enabled the explosive growth in population, per capita consumption, and destructive technologies that many analysts of the environmental condition point to as drivers of environmental harm. These underlying conditions, he argues, must also be understood if humanity hopes to better appreciate and grapple with the changing character of New Earth politics.

Conca identifies three key "inflection points" that help us better understand these beyond-growth explanations of environmental degradation. First, he suggests, it is not just the fact of economic growth that needs attention, but the complications and structural changes that have arisen from the pairing of economic growth with globalization. Most notably, Conca argues that these "complications of economic globalization" present profound challenges to the regulation of environmental problems at the domestic and local levels. Second, although the 1980s heralded the beginning of a twenty-year era of vigorous international environmental cooperation, Conca highlights that the world has largely failed to construct a robust architecture of international environmental law. This policy window, he laments, has been narrowed, if not forced closed entirely, by, among other things, the complications of economic globalization, making it increasingly difficult to sustain environmental cooperation of a robust character. Finally, Conca contends that there is a decline in movement toward sustainable communities and lifestyles, with more clear evidence of movements toward modes of social organization characterized by overconsumption or economic and ecological marginalization.

Daniel Deudney and Elizabeth Mendenhall in chapter 2 follow Conca's reflections on the causes of environmental harm by pivoting to an optimistic narrative that casts the nature of politics on a New Earth in a different light. They point out that the New Earth is characterized not only by more severe environmental conditions but also by a vibrant body of environmentally informed theory and practice. So far reaching is this environmentalism in terms of scale (individual to global) and scope (mundane to cosmic) that it constitutes, they argue, an emerging "civilization."

With climate change at the fulcrum and serving as a crystallizing agent, Deudney and Mendenhall argue that this "green civilization" weaves together elements of science, religion, economy, community, technology, and more to set guidelines for the future of life and politics on the New Earth. Noting that the Earth has been "remade" by this emergent civilization, they caution that our existing human practices and institutions have yet to adjust to life on the New Earth. Furthermore, a full transition to a green civilization, they argue, will occur only if this rising civilizational form proves superior in addressing the new field of problems, such as climate change, that afflict the planet.

Framing Questions Posed to the Authors in Section 1

- How do you characterize the current environmental condition? What are the most pressing environmental challenges facing the New Earth? Are they different from the challenges that sparked the contemporary environmental movement following World War II?
- What are the most important political, economic, and ideational drivers of environmental harm? Have these changed over time?
- What are the most important barriers to overcoming or ameliorating today's most pressing environmental challenges? How big are these barriers, and can they be overcome with our existing institutions, geopolitical arrangements, narrative frames, and emerging social movements?

1 The Changing Shape of Global Environmental Politics

Ken Conca

A simple way of characterizing the world's current environmental condition is to start with the explosive growth trends—in population, consumption, and environmentally harmful technologies—of the post–World War II era. In this view, there are simply too many people, chasing too many things, and using too many technologies that are inefficient, or toxic, or both. These trends are seen to strain against the carrying capacity of individual nations, entire regions, and, at least in the long run, the planet as a whole. The challenge implicit in this perspective follows directly. We must find a way to accommodate the needs and desires of some 9 billion to 12 billion people as efficiently as possible in order to minimize the damage to life-supporting systems and give nature a fair shot at coexistence with us.

This idea of a race between growth trajectories and our capacity to adapt is not particularly new. As Gandhi noted in 1928, "God forbid that India should ever take to industrialism after the manner of the West. ... If an entire nation of 300 million took to similar economic exploitation, it would strip the world bare like locusts." Secretary-General U Thant told the UN General Assembly in 1970, "As we watch the sun go down, evening after evening, through the smog across the poisoned waters of our native Earth, we must ask ourselves seriously whether we really wish some future universal historian on another planet to say about us: 'With all their genius and with all their skill, they ran out of foresight and air and food and water and ideas.'"[1]

Several broad trends over the past five or six decades offer some support for this broad-brush view. Worldwide, the annual production of light motor vehicles (cars and small trucks) has grown from fewer than 10 million in 1950 to more than 70 million today. During that same period, air travel has grown from a negligible amount to over 3 billion passenger flights annually. The world's mobile telephone matrix, which was nonexistent in the early postwar years, contains some 7 billion nodes, and there are perhaps 2 billion computers currently in use. Since World War II, the global production of meat has increased more than sixfold. As the UN Environment Programme put it in its most recent *Global Environmental Outlook* report, "The scale, spread, and rate of change of global drivers are without precedent. Burgeoning populations and growing economies are pushing environmental systems to destabilizing limits."[2]

Obviously these trajectories of growth cannot occur without an astounding level of human intervention in the background processes and cycles of natural systems. Human beings now liberate amounts of carbon and nitrogen that rival or exceed the natural background flows of these key nutrients. We trap and use perhaps half of the globally available water runoff.[3] As Simon Nicholson and Sikina Jinnah note in the introduction to this book, we live in an era that scientists call the "sixth extinction" for the scope and abruptness of the loss of biodiversity we are experiencing. And we are threatening to alter the planet's climate to a degree that could increase sea level by as much as 7 meters over the next millennium.[4] Such disruptive environmental change has profound consequences for people's lives. Some 2.4 million people die prematurely each year from air pollution.[5] An estimated one-third of the world's population extracts its livelihood from degraded land that has suffered a long-term loss of ecosystem functions and services.[6]

We ignore the blunt truths about planetary health and livability embedded in these global trajectories at our peril. Still, extrapolating from global trends can also cause us to miss important inflection points in what may seem inexorable patterns of growth. Deforestation from the clear-cutting of timber has decreased dramatically in the Amazon in the past decade. The global trend of increasing land conversion for agriculture has reversed, with the global area devoted to cropland flatlining over the past decade and the area dedicated to pastureland actually decreasing. Growth in water consumption has not followed the dire warnings of the 1970s and 1980s; overall demand has proven far more price elastic than was once thought possible (even as almost 1 billion people still lack clean water, and over 2 billion lack sanitation).[7]

More important, global growth trends also tell us little about the underlying structure of activity, and may mask important shifts in that structure. The eightfold increase in the world's fish catch since 1950 parallels the growth trends for cars, air travel, and meat consumption. Yet it also masks an important underlying shift: the growth of aquaculture has offset the flatlining trend in the volume of wild fish catches and now accounts for fully half of the world's annual seafood harvest.[8] Or consider atmospheric carbon. Emissions since 1990 have grown at a rate slightly outpacing population growth, invoking the familiar twin drivers of growing population and growing per capita consumption. Yet looking inside that aggregate trend, we see underlying it a striking structural transformation. As overseas investment and trade have grown, the emissions embedded in international trade have outpaced overall emissions growth, adding an increasingly transnational element to the carbon problem. Probing further still, we find the real story: there has been an extraordinary offshoring of carbon emissions during this period in the form of large net emissions transfers from developed country to developing country economies. Whether the growing transnationalism and North-to-South transfer bode well or ill for controlling carbon emissions, they probably doom to failure Kyoto-style diplomacy, with its quest to regulate carbon through national emission targets. Such diplomacy answers the question. "Whose carbon?" in far too simplistic and misleading a fashion for the contemporary world economy.

Three Inflection Points

To understand the changing character of the politics of a New Earth, then, we must look both beyond and beneath broad global trajectories. We must seek to identify inflection points in the underlying political, economic, social, and technological conditions that lay behind these macrotrends. I see three important forms of nonlinearity or discontinuity that seem likely to condition the environmental politics of the New Earth in important ways: the ongoing restructuring of the world economy in ways that profoundly complicate the traditional grand strategy of liberal-internationalist environmentalism; the closing of the window of political opportunity that was afforded by the end of the Cold War and the early onset of global economic and political restructuring in the 1980s and 1990s; and the continuing decline of what might loosely be termed the world's "environmental middle class."

Complications of Economic Globalization

I have argued elsewhere that since the late 1980s, the grand strategy of liberal-international environmentalism has been to promote two broad types of reform: better international environmental law between nations and better (read: "sustainable") development within them.[9] This strategy, which I refer to here as the law-and-development approach to global environmental governance, first coalesced in the 1980s around the Brundtland Commission's report, *Our Common Future* (1987), and the surprisingly successful treaty negotiations to protect the stratospheric ozone layer, which shields the Earth from damaging ultraviolet radiation. The strategy reached its apogee with the ambitious outputs of the 1992 Earth Summit, including international legal accords on climate change and biodiversity and the voluminous Agenda 21 blueprint for national policy reforms to promote sustainable development.

The law-and-development approach, however, has proven fundamentally problematic in a world marked by accelerating economic globalization. The proliferation of transnational investment, the growth and intensification of trade, and the emergence of a genuinely global communications and transportation infrastructure have created systems of production, exchange, and consumption that follow an increasingly global logic. The most obvious manifestations of this trend are the increasingly globalized commodity chains that snake across national borders in ways that confound regulatory strategies at the international or domestic level.

Although economic globalization is typically understood as simply an intensification of flows across borders, with a particular focus on trade and financial flows, this view confuses cause and effect. Rather, the intensification of transactions is a by-product of globalization, the essence of which lies in the construction of fundamentally global platforms of production and the parallel manufacturing of global consumer aspirations. The building of this world economic architecture dates to the exhaustion of postwar middle-class economic growth in the 1970s. Far from being a natural evolution toward some inevitable new stage of capitalism, it has been very much a product of policy changes: liberalized rules on capital investment, floating exchange rates among the world's major currencies, the exploitation of the debt crisis to leverage "structural adjustment" and neoliberal economic policy reforms in the economies of key developing countries, the rise of the World Trade Organization as the focal point for aggressive expansion of world trade, and the speedy embrace of thinly regulated market economies across virtually all of the formerly socialist world. The financial turmoil seen at the end of the first decade of the twenty-first century reflected the latent instability and managerial challenges of this system, but did not fundamentally derail it or significantly alter the legal, regulatory, and public policy frameworks that make it possible.

This new economic order differs fundamentally from the largely distinct national economies of an earlier era. Its environmental impacts may not be all bad: where natural resource inputs are a significant component of costs, shifting patterns of production may yield gains in efficiency (while also imposing severe social dislocations on downsized and outsourced people and communities). Any such gains, however, are undercut by the subsidizing distortions governments apply to resource prices and the failure to internalize the costs of pollution and resource depletion in the market price of goods. The seeming "comparative advantage" that can result from measures such as underregulating pollution or oversubsidizing natural resource extraction is actually a mechanism for propelling domestic mismanagement and the undervaluation of environmental quality into the international realm. The vast and subsidized energy consumption of the global trade and transport system also renders many seeming environmental gains from trade less robust, if not illusory. Even if it were somehow more efficient to bottle water in Fiji, it cannot possibly make ecological sense to ship those bottles halfway around the world to Los Angeles for consumption. And it requires an astonishing set of market distortions, subsidies, failures of the public water system, and fear-based, myth-ridden advertising to make it economically profitable to someone.

The larger implication of this form of economic (re)organization is its profound challenge to strategies for regulating environmental problems at the national and local levels.[10] Places with weak state capacity or little enthusiasm for controlling environmental harm sit stubbornly beyond the reach of the law-and-development approach and its quest to turn international goals into national standards and local implementation. Moreover, commodity chains can and do shift in a highly dynamic fashion when regulatory controls are adopted at any particular node in the chain. Thus, the implementation of controls on waste disposal in the United States and Europe in the 1970s led to a burgeoning North–South trade in hazardous waste in the 1980s, which led to a global regulatory regime (the Basel Convention) to address the waste trade problem in the 1990s, which has led in turn to the exploitation of recycling loopholes and an expanding South-South waste trade.[11] The dynamism of such shape-shifting responses to controls and the complexity of the chains themselves also complicate efforts to regulate by using consumer power through green product certification and chain-of-custody approaches.[12] Too often, the regulatory response is like squeezing a balloon: applying controls in one place causes the problem to swell outward somewhere else in the system. In the end, there are just too many locations to which rich consumers can export the harmful environmental effects of their consumption. As Judith Shapiro points out in chapter 12, much of the explosive growth of pollution in China, which is rightfully alarming to global trend watchers, stems from production that serves a global class of consumers who live for the most part outside China.

Consider the example of California, one of the planet's wealthiest regions in per capita terms (despite persistent pockets of poverty in both rural and urban areas). The state enjoys a bounteous endowment of natural resources that were tapped throughout the nineteenth and twentieth centuries to fuel its growth. More recently, the state has become the leading edge of North American environmentalism: expanding its protected areas, limiting offshore resource development, mandating cutting-edge efficiency standards on fuel and water use, and developing innovative methods of environmental impact assessment and decision making. California is also at the front of the financial machinery of environmentalism: Hollywood stars and entertainment firms fill out the boards of the major US environmental organizations, and the state's liberal pockets around Los Angeles and San Francisco are major fundraising targets. California thus epitomizes several of the social-cultural shifts of "planetary civilization" posited by Daniel Deudney and Elizabeth Mendenhall in chapter 2.

Yet California's green identity coexists with a voracious appetite for consumer culture and natural resource use. According to the Global Footprint Network, the state's environmental footprint is more than five times larger than its available ecological resources.[13] As protections on California's environmental assets—its forests, fisheries, pastures, mountains, coastline, and rivers—have multiplied, so too has the outsourcing of its resource demands.[14] The United States has declined to ratify several of the most important international environmental treaties, leaving Californians unbound by much of the existing body of international environmental law. A second important gap in the fabric of international law—the failure to articulate environmental protection as an explicit human right—is also relevant: it enables Californians largely to ignore the ethical implications of exporting the ecological costs of their consumption.

In a previous work, several colleagues and I noted that the law-and-development approach, and the broader Stockholm-to-Rio trajectory of mainstream global environmental governance, has largely failed to grapple with this emergent global political economy: "The Rio process underestimated—indeed, ignored—the dynamic trajectory of industrial civilization in the second half of the twentieth century and failed to account for the underlying, reinforcing dynamics of economic growth and technological diffusion that have come to define industrial development on an increasingly global scale."[15] Indeed, the Brundtland Commission overlooked this restructuring of world economic activity when writing *Our Common Future*, though the trend was quite evident by the mid-1980s. Since that time, a string of global summits have mostly preserved the fiction of largely separate and independently manageable national economies. Nominally new initiatives, such as those on "sustainable consumption" and "the green economy," have done little to counteract this tendency.

Missing the Political Window

When future chronicles of the planet's environmental circumstances are written, the period from the late 1980s to the early 2000s is likely to merit a simple title: *Blowing It*. With the benefit of hindsight, it is clear that this period enjoyed an unusually favorable convergence of hopeful circumstances for global environmental governance. A powerful new paradigm of sustainability emerged to guide understanding of both the problem and the response in ways that created cooperative possibilities across the North–South divide in world politics. Less developed countries, previously inclined to reject the environmental agenda as the latest wave of neocolonial intrusion, began to take the issue seriously. The industrialized world, slow to recognize the very different environmental realities embedded in a pollution of poverty, learned the value of making environment-development linkages. A new breed of professional environmentalist began to emerge—as likely to be a geographer or a sociologist as a lawyer and as likely to wield techniques of participatory appraisal and social cost–benefit analysis as the traditional tools of environmental impact assessment or conservation planning. More broadly, favorable conditions also came together in the "enabling environment" of environmentalism. The UN began to find its post–Cold War legs under the leadership of a secretary-general, Kofi Annan, who understood media power and the bully pulpit, and the global organization started to gain traction on challenges ranging from peacekeeping missions to its own institutional reform. Democracy spread and took root from Brazil to South Africa to Indonesia. Favorable conditions of steady economic growth obtained. And of course, the Cold War ended.

Yet far from seizing the moment, those who converged on Rio de Janeiro in 1992 as the would-be architects of a new institutional apparatus of global environmental governance built surprisingly little that has been of lasting use in reshaping our relationship with the natural world. The would-be regulatory regime set in motion by the Earth Summit's climate treaty is teetering; the regime inscribed in the biodiversity treaty has been more about framing biotech development than promoting conservation. Plans for a new financial architecture for sustainable development ran aground on disputes over the "additionality" of aid and funding promises that have not been kept. Agenda 21, the Earth Summit's forty-chapter blueprint for promoting sustainability at the national level, has not fared much better. In the run-up to the Rio+20 summit of 2012, the Stakeholder Forum for a Sustainable Future reached the following grim conclusion:

Humanity has not progressed on the road to sustainability as far as hoped in 1992. We can celebrate some notable successes, in particular the fact that hundreds of millions of people have been lifted from poverty during the last two decades. Yet, many of the global problems we are facing today are more acute or larger in scale than they were in 1992. The political deal that emerged from the Earth Summit in 1992 has, for various reasons, never been fulfilled. Neither the expected outcomes—elimination of poverty, reduction in disparities in standard of living, patterns of consumption and production that are compatible with the carrying capacity of ecosystems, sustainable management of renewable resources—nor the agreed means to achieve them, have materialized.[16]

Stakeholder Forum's assessment of chapter-by-chapter progress on Agenda 21, summarized in table 1.1, was able to score only five of Agenda 21's forty chapter-level themes as "good progress/on target," and those with among the lowest scores included such critical focal points as protecting the atmosphere, changing consumption patterns, and promoting sustainable human settlements.[17]

International environmental law has also lost much of its momentum. The rate of formation of new multilateral agreements on the environment

Table 1.1
Stakeholder Forum assessment of progress on Agenda 21

Score	Definition	Agenda 21 chapters receiving score
Blue	"Excellent progress/ fully achieved"	None
Mixed green/ blue		28. Major Groups—Local Authorities 38. International Institutional Arrangements
Green	"Good progress/on target"	27. Major Groups—NGOs 35. Science for Sustainable Development 39. International Legal Instruments and Mechanisms
Mixed yellow/ green		19. Environmentally Sound Management of Toxic Chemicals, including Prevention of Illegal International Traffic in Toxic and Dangerous Products 23. Major Groups—Preamble 31. Major Groups—Science & Technology

Table 1.1 (continued)

Score	Definition	Agenda 21 chapters receiving score
Yellow	"Limited progress/far from target"	2. International Cooperation to Accelerate Sustainable Development in Developing Countries and Related Domestic Policies 3. Combating Poverty 5. Demographic Dynamics and Sustainability 6. Protecting and Promoting Human Health Conditions 8. Integrating Environment and Development into Decision-making 11. Combating Deforestation 12. Managing Fragile Ecosystems: Combating Desertification and Drought 13. Managing Fragile Ecosystems: Sustainable Mountain Development 14. Promoting Sustainable Agriculture and Rural Development 15. Conservation of Biological Diversity 16. Environmentally Sound Management of Biotechnology 17. Protection of the Oceans, All Kinds of Seas, including Enclosed and Semi-enclosed Seas, and Coastal Areas and the Protection, Rational Use and Development of their Living Resources 18. Protection of the Quality and Supply of Freshwater Resources: Application of Integrated Approaches to the Development, Management and Use of Water Resources 20. Environmentally Sound Management of Hazardous Wastes, Including Prevention of Illegal International Traffic in Hazardous Wastes 21. Environmentally Sound Management of Solid Wastes and Sewage-related Issues 22. Safe and Environmentally Sound Management of Radioactive Wastes 24. Major Groups—Women 25. Major Groups—Children & Youth 26. Major Groups—Indigenous Peoples 30. Major Groups—Business & Industry 32. Major Groups—Farmers 33. Financial Resources and Mechanisms 34. Transfer of Environmentally Sound Technology, Cooperation and Capacity-building 36. Promoting Education, Public Awareness and Training 37. National Mechanisms and International Cooperation for Capacity-building in Developing Countries 40. Information for Decision Making

Table 1.1 (continued)

Score	Definition	Agenda 21 chapters receiving score
Mixed red/ yellow		10. Integrated Approach to the Planning and Management of Land Resources 29. Major Groups—Workers & Trade Unions
Red	"No progress or regression"	4. Changing Consumption Patterns 7. Promoting Sustainable Human Settlement Development 9. Protection of the Atmosphere

Source: Stakeholder Forum for a Sustainable Future, *Review of Implementation of Agenda 21 and the Rio Principles. Synthesis Report,* (January 2012), Table 2, pp. 22–39. January 2012.

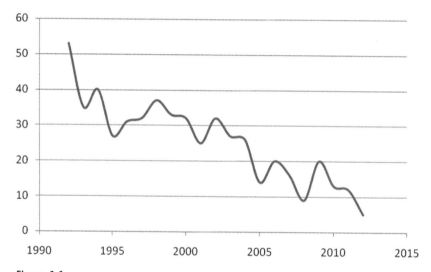

Figure 1.1
Annual multilateral environmental agreements and amendments. Note: "Agreements" includes new conventions and new protocols to existing conventions; "amendments" includes amendments and modifications to preexisting conventions and protocols. *Source:* International Environmental Agreements (IEA) Database Project

has fallen off dramatically since 1992 (figure 1.1). Bilateral diplomacy, which peaked in the Earth Summit era of the early- to-mid-1990s, has seen an equally precipitous decline (figure 1.2). The notion that this attenuation of legal and diplomatic activity is a natural development, the result of having successfully built an adequate apparatus of international environmental law, seems wildly optimistic.

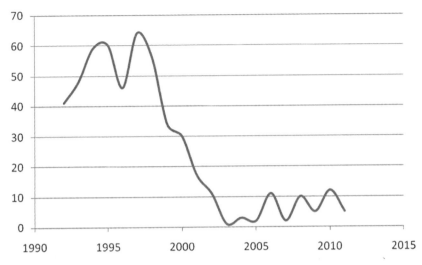

Figure 1.2
Annual bilateral environmental agreements and amendments, 1992–2011. Note: "Agreements" includes new conventions and new protocols to existing conventions; "amendments" includes amendments and modifications to preexisting conventions and protocols. *Source:* International Environmental Agreements (IEA) Database Project

The decline in new accords would be less troubling if existing agreements were showing robust capability for adaptation and innovation. Indeed, one of the great contributions of international environmental law in the 1980s and 1990s was the development of dynamic regimes that in principle could adapt to new understandings and shifting problem structures through mechanisms such as periodic reviews and conferences of the parties. As indicated in figure 1.3, however, the "amendment rate" for existing accords has fallen by more than 50 percent since the early 1990s, suggesting a lack of dynamic innovation in existing agreements.

Twenty years after the original Earth Summit, when global environmental summitry returned to Rio, what should have been a sober stock-taking and fine-tuning exercise was forced instead to confront a broken climate regime, enduring bickering over financial responsibilities, failure to implement the most ambitious and important elements of Agenda 21, and an institutional apparatus (e.g., UN Environment Programme, GEF, UN Commission on Sustainable Development) that has been able to do little more than tinker at the margins. The summit's outcome document, which implicitly reflects the lack of institutional traction from the original Earth Summit as it meanders through a laundry list of

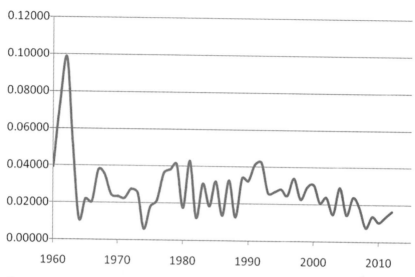

Figure 1.3
Number of amendments annually per existing environmental agreement, 1960–2012. Note: "Agreements" includes new conventions and new protocols to existing conventions; "amendments" includes amendments and modifications to preexisting conventions and protocols. *Source:* International Environmental Agreements (IEA) Database Project

aspirations, was titled *The Future We Want*. A more appropriate sobriquet would have been *The Past We Wish We'd Had*. In the end, the governments assembled at Rio settled for least-common-denominator statements of aspiration and passed all the key decisions on the summit agenda off to the UN General Assembly without clear resolution—as though the General Assembly were not composed of precisely the same governments meeting in Rio.

The seeming closure of this relatively favorable political window can be linked directly to the earlier comments about global economic restructuring. Simply put, by the early 1990s, the world was just globalized enough to see that it had a problem and to envision the broad outlines of a response. But it was not so very globalized that it lacked the capacity for diplomatically centralized decision structures that could overcome barriers to collective action. Indeed, the ability of such decision structures to function collectively was a key element in the genesis of economic globalization. That moment appears to have passed in terms of the prospects for rebuilding the world's economic architecture and creating significant mechanisms of global environmental governance. If this analysis is correct, then global economic recovery, restabilization of the euro zone, and resolution of the domestic political paralysis that currently sidelines the United States from serious international discussions, while helpful, will likely not be enough to recapture momentum.

The Decline of the Sustaining Middle

In 1992 Alan Durning, then affiliated with the Worldwatch Institute, published a short, provocative book titled *How Much Is Enough? The Consumer Society and the Future of the Earth.*[18] In it, he made two powerful observations. First, he argued that it made more sense to think ecologically about a world with three broad strata of consumption patterns, rather than the more familiar dichotomization of affluent North and impoverished South. Second, he suggested that these three strata, which I depict and label in figure 1.4, could be characterized by basic practices of consumption in daily life. Essentially, if you drive a car, eat lots of meat, and experience year-round air-conditioning, you are an over-consumer; if you walk, suffer a protein-deficient diet, and suffer in the heat, you are among the economically marginalized; and if you enjoy low-impact mobility (think buses and bikes), have access to a balanced and protein-rich diet (think beans and rice), and have seasonally appropriate climate control (think ceiling fans and well-made windows), you occupy a middle stratum we might think of as sustainers. Durning speculated at the time that in a circa 1990

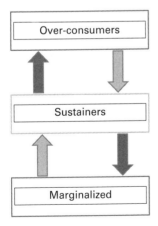

Figure 1.4
Three global strata of consumers

world of about 5 billion people, perhaps 1 billion occupied the overcon-
suming ranks, another 1 billion constituted the marginalized poor, and the
rest fell somewhere in between.

This framework has some problems. First, from a sustainability point of
view, there is no reason to think of the sustainers as a middle stratum; this
reflects the enduring pull of per capita income levels on our imagination.
Second, as my preceding argument suggests, the structure of consumption
is in many ways derivative of the structure of production and the manufacturing of demand; using it as the basis for analysis risks privileging the
individual or household scale over more aggregate scales and may presume
more capacity for effective agency than many people currently enjoy,
embedded as they are in economic systems they lack the ability to control
or even diagnose. Nonetheless, it provides a rough first cut at thinking
about where models for sustainability may be found.[19]

More important, however, is the matter of change. As we look for inflection points in global sustainability trends, this framework can be useful in
posing a critical question: What social processes move individuals, households, and entire communities from one stratum to another? Figure 1.5
presents some of the key processes of social transformation that cause
movement into or out of the ranks of the stratum of nominal sustainers,
corresponding to the arrows in figure 1.4. Most, if not all, of the "civilizational" transformations noted by Deudney and Mendenhall in chapter 2

Social transformation: rising incomes combined with embrace of
consumer lifestyles
Prototypical measures: ownership of automobiles and cellular telephones

Social transformation: efficiency-oriented innovations; community-
oriented investments in environmental public goods; "voluntary
simplicity"; post-materialism; corporate social responsibility
Prototypical measures: mass transit; farmer's markets; carbon neutrality

Social transformation: enhanced human security and community
resilience; reduced vulnerability
Prototypical measures: stabilized livelihoods; disaster risk reduction;
improved public health; access to water and sanitation

Social transformation: Marginalization, impoverishment, displacement
Prototypical measures: violent conflict; economic and environmental
refugees; down-sizing and out-sourcing of livelihoods; loss of access to
productive resources

Figure 1.5
Key processes of social transformation in global consuming strata

correspond to the arrow moving from the over-consumer stratum to the sustainer stratum. The figure cautions, however, that other equally important processes of social and economic transformation are also at work—not all of them involving current over-consumers and not all of them positive for sustainability.

It is difficult to use currently available statistics, based as they are primarily on national averages, to systematically measure the key processes identified in figures 1.4 and 1.5. Poverty reduction statistics speak most directly to the marginalized-to-sustainer process in figure 1.5, and they draw an ambiguous picture. Conventional measures such as growth in per capita income suggest that global poverty has been reduced substantially over the past few decades. The World Bank estimates that the number of people living on $1.25 or less per day has been halved since 1990, to about 1 billion.[20] Yet only a handful of the Millennium Development Goals (MDG) that offered specific targets for improvements by 2015 have been attained on a global scale. And the global totals, which can be skewed by strong gains in a few large countries, shows the limits to progress in many countries and regions and the extent to which material improvements have lagged the income gains that have reduced extreme income poverty in many countries.

Moreover, any such gains must be measured against downward mobility into the ranks of the marginalized. The aforementioned poverty-reduction and MDG data are all net trends that tell us little about downward mobility. Nor do they capture the impacts on social capital and the fabric of community. Consider, for example, the role of war and disaster in driving people from living relatively sustainable lifestyles into the ranks of the marginalized. According to the organizers of the UN World Conference on Disaster Risk Reduction, "Exposure of people and assets in all countries has increased faster than vulnerability has decreased, thus generating new risk and a steady increase in disasters losses, with significant socio-economic impact in the short, medium and long terms, especially at the local and community level."[21] War imposes a similar burden: ongoing violence in settings as diverse as Afghanistan, Colombia, the Democratic Republic of Congo, Iraq, Myanmar, Somalia, Sudan, and Syria has caused the forcible displacement of a record 51 million people, according to the UN High Commissioner for Refugees.[22] Moreover, we are learning that conflict and disaster are linked in ways that mutually reinforce vulnerability and human insecurity. Significant disaster episodes have been shown to be a risk factor for the subsequent occurrence of violent conflict in both the short and medium term and for both low- and middle-income countries.[23] Similarly, conflict enhances vulnerability to the effects of disasters. Government institutions are weakened or destroyed by conflict, people are displaced, and vital ecosystems that provide "natural security" may be overwhelmed by the effects of disaster or the survival needs of refugees.[24] All but one of forty-one UN peacekeeping missions in the field between 1980 and 2010 experienced at least one natural disaster while operating in the host country.[25] Obviously climate change adds a worrisome driver to this already volatile mix. The Fifth Assessment Report of the Intergovernmental Panel on Climate Change projects increases in intensity and duration of droughts and frequency of extreme precipitation events.[26]

Wars and disasters also tear at the fabric of community and at models that seek collective, public goods solutions to problems. In the wake of Hurricane Katrina in 2005, New Orleans essentially demolished its public school system, firing all of the system's teachers and turning most of the work of education over to charter schools. The predictable result has been a two-tiered structure in which test score improvements have come at the expense of shunting the challenged, the disabled, and others who don't fit the model into the shrunken remains of a nominally public school system. Community-based clinics and the city's main public hospital, also devastated by the flooding, have been replaced with "medical homes"— decentralized care sites with health-care teams headed by a primary-care physicians, as opposed to a more traditional clinic model—that have struggled to sustain safety net care after the initial grant funding for system transformation ran out.[27]

The model of three consuming strata also calls our attention to change at the top end of the income spectrum, in the relationship between the sustainer and over-consumer strata. Given the emphasis governments place on tracking consumption, it is relatively easy to identify movements into the ranks of overconsumption, including through some of the global growth trends such as the spread of autos and mobile phones.[28] Movement toward sustaining lifestyles is harder to measure and relies on partial evidence—for example, the quadrupling in the number of farmers' markets in the United States in the past twenty years or the growth of investment in solar and wind energy systems.[29]

The Challenge Ahead

If these three clusters of observations—on the complications of globalization, a missed political window in world politics, and the decline of the sustaining middle—do in fact represent inflection points in the quest for a more sustainable world, then many of the tactics and strategies of the modern environmental movement are unlikely to yield traditional results in this new context. Efforts to forge new international agreements founder on the political shoals of a world fragmented by ebbing state authority and capacity challenges that make credible commitments difficult. Those supranational regulatory efforts that can be established—regional or global, mandatory or voluntary—seem endlessly to chase the dynamic border-crossing commodity chains they seek to control without ever really catching up. Meanwhile, the search to find and learn from existing models of low-throughput, high-quality lives too often finds a note pinned to the door that says, "Sorry, upscaled to consumerism" or "Outsourced—new quarters on Vulnerability Street." Even if we are in the early stages of the type of hopeful culture-shift that Deudney and Mendenhall posit in the following chapter, it must grapple with the fact that we have rapidly been dismantling existing practices of sustainability at an alarming rate—chiefly by removing or allowing the wider conditions of proximity, time, access, localized knowledge, and public goods provisioning that had supported them to decay.

None of this is to suggest that we would be better off without international environmental law, or the post-Brundtland sustainability movement, or the tools and techniques of late-twentieth century environmental management. But it does suggest that both new tools and new strategies are required. Among these, three seem critical. First and foremost is to infuse new energy and bolder support into the quest for environmental human rights.[30] Without global recognition that people and communities have a right to a safe, quality environment, there will always be another country, or region, or community onto which the noxious by-products of globalized production-consumption systems can be dumped and where the plunder of natural resources can proceed apace. While recognizing environmental human rights is simply a first step, it is an important one, in that it creates new tools to hold both governments and end-of-the-chain consumers accountable for their actions.

A second key shift involves recognizing a broader paradigm shift that is already well underway. Across a range of resource sectors, including food, water, and energy, there is a marked movement away from the idea of optimizing systems under conditions of relative certainty and toward risk management approaches, which (as a general rule) seek strategies that are robust across a wide range of scenarios in an uncertain future. Financial instability and looming uncertainties of climate change are key drivers of this shift. To the extent that it yields more flexible and decentralized responses—one hundred projects to generate 10 megawatts rather than one to generate 1,000 megawatts—this is a very hopeful adjustment. However, the barriers to making such adjustments are not trivial. Consider the world of water, where much of my own recent work is concentrated. Water is the delivery mechanism for the effects of climate change on people, communities, and ecosystems—be it through changing patterns of precipitation, evaporation, and runoff; effects on soil moisture; or the frequency and intensity of flood and droughts. Climate adaptation schemes that produce more sensible use of water and resilience in the face of these stressors could do much to enhance the positive dynamics in figures 1.5 and 1.6 and to reduce the negative flows. Water is also a sector that has seen large, traditional infrastructure projects increasingly destabilized by financial uncertainty, again favoring new thinking and decentralized, lighter-impact responses.

However, efforts to move in this direction in the water world encounter some large obstacles.[31] First is the existing institutional landscape. We have just passed through an era, beginning in the early 1990s, of promoting a paradigm of integrated water resources management (IWRM) that has created a newly built structure of laws, institutions, regulations, and information systems for water management in dozens of countries. The main emphasis in IWRM has been on building more complex, ambitious, interlinked, and comprehensive management tools to optimize water use through tighter coupling and coordination across different sectors and users. Despite their many advantages, such reforms are not obviously designed for flexible adaptation. Second, powerful economic actors in the water world are busy building water risk management tools that tend to financialize corporate risk—managing their financial exposure without for the most part addressing the underlying changes to the water cycle that are its ultimate source. Effective strategies on water must learn to navigate, and challenge when necessary, this built landscape of institutions and political economy, which recognize and privilege the managing of some risks over others.

Third, this rights-and-risks approach[32] also suggests new approaches to conceptualizing and framing the tasks of the global environmental movement. Rights are inherently tools for individuals, households, and local communities. Risks cannot be understood outside the context of specific places, particular social relations, and the rich fabric of the lives of real people. To use these tools effectively on the New Earth, our frameworks must move from people to planet, and not simply vice versa.

Notes

1. UN Environment Programme, *GEO 5*, 2.

2. Ibid., 4.

3. Jackson et al., "Water in a Changing World."

4. UN Environment Programme, *Global Environmental Outlook*, 64, citing the Intergovernmental Panel on Climate Change.

5. Ibid., 52, citing the World Health Organization.

6. Ibid.

7. Conca, "Global Water Prospects."

8. Jacquet et al., 2010.

9. Conca, *An Unfinished Foundation*.

10. Conca, "Consumption and Environment in a Global Economy." This section also draws on Conca, *An Incomplete Foundation*, chap. 3.

11. Clapp, *Toxic Exports*.

12. See, for example, Horne, "Limits to Labels"; Jacquet et al., "Conserving Wild Fish in a Sea of Market-Based Efforts"; Franze and Ciroth, "A Comparison of Cut Roses from Ecuador and the Netherlands"; Raynolds, "Fair Trade Flowers."

13. Global Footprint Network, "Highlights of California's First Ecological Footprint Report."

14. See "State of Denial," a special report published in the *Sacramento Bee*.

15. Park, Conca, and Finger, "The Death of Rio Environmentalism," 6.

16. UN Department of Economic and Social Affairs, *Back to Our Common Future*, iii, emphasis in original.

17. Stakeholder Forum for a Sustainable Future, *Review of Implementation of Agenda 21*.

18. Durning, *How Much Is Enough?*

19. I developed an earlier variant of this argument in "Beyond the Statist Frame."

20. World Bank Group, *Global Monitoring Report 2014–15*, 18.

21. UN World Conference on Disaster Risk Reduction, "Development of the Post-2015 Framework for Disaster Risk Reduction."

22. UN High Commissioner for Refugees, "World Refugee Day."

23. Nel and Righarts, "Natural Disasters and the Risk of Violent Civil Conflict."

24. Stolton, Dudley, and Randall, *Natural Security*.

25. UN Environment Programme, *Greening the Blue Helmets*, 13.

26. Intergovernmental Panel on Climate Change, *Climate Change 2014 Synthesis Report*.

27. Commonwealth Fund, "The Post-Katrina Conversion of Clinics in New Orleans."

28. Dauvergne, "The Problem of Consumption"; Princen, Conca, and Finger, eds., *Confronting Consumption*.

29. On US farmers' markets, see US Department of Agriculture Economic Research Service, "Number of U.S. Farmers' Markets Continues to Rise."

30. Conca, "Environmental Human Rights."

31. Conca, "Which Risks Get Managed?"

32. The phrase "rights and risks" was coined by the World Commission on Dams. See its *Dams and Development*.

Bibliography

Clapp, Jennifer. *Toxic Exports: The Transfer of Hazardous Wastes from Rich to Poor Countries*. Ithaca, NY: Cornell University Press, 2001.

Commonwealth Fund. "The Post-Katrina Conversion of Clinics in New Orleans to Medical Homes Shows Change Is Possible, But Hard to Sustain." August 6, 2012.

Conca, Ken. "Beyond the Statist Frame: Environment in a Global Economy." In *Nature, Production, Power: Towards an Ecological Political Economy*, edited by Fred P. Gale and R. Michael M'Gonigle. Cheltenham, UK: Elgar, 2000.

Conca, Ken. "Consumption and Environment in a Global Economy." *Global Environmental Politics* 1, no. 3 (2001): 53–71.

Conca, Ken. "Environmental Human Rights." In *Handbook of Global Environmental Politics*, edited by Peter Dauvergne. Cheltenham, UK: Elgar, 2012.

Conca, Ken. "Global Water Prospects." In *From Resource Scarcity to Ecological Security: Exploring New Limits to Growth*, edited by Dennis Pirages and Kenneth Cousins, 59–82. Cambridge, MA: MIT Press, 2005.

Conca, Ken. "Which Risks Get Managed? Addressing Climate Effects in the Context of Evolving Water-governance Institutions." *Water Alternatives* 8, no. 3 (2015): 301–316.

Conca, Ken. *An Unfinished Foundation: The United Nations and Global Environmental Governance*. New York: Oxford University Press, 2015.

Dauvergne, Peter. "The Problem of Consumption." *Global Environmental Politics* 10, no. 2 (2010): 1–10.

Durning, Alan. *How Much Is Enough? The Consumer Society and the Future of the Earth*. New York: Norton, 1992.

Franze, Juliane, and Andreas Ciroth. "A Comparison of Cut Roses from Ecuador and the Netherlands." *International Journal of Life Cycle Assessment* 16 (2011): 366–79.

Global Footprint Network. "Highlights of California's First Ecological Footprint Report." Retrieved December 30, 2013, from http://www.footprintnetwork.org/en/index.php/newsletter/det/ca.

Horne, Ralph E. "Limits to Labels: The Role of Eco-Labels in the Assessment of Product Sustainability and Routes to Sustainable Consumption." *International Journal of Consumer Studies* 33 (2009): 175–82.

Intergovernmental Panel on Climate Change. *Climate Change 2014 Synthesis Report: Summary for Policy Makers*. Geneva: IPCC, 2014.

Jackson, Robert B., Stephen R. Carpenter, Clifford N. Dahm, Diane M. McKnight, Robert J. Naiman, Sandra L. Postel, and Steven W. Running. "Water in a Changing World." *Ecological Applications* 11 (2001): 1027–45.

Jacquet, Jennifer, John Hocevar, Sherman Lai, Patricia Majluf, Nathan Pelletier, Tony Pitcher, Enric Sala, Rashid Sumaila, and Daniel Pauly. "Conserving Wild Fish in a Sea of Market-Based Efforts." *Oryx* 44:1 (2010): 45–56.

Nel, P., and M. Righarts. "Natural Disasters and the Risk of Violent Civil Conflict." *International Studies Quarterly* 52 (2008): 159–85.

Park, Jacob, Ken Conca, and Matthias Finger. "The Death of Rio Environmentalism." In *The Crisis of Global Environmental Governance: Toward a New Political Economy of Sustainability*, edited by Jacob Park, Ken Conca, and Matthias Finger, 1–12. New York: Routledge, 2009.

Princen, T., K. Conca, and M. Finger, eds. *Confronting Consumption*. Cambridge, MA: MIT Press, 2002.

Raynolds, Laura T. "Fair Trade Flowers: Global Certification, Environmental Sustainability, and Labor Standards." *Rural Sociology* 77 (2012): 493–519.

Stakeholder Forum for a Sustainable Future. *Review of Implementation of Agenda 21 and the Rio Principles. Synthesis Report*. January 2012.

"State of Denial." *Sacramento Bee,* April 27, 2003. http://www.sacbee.com/static/live/news/projects/denial/text.html.

Stolton, S., N. Dudley, and J. Randall. *Natural Security: Protected Areas and Hazard Mitigation.* Gland, Switzerland: WWF, 2008.

UN Department of Economic and Social Affairs. *Back to Our Common Future: Sustainable Development in the 21st Century Project. Summary for Policy Makers.* New York: UNDESA, 2012.

UN Environment Programme. *Global Environmental Outlook: Environment for Development (GEO 4).* Nairobi: UNEP, 2007.

UN Environment Programme. *GEO 5: Global Environmental Outlook.* Nairobi: UNEP, 2012.

UN Environment Programme. *Greening the Blue Helmets: Environment, Natural Resources and UN Peacekeeping Operations.* Nairobi: UNEP, 2012.

UN High Commissioner for Refugees. "World Refugee Day: Global Forced Displacement Tops 50 Million for First Time in Post–World War II Era." Press release, June 20, 2014.

UN World Conference on Disaster Risk Reduction. "Development of the Post-2015 Framework for Disaster Risk Reduction." Co-Chairs' pre-zero draft, 2. http://www.wcdrr.org/preparatory/post2015.

US Department of Agriculture Economic Research Service. "Number of U.S. Farmers' Markets Continues to Rise." 2014.

World Bank Group. *Global Monitoring Report 2014–15: Ending Poverty and Sharing Prosperity.* Washington, DC: World Bank, 2014.

World Commission on Dams. *Dams and Development: A New Framework for Decision Making.* London: Earthscan, 2000.

2   Green Earth: The Emergence of Planetary Civilization

Daniel Deudney and Elizabeth Mendenhall

Green Civilization Emergent

Over the past half-century, there has been an explosive growth in concern about the negative consequences of human activity and efforts to address them, propelled by the stark fact that the anthropogenic impact on Earth's biosphere has become increasingly disruptive. The rapid rise in human population, from 2 billion around 1930 to over 7 billion today, the major expansion of economic activities made possible by technological advance, and the growing ability of humans to wrest energy and minerals from the Earth, have combined to produce not just unprecedented "progress" in making life better for vastly larger numbers of people, but also a catastrophic stress on the planet's natural life support systems. In sum, modern scientific technological industrial civilization is on a collision course with the Earth's biosphere, and humans now inhabit a starkly unsettled New Earth.[1]

As a result, environmentalism has emerged in virtually every dimension of human life, virtually everywhere. Environmental practice has rapidly grown into a sprawling body of initiatives, activities, and innovations that seem to defy any simple summary or description. The breadth of environmentalist critique and agendas is staggering. They range from proposals for international treaties to individual lifestyle changes, and from cosmologies and metaphysics to programs for mundane human domestic life. Environmentalists have pioneered green architecture and ecopsychology, fought to establish wilderness areas, and reenvisioned economic systems and industrial processes. Every discipline now has a branch devoted to engaging the environment, from architecture to zoology. But environmentalism is so dizzyingly kaleidoscopic that it seems both fragmented and internally conflicted. However, this very plurality and heterogeneity tells us something about environmentalism that has not been fully appreciated.

In this chapter, we make the case that the numerous sprawling and diverse parts of environmentalism can be best understood as an emergent civilization, the largest and most encompassing category for analyzing human historical formations. Civilizations have distinctive social, cultural, religious, economic, and political forms. A civilization is marked by a unity that is embodied in a narrative, a story that links past, present, and future. A civilization speaks to all aspects of human life, from the high to the low, and encompasses arrangements from the micro to the macro. It is comprehensive in both scope and scale, from the mundane to the profound, and from the spatially very small to the size of the planet. Civilizations range in scope from cosmological and metaphysical systems to pragmatic routines for conducting the most mundane domestic material bodily activities. Civilizations range in scale from world order architectures to individual identities and practices.[2] In short, to say that there is an emergent green civilization is to say that the environmental agenda significantly touches on all aspects of human life in a manner that is logically interconnected.

In making the case for an emergent green civilization, we point to the ways in which environmentalists, in their theory and practice, have pioneered arrangements that span both the axis of scope and significance and the axis of size and spatial scale (see figure 2.1). Viewing the sum of environmental theory and practice as an emergent civilization enables us to see a whole that combines their otherwise bewilderingly diverse parts. Similarly, viewing environmentalism as an emergent civilization helps combat pessimism and defeatism among environmentalists by showing that their efforts are weaving something that goes beyond the particular struggles in which they are engaged. It also demonstrates that the whole is more than the sum of the parts and that there are unappreciated alliances to be forged. In making this case, it is important to emphasize that we do not claim that this emergent green civilization is yet dominant on the Earth, or even that it inevitably will become so, or deny that environmental problems have continued to get worse overall during the first decades of its gestation and emergence.

Environmentalism has not only been diverse in the scope of its significance and spatial reach, but also has been rapidly evolving over the past half-century. Much of early environmentalism can be characterized as a first impulse, marked by an emphasis on critique, resistance, and rejection. This negative moment of environmentalism remains vital in driving efforts to oppose, subvert, and deconstruct the established hegemonic modern civilizational forms that are assaulting the natural world. But across virtually every environmental topic and domain, this deconstructive first move

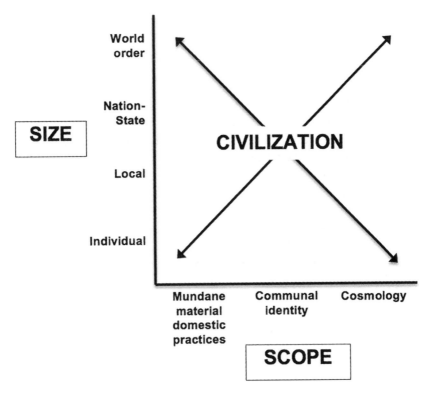

Figure 2.1
The Domain of Green Civilization

has increasingly evolved into, or been complemented by, a constructive agenda that advances positive green alternatives. For example, early environmentalism focused on the harms caused by various types of fossil fuel extraction and use, but very quickly environmentalists were faced with the question, "What do you propose instead?" and thus began to conceptualize and promote energy alternatives centered on efficiency and renewables. It is the sum of these alternative positive agendas that, we argue, composes the emergent green civilization.

Our approach of conditional optimism differs in several ways from the nearly comprehensive pessimistic assessment that Ken Conca offers in chapter 1. We are in agreement that efforts to solve environmental problems have been insufficient and that the full implementation of solutions is not inevitable. But our approach looks at the contemporary landscape of environmental problem solving and sees a wealth of visions and ideas, new sustainable practices, and institutional arrangements that are, in partial ways, solution sets to the overarching environmental problem. In short, the sum of the present is inadequate, but parts of the present, if greatly expanded, hold the promise of effective global response. We anticipate that environmentalism, like other major historical movements, will pass through, as it has, a long gestation period in which its initiatives are resisted and its defeats exceed its victories before it makes a breakthrough to being civilizationally dominant. For example, no one looking at the brutal and comprehensive persecution of the Christians in the Roman Empire for nearly a century would have predicted that the Roman Empire itself would come to be headed by a Christian and the full weight of Roman institutions placed behind Christianity. Furthermore, we look at environmentalism itself not as a static agenda that has successively been losing to developers and exploiters, as does Conca, but rather as a protean and multidimensional agenda that has been rapidly evolving and mutating over the course of the past half-century. And finally, we agree with Conca's characterization of the limits of the law and development approach to environmentalism, but we look beyond institutions to religion, identity, and cosmology, where revolutionary ideas with wide implications for practice have been gaining ground and growing in their power.

A full appreciation of the many important facets of environmentalism that, woven together, constitute an emerging civilization is an undertaking beyond the scope of this chapter. Unable to be fully comprehensive, we strategically focus on some of the most important dimensions of environmentalism as a civilizational form, starting with its temporal and spatial extension. Then we examine a select set of three important facets of environmental critiques and agendas: religion and cosmology, capitalism and economy, and industrial technology. We then make the case that the emergence of climate change as the central environmental problem has provided a unifying imperative connecting previously disparate environmental agendas, while at the same time forcing revisions, sometimes dramatic, in environmentalist conceptualizations of alternatives. We end with a reflection on the emergence of green civilization in the light of civilizational transitions more generally.

Time: Novel Problems, Environmental History, and Big History

A central feature of every civilizational formation is that it has a narrative about the past that is both temporally deep and contemporarily useful. Over the past half-century, environmental thinking about novelty, history, and time has undergone a dramatic evolution. During the 1960s when the modern environmental movement, according to virtually every account, first emerged, environmental thinking emphasized that modern technological civilization was faced with a fundamentally new and unprecedented set of problems. Iconic works such as Rachel Carson's *Silent Spring*, Barry Commoner's *The Closing Circle*, and Paul Ehrlich's *The Population Bomb* underscored the novelty of new forms of pollution stemming from pesticides and other industrial agricultural chemicals and the growth in human numbers resulting from advances in medicine, sanitation, and agriculture.[3] These accounts, often alarmist or even apocalyptic in their tone and rhetoric, naturally led to deconstructive oppositional programs to halt, and where possible reverse, the direct causes of these human impacts on the environment.[4] Similarly, the threat of the ecological and health effects of radiation and fallout, produced by the completely novel technology of nuclear fission, played a catalytic role in forming environmental consciousness and stimulating environmental resistance movements. But from the outset, these claims about the novelty of these environmental problems were suspect due to the long presence of conservation efforts from the late nineteenth and early twentieth centuries.[5]

Rising awareness of new environmental problems also stimulated an entire new discipline, environmental history. Historians already had been increasingly doing "history from below," examining the role of social classes and conflicts, and displacing the older "high history" centered on wars, monarchs, treaties, and constitutions.[6] The new environmental history was history from even further below. It looked, to use a theatrical analogy, not just at the cast and chorus as well as the leads, but also at the stage or set and its influence on the plot. Much of environmental history wove a narrative in which environmental degradation and human advance were closely intertwined, pushing the temporal horizon for understanding the human assault on nature back to the dim mists of prehistoric human use of fire and hunting tools.[7] The new environmental history, in works by Alfred Crosby and others, also brought to light the extent to which the large patterns of human historical development were profoundly shaped by ecological factors, such as variations in climate and rainfall, patterns of disease, and animal domestication.[8] But as the fuller picture of humanity's long interaction with the natural world came into more complete view, some historians, such as Joachim Radkau and others, began to emphasize that human historical development, particularly agriculture and urbanization, not only degraded the environment but was also fundamentally dependent on the development and implementation of knowledge and practices to sustain and make urban spaces habitable by combating soil infertility, air and water pollution, and other degradations of the immediate environment on which humans depended.[9]

Both the new industrial technological forms of environmental degradation and the histories of previous human-environment interactions clearly establish that the history of civilization has been from its outset the story of grappling, sometimes successfully and sometimes not, with environmental problems, thus making the contemporary task of global-scale environmental rescue essentially the continuation of a much older story on a newly enlarged scale. Environmental history, by capturing the past, provided a larger temporal frame that could encompass the bewildering diversity of human historical experience. Environmental history is thus a history from far below that also stretches far back and is intimately intermingled with the history of life on Earth. In the recent "big history" movement, historians and natural scientists have sought to construct a unifying narrative that puts the human, and human interaction with the Earth, in a cosmic temporal story.[10] This big history begins with astronomical history, proceeds through the evolutionary emergence of life on Earth, and brings the story to the emergence of humans and their progression from a rare mammal to a force of planetary transformation. It aims not simply at unifying knowledge of the historical interactions between nature and human development, but doing so in a way that is suitable for wide vernacular knowledge, thus providing a unifying educational framework that integrates all disciplines of knowledge into one intelligible whole.[11]

Not only has environmental thinking provided the Earth with a new past; it has also outlined a new future. A defining temporal aspect of emergent green theory and practice is the appeal to the interests of future generations of humans. During the first wave of environmentalism, the perils of nuclear power loomed large, and the fact that nuclear materials would remain hazardous for millennia meant that decision making about the production and disposition of nuclear waste had an unprecedentedly lengthy temporal horizon. Similarly, human impacts have been producing the extinction of plant and animal species in an effectively permanent transformation of the Earth's living biospheric resources. This is occurring at such an accelerated rate that biologists speak of the industrial era as the sixth great extinction event, placing human impacts in a geological deep time frame comparable to such planetary disasters as the extinction of the dinosaurs 65 million years ago by an asteroidal collision with the Earth.[12] Furthermore, as the dimensions of atmospheric carbon loading and their impacts on the Earth's atmospheric, oceanic, and living systems have become clear, the horizon of consequence has leaped many centuries, if not millennia, into the future. Thus, decisions today about generating energy from nuclear fission and fossil fuels define not only a footprint of impact on the current generation, but also are in a very real and substantial way defining the environmental possibilities for generations of humans stretching far into the future. In the language of the American pragmatist, political theorist John Dewey, the temporal scope of contemporary technological impacts has created a "transgenerational public."[13]

This situation is compellingly captured in the (apparently apocryphal) American Indian proverb, "We have not inherited the Earth from our ancestors, but borrowed it from our descendants." In the face of these expanded temporal horizons, environmentalists argue that nuclear power, species loss, and carbon atmospheric loading are robbing future generations of their birthrights.[14] Thus, environmental thinkers conceptualize transgenerational stakeholder groups and attempt to conceptualize mechanisms for the representation of their interests in contemporary decision making and have sought to reemploy constitutional forms as a means to put restraints on the predations of the present on the future.[15] Environmental thinking and practice have been forced to think about policy alternatives in time frames that are far beyond those that mark decision making in other policy domains. In Deweyian terms, environmental theory is thus attempting to conceptualize forms of government appropriate to this new planetary-scale intergenerational public.

Taken together, the knowledge produced by the new environmental history, the unifying frames of the new big history, and the policy implications of intergenerational publics and stakeholder groups constitute a civilizational-grade temporal narrative. Like the architectonic temporal stories of previous civilizations, this new historical narrative is comprehensive, while at the same time being rooted in science rather than inspired prophecy and supernatural revelation.

Space: From the Local to the Global and Back Again

A second defining feature of civilizational formations is the presence of a distinctive geographic narrative about place and space.[16] Such civilizational spatialities make actions at the smallest spatial scale intelligible and appropriate by reference to frameworks at the largest spatial scale. The ubiquitously articulated motto of environmental thinking and practice, "act locally and think globally," is the seed of the emergent green civilizational reconfiguration of place and space. This simple green dictum orients a myriad of diverse local practices and activities on the basis of a macrospatial conceptualization of global space and place.

In thinking globally in a way that is accessible to dispersed local actors, the "whole Earth" photograph has assumed iconic vernacular status in green movements. The first photograph of the entire planet Earth was taken from space by NASA astronauts in late 1968 and assumed its central role in alternative environmentalist representations of space and place during the first Earth Day in 1970. For the emerging environmental movement, the "whole Earth" pictures became powerful symbols of Earth system science. The image seemed to reveal the Earth "as it actually was," showing the fluidity of the atmosphere and oceans, and its cosmic isolation and fragility, but not showing sharp lines and spatial compartmentalizations. Thus, it looked radically different from previous maps, particularly of state territorial borders.[17]

The fact that the "whole Earth" photograph was produced by the space program is also revealing. The picture stands as the central trope in how the anticipated Space Age became the Earth Age.[18] The space program was the crown jewel and the cutting edge of the modern scientific-technological civilization and embodied its agenda of endless progress and expansion.[19] The opening of the high frontier of space played a central role in this civilization's confident belief that there were no ultimate limits to growth and that the Earth was a launch pad staging site for the cosmic emergence of humanity from its natal cradle.[20] Representing more than just the abstract expansion of humanity into new places, visions for extracting resources and energy and colonies in space hover discreditingly over green terrestrial agendas to adjust to limits to growth.[21] In contrast to these expectations, as the *Apollo* 8 astronaut William Anders put it, the most important consequence of space exploration is that "we discovered the Earth."[22] The expectation that technological advance would enable humanity to pour across the high frontier and replicate its exploitative expansionist pattern on Earth into the "fertile stars" has been rudely subverted by the cosmic geography mapped by space explorers, human and robotic, during the second half of the twentieth century and beyond.[23] This essential finding is captured by *Apollo* astronaut Edwin "Buzz" Aldrin, the second human to set foot on the moon, who described it as a "magnificent desolation."[24] Thus, the Space Age became the Earth Age when space exploration provided a new view of the fragility, interconnectedness, and closed character of the Earth and revealed the existence not of a new frontier but of a forbiddingly steep and strong natural barrier.

The "whole Earth" image defines the macrospatial end of the emergent green civilization's geography. But it also poses a set of fundamental problematics that environmental thinking and practice have been wrestling with about how concrete local actions are to be oriented in this new planetary spatial frame.[25] Environmental practice, while heavily weighted toward actions and agendas that are centered in and built from the local, remains unresolved in how the connection between local action and global thinking actually occurs. There are strong environmentalist strands of antiglobalist activism, and some environmental thinkers, notably Wendell Berry, reject global frames as "globaloney."[26] Another approach argues that the intensity of global interdependence, captured in notions of a global village, indicates that the Earth as a whole now has place-like local characteristics previously associated only with much smaller spatial scales.

The most powerful way in which the local and the global are connected in green theory and practice is through Earth systems science, which emerged in the latter part of the twentieth century from the integration of the sciences of geology, biology, ecology, oceanography, and atmospheric science.[27] In practical terms, the question of what to do locally is mediated by knowledge about planetary-scale interconnections as revealed by these Earth system sciences.[28] Thus, local actions by individuals, municipalities, corporations, and cities to address climate change depend on scientific understandings of the extended spatial consequences of particular built structures, transportation systems, and land use patterns. With climate change, for example, people experiencing drought or extreme weather can connect such developments to the emissions of their tailpipes and chimneys only through the knowledge of Earth system science. An emergent green civilization thus builds on the modern technological civilization because it attempts to base widespread dispersed actions on a vernacular knowledge of scientifically revealed causal links, making it in the eyes of some observers a type of "reflexive modernity."[29]

At the smallest spatial scale stands the individual as a locus for environmental practices. Like any other civilization, the emergent green one has a robust appreciation for the ability of individual actions to reproduce or undermine larger-scale systems—in effect, a green "civic personality," green "ways of life" and green virtues, citizenship, and sacrifices.[30] Individual practices such as recycling, composting, vegetarian diets, and reproductive restraints constitute a set of green virtues. The locus of this green virtue is robustly material, focusing on intimate and domestic individual bodily practices. As with "acting locally," these individual practices are oriented on the basis of understandings of global-scale causal chains of extended consequence. Environmental activists often start as "NIMBYs" ("Not In My Backyard") and then frequently evolve into "NOPEs" ("Not On Planet Earth") as their knowledge of extended causal linkages grows.[31] Similarly, the environmental practice of composting connects a local, and quite ancient, insight about the necessity for maintaining soil fertility through waste recycling with a new Earth system science understanding of the effects of methane on global climate. These forms of "glocality" are based on the distant proximities created by modern technological empowerment and illuminated by ecological and Earth systems science.[32]

The local and global spatial framing of emergent green civilization envisages not the elimination of intermediary-scale forms such as nation-state governments and international organizations, but rather their reorientation on the basis of whether they hinder or support the local reconfigurations necessary for environmentally sound material practices.[33] Despite the centrality of the global scale, most green political thought and action does not look to the erection of heavy institutional architectures at larger spatial scales, such as world governments or world federal unions. Instead, the international-scale green agenda has mutated into a "global governance" format that emphasizes the ways in which large numbers of local actors are informationally networked and in which international regimes embody bottom-up emergent commitments without central enforcement capacities and authorities.[34] Even as the states have been gridlocked in negotiating top-down agreements, vibrant networks of substate actors, most prominently cities, have pushed ahead to forge horizontal alliances and develop innovative sustainable practices. Furthermore, when transnational activism of this extent is occurring beneath the level of interstate politics, it can potentially trigger rapid change in the realm of high politics, as took place with the sudden end of the Cold War. In all of these emergent practices, the tendency is not to replace de novo but instead to repair, reuse, reorient, and reconfigure existing authorities and capacities at all spatial scales.

Identity and Community: Green Religion and Earth Nationalism

Another defining attribute of civilizational-grade human formations is that they offer identity and community narratives grounded in hierarchical claims of sacred order and special place. Scientific-technological civilization is distinctive from all its premodern successors because it has attempted to build forms of community and identity on utilitarian, instrumental, and atomistic foundations. Similarly, this civilization has, unlike its predecessors, grounded itself on a "disenchanted" nature and cosmos.[35] This project, while immensely powerful, has never fully displaced its predecessors, and never generated identities and communities as thick and compelling as they possessed. And the form of identity and community that has flourished in the civilization of modernity paradoxically has been the nation, a form of communal identity that is widespread, conceptually illusive, and perpetually problematic for the full modernist Enlightenment worldview.

Although much of environmentalism is cast instrumentally and is focused on the reconfiguration of the mundane material human world, environmental thinking and practice also encompass powerful emergent alternative formations of individual and group identity and community. The nascent green civilizational project contains a variety of sacred and spiritual dimensions, and green identity and community are grounded in strong value claims and various natural reenchantments of place.[36]

The community and identity narratives of the nascent green civilization are grounded in, not antagonistic to, the understandings of nature produced by modern science. Modern civilization privileged science as the supreme and unique pathway to the generation of reliable knowledge about reality. For much of the modern era, scientific advance powerfully subverted the cosmological foundations of premodern religions and cultures. The Copernican displacement of the Earth from the center of the universe, the Cartesian and Newtonian models of mechanical nature, and the Darwinian evolutionary dethroning of humanity as the "crown of creation" dealt successive blows to the credibility of premodern religious cosmologies and the communal identities they supported.[37] In the second half of the twentieth century, natural scientific advances, most notably in ecology, Earth systems science, and chaos and complexity theory, have produced radically new understandings of nature that are congruent with green worldviews and have created opportunities for grounding the full green project in natural science.[38]

The greening of religion, and green religions, have been a salient feature of environmental theory and practice. The word *religion*, coming from the Latin *re-ligio*, meaning to "bound back," has been recast into Earth-bound spiritual and ritual practices and sacred hierarchies and places. In the nineteenth century, long before the emergence of modern environmentalism, Romantic theories of aesthetics laid the foundations for the valuation of the extremes of nature as evoking the spiritually edifying "sublime."[39] Environmental pioneers such as John Muir and Aldo Leopold deployed religious claims of "sanctuary," "cathedrals of nature," and "sacred fires" in their pioneering formulations of the proposition that nature had value and claim beyond serving as an instrumental and utilitarian resource for human appropriation, and such tendencies have flourished and expanded in environmentalism over the past half-century.[40] Initial indictments of the currently dominant religious traditions by Lynn White Jr. and others quickly gave way to a widespread rereading of their texts and traditions and the discovery of a variety of powerful green strands and dimensions. Radical green religious theory and practice has also pioneered new forms of sacred ritual and spiritual practice.[41] While often miscast by critics as "New Age," such tendencies are, in a more basic way, extremely "Old Age" because they attempt to refurbish and extend religious forms marginalized as primitive, such as the Earth Mother cult and various forms of spirituality found in indigenous cultures, the "first nations" that have persisted at the underdeveloped margins of modern globalizing industrial civilization.[42]

National identity, so prevalent in the modern world, has also been subject to a similar pattern of subversion, deconstruction, and reconstruction in emergent environmental theory and practice. The rhetoric of the national is highly naturalistic. The word *nation*, meaning "to be born," asserts that there is something biologically and prepolitically natural in associations that are in fact historical and bolstered by state interests, warmaking, and official education. Naturalization is the process by which "aliens" become citizens. The state and nation are cast as the motherland and the fatherland. Nations also evoke claims of particular places and affiliations to place—what geographers refer to as "topophilia."[43] In contrast to these essentially unnatural "imagined communities," green movements assert identities and communities that actually have substantial biological and natural foundations, as well as claims to place. Ecologically inflected environmental thinking and practice assert that human bodies and human practices are deeply enmeshed in natural flows and processes, and Earth system science establishes the intimate material connectivity of humans across the lines drawn on the Earth by national states. Similarly, environmental theory and practice evoke a variety of topophilic claims, stretching from the bioregion to the whole Earth as a distinct place to which human attachments are most appropriately directed.

Taken together, these emerging green naturalistic discourses and practices, combined with the new ecological Earth system "chaoplexic" sciences, provide robust new forms of identity and community of a civilization-grade scope.

Greening Economics: From Anticapitalism to Natural Capitalism

In speaking of an emergent green civilizational formation that spans the spectra of spatial scale, from the individual to the planet, and of topical scope, from the quotidian to the cosmological, questions about mundane material activities and their impacts have a practical primacy. The reason humans are having such a significant impact on nature is that human technologies have been deployed for the purposes of production and consumption in ways that displace and disrupt natural systems. Fixing the environmental problem is essentially a task of reconfiguring the human relationship to these material flows, thus recasting the human role in the planetary metabolism.[44] The expansion of technological capabilities and the enlargement of the human population, occurring in a finite space, have turned previously local and regional impacts into planetary ones. However, a focus on the actual ("where the rubber meets the road") interface between humans, their technology, and nature must grapple with the patterns and institutions of economic systems that so powerfully shape them.

When modern environmentalism emerged in the 1960s, two distinct economic systems—state socialism and market capitalism—were both environmentally destructive.[45] With the collapse of the socialist project in the last decades of the twentieth century, capitalism was not only left standing but also was able, under the rubrics of "free trade," "globalization," and "transitions to market economies," to become the single dominant economic form on the planet. First-impulse environmentalism was highly critical of capitalism and socialism, and the industrialism that both were firmly committed to. Criticisms of capitalism, actually existing socialism, and industrialism were an opening of the powerful deconstructive and antihegemonic moment in the emergence of modern environmentalism.[46] And with the accelerated spread of market economies over the past several decades, criticisms of globalization have become a central facet of environmental theory and practice. From the beginning of the modern environmental movement through the present, the spread of market relations and the industrialization of natural resources, such as the opening of mines, the construction of pipelines, the damming of rivers, the filling of wetlands, and the conversion of rain forest into pastures, have been decisive battlegrounds for the green project. And despite nontrivial particular victories, the overall tide of these encounters has been relentlessly on the side of capitalism, industrialism, and globalization.

In the face of the primacy of capitalism and the globalization of economic activities, environmental economic thinking becomes a primary part of the emergent environmental project. A variety of radical critiques, reforms, and reconfigurations have been developed by green-oriented economic thinkers. Some, such as ecoanarchists and local communitarians, envisage the dismantlement of large-scale economic systems and their reconstruction on local and municipal scales.[47] Others advance a refurbished Marxism and ecosocialism.[48] A central axis of concern in ecoeconomics has been the question of limits to growth, an approach that was particularly salient in the late 1960s and 1970s and gained wide currency with the 1972 report by the Club of Rome, *Limits to Growth*. This study triggered an ongoing debate between the limits-to-growth position and various technological "cornucopians" such as Julian Simon and Bjørn Lomborg.[49] Others, such as Herman Daly and his school, attempted to reconstruct economics along ecologically more satisfactory lines.[50]

A particularly useful and influential way of framing the economic implications of ecological finitude is the economist Kenneth Boulding's distinction between a "cowboy economy" and a "spaceship economy."[51] The cowboy economy is marked by the presence of an expanding frontier for resource extraction and the presence of natural sinks for the dispersal of wastes. Conversely, a spaceship economy is one in which there is no outside into which extraction can expand and in which the absorptive capacity of sinks, such as the ocean and the atmosphere, has been exhausted. Boulding argued that economic practices and institutions needed to evolve from the cowboy to the spaceship model economy.

Transitioning from a cowboy to a spaceship economy requires not the abolition or replacement of capitalism but rather its reconfiguration.[52] And much of environmental economic theory and practice has been oriented toward this task. In this approach, the sophisticated tools of neoclassical economics, developed to explain free market economies, are both insufficient and vital. Neoclassical economics has no satisfactory account of what resources are appropriately made into property and generally relies on the squatters' rights approach at the expense of traditional users and ecological limits.[53] Similarly, neoclassical economics reflects the short-term time horizons of market-driven actors and thus discounts potential future impacts, a disastrous limitation for framing choices with intergenerational and millennial time horizons. Also, market economies have a systemic problem when the concentrated interests of producers can be more readily mobilized and brought to bear on political decision making than the dispersed and less intense interests of those harmed by producer activities.

Neoclassical economics nevertheless provides powerful insights and tools to arrest environmental problems. Most important is the concept of externality, which refers to situations in which the costs (or benefits) of the decisions of market actors are imposed on unwilling third parties. The presence of negative externalities such as pollution is a "market imperfection," and economists have developed a powerful set of tools to understand and correct them, ranging from direct regulation to effluent taxes and tradable permit schemes. All of these internalization strategies, however, depend on state action, which is itself subject to a host of government imperfections, most notably capture by special interest groups.[54] Furthermore, market competition has historically been tremendously stimulative of technological innovations of the sort vital for the construction of a spaceship economy.

Another particularly illuminating redeployment of the conceptual apparatus of economics for a spaceship system is the notion of natural capital— the idea that nature is a capital stock that provides a flow of valuable services to humanity that are unpriced, and thus overconsumed and not taken into account in calculations of aggregate growth and well-being. These flows, estimated to be in the neighborhood of $33 trillion a year, roughly equal to half the monetarized gross world product, depend on the stock of "natural capital," which no one owns but which on conservative calculations of flow-to-stock value ratios would be worth nearly $500 trillion.[55] Such a "natural capital" framework for conceptualizing spaceship economies tells us that the existing economic system, although called "capitalism," is actually a form of consumerism that is diminishing capital stocks and thus is really anticapitalism.[56] Thus natural capital provides a crucial conceptual building block for a spaceship economy.

The approach that we have outlined here differs from the pessimism of Conca's view in several ways. First, we see capitalism itself as having a mix of both negative and positive relations to sustainability, while he emphasizes solely the negative ones. Furthermore, we see a greater plasticity to capitalist institutions than does Conca, and we point to the fact that capitalism has historically been combined with a wide variety of other political, social, and economic arrangements. This means that there is no "capitalism," only many "capitalisms." The accelerated globalization of market activity over the past several decades has indeed set back sustainability goals, as Conca claims, but the space for further races to the bottom is rapidly closing as even the poorest countries are beginning to experience nature's backlash in acute forms. Furthermore, green enclaves such as California, which Conca points to as insufficient and based on the export of nongreen economic activities, are being increasingly superseded by an awareness that the relevant unit for sustainability is the planet itself and that the agenda is to globalize the practices pioneered in these green enclaves. And finally, the increasing connection between global poverty and environmental destruction highlighted by Pope Francis's encyclical Laudato Si' (2015) points to the merging of the global justice and global sustainability movements in a way that could further foreclose the externalization of environmental harms to the regions inhabited by the poor and weak.

Technology: From Pristine Nature and Anti-Industrialism to Green Urbanism and Industrial Ecology

Closely related to the green economic agenda is the question of technology. From its earliest conceptualizations by Francis Bacon and others, the science of the moderns promised a transformation of the human estate through technological advance.[57] With the new sciences based on "torturing nature," humanity would "conquer nature." The modern world's unrestrained embrace of this project led to the amplification of human powers and numbers that has wreaked ruin on the planet's biosphere. Thus, not surprisingly, the emergence of environmental awareness in the middle years of the twentieth century heavily centered on a strong critique and near complete rejection of technological modernization. Modern environmentalism arose in response to the unanticipated negative second-order consequences of industrial technologies such as pesticides and fertilizers, automobiles and power plants, and jet airplanes and nuclear power. First-impulse environmentalism was strongly technophobic, and theorists such as Lewis Mumford, Jacques Ellul, and Langdon Winner sketched a comprehensive indictment of technological modernity running amok.[58] Earlier environmentalist thinking valued the pristine in nature and saw the city as the site of loss and corruption. From this orientation, there emerged agendas of wilderness preservation, back-to-the-land movements, and the rejection of complex and advanced technologies. But over subsequent decades, a very different orientation has emerged that proposes not anti-industrialism but industrial ecology, and not the rejection of cities but green urbanism.

While first-wave environmentalism embraced the pristine and valorized the wilderness, it became evident that strategies of preservation and complete containment, while valuable, would have modest impacts on ameliorating or reducing anthropogenic damage to the biosphere. And in recent decades, the city has emerged as the central locus for the emergence of new sustainable practices and arrangements with global-scale leverage.[59] Cities, being where most consumption occurs, can greatly lower their footprint by reconfiguring their infrastructures. Particularly notable has been the rise of green architecture and green buildings that dramatically lower consumption of materials, energy, and water through innovative designs.[60] These moves exploit the fact that the density of cities, initially decried as intrinsically antienvironmental, has immense intrinsic advantages for reducing energy and materials use, in contrast to the sprawl associated with suburban and rural infrastructures.[61] Shaped by farsighted municipal policies in zoning, taxation, and regulation, the infrastructures of cities are becoming increasingly frugal in their environmental impacts.[62]

The automobile and the automobilization of transportation had immensely negative effects on the air and on land use, and required the production of large quantities of steel, plastics, and fossil fuels. First-wave rejectionist environmental thought elevated the automobile into the reigning icon of things gone wrong. Subsequently, however, environmental thinking and practice have focused on essentially reinventing the automobile through design changes to increase the efficiency of fuel use by reducing weight and aerodynamic drag, eventually leading to "hypercars" that use comparatively minuscule resource inputs. A lesser reliance on even improved automobiles remains a central goal of environmentalists, and a great effort has been placed on building mass transit systems and reconfiguring urban infrastructure to make bicycling and walking more attractive.

A similar pattern of evolution from rejectionism and dismantling to thorough reconstitution and reconfiguration is visible with industrial production, where first-wave environmentalism was strongly anti-industrial but has increasingly given way to industrial ecology, an attempt to redesign basic industrial processes to use fewer virgin materials and less energy, and to generate less waste. At its furthest reaches, industrial ecology aims to make the metabolism of industry suitable for the completely closed "spaceship" economy in which the waste streams of one industry become the resource streams of another.[63]

The case for viewing emergent environmental theory and practice with regard to technology as a civilizational dimension rests on the comprehensive character of the green agenda for the reconfiguration of the mundane material world—the system of physical infrastructures, artifacts, and flows on spatial scales that span from the micro to the planetary. The material program of previous civilizations often penetrated into individual daily dietary and reproductive practices, but their overall material imprint was

largely a mixture of monumental buildings and ceremonial city infrastructures, combined with the unintentional and unscripted effects on the
broader metabolic human-machine-nature complex. In contrast, the green
program is literally an agenda for a comprehensively remade world, not just
with regard to consciousness and institutions but also for the entire material fabric of the Earth as a place.

The Ascent of Climate Change: From Human Impacts on Nature to the Anthropocene

Among the myriad issues and topics that environmentalism has been grappling with or seeking to address, climate change has rapidly emerged in the
last two decades, as the issue of issues, the most important environmental
problem, and the problem that connects all other problems in intimate and
unexpected ways.[64] Carbon loading of the atmosphere changing the Earth's
climate has been a topic of concern for environmentalists since the 1960s,
but until two decades ago, it tended to be an issue for the distant or perhaps
midterm, but not near-term, future. Furthermore, scientific understanding
of the consequences of rising greenhouse gases, immensely complicated,
has matured more slowly than knowledge about more localized environmental problems.[65] Over the past two decades, knowledge about the climate has rapidly advanced and clarified the very negative consequences of
climate change, at the same time that rapid economic growth, fueled by
rocketing fossil fuel use in China, India, and elsewhere, has brought the
time frame for dire consequences much closer.

This rapid arrival of climate change as a severe problem has three profound and far-reaching implications for the green civilizational project.
First, it unifies all other environmental agendas in a much more complete
manner than ever before. Second, it forces reconsideration and reprioritiza-
tion, sometimes radically, of all other green programs. Third, it raises the
salience and visibility of environmental problems to a new level, potentially crossing a threshold to galvanize far-reaching and substantial implementation of environmental agendas.

Climate change as a problem, and decarbonization as an agenda, powerfully unifies green agendas for the first time. An indicator of the unifying
effect of climate change is the emergence of the category of the Anthropocene as an Earth geologic period defined by human impacts, thus replacing
earlier attempts to provide an overall picture of human effects on the environment, which tended to be a composite list.[66] Climate change brings
about comprehensive change in the Earth's air, water, and land, and thus

affects in a fundamental way everything, everywhere. Environmental problems that have been salient in environmental thinking and practice in the past have been spatially more limited and concentrated in their effects on different ecological and geophysical domains. Carbon loading of the atmosphere and the warming of the planet from the greenhouse effect will alter the atmosphere and its patterns of mesoscale flows, such as the East and South Asian monsoons, the Atlantic Gulf Stream, and the North American Jet Stream. This will result in substantial changes in the weather in virtually every part of the world, affecting patterns of rainfall and the range of temperature variation, increasing the severity of extreme weather events (tornados, hurricanes, floods), and altering their distribution.[67] The ocean will also be dramatically affected by alterations in the massive water flows of the thermo-haline circulation system. Climate change also acidifies the ocean, with far-reaching implications for fisheries and coral reefs. Climate change has profound impacts on the land as well, as changing rainfall patterns turn agricultural areas into steppes and deserts, as changing temperatures alter the ranges of species habitats and melt glaciers, and as rising sea level floods low-lying coastal areas in which many of the world's largest cities and population concentrations are located. Taken as a whole, climate change poses a catastrophic threat to existing human civilization in a way that no previous problem, with the exception of general nuclear war, has ever done.

Second, climate change largely obviates many of the environmental accomplishments to date. As rainfall and temperate patterns change, the various wilderness areas and wildlife preserves will be massively perturbed. As climate changes, the zones of habitability for different species change, forcing either extinctions or migrations. As the ocean level rises, preserved wetlands will be inundated, eliminating their ecological value. As the ocean acidifies, coral reefs protected from dredging or development will be decimated by the changes to the water itself. In sum, climate change radically subverts the viability of local and regional-scale arrangements for environmental protection.

As climate change has rapidly emerged as the master environmental problem, previous environmentalist programs are subject to fundamental reassessment and sometimes radical reversal. The most important such case is nuclear power, which environmentalists have been attempting to restrain and eliminate since the 1960s. Increasingly many leading environmental thinkers and analysts realize that large-scale reliance on nuclear power may be the only short- and midterm energy alternative capable of replacing the currently massive reliance on fossil fuels, particularly coal. Compared to climate change, the environmental problems of nuclear power appear far less threatening and more manageable. For environmentalists to begin supporting, instead of resisting, nuclear power marks a profound reversal in the green agenda, one that many environmentalists have been reluctant to fully make. Thus, green antinuclearism, a defining feature of first-wave environmentalism, is giving way to a pro-nuclear second wave environmentalism in the shadow of emergent climate catastrophe. In this case, the second wave constructive technological agenda unexpectedly embraces the defining technology rejected by first impulse environmentalism.[68]

Third, the rise of climate change pushes the harms from environmental deterioration across a threshold of importance, and this is likely to elevate the environmental agenda into the central political and economic concern of the world. If global mean temperature passes the 2°C threshold, the human population in large parts of the world will be profoundly and adversely affected through coastal zone flooding, drought-caused agricultural decline, the spread of tropical diseases, and political and economic disruptions that may ensue. This enlarged horizon of negative consequence strengthens the credibility of the environmentalist critique and the appeal of its alternatives in an unprecedented manner. Furthermore, as climate change alters weather patterns, people everywhere will experience this as an actual problem rather than an abstract hypothetical future problem, making possible much larger-scale mobilization of public support and resources for green agendas. The rise of climate change and the comprehensive character of its impacts make the green program into a civilizational alternative with immediate and urgent practical appeal. Unfortunately, the window for preventing the worst of climate change may have already closed, or be closing, more rapidly than responses can be mobilized. It is also possible that worst-case scenarios of runaway climate change triggered by geophysical mechanisms of positive feedback may make the problem vastly greater very rapidly, thus overwhelming even greatly enhanced efforts of response.[69] Should these worst-case scenarios materialize and much of industrial civilization collapse, and most of the human population die off, it seems reasonable to think that the remnant civilization will be sobered into becoming, by harsh necessity, a green civilization.

Civilizational Transitions and the Green Horizon

In this chapter, we have sketched out the case for viewing the immense diversity of green theory and practice as constituting a nascent civilizational formation, outlined some of the ways in which this emergent green civilization has been internally evolving, and described the catalytic role of climate change in crystallizing this transition. It is appropriate to think about green theory and practice as a civilizational-grade formation because it encompasses strong components along an axis of size from the individual and the municipal, through the region and nation-state, to world order as well as an axis of scope of significance spanning from the mundane to the cosmological. Furthermore, this emergent green civilization includes a robust narrative about time, connecting the present with the past and the future, as well as about space, connecting the microlocal with the full planetary. This civilization is centered on the features of the planet Earth and offers comprehensive guidelines for sustainable human habitation with the New Earth. Over the past half-century, green theory and practice have evolved from an initial posture of opposition, resistance, and deconstruction into one that is affirmative, alternative, constructive, and reconstructive. This evolution has been particularly pronounced in green thinking about economics and technology. Its claim to civilizational status is furthered by its rich narratives about identity and community and its spiritual, religious, and cosmological dimensions.

The Earth has been remade by scientific-technological civilization into a New Earth, but the full slate of human practices, identities, and institutions has yet to adjust to the new planetary situation. In thinking about civilizational transitions, many of the existing conceptual frameworks for thinking about change, evolution, and revolution in politics are an inadequate guide. Civilizational transitions are infrequent and, almost by definition, qualitatively different from one another. The largest subcivilizational model of change, of interstate hegemonic transitions and successions, captures the important antagonism between the rising new and the declining old and the contentious political struggles over priorities, resources, and policies. But it leaves out an essential aspect of civilizational transition: that civilizational change emerges not from shifts in power but rather from shifts in the field of fundamental problems that afflict the human world. And the ultimate motor for transition is the superior ability of the rising civilizational formation to address such problems.

A parting image of the transition from globalizing scientific-technological modern civilization to the emergent planetary Earth-centered civilization helps captures the epochal shift that is underway. The modern industrial civilization can be likened to a molded but immobile massive infrastructure of concrete. Its rudely thoughtless intrusion into the landscape has caused a cascade of environmental problems, and as a result this concrete edifice has come to be cracked and crumbling. But a new order is starting to emerge everywhere in its ruins. Its surfaces are mottled with a thickening carpet of lichens, which are slowly but surely dissolving and digesting its imposing structures. Within the cracks of the concrete and nourished by the soil-producing lichens, vibrant green weeds are sprouting everywhere. Some are growing into riotous, thorny bushes, and a precocious few are growing into stout but flexible saplings and trees. How soon the crushing immobility of the concrete of the old order will fully give way to the fecundity and the fertility of its burgeoning green successor is hard to say, but that such a transition is underway is hard to deny.

Notes

This chapter benefited from comments on earlier drafts from Margaret Keck, Peter Haas, Peter Katzenstein, and members of the Johns Hopkins Sustainability Roundtable.

1. Homer-Dixon, *The Upside of Down*.

2. A large literature exists with many strong disagreements. We follow Toynbee's seminal mid-twentieth-century formulation in holding that a modern civilization centered on Enlightenment rationality emerged in Europe in the early modern period and that it first killed Latin Christendom and in its subsequent globalization has killed all sister agricultural urban civilizations, ranging from the Aztec and Inca through the Islamic, Hindu, and Confucian. Samuel P. Huntington's prominent argument about the emerging "clash of civilizations" thus mistakes cultural zones for a civilization. In terms of Peter Katzenstein's formulation, emergent green civilization is an alternative or multiple modernity. Toynbee, *A Study of History*; Huntington, *The Clash of Civilizations*; Katzenstein, *Civilizations in World Politics*.

3. Carson, *Silent Spring*; Ehrlich, *The Population Bomb*; Hays, *Beauty, Health, and Permanence*.

4. John Robert McNeill, *Something New under the Sun*; Michael, *Planetary Overload*.

5. Hays, *Conservation and the Gospel of Efficiency*.

6. Braudel, *Capitalism and Material Life*.

7. Flannery, *Here on Earth*.

8. Crosby, *Ecological Imperialism*.

9. Radkau, *Nature and Power*.

10. Christian, Brown, and Benjamin, *Big History*; Rudwick, *Earth's Deep History*.

11. Orr, *Earth in Mind*.

12. Kolbert, *The Sixth Extinction*.

13. Dewey, *The Public and Its Problems*.

14. Kellert, *Birthright*.

15. Weiss, ed., *In Fairness to Future Generations*.

16. Cosgrove, *Apollo's Eye a Cartographic Genealogy of the Earth*.

17. Poole, *Earthrise*; Denis Cosgrove, "Contested Global Visions."

18. Heise, *Sense of Place and Sense of Planet*.

19. Burrows, *This New Ocean*.

20. Zubrin, *Entering Space*.

21. Zubrin, *Merchants of Despair*; O'Neill, *The High Frontier*.

22. Chaikin, *A Man on the Moon*.

23. Deudney, *Space the High Frontier in Perspective*.

24. Aldrin, *Magnificent Desolation*.

25. Jasanoff and Long, *Earthly Politics*.

26. Berry, "Out of Your Car, Off Your Horse"; Mittelman, The Globalization Syndrome; Veseth, *Globaloney*.

27. Lovelock, *Gaia*.

28. Alker and Haas, "The Rise of Global Ecopolitics."

29. Beck, *Risk Society*; Beck, *World at Risk*.

30. Maniates and Meyer, eds., *The Environmental Politics of Sacrifice*; Dobson and Bell, eds., *Environmental Citizenship*.

31. Gerlach, "Negotiating Ecological Interdependence through Societal Debate."

32. Rosenau, *Distant Proximities*.

33. Robyn Eckersley, *The Green State*.

34. Wapner, *Environmental Activism and World Civic Politics*; Young, *International Cooperation*; Keohane and Victor, "The Regime Complex for Climate Change"; Conca, *Governing Water*.

35. Bennett, *The Enchantment of Modern Life*.

36. Daniel Deudney, "Ground Identity"; Berman, *The Reenchantment of the World*.

37. Toulmin, *Cosmopolis*.

38. Botkin, *Discordant Harmonies*; Nadeau, *Rebirth of the Sacred*.

39. Nicolson, *Mountain Gloom and Mountain Glory*.

40. Nash, *The Rights of Nature*.

41. Taylor, *Dark Green Religion*.

42. Hallman, *Ecotheology*.

43. Tuan, *Space and Place*.

44. Luke, "Urbanism as Cyberorganicity."

45. Feshbach and Friendly, *Ecocide in the U.S.S.R*; Shapiro, *Mao's War against Nature*.

46. Commoner, *The Closing Circle*.

47. Bookchin, *Social Ecology and Communalism*.

48. Benton, *The Greening of Marxism*.

49. Simon, *The Ultimate Resource 2*; Lomborg, *Global Crises, Global Solutions*.

50. Daly and Townsend, *Valuing the Earth*.

51. Boulding, "The Economics of the Coming Spaceship Earth."

52. Grubb, *Planetary Economics*; Sachs, *Common Wealth*.

53. Pearce, *The Land Grabbers*.

54. Bernstein, *The Compromise of Liberal Environmentalism*.

55. Hawken, Lovins, and Lovins, *Natural Capitalism*; Costanza et al., "The Value of the World's Ecosystem Services and Natural Capital."

56. Hawken et al., *Natural Capitalism*.

57. Bacon, *The Great Instauration*.

58. Mumford, *The Pentagon of Power*; Ellul, *The Technological Society*; Winner, *Autonomous Technology*.

59. Barber, *If Mayors Ruled the World*.

60. Chambers, *Urban Green*.

61. Meyer, *The Environmental Advantages of Cities*.

62. Brand, *Whole Earth Discipline*.

63. Socolow et al., *Industrial Ecology and Global Change*.

64. Gardiner, *A Perfect Moral Storm:*.

65. Weart, *The Discovery of Global Warming*.

66. Thomas, *Man's Role in Changing the Face of the Earth.*

67. McKibben, *The End of Nature.*

68. Brand, *Whole Earth Discipline.*

69. Pearce, *With Speed and Violence.*

Bibliography

Aldrin, Buzz. *Magnificent Desolation: The Long Journey Home from the Moon.* New York: Three Rivers Press, 2010.

Alker, Hayward R., and Peter M. Haas. *"The Rise of Global Ecopolitics."* In *Global Accord: Environmental Challenges and International Responses*, edited by Nazli Choucri. Cambridge, MA: MIT Press, 1995.

Bacon, Francis. *The Great Instauration.* Calgary: Theophania Publishing, 2011. (1620).

Barber, Benjamin R. *If Mayors Ruled the World: Dysfunctional Nations, Rising Cities.* New Haven, CT: Yale University Press, 2014.

Beck, Ulrich. *Risk Society: Towards a New Modernity.* London: Sage, 1992.

Beck, Ulrich. *World at Risk.* Cambridge: Polity Press, 2009.

Bennett, Jane. *The Enchantment of Modern Life: Attachments, Crossings, and Ethics.* Princeton, NJ: Princeton University Press, 2001.

Benton, Ted. *The Greening of Marxism.* New York: Guilford Press, 1996.

Berman, Morris. *The Reenchantment of the World.* Ithaca, NY: Cornell University Press, 1981.

Bernstein, Steven F. *The Compromise of Liberal Environmentalism.* New York: Columbia University Press, 2001.

Berry, Wendell. "Out of Your Car, Off Your Horse." *Atlantic* (February 1991):1.

Bookchin, Murray. *Social Ecology and Communalism.* Edinburgh: AK Press, 2007.

Botkin, Daniel B. *Discordant Harmonies: A New Ecology for the Twenty-First Century.* New York: Oxford University Press, 1990.

Boulding, Kenneth. *"The Economics of the Coming Spaceship Earth."* In *Environmental Quality in a Growing Economy*, edited by Henry Ed Jarrett. Baltimore, MD: Johns Hopkins University Press, 1966.

Brand, Stewart. *Whole Earth Discipline: An Ecopragmatist Manifesto.* New York: Viking, 2009.

Braudel, Fernand. *Capitalism and Material Life, 1400–1800*. New York: Harper and Row, 1973.

Burrows, William E. *This New Ocean: The Story of the First Space Age*. New York: Modern Library, 1999.

Carson, Rachel. *Silent Spring*. Boston: Houghton Mifflin, 2002.

Chaikin, Andrew. *A Man on the Moon: One Giant Leap*. Alexandria, VA: Time-Life Books, 1999.

Chambers, Neil B. *Urban Green: Architecture for the Future*. New York: Palgrave Macmillan, 2011.

Christian, David, Cynthia Stokes Brown, and Craig Benjamin. *Big History: Between Nothing and Everything*. New York: McGraw-Hill, 2014.

Commoner, Barry. *The Closing Circle: Nature, Man, and Technology*. New York: Knopf, 1971.

Conca, Ken. *Governing Water: Contentious Transnational Politics and Global Institution Building*. Cambridge, MA: MIT Press, 2006.

Cosgrove, Denis E. *Apollo's Eye a Cartographic Genealogy of the Earth in the Western Imagination*. Baltimore, MD: Johns Hopkins University Press, 2001.

Cosgrove, Denis. "Contested Global Visions: One-World, Whole-Earth, and the Apollo Space Photographs." *Annals of the Association of American Geographers* 84 (1994): 270–94.

Costanza, Robert, Ralph d'Arge, Rudolf de Groot, Stephen Farber, Monica Grasso, Bruce Hannon, Karin Limburg, "The Value of the World's Ecosystem Services and Natural Capital." *Ecological Economics* 25, no. 1 (April 1998): 3–15.

Crosby, Alfred W. *Ecological Imperialism: The Biological Expansion of Europe, 900–1900*, 2nd ed. Cambridge: Cambridge University Press, 2004.

Daly, Herman E., and Kenneth N. Townsend. *Valuing the Earth: Economics, Ecology, Ethics*. Cambridge, MA: MIT Press, 1993.

Deudney, Daniel. "Ground Identity: Nature, Place, and Space in Nationalism." In *The Return of Culture and Identity in IR Theory*, edited by Yosef Lapid and Friedrich Kratochwil, 129–45. Boulder, CO: Lynne Rienner, 1996.

Deudney, Daniel. *Space the High Frontier in Perspective*. Washington, DC: Worldwatch Institute, 1982.

Dewey, John. *The Public and Its Problems an Essay in Political Inquiry*. University Park: Pennsylvania State University Press, 2012.

Dobson, A., and D. Bell, eds. *Environmental Citizenship*. Cambridge, MA.: MIT Press, 2006.

Eckersley, Robyn. *The Green State: Rethinking Democracy and Sovereignty*. Cambridge, MA: MIT Press, 2004.

Ehrlich, Paul R. *The Population Bomb*. Cutchogue, NY: Buccaneer Books, 1995.

Ellul, Jacques. *The Technological Society*. New York: Vintage Books, 1964.

Feshbach, Murray, and Alfred Friendly Jr. *Ecocide in the U.S.S.R.: Health and Nature under Siege*. London: Aurum Press, 1992.

Flannery, Tim F. *Here on Earth: A Natural History of the Planet*. New York: Atlantic Monthly Press, 2010.

Gardiner, Stephen. *A Perfect Moral Storm: The Ethical Tragedy of Climate Change*. New York: Oxford University Press, 2011.

Gerlach, Luther P. "Negotiating Ecological Interdependence through Societal Debate: The 1988 Minnesota Drought." In *The State and Social Power in Global Environmental Politics*, edited by Ronnie D. Lipschutz and Ken Conca. 185–220. New York: Columbia University Press, 1993.

Grubb, Michael. *Planetary Economics: Energy, Climate Change and the Three Domains of Sustainable Development*. New York: Routledge, 2013.

Hallman, David G. *Ecotheology: Voices from South and North*. Eugene: Wipf & Stock Publishers, 2009.

Hawken, Paul, Amory B. Lovins, and L. Hunter Lovins. *Natural Capitalism: Creating the next Industrial Revolution*. Boston: Little, Brown, 1999.

Hays, Samuel P. *Beauty, Health, and Permanence: Environmental Politics in the United States, 1955–1985*. Cambridge: Cambridge University Press, 1989.

Hays, Samuel P. *Conservation and the Gospel of Efficiency: The Progressive Conservation Movement, 1890–1920*. Pittsburgh: University of Pittsburgh Press, 1999.

Heise, Ursula K. *Sense of Place and Sense of Planet: The Environmental Imagination of the Global*. Oxford: Oxford University Press, 2008.

Homer-Dixon, Thomas F. *The Upside of Down: Catastrophe, Creativity, and the Renewal of Civilization*. Washington, DC: Island Press, 2006.

Huntington, Samuel P. *The Clash of Civilizations and the Remaking of World Order*. New York: Simon and Shuster, 2011.

Jasanoff, Sheila, and Marybeth Long. *Earthly Politics: Local and Global in Environmental Governance*. Cambridge, MA: MIT Press, 2004.

Katzenstein, P., ed. *Civilizations in World Politics: Plural and Pluralist Perspectives*. New York: Routledge, 2010.

Kellert, Stephen R. *Birthright: People and Nature in the Modern World*. New Haven, CT: Yale University Press, 2014.

Keohane, Robert O., and David G. Victor. "The Regime Complex for Climate Change." *Perspectives on Politics* 9, no. 1 (2011): 7–23.

Kolbert, Elizabeth. *The Sixth Extinction: An Unnatural History*. New York: Holt, 2014.

Lomborg, Bjørn. *Global Crises, Global Solutions*. Cambridge: Cambridge University Press, 2009.

Lovelock, J. E. *Gaia: A New Look at Life on Earth*. Oxford: Oxford University Press, 1979.

Luke, Timothy W. "Urbanism as Cyberorganicity." In*New Geographies 06: Grounding Metabolism*, edited by Daniel Ibañez and Nikos Katsikis. Cambridge, MA: Harvard University Press, 2014.

Maniates, M., and J. M. Meyer, eds. *The Environmental Politics of Sacrifice*. Cambridge, MA: MIT Press, 2010.

McKibben, Bill. *The End of Nature*. New York: Random House, 2006.

McNeill, John Robert. *Something New under the Sun: An Environmental History of the Twentieth-Century World*. New York: Norton, 2000.

Meyer, William B. *The Environmental Advantages of Cities: Countering Commonsense Antiurbanism*. Cambridge, MA: MIT Press, 2013.

Michael, A. J. *Planetary Overload: Global Environmental Change and the Health of the Human Species*. Cambridge: Cambridge University Press, 1993.

Mittelman, James H. *The Globalization Syndrome: Transformation and Resistance*. Princeton, NJ: Princeton University Press, 2000.

Mumford, Lewis. *The Pentagon of Power: The Myth of the Machine*. San Diego, CA: Harcourt Brace Jovanovich, 1970.

Nadeau, Robert. *Rebirth of the Sacred: Science, Religion and the New Environmental Ethos*. New York: Oxford University Press, 2013.

Nash, Roderick F. *The Rights of Nature: A History of Environmental Ethics*. Princeton, NJ: University of Wisconsin Press, 2007.

Nicolson, Marjorie Hope. *Mountain Gloom and Mountain Glory: The Development of the Aesthetics of the Infinite*. Seattle: University of Washington Press, 1997.

O'Neill, Gerard K. *The High Frontier: Human Colonies in Space*. Princeton, NJ: Space Studies Institute Press, 1989.

Orr, David W. *Earth in Mind: On Education, Environment, and the Human Prospect.* Washington, DC: Island Press, 2004.

Pearce, Fred. *The Land Grabbers: The New Fight over Who Owns the Earth.* Boston: Beacon Press, 2012.

Pearce, Fred. *With Speed and Violence: Why Scientists Fear Tipping Points in Climate Change.* Boston: Beacon Press, 2007.

Poole, Robert. *Earthrise: How Man First Saw the Earth.* New Haven, CT: Yale University Press, 2008.

Radkau, Joachim. *Nature and Power: A Global History of the Environment.* Cambridge: Cambridge University Press, 2008.

Rosenau, James N. *Distant Proximities: Dynamics beyond Globalization.* Princeton, NJ: Princeton University Press, 2003.

Rudwick, M. J. S. *Earth's Deep History: How It Was Discovered and Why It Matters.* Chicago: University of Chicago Press, 2014.

Sachs, Jeffrey. *Common Wealth: Economics for a Crowded Planet.* New York: Penguin, 2009.

Shapiro, Judith. *Mao's War against Nature: Politics and the Environment in Revolutionary China.* Cambridge: Cambridge University Press, 2001.

Simon, Julian Lincoln. *The Ultimate Resource 2.* Princeton, NJ: Princeton University Press, 1996.

Socolow, Robert H., *Industrial Ecology and Global Change.* Cambridge: Cambridge University Press, 1997.

Taylor, Bron Raymond. *Dark Green Religion: Nature Spirituality and the Planetary Future.* Berkeley, CA: University of California Press, 2010.

Thomas, W. L. *Man's Role in Changing the Face of the Earth.* Chicago: University of Chicago Press, 1971.

Toulmin, Stephen. *Cosmopolis: The Hidden Agenda of Modernity.* Chicago: University of Chicago Press, 1992.

Toynbee, Arnold J. *A Study of History*, 12 vols. New York : Oxford University Press, 1935.

Tuan, Yi-Fu. *Space and Place: The Perspective of Experience.* Minneapolis: University of Minnesota Press, 1977.

Veseth, Michael. *Globaloney: Unraveling the Myths of Globalization.* Lanham, MD: Rowman & Littlefield, 2006.

Wapner, Paul. *Environmental Activism and World Civic Politics*. Albany: State University of New York Press, 1996.

Weart, Spencer R. *The Discovery of Global Warming*. Cambridge, MA: Harvard University Press, 2008.

Weiss, E. B., ed. *In Fairness to Future Generations: International Law, Common Patrimony, and Intergenerational Equity, Innovation in International Law*. New York: Transnational Publishers, 1989.

Winner, Langdon. *Autonomous Technology: Technics-out-of-Control as a Theme in Political Thought*. Cambridge, MA: MIT Press, 1978.

Young, Oran R. *International Cooperation: Building Regimes for Natural Resources and the Environment*. Ithaca, NY: Cornell University Press, 1989.

Zubrin, Robert. *Entering Space: Creating a Spacefaring Civilization*. New York: Putnam, 2000.

Zubrin, Robert. *Merchants of Despair Radical Environmentalists, Criminal Pseudo-Scientists, and the Fatal Cult of Antihumanism*. New York: Encounter Books, 2012.

Section 2   Scholarship as Engagement

One of the many questions facing students and scholars of global environmental politics is how best to bridge the worlds of scholarship and practice. The scholarly endeavor is often caricatured as insular and removed—as a set of activities that have little to do with the "real world." Not so with the study of global environmental politics. Students and scholars of global environmental politics are concerned about worldly realities in a most direct way. Our work, after all, seeks to understand environmental problems and develop responses that can ameliorate harm to both human and nonhuman life. Global environmental politics scholarship therefore tends to be engaged, in the sense that our scholarly pursuits are often animated and informed by pressing real-world challenges.

Still, it is one thing to study environmental matters, even in the engaged sense described above, and quite another to take the leap to acting on that scholarly work. Yet action is demanded at a time of growing environmental dangers. In preparing this book, we, the editors, felt compelled to ask, is it enough now for those of us who focus on global environmental politics to occupy the traditional role of scholar? Or does this moment call for something more? What role is there for students and scholars of global environmental politics in the world of praxis—the practical application of our scholarly activities?

This section brings together two pioneers in the field of global environmental politics to help us understand the differing approaches to engagement at the interface of scholarship and praxis. In chapter 3, Oran Young offers an autobiographical account of his distinguished career spent on what he calls the science/policy interface. Young is a theoretician of environmental regimes—of the international agreements and institutions that have emerged as a form of response to environmental harm. At the same time, he has been, among other things, an active architect of agreements to protect the Arctic and of a new set of Sustainable Development Goals developed by the United Nations. Young, in his reflections on a life spent moving between theory building and praxis, extends the view that good scholarship and effective public engagement are mutually reinforcing endeavors.

In chapter 4, similarly an autobiographical essay, Richard Falk distinguishes his own modes of praxis from those favored by Young. Falk describes his role as an engaged citizen, in contrast to the "expert" role he ascribes to Young. Falk argues that experts work within "horizons of feasibility" to engender incremental change. Yet the New Earth, he says, requires a critical and motivated citizenry to pursue "horizons of necessity," to complete the improbable work of large-scale cultural and social revolution.

These two powerful chapters teach us that engaged scholarship can be many things. Indeed, as other chapters in the book make clear, traditionally scholarly activities can themselves, in the right hands and wielded in pursuit of the right ends, be potent forms of action, or at least the precursors to more effective political engagement. Communities of scholars, teachers, and students, working together through classroom conversation and research, can shed essential light on the drivers of environmental harm (see section 1), help to prepare the next generation of engaged citizens (see section 3), pull back the curtains on institutions and the work of civil society actors (sections 4 and 5), and help craft new, potent ways of understanding and speaking about the world (section 8). Such is the work demanded of global environmental politics scholars on the New Earth.

Framing Questions Posed to the Authors in Section 2

- Looking across the global environmental politics field, what is the relationship between scholarship and praxis? How, over the field's history, have scholars of global environmental politics contributed to efforts to respond to environmental challenges?
- What, to your mind, are the shortcomings of global environmental politics scholarship, and with efforts by global environmental politics scholars to engage beyond their scholarship? What are the epistemological or institutional barriers, or both, to action-oriented scholarship, and how might any barriers be overcome?
- What types of questions should scholars of global environmental politics be asking, and what kinds of actions should they be taking to rise to the challenge of environmental problems on the New Earth?

3 The Co-production of Knowledge about International Governance: Living on the Science/Policy Interface

Oran R. Young

Discussions of usable knowledge in the field of international relations and, for that matter, many other fields commonly start with a clear separation between analysis and praxis. On one side are the analysts who seek to formulate and test general propositions about international relations. On the other are the practitioners who devote their attention to specific situations and seek to advance the interests of the states or nonstate actors that employ their services. The analysts are motivated by a desire to contribute to the development of general knowledge regarding international relations; their incentives center on rewards associated with the growth of their disciplines and with their own advancement in the world of higher education and research. The practitioners strive to make progress in addressing specific problems; they are often rewarded for moving the system toward achievement of the goals of their employers. From this perspective, it is natural to think of analysts and practitioners as belonging to separate cultures, exhibiting divergent outlooks, and experiencing differing incentives that impede communication, much less cooperation, across the resultant divide.

Yet this account of the gap between analysis and praxis in the field of international relations is too stark. Pure praxis and analysis constitute extreme types; they are the end points of a continuum that has a range of intermediate points. Some practitioners have a reflective cast of mind and proceed to develop accounts of important phenomena based on their experience with real-world problems that are of general interest. Richard Benedick's analysis of the negotiation process involved in crafting international environmental regimes derived from his experience as chief US negotiator on the 1987 Montreal Protocol is a prominent example.[1] Others operate from a vantage point closer to analysis but find themselves deeply engaged in efforts to contribute to solving real-world problems. Some (e.g.,

Gus Speth) are able to move back and forth between the worlds of analysis and praxis with relative ease.[2]

Here, I focus on issues relating to governance in international society to develop a stronger argument. Life on the science/policy interface can engender synergy benefiting analysis and praxis at the same time and contributing to the coproduction of knowledge.[3] Analysis produces propositions that can help to solve specific problems; praxis can generate insights of broader significance. To explore this argument, I draw on my experience starting in the 1980s with the effort to promote environmental protection and sustainable development in the Arctic and on my more recent experience with the effort to fulfill the mandate of the 2012 UN Conference on Sustainable Development to adopt a set of Sustainable Development Goals.

Maintaining the Arctic as a Zone of Peace

On October 1, 1987, Mikhail Gorbachev, then both president of the Soviet Union and general secretary of the Communist Party of the Soviet Union, delivered a speech in the northern city of Murmansk in which he called for recognizing the Arctic as a zone of peace and identified a suite of issues providing opportunities for mutually beneficial cooperation in the region.[4] With the winding down of the Cold War and the subsequent collapse of the Soviet Union at the end of 1991, initiatives aimed at encouraging international cooperation in the circumpolar North flourished. A stream of cooperative steps followed, including such highlights as the launching of the International Arctic Science Committee in 1990, the establishment of the Arctic Environmental Protection Strategy in 1991, the initiation of the Northern Forum in 1991, the creation of the Barents Euro-Arctic Region in 1993, the inception of the Arctic Council in 1996, and a series of measures unfolding under the auspices of the council, including the Arctic Climate Impact Assessment (2004), the Arctic Human Development Report (2004), the Arctic Marine Shipping Assessment (2009), and the legally binding Agreements on Cooperation on Aeronautical and Maritime Search and Rescue (2011) and Cooperation on Marine Oil Pollution Preparedness and Response (2013).

In retrospect, the 1990s and the 2000s may come to be seen as an exceptional period with regard to the politics of the Arctic region.[5] The end of the Cold War and the collapse of the Soviet Union had the effect of moving the Arctic to the periphery of global politics. No longer a critical theater for the deployment of advanced weapon systems, the region also seemed somewhat marginal in economic and environmental terms. But the inter-acting forces of global environmental change and economic globalization have moved the region once again to center stage in global terms.[6] The impacts of climate change are being felt more dramatically in the Arctic than anywhere else on the planet. One consequence of this is an increase in the accessibility of Arctic hydrocarbons and mineral resources of interest to the industrialized nations of East Asia (e.g., China, Japan, Korea) as well as the traditional powers of Europe and North America. The Arctic has reemerged as a focus of global attention, though this time interest in the region has more to do with economic and environmental concerns than with matters of military security.

My own involvement in Arctic politics spans the same period. During the week in which Gorbachev delivered his Murmansk speech, I received a grant from the MacArthur Foundation to launch what became known as the Working Group on Arctic International Relations (WGAIR). The group brought together a mix of analysts and practitioners from all the Arctic states. It met on a number of occasions in various Arctic locations to discuss issues like environmental protection and sustainable development but also to cultivate relations of mutual understanding and trust among well-placed individuals in the Arctic states. Meeting for the first time in spring 1988, the WGAIR got underway at just the right time to make a difference in the international relations of the post–Cold War Arctic.[7] During the 1990s, I served as a vice president of the International Arctic Science Committee and played a major role in the launching of the University of the Arctic, an entity that came into existence with the explicit blessing of the Arctic Council in 1998.[8] In 2001, I became the first chair of the university's board of governors. I served also as cochair of the 2004 Arctic Human Development Report, a project of the Arctic Council's Sustainable Development Working Group that helped to provide a road map guiding the agenda of the group in the following years.[9]

In the 1990s and the 2000s, I carried out projects for the Standing Committee of Parliamentarians of the Arctic Region, a remarkable group of individuals from the policy community who have played a role in bringing innovative ideas to bear on the process of devising governance arrangements for the Arctic region. From 2008 through 2010, I chaired the steering committee of the Arctic Governance Project (AGP), an initiative supported by a coalition of private funders known as the Arctic Funders Group and structured to engage individuals from the policy community, government agencies, the nongovernmental world, indigenous peoples' groups, and the academic community. The AGP produced a widely used website containing documents relating to Arctic governance and a series of recommendations aimed at strengthening existing arrangements in this realm.[10] The project's timing was fortuitous; it had the good fortune of being able to project a reasoned approach falling between the views of those calling for more radical reforms and those content to support the status quo. Recent developments, especially those relating to the evolution of the Arctic Council, are very much in line with the AGP's recommendations. It would be wrong to exaggerate the influence of the AGP. But it seems clear that the project made a difference with regard to developments in the realm of Arctic governance. Overall, it has been a privilege for me to be able to play a number of applied roles relating to Arctic governance, while continuing my more theoretical work on needs for international governance and the conditions likely to determine the effectiveness of international regimes created to address these needs.[11]

To explore the synergy between analysis and praxis in this setting, I focus on two substantive issues that have arisen in specific terms in the Arctic but are of more general significance: the functions or roles of international regimes or governance systems and the conditions under which it is or is not appropriate to push for the negotiation of legally binding agreements at the international level. My contribution has been to highlight the importance of the Arctic Council's nonregulatory roles and articulate the case against seeking to negotiate an Arctic treaty.

Most of those who think about international regimes start with an expectation that they are largely regulatory arrangements in the sense that they spell out requirements, prohibitions, and permissions needed to address collective-action problems or to resolve conflicts of interest among actors seeking to use the same resources for incompatible purposes.[12] Some international regimes do take this form. Most regional fisheries management organizations, for example, set forth rules dealing with matters like seasons, open and closed areas, gear types, and so forth. But an examination of needs for governance and the regimes created to deal with these needs makes it clear that regimes can and often do fulfill other functions.

Among the most important of these is a generative function.[13] This function centers on efforts to identify emerging issues, frame these issues for consideration in policy arenas, and move them up the policy agenda to the point where they become actionable within the framework of identifiable governance systems. In many cases, this agenda-setting function turns out to be every bit as important as more familiar regulatory functions.[14] Importantly, success regarding this function may not require the formal features (e.g., recognized legal personality, a dedicated secretariat, a secure revenue stream) we commonly think of in assessing the performance of regulatory regimes.

The negotiations that led to agreement on the terms of the 1996 Ottawa Declaration on the Establishment of the Arctic Council were often difficult, and the eventual outcome was disappointing to many.[15] The essential challenge was to engage the United States, which was determined to avoid addressing military security in this forum, suspicious about the inclusion of a mandate to address sustainable development, and hesitant to agree to language that could be read as acknowledging an expansive interpretation of the rights of indigenous peoples. As a result, the Ottawa Declaration is an informal instrument having no legal status and little substantive content. It establishes the Arctic Council as a "high-level forum" rather than an intergovernmental organization. Under the terms of the declaration, the council must operate on the basis of consensus, has no regular budget to support its activities, and lacks a permanent secretariat.[16] Those familiar with efforts to reach agreement on the terms of instruments like the 1987 Montreal Protocol on Substances that Deplete the Ozone Layer or the various agreements underlying the World Trade Organization consequently had low expectations regarding the performance of the Arctic Council.

Yet the performance of the Arctic Council has exceeded these low expectations by a considerable measure.[17] Why is this the case? In essence, it has to do with the success of the council in performing the generative function. During the 1990s, the council succeeded in documenting the impacts of contaminants like persistent organic pollutants (POPs) and heavy metals in a manner that influenced the negotiation of the 2001 Stockholm Convention on POPS and, more recently, the 2013 Minamata Convention on mercury.[18] The report of the Arctic Climate Impact Assessment, delivered in 2004, not only demonstrated the dramatic impacts of climate change in the high latitudes; it also dramatized the reality of climate change more generally at a time when much of the analysis of climate change was based on simulation models.[19] The 2004 Arctic Human Development Report directed attention to aspects of human well-being not captured in measures like gross domestic product or the UN Human Development Index. Specifically, it presented evidence regarding the importance of matters like meaningful contact with nature, the existence of a vibrant social network, and fate control.[20] The Arctic Marine Shipping Assessment, completed in 2009, brought a reasoned assessment of a host

of issues relating to shipping in the Arctic at a time when all sorts of alarming projections were appearing in the popular press.[21] Many of these issues
remain on the active agenda of the Arctic Council and other bodies like
the International Maritime Organization.

It is important not to exaggerate the significance of these generative
activities. But it is equally important not to ignore their influence or take
steps that would diminish the capacity of the Arctic Council to engage in
such activities going forward. An interesting question in this connection
arises from recent efforts to enhance the ability of the council to engage in
policymaking in contrast to policy shaping and to endow the council with
the conventional attributes of an intergovernmental organization (e.g., a
permanent secretariat). Most observers have treated these steps as indicators of progressive development, and there is no doubt that they are turning the council into a more "normal" intergovernmental organization.
There is something to this argument: the permanent secretariat in particular has gotten off to a good start. But I have argued that these steps may
prove costly in terms of the council's continued effectiveness as a generative mechanism. The growing interest in regulatory measures in such forms
as the search-and-rescue agreement and the agreement on oil spill preparedness and response need not conflict with generative efforts. But an
increased emphasis on regulatory measures may sidetrack the efforts of the
council's working groups, which are the engines of its generative activities.
More generally, international regimes have a finite capacity to handle distinct functions at the same time. As a result, the move toward a traditional
regulatory role could well come at the expense of continued effectiveness in
generative terms. Implicitly if not explicitly, most players in the system
place a higher value on regulatory activities than on generative activities.
Yet this could turn out to be a poor bargain in the case of the Arctic Council.
An outstanding performance in generative terms may make a greater contribution toward the maintenance of the Arctic as a zone of peace than a
pedestrian performance in regulatory terms.

Influenced by the success of the 1959 Antarctic Treaty and the governance system that has grown up around it, many policymakers and
representatives of nonstate actors have called for the negotiation of a comprehensive and legally binding treaty for the Arctic.[22] Yet initiatives along
these lines have met with little success, and there is little prospect of
movement toward the negotiation of an Arctic treaty during the foreseeable future. I have been among those arguing that there are fundamental
differences between the two polar regions in these terms and that the case

for pursuing an Arctic treaty is not compelling at this time.[23] Why is this the case?

There are fundamental differences between the two regions in jurisdictional terms. Whereas one of the principal goals of the Antarctic Treaty was to avoid the solidification of (sometimes conflicting) jurisdictional claims to slices of the continent, the jurisdictional status of the Arctic is, for the most part, well defined and undisputed. The terrestrial parts of the Arctic lie securely within the jurisdiction of the Arctic coastal states. The 1982 UN Convention on the Law of the Sea (UNCLOS) provides a solid foundation for the governance of the region's marine areas. Even in cases where there are unresolved jurisdictional issues (e.g., claims to jurisdiction over the seabed beyond the limits of coastal state exclusive economic zones), there is general agreement that these claims are to be resolved through the procedures established under the terms of Article 76 of UNCLOS. There is no political vacuum in the Arctic or, to put it another way, there are no needs for governance that cannot be met under the terms of existing constitutive arrangements covering the relevant terrestrial and marine spaces.

The Arctic and the Antarctic differ in other important respects as well.[24] There are world-class economic activities (e.g., mining and oil and gas development) in the Arctic; there is no industrial development in the Antarctic. The Arctic continues to be a theater of operations for advanced weapons systems despite the end of the cold war; Antarctica is for all practical purposes demilitarized. Above all, the Arctic has a sizable population of permanent human residents, including numerous groups of indigenous peoples for whom the region is a cherished homeland; Antarctica has no permanent human residents. Far-reaching environmental changes are occurring at a more rapid pace in the Arctic than in the Antarctic. Aside from the fact that they share certain biophysical features as the Earth's antipodes, therefore, the circumstances prevailing in the two polar regions are not parallel.

Beyond this lies a major gap between the ideal and the actual with regard to the prospects for an Arctic treaty. Those who call for the negotiation of such a treaty normally think in terms of an ideal arrangement that is legally binding, includes all relevant parties, is relatively deep in substantive terms, creates effective regulatory and procedural arrangements, and is capable of adapting quickly and efficiently to rapidly changing circumstances. But there is no prospect of establishing a governance system for the Arctic that resembles this ideal type. The five Arctic coastal states are uniformly and vigorously opposed to moving in this direction.[25] There is no agreement about whether such an arrangement should include other states, as either full consultative parties or nonconsultative parties. It is safe to assume that any legally binding agreement regarding Arctic governance would be thin in substantive terms. There are good reasons to doubt whether such a treaty would actually enter into force. The United States, which has failed to ratify UNCLOS, might well refuse to ratify an Arctic treaty. Moreover, such a treaty would almost certainly prove difficult to adjust, a serious drawback in a region that is experiencing rapid change in biophysical and socioeconomic terms.

Many of us have concluded, under the circumstances, that the pursuit of an Arctic treaty would prove costly in terms of time and energy, disappointing in terms of the probable outcome, and diversionary in terms of getting on with the day-to-day issues of governance in the region. The existing system seems unsatisfactory to those who are used to thinking in terms of the rule of law and measure progress in terms of movement toward the creation of coherent and legally binding governance systems. But this system may well prove effective in terms of meeting emerging needs for governance in the Arctic and, in the process, maintaining the region as a zone of peace.[26] The existing system has the additional virtue of being relatively easy to adjust to address evolving needs for governance in a rapidly changing setting.

The message from my experience with governance arrangements in the Arctic is that we need to adopt what Elinor Ostrom calls "a diagnostic approach for going beyond panaceas," to think hard about the fit or match between the needs for governance arising in specific settings and the governance arrangements capable of addressing them, and to break the grip of our biases favoring arrangements that are formal, coherent, and legally binding.[27] No doubt, some will find this conclusion disappointing; there is no basis here for detecting a move in the direction of government in contrast to governance without government at the international level.[28] From another perspective, however, the conclusion is encouraging. Experience in the Arctic makes it clear that it does not make sense to regard international society as an anarchic society.[29] Many governance systems are operative in this setting; some of them clearly make a difference regarding the trajectory of human/environment relations. Whether we are gaining the experience needed to cope successfully with the challenges of Earth system governance in the Anthropocene is another matter.[30] But we are not lacking in relevant experience to draw on as we begin to confront these challenges.

Crafting Sustainable Development Goals

In September 2000, the UN General Assembly adopted the UN Millennium Declaration setting forth a series of broad goals that have become known as the Millennium Development Goals (MDGs) and calling for a concerted effort to fulfill these goals by 2015.[31] In retrospect, it seems clear that the articulation of the MDGs constituted an effort on the part of world leaders to respond to the most pressing concerns of the developing countries following a decade of initiatives, including the negotiation and entry into force of the UN Framework Convention on Climate Change and the Convention on Biological Diversity, regarded by many as efforts to address priority concerns of the advanced industrial countries.[32] Focusing on issues like poverty reduction, the provision of freshwater and adequate sanitation, and the enhancement of education, the MDGs have come to symbolize the importance of a global effort to address the most urgent priorities of the developing world.

Have the MDGs succeeded?[33] This is not an easy question to answer. The number of people living in extreme poverty has declined in the years since the adoption of the MDGs, a good development and a promising sign with regard to the effectiveness of the MDGs. Yet a large portion of this achievement has occurred in China and is attributable to the remarkable pace of economic development in that country rather than to any activities associated with the MDGs. Overall, it is probable that the net effect of the MDGs has been positive but modest. Nevertheless, in a world in which it is hard to find bright spots in efforts to address the concerns of the developing countries, it is understandable that many have come to think of the MDGs in progressive terms and to regard this initiative as a success story in the context of the efforts of the United Nations to play a significant role in the domain of economic and social affairs.

It is not difficult to comprehend the thinking of those who worked hard during the run-up to the UN Conference on Sustainable Development (Rio+20) to gain acceptance for the idea of articulating a set of goals to guide the efforts of those seeking to promote sustainable development over the period from 2015, the terminal point of the MDGs, through 2030. As the effort to make progress on other issues flagged, the idea of articulating a set of sustainable development goals (SDGs) became increasingly prominent. The results are reflected in paragraphs 245 to 249 of the Rio+20 outcome document.[34]

Paragraph 245 begins by stating, "We underscore that the MDGs are a useful tool in focusing the achievement of specific development gains as part of a broad development vision and framework."[35] Treating this as a point of departure, paragraph 246 then asserts that "the development of goals could also be useful for pursuing focused and coherent action on sustainable development." To this end, these "goals should address and incorporate in a balanced way all three dimensions of sustainable development and their inter-linkages."[36]

The objective is to frame the SDGs in a form suitable for incorporation in a UN General Assembly resolution to be adopted in fall 2015. To achieve this outcome, paragraph 248 of "The Future We Want" calls for the establishment of "an inclusive and transparent intergovernmental process on SDGs that is open to all stakeholders with a view to developing global sustainable development goals to be agreed by the United Nations General Assembly. An open working group shall be constituted no later than the opening of the 67th session of the UNGA ... with the aim of achieving fair, equitable and balanced geographic representation." The open working group "will submit a report to the 68th session of the UNGA containing a proposal for sustainable development goals for consideration and appropriate action."[37] In fact, the open working group began its work in March 2013 under the chairmanship of the representatives of Hungary and Kenya.

This is where I became involved in the process. I have participated in a project sponsored by the Japanese Ministry of the Environment and organized by the United Nations University and the Earth System Governance Project designed to produce a volume of analytic papers dealing with the processes involved in formulating the SDGs and with the factors that are likely to determine the success of this effort. At the same time, I have participated in workshops designed to promote interaction between members of the open working group and members of the science community to encourage cross-fertilization of ideas. I have played a role in an effort on the part of the UN Environment Programme (UNEP) (see also chapter 8, this volume) to ensure that the SDGs as approved by the General Assembly in 2015 are framed in such a way that they are sensitive to the concerns of UNEP. My work on the SDGs spans a much shorter period than my engagement with issues of governance in the Arctic. Even assuming that the process yields agreement on a set of SDGs that are suitable for adoption in the form of a General Assembly resolution, it will be impossible for some years to make any well-informed judgment regarding the success of this initiative. Nevertheless, work on the SDGs has provided me with a second, and substantially different, opportunity to experience life on the science/policy interface. Here, too, I have learned a lot about both the development of usable knowledge relating to international governance and the practice of addressing matters of international governance under real-world conditions.

A fundamental insight that has guided my contribution to both analysis and praxis in this realm is that goal setting is a form of governance.[38] If we treat governance as a matter of social steering, it is easy to see that goal setting is a means of drawing attention to major issues, providing incentives to adjust behavior to make progress toward addressing these issues, and reminding actors of the importance of longer-term goals when short-term diversions threaten to derail efforts to deal with more important needs for governance. In Western thinking and especially in American approaches to governance, there is a tendency to assume that governance is a matter of rule making rather than goal setting. This regulatory approach emphasizes the formulation of requirements and prohibitions that serve to guide behavior in such a way as to meet needs for governance. The classic examples are introducing rules that allow social groups to avoid collective action problems like the tragedy of the commons or to protect innocent bystanders from the unintended impacts of the actions of those pursuing their own interests regardless of their effects on the welfare of others.[39]

In contrast to rule making, goal setting is a matter of establishing targets, laying down time lines for their achievement, identifying benchmarks to check on progress, and prioritizing efforts to meet the goals in contrast to allocating resources to other matters. Goal setting is an intuitively appealing way to think about steering. As individuals, we all have experience with goal setting, whether it involves mastering the skills needed to pursue a profession, saving money to buy a house, or setting aside funds to pay for children's education. But goal setting is also an important steering mechanism in social or group settings. Perhaps the most prominent examples occur in planned economies where comprehensive plans are used as devices for establishing societal targets and allocating both natural and human resources to make progress toward reaching them.[40] This requires both a means of establishing societal targets authoritatively and the capacity to ensure that members of society adjust their behavior in the manner required to meet the targets. As the examples of the Soviet Union and China suggest, this often involves top-down initiatives that are carried out in an authoritarian manner. This helps to explain why goal setting has not been a popular approach to governance in a country like the United States in which the idea of central planning has never become a potent political force. Even in the case of the United States, however, there are exceptions to this generalization. During World War II, the United States emerged as the "arsenal of democracy" through a process in which the state controlled the means of production, imposed rationing on consumers, and steered the resources of the entire society toward the overarching goal of defeating the Axis powers.[41]

If goal setting is challenging in political systems that have no tradition of top-down direction, it is easy to understand how much more difficult it is likely to be at the international level. Paragraph 247 of "The Future We Want" says that the "... SDGs should be action oriented, concise and easy to communicate, limited in number, aspirational, global in nature, and universally applicable to all countries, while taking into account different national realities, capacities and levels of development and respecting national policies and priorities."[42] This is a tall order. Unlike the MDGs, which were designed to be responsive to the needs of the developing world during a period otherwise dominated by global issues like climate change and the loss of biological diversity, the SDGs are intended to address the full suite of economic, social, and environmental issues in a world in which the current human population of 7 billion is projected to rise to 9 or 10 billion during this century. Despite the superficial impression that the formulation of the SDGs constitutes a logical sequel to the development of the MDGs, therefore, the two processes are fundamentally different.

Framing the SDGs is in essence a bargaining process. While the open working group is limited to thirty members, "The Future We want" specifies that the working group should endeavor "to establish an inclusive and transparent intergovernmental process on SDGs" that provides for "the full involvement of relevant stakeholders and expertise from civil society, the scientific community and the UN system in its work in order to provide a diversity of perspectives and experience."[43] Such processes typically yield agreements that include something for everyone and are framed in general terms that defer many of the toughest decisions to the stage of implementation. This obviously compromises the effectiveness of goal setting as a means of addressing needs for governance. But it is properly understood as a response to the realities of the relevant social setting rather than as a defect of goal setting as a means of responding to needs for governance.

In the case of the SDGs, the critical challenge is to find a way to address simultaneously systemic concerns like climate change or the loss of biological diversity and the concerns of particular segments of the human population, and especially those often referred to as the bottom billion.[44] This is difficult in part because it requires allocating scarce resources among competing goals—and this is only one feature of the challenge. Equally challenging is the fact that the steps required to meet the needs of the developing world (e.g., industrial development, more intensive agriculture) may well conflict with efforts to address the systemic issues by increasing emissions of greenhouse gases, converting more land to agricultural production, and creating conditions that threaten a growing number of species with extinction. To make this problem concrete, consider the political problems that would accompany any effort to tell the Chinese, the Indians, or the Brazilians that they should forgo rapid economic development needed to lift large numbers of people out of extreme poverty due to the impacts of such measures on the Earth's climate system or the loss of biological diversity. Undoubtedly this accounts for the attractions of the idea of a green economy, which envisions economic development in some more environmentally friendly fashion and was adopted as a central theme of the Rio+20 process.[45] But as the outcome of the conference makes clear, no one has produced a realistic strategy for making progress toward economic development in a manner that differs profoundly from the strategy that today's advanced industrial countries followed.

Assuming that the UN General Assembly adopts a resolution in fall 2015 setting forth a set of SDGs, attention will then shift to issues of implementation. In centrally planned systems, implementation ordinarily involves top-down command-and-control decisions regarding the allocation of society's resources, combined with rewards provided to those who perform particularly well in terms of efforts to meet the goals of five-year plans. But it is unlikely that this strategy will work as an approach to the implementation of the SDGs. No central body possesses either the authority or the capacity to engage in such top-down measures. This means that efforts to pursue the SDGs will need to rely to a large degree on bottom-up processes. The most relevant experience in this regard involves the growth of social movements of the sort that played a role in putting an end to slavery, promoting women's suffrage, and breaking down the barriers to same-sex marriage.[46] So far, there are few examples of effective social movements operating on an international or global scale. But this is not to say that such movements will not arise during the current era of global needs for governance.[47]

Efforts to assess the effectiveness of the SDGs will confront fundamental problems. These problems are not unique to goal setting in contrast to other ways of addressing needs for governance. They center on the difficulties of establishing causal connections in situations in which universes of cases are small, responses to needs for governance must be tailored to the attributes of specific situations, and opportunities to make use of counterfactuals are limited.[48] As the case of the MDGs makes clear, enthusiasm for goal setting as a governance strategy may owe as much to the absence of other appealing governance strategies as to evidence regarding the efficacy of goal setting. Still, it is important to acknowledge that the existence of these problems does not guarantee that the SDGs will be ineffective as a way of addressing needs for governance on a global scale. All governance systems operate as elements in interacting collections of forces that determine societal trajectories. This poses a challenge for the analyst seeking to separate out the impacts of governance systems from the effects of other forces. But it should not deter the practitioner striving to make progress toward meeting concrete needs for governance.

Overall, I am skeptical about the efficacy of the effort to devise SDGs that make a difference. Yet it is hard to deny the enthusiasm associated with the MDGs, and there are compelling reasons to pursue all potentially effective leads in addressing the needs for governance arising in the Anthropocene.[49] This may be a case of embracing what Reinhold Niebuhr characterized as the "impossible possibility." As Niebuhr observed in his theological writings, the nature of human nature makes it difficult or even impossible to achieve success in the pursuit of transcendent goals like peace, environmental security, and social justice. But we must continue to strive to achieve these goals, even when we are aware that ultimate success is unlikely or even impossible.[50]

Comparative Advantages

Drawing on this account of the interaction between analysis and praxis, let me turn to the distinction Richard Falk draws in chapter 4 between what he describes as "horizons of feasibility" and "horizons of necessity." He directs attention to the challenge of solving profound problems confronting the human enterprise, problems that have intensified greatly since the publication of his prescient volume, *This Endangered Planet*, in 1971.[51] To meet this challenge, Falk asserts that "only a revolution in human consciousness can summon the political will needed to make the necessary adjustments to an endangered planet." The resultant transformative politics, he says, "must come from below." It will require a form of "engaged citizenship" focusing on values and dedicated to the development of a new discourse in contrast to the application of expert knowledge "reinforced by careful analysis and rational argument."

I sympathize with this view. I have said somewhat similar things, albeit in less evocative language, in my recent writings on international relations in the Anthropocene.[52] But what are we to do while waiting for the needed revolution in human consciousness to occur? Peering into the abyss, Falk reaches "the unhappy conclusion that the will of the species to survive is rather weak, that is, the dangers of catastrophic happenings induce what might be described as a new normal rather than a social demand to minimize risks." My own view is that we need to practice the sort of engagement between analysis and praxis I have described in this chapter, even while we do what we can to promote the required revolution in human consciousness. It does make a difference whether we can find ways to ensure that the Arctic remains a zone of peace. There is a difference between getting the SDGs right and failing to take advantage of this opportunity for international cooperation arising in the wake of Rio+20.

It may be that there is a case for developing a productive division of labor regarding such matters and that this division should reflect our comparative advantages. Richard Falk and I have known each other and admired each other's work for almost fifty years. During that time, his association with what he calls horizons of necessity has deepened and grown more profound. My efforts to pursue the horizons of feasibility have grown more sophisticated and become more influential.

One of the things I have learned in my life on the science/policy interface is that it is helpful to keep in mind the policy cycle or the knowledge-to-action cycle. Although the boundaries are fuzzy, we can identify different phases or stages of this cycle and recognize that the skills needed to address the individual phases successfully are distinct. The ideas phase, for example, benefits from an ability to consider unconventional perspectives, assemble data in novel ways, and generate innovative formulations of issues to be added to the policy agenda. This is why analysts have been able to make useful contributions to the activities of the Arctic Council and the effort to frame the SDGs. Both cases involve generative activities well suited to the skills of those who bring analytic perspectives to the tasks.

By contrast, the choices phase requires the concentrated attention of practitioners who are able to follow the dynamics of negotiation processes closely and are skilled at crafting formulations of key provisions that can turn apparent conflicts of interest into initiatives that are broadly appealing. The implementation phase is another matter. Analysts seldom make good administrators. Much the same is true of practitioners whose forte is diplomacy or the crafting of language addressing the key points of international agreements. Yet there are those whose skills come to the fore once an international agreement is signed and the challenge turns to moving the provisions of governance systems from paper to practice.

One aspect of life on the science/policy interface that I have found problematic has to do with the role of advocacy. Many of those who engage in activities like the creation and operation of the Arctic Council or the framing of the SDGs are members of national delegations. Although not all national delegations operate in the same way, the normal expectation is that delegation members will follow instructions provided by the head of delegation (and ultimately the foreign ministry) and make a concerted effort to pursue outcomes that advance the national interest. There is nothing wrong with playing this role. But for those who are more interested in enhancing the effectiveness of international governance systems in general than in the extent to which they reflect the preferences of a particular member country, serving as a member of a national delegation is not a comfortable role. With rare exceptions, I have avoided this role. That is why I have consistently opted for alternative roles like cochairing the Working Group on Arctic International Relations, chairing the steering committee of the Arctic Governance Project, and serving on the experts panel advising the open working group on the SDGs.

Be that as it may, I have found life on the science/policy interface with regard to matters of international governance deeply rewarding. I believe I have been able to make a constructive contribution, at least at the margin, in steering the course of international cooperation in the post–Cold War Arctic. It is too early to assess the results of the effort to frame SDGs. Theoretical arguments about a number of issues (e.g., the functions of governance systems, the problem of fit, the nature of social practices) have proven invaluable in the development of my thinking about more applied concerns. Conversely, the opportunity to work back and forth between theory and practice has been enormously helpful to my work on the broad theme of governance in stateless settings. Applications to cases like climate change and fisheries management, as well as the polar regions, have played a key role in sharpening and vetting my thinking about international governance.

Notes

1. Benedick, *Ozone Diplomacy*.

2. Speth, *Red Sky at Morning*.

3. Jasanoff, ed., *States of Knowledge*.

4. Gorbachev, "Speech in Murmansk."

5. Young, "Arctic Politics in an Era of Global Change."

6. Young, Kim, and Kim eds., *The Arctic in World Affairs*.

7. Young, "The Work of the Working Group on Arctic International Relations."

8. Iqaluit Declaration, "First Ministerial Meeting."

9. AHDR, *Arctic Human Development Report*. A second edition of the *Arctic Human Development Report* is slated for completion during summer or fall 2014.

10. Arctic Governance Project, "Arctic Governance in an Era of Transformative Change."

11. Young, "The Effectiveness of International Environmental Regimes."

12. Chayes and Chayes, *The New Sovereignty*.

13. Young, *Governance in World Affair*.

14. Kingdon, *Agenda, Alternatives, and Public Policies*.

15. Ottawa Declaration, "Declaration on the Establishment of the Arctic Council."

16. A permanent secretariat agreed to in 2011 began operations officially in early 2013.

17. Kankaanpää and Young, "The Effectiveness of the Arctic Council."

18. AMAP, *State of the Arctic Environment Report*.

19. ACIA, *Impacts of a Warming Arctic*.

20. AHDR, *Arctic Human Development Report*.

21. AMSA, *Arctic Marine Shipping Assessment*.

22. Koivurova and Molenaar, *International Governance and Regulation of the Marine Arctic*.

23. Young, "If an Arctic Treaty Is Not the Solution, What Is the Alternative?"

24. Berkman and Vylegzhanin, eds., *Environmental Security in the Arctic Ocean*.

25. Ilulissat Decalaration, "Declaration from the *Arctic Ocean Conference*."

26. Young, "Building an International Regime Complex for the Arctic."

27. Ostrom et al., "A Diagnostic Approach to Going beyond Panaceas."

28. Rosenau and Czempiel, eds., *Governance without Government*.

29. Bull, *The Anarchical Society*.

30. Young, *On Environmental Governance*.

31. Millennium Declaration, "UN General Assembly Resolution 55/2."

32. Young and Steffen, "The Earth System."

33. Collier, *The Bottom Billion.*

34. Future We Want, "Outcome Document of the UN Conference on Sustainable Development."

35. Ibid., para. 245.

36. Ibid., para. 246.

37. Ibid., para. 248.

38. Young, "Goal-Setting vs. Rule-Making as Strategies for Earth System Governance."

39. Some governance systems feature combinations of rule making and goal setting. Consider, for example, fisheries regimes that combine a variety of requirements and prohibitions with the goal of achieving maximum sustainable yield.

40. Gregory and Stuart, *Comparing Economic Systems in the Twenty-First Century.*

41. Goodwin, *No Ordinary Time.*

42. Future We Want, para. 247.

43. Ibid., para. 248.

44. Collier, *The Bottom Billion;* Stern, *The Global Deal.*

45. UNEP, *Toward a Green Economy.*

46. Goodwin and Jasper, eds., *The Social Movement Reader.*

47. For the example of 350.org, see McKibben, *Oil and Honey.*

48. Young, "The Effectiveness of International Environmental Regimes.

49. Young, 2013, *The Economist* "Welcome to the Anthropocene," 399, no. 8735, (28 May-3 June 2011).

50. Niebuhr, *An Interpretation of Christian Ethics.*

51. Falk, *This Endangered Plane.*

52. Young, "International Relations in the Anthropocene."

Bibliography

ACIA. *Impacts of a Warming Arctic: Arctic Climate Impact Assessment.* Cambridge: Cambridge University Press, 2004.

AHDR. *Arctic Human Development Report.* Akureyri: Stefansson Arctic Institute, 2004.

AMAP. *State of the Arctic Environment Report.* Oslo: AMAP, 1997.

AMSA. *Arctic Marine Shipping Assessment* . 2009. www.arctic-council.org.

Arctic Governance Project. "Arctic Governance in an Era of Transformative Change: Critical Questions, Governance Principles, Ways Forward." 2010. www. arcticgovernance.org.

Benedick, Richard E. *Ozone Diplomacy: New Directions in Safeguarding the Planet.* Cambridge, MA: Harvard University Press, 1998.

Berkman, P. A., and A. Vylegzhanin, eds. *Environmental Security in the Arctic Ocean.* Dordrecht: Springer, 2012.

Bull, Hedley. *The Anarchical Society: A Study of Order in World Politics.* New York: Columbia University Press, 1977.

Chayes, Abram, and Antonia Handler Chayes. *The New Sovereignty: Compliance with International Regulatory Agreements.* Cambridge, MA: Harvard University Press, 1995.

Collier, Paul. *The Bottom Billion: Why the Poorest Countries Are Failing and What Can Be Done about It.* Oxford: Oxford University Press, 2007.

Falk, Richard. *This Endangered Planet: Prospects and Proposals for Human Survival.* New York: Random House, 1971.

Future We Want. "Outcome Document of the UN Conference on Sustainable Development." 2012. http://www.un.org/en/sustainablefuture/.

Goodwin, Doris Kearns. *No Ordinary Time: Franklin and Eleanor Roosevelt: The Home Front in World War II.* New York: Simon and Schuster, 1994.

Goodwin, J., and J. M. Jasper, eds. *The Social Movement Reader.* Chichester, UK: Blackwell, 2009.

Gorbachev, Mikhail. "Speech in Murmansk on the Occasion of the Presentation of the Order of Lenin and the Gold Star to the City of Murmansk. 1987. http://wws .barentsinfo.fi/docs/Gorbachev_speech.pdf.

Gregory, Paul R., and Robert C. Stuart. *Comparing Economic Systems in the Twenty-First Century.* Mason, OH: Cengage Learning, 2003.

Ilulissat Declaration. "Declaration from the *Arctic Ocean Conference,* 28 May 2008." http://www.arcticgovernance.org/the-illulissat-declaration.4872424.html.

Iqaluit Declaration. "First Ministerial Meeting of the Arctic Council, September 17–18, 1998." http://www.arctic-council.org.

Jasanoff, S., ed. *States of Knowledge: The Co-Production of Science and the Social Order.* New York: Routledge, 2004.

Kankaanpää, Paula, and Oran R. Young. "The Effectiveness of the Arctic Council." *Polar Research* 31 (2012). doi:.10.3402/polar.v31i0.17176

Kingdon, John W. *Agenda, Alternatives, and Public Policies.* 2nd ed. Boston: Addison-Wesley, 1995.

Koivurova, Timo, and Erik J. Molenaar. *International Governance and Regulation of the Marine Arctic.* Oslo: WWF International Arctic Programme, 2009.

McKibben, Bill. *Oil and Honey: The Education of an Unlikely Activist.* Collingwood, Australia: Black, 2013.

Millennium Declaration. "UN General Assembly Resolution 55/2." September 8, 2000.

Niebuhr, Reinhold. *An Interpretation of Christian Ethics.* New York: Scribner, 1935.

Orsini, Amandine, Jean-Frederic Morin, and Oran R. Young. "Regime Complexes: A Buzz, a Boom, or a Boost for Global Governance." *Global Governance* 19 (2013): 27–39.

Ostrom, Elinor, "A Diagnostic Approach to Going Beyond Panaceas." *Proceedings of the National Academy of Sciences of the United States of America* 104 (2007): 15181–87.

Ottawa Declaration. "Declaration on the Establishment of the Arctic Council." 1996. www.arctic-council.org.

Rosenau, J. N., and E.-O. Czempiel, eds. *Governance without Government: Order and Change in World Politics.* Cambridge: Cambridge University Press, 1992.

Speth, James G. *Red Sky at Morning: America and the Crisis of the Global Environment.* New York: Oxford University Press, 2004.

Stern, Nicholas. *The Global Deal: Climate Change and the Creation of a New Era of Progress and Prosperity.* New York: Public Affairs Press, 2009.

UNEP. *Towards a Green Economy: Pathways to Sustainable Development and Poverty Eradication.* 2011. www.unep.org/greeneconomy.

"Welcome to the Anthropocene. " *Economist,* May 28–June 3, 2011.

Young, Oran R. "The Work of the Working Group on Arctic International Relations." *Northern Notes: Occasional Publication of the Dickey Center Institute of Arctic Studies* 4 (1996): 1–19.

Young, Oran R. *Institutional Dynamics: Emergent Patterns in International Environmental Governance.* Cambridge, MA: MIT Press, 2010.

Young, Oran R. "If an Arctic Treaty Is Not the Solution, What Is the Alternative?" *Polar Record* 47 (2011): 327–34.

Young, Oran R. "Arctic Politics in an Era of Global Change." *Brown Journal of World Affairs* 19 (2012): 165–78.

Young, Oran R. *Governance in World Affairs.* Ithaca, NY: Cornell University Press, 1999.

Young, Oran R. "Building an International Regime Complex for the Arctic: Current Status and Next Steps." *Polar Journal* 2 (2012): 391–407.

Young, Oran R. "The Effectiveness of International Environmental Regimes: Existing Knowledge, Cutting-Edge Themes, and Research Strategies." *Proceedings of the National Academy of Sciences of the United States of America* 108 (2011): 19853–60.

Young, Oran R. "Goal-Setting vs. Rule-Making as Strategies for Earth System Governance." In *Governance through Goals*, edited by Norichika Kanie and Frank Biermann. Forthcoming.

Young, Oran R. "International Relations in the Anthropocene: The Twilight of the Westphalian Oder." In *International Relations Theory Today*, edited by Ken Booth and Toni Erskine. Forthcoming.

Young, Oran R. *On Environmental Governance: Sustainability, Efficiency, and Equity*. Boulder, CO: Paradigm Publishers, 2013.

Young, O. R., J. D. Kim, and Y. H. Kim, eds. *The Arctic in World Affairs: A North Pacific Dialogue on Arctic Marine Issues*. Seoul: Korea Maritime Institute, 2012.

Young, Oran R., and Will Steffen. "The Earth System." In *Principles of Ecosystem Stewardship*, edited by F. Stewart Chapin, Gary Kofinas, and Carl Folke, 295–315. New York: Springer, 2009.

4 Scholarship as Citizenship

Richard Falk

My perspective on New Earth follows the line set forth by the book editors: that the earth as an integrated image and reality is imperiled by the interactive dynamics of globalization. One result of this development is a growing and harmful human footprint. The consequences of such circumstances are giving rise to unprecedented risks of human disaster, as well as to widely shared perceptions of human responsibility for several centuries of complacent stewardship of the planet. Society is being severely challenged to come up with answers. Conservative and restorative policies will be needed to alleviate the multiple crises that are present in ways that are sensitive to the imperatives of ecological justice and societal equity. In some serious sense "New Earth" entails "whole earth," that is, a refocusing of attention to carry forward this mandate of engagement in a manner that is better attuned to the ecology of the planet and less given over to its customary statist and geopolitical preoccupations. In advocating such a process of adjustment, I address particularly the question of how scholars and scholarship might best contribute, configuring their vocational specialties in light of this interpretation of the holistic originality of our era that underlies this New Earth sense of emergency.

I do this from an outlook that is skeptical about the problem-solving capabilities of governmental institutions today, especially when seeking cooperative responses to challenges of global scope that serve human interests as distinct from the aggregation of national interests. I show in the course of this chapter that only a revolution in human consciousness can summon the political will needed to make the necessary adjustments to an endangered planet and that such a transformative politics will come, if at all, from the political mobilization of society.[1] Governmental institutions are too embedded in the extremely uneven particularities of national experience and hampered by special interests and bureaucratic rigidities to have the energy and imagination needed to find solutions unless pushed hard by the citizenry. Governmental responsiveness to the New Earth agenda is blocked by a variety of entrenched interests and by nationalist approaches to decision making. The proposed changes seem unlikely to take place without the strong backing of a transnational popular movement that is creative in the ways that challenge the established order in fundamental respects. This recommended reorientation of government is already latent in the body politic, yet until the peoples of the world, especially the youth, awaken to its urgent necessity, the leaders will remain at a loss as to how this potential can be activated for the benefit of New Earth.

Scholars, Experts, and Activists

In reading chapter 3 by Oran Young, I was deeply impressed by his extraordinary range of contributions, especially in an Arctic setting. He works at the interface between scholarly expert and policy practitioner. This has meant exerting influence in a variety of policymaking settings with respect to devising schemes, guidelines, and recommendations associated with the agenda of environmental governance. I was also interested by Young's sensitivity to political constraints that need to be respected by those policymakers seeking to be effective in such settings. Above all, such sensitivity involves an acute awareness of the limits on policymaking that derive from considerations of feasibility. The acceptance of such limits will usually require a willingness to focus on incremental and indirect dynamics of adaptation and reform, as well as the avoidance of harsh criticism of the powers that be. This is how I interpret Young's assertion that the effectiveness of an expert in policy realms presupposes deference to what he calls "real-world conditions." Such an orientation accepts the structure of relations as one finds them, which includes the following features: the primacy of geopolitics in most, if not all, global policymaking domains; respect for the constraints of national interests and private sector leverage; and avoidance of criticism directed at the ideological premises and operating procedures of neoliberalism (a shorthand designation for world capitalism in the period following the end of the Cold War). The policy-minded expert, whatever his or her actual beliefs, must operate within this structure to be effective.

I mention these features of Young's work, which I admire for its clarity, coherence, and practicality, while at the same time situating my form of engagement in very different, perhaps even contrasting, ways. My own form of engagement is best expressed as engaged citizenship, by which I mean an interest in affecting the public discourse relating to the New

Earth agenda, encouraging radical critique of political, economic, cultural, and ideological structures. I am skeptical about devoting energy to exerting influence on national governments as now oriented, especially here in the United States, being distrustful of the viewpoints and control exerted by entrenched bureaucratic and market elites with respect to the promotion of fundamental change. I believe that world politics as practiced is beholden, by and large, to the ethos and praxis of "old earth," which means the primacy of national interests as modified by the priorities of economic globalization and its receptivity to technological innovation. It also may be relevant to acknowledge that my academic career has not been nearly as focused on meeting environmental challenges as has that of Young.

The policy practitioner generally functions much more as an expert or resource person than does the engaged citizen. I would not overstate this distinction as there are often overlaps in both directions. I note that Young describes his own reluctance to subsume his undertakings within the constraints offered by membership in national delegations or groupings that take their policy direction from the governments of sovereign states. Presumably he seeks the independence of an unaffiliated specialist. In my case, I have been willing, although rarely given the chance, especially in recent years, to offer my views on international issues to congressional committees as an expert witness or to give talks at institutions associated organizationally with the government. At the same time, I think there is a big difference between being an expert who may represent civil society actors and being a radical critic who is not often concerned with short-term incremental policy choices and unlikely to be consulted by the powers that be.

For the expert, information and knowledge become the principal modalities of engagement, reinforced by careful analysis and reasoned policy assessments. In contrast, the engaged citizen is more likely concerned with normative dimensions of whatever problem is being addressed. As such, the emphasis is placed on ethics, values, and justice. The overall outlook seeks what might be identified as wisdom, invoking law, rights, experience, aspiration, and heritage to whatever extent relevant. The prevailing academic constraints on epistemological freedom create little professional tension for the policy practitioner who is performing within the confines of the discipline acquired during the latter stages of graduate school and through the tribulations of faculty apprenticeship. The engaged citizen is less likely to be so prepared to play her or his chosen role, especially if wishing to deploy scholarship for political purposes and thus allowing his or her contributions to stray from the objectifying mantras of science, even in the relaxed formats of social science.

My own stance is synthetic in the sense of accepting both normative and scientific approaches as appropriate for seeking desirable policy results, but confining my own work mainly to normative domains, seeking a convergence of knowledge and wisdom even if that casts to one side any prospects of short-term influence in the corridors of power. This choice of epistemological posture is important, however, as an indicator of whether a particular person is willing to accept the existing mechanisms of problem solving bearing on the New Earth agenda, or claims that only by reaching for the stars can one hope to be relevant to the needs of the earth. My own fragmentary experience in relevant policy domains came as a member of the Turkish delegation at the 2010 Cancun and 2012 Doha UN multilateral climate change global conferences among states. These gatherings of more than 190 states were demonstrations of the extent to which the pursuit of short-term national perceived interests was in command. This necessarily caused the marginalization of what might be understood as the global public interest pertaining to climate change, which presupposed both a global outlook and a long-term time frame. To the extent that global public interests were treated as relevant by the representatives of national delegations, it was by way of their rhetoric in public sessions, words often spoken with audiences back home primarily in mind, a rhetoric that was at odds with the pragmatic bargaining stance in conference rooms behind the scenes, and out of view of the media. Global public interests were given sustained attention only in venues set aside for nongovernmental voices, which were located spatially and, even more so, politically at the inconvenient outer margins of the luxury hotels that provided the governmental delegations with their meeting halls and lodgings.

New Earth Scholarship

In my view, the center of gravity of New Earth scholarship has been moving in the direction of biopolitics and spiritual renewal as vital ingredients of a restorative ecological response.[2] I find such a repositioning of outlook to be an important part of my own engaged citizenship that has been generated by a number of influences: participation for many years as a member of the Lindisfarne Fellowship founded by William Irwin Thompson, skepticism about horizons of feasibility as the appropriate limit for public policy in settings that shape the intergovernmental political landscape (including the war system), the degree to which policy responses must defer to the iron law of economic growth or, put differently, media encouragement to accept captivity within the iron cage of predatory capitalism as a precondition of responsible advocacy.[3]

Let me explain this turn toward the spiritual and biopolitical. It is associated with a conviction borne of analysis and experience that horizons of feasibility will not achieve the kinds of change that seems required if we consider New Earth challenges from the perspectives of horizons of necessity, that is, what needs to be done given the nature of the challenge. This gap between feasibility and necessity cannot be closed in my judgment except by a revolutionary or nonincremental jump that is transformational as far as feasibility is concerned, and this will not occur without a post-Marxist social mobilization from below.[4] In other words, such transformation depends on a populist mobilization, but not in the Marxist form of a rising of the workers of the world. What form is not clear at this point, although a movement built around a New Earth synthesis would be one relevant possibility. There are some examples of populist pressures based on conceptions of necessity altering the horizons of feasibility in benevolent directions. Among the most notable of these in the political domain have been the liberation of East European societies at the end of the Cold War and the American civil rights movement. In the environmental domain, agitation against pollution often powered by local movements as well as pressures to protect the ozone layer in the atmosphere from chemical dissolution is illustrative of closing the gap between what is feasible and what is necessary.

As far as biopolitics is concerned, I have been affected by the inability to achieve much traction in civil society on the basis of the scientific warnings about global warming and climate change. The resistance on the part of entrenched elites was to be expected due to the embedded assumptions of modernity, including the links between economic growth and human well-being, as well as the pressures mounted by special corporate and financial interests that would be threatened by the enactment of New Earth politics. The passivity of the public is more surprising, even taking account of the alignments between dominant global media and entrenched elites, and seems to reflect a combination of preoccupations with immediacies of the short run and the pressures of everyday life with a kind of widely shared cultural assumption of the modern world that if the problems are as serious as most climate experts claim, science and technology will devise a timely rescue. Partly on the basis of the analogous failure to take steps to reduce the risks of nuclear warfare, I have reached the unhappy conclusion that the will of the species to survive is rather weak, that is, the risks associated with the possibilities of catastrophic happenings induce what might be described as an acceptance of a new normal rather than a social demand to minimize risks.[5]

Narrating Citizen Engagement Prior to New Earth Agenda

Given this undertaking of depicting a personal approach to an academic vocation in relation to the New Earth agenda, it seems relevant to include a brief autobiographical sketch. My focus is on what led me to an embrace of engaged citizenship. It is an outgrowth, especially, of my experience as an opponent of the Vietnam War.

My opposition to the Vietnam War started in the mid-1960s and was grounded initially on what might be called realist calculations, reinforced by a belief that national interests, even for the United States, were better served by compliance with the UN Charter and international law than by subscribing to the view that the more belligerent geopolitics of the Cold War should be a guide for policymakers in the West. I wrote frequently along these lines in scholarly journals, debated in academic settings, and served as an expert witness in litigation arising from opposition to the war and in the context of congressional debate.[6] I was also active in the main professional association concerned with international law (American Society of International Law), heading up a panel that tried to call attention to the relations between international law and military interventions in foreign societies.

In a move toward engaged citizenship beyond scholarly endeavor was my willingness to chair a committee of international law scholars that took a full-page ad in the *New York Times* to protest the military intervention in the Vietnam War by reference to law governing the conduct of warfare.[7]

As a result of this appeal to public conscience, I was invited to visit North Vietnam in 1968 at a time when there were growing doubts through-out the United States about whether the war was worth its costs and whether it was proceeding as successfully as its most ardent supporters claimed. Going to "the enemy" during a period of war, although unde-clared, was the most radical act of citizen defiance that I had undertaken up to that time, and it was highly controversial given the strong emotions prevalent in the United States for and against the war. I had some appre-hension that I would be prosecuted under an old and dormant law that prohibited private diplomacy because I was scheduled to meet with some

Vietnamese leaders. Prior to my departure for Hanoi, I was informally asked to visit the Pentagon to discuss the trip. Two fairly senior advisors to the secretary of defense, both of whom later became prominent, met with me, described their own skepticism toward the war at its present stage, and offered to entrust a joint letter from their boss, the secretary of defense, and the secretary of state to the North Vietnamese leaders if I would agree to stop opposing the war in public. Their unstated reasoning seemed to be that it would be awkward for the government to be using an antiwar activist as a back-channel contact with the North Vietnamese. I was unwilling to do this, and hence never saw the letter, and never regretted the decision to forgo this co-opting temptation.

The trip in 1968 to North Vietnam had a permanent transformative impact on my understanding of what engaged citizenship meant, which came to include to a far greater extent than earlier what might be called the imperatives of conscience. In this respect, to be a good American citizen for me came to mean fidelity to conscience far more than obedience to government fiat or even an uncritical acceptance of the patriotic impulse to view the adversary of my government as automatically my enemy. These reflections surfaced in Vietnam as I witnessed the total vulnerability of a peasant society to high-technology warfare waged from air, sea, and land. These strong impressions were reinforced by the warm hospitality of ordinary Vietnamese people who had been taught by their leaders to distinguish between the US government, which was bombing their homeland, and the American people, who were not held responsible.

I was also influenced to this day by an understanding that the Vietnamese people were primarily fighting for their political independence and the end of foreign control of their homeland. The elaborate ideological justifications for the Vietnam War in America appeared to me increasingly irrelevant. From such a perspective, it seemed not to matter whether the leadership of the Vietnamese nationalist movement was Communist. The American geopolitics used to justify killing and dying was tone deaf in relation to the dominant historical trend of the period, which was moving strongly in the direction of anticolonialism and national self-determination. In this atmosphere, I came to adopt the outlook of the Vietnamese people in relation to such wars of national liberation and abandoned the notion that the war was wrong because it was being lost or that it was not worth the effort because the Vietnamese we supported were corrupt and were former collaborators with French colonialism or that better tactics might have allowed the intervention to succeed.

My shift from being a realist opponent of the American policy in Vietnam to becoming a supporter of Vietnamese goals in the conflict was treated as irrelevant and of no interest by a series of prominent liberal journalists who interviewed me on my return. Such journalists shared my hostility to Washington's war policies, but purely on pragmatic grounds of winning and losing, as well as in light of their perception of a widening credibility gap between the rosy picture political leaders were painting in public and the far darker realities that were deliberately hidden from the American people. From that point on, I became an unwelcome critic who spoke from outside the responsible mainstream and was no longer usable as an expert, although in my own mind I was no less committed to the academic life or to my primary political identity as an American citizen, and really more valuable as a critical voice because of joining these considerations of the heart to those of the mind. Despite my academic inquiries into the nature of a just world order beneficial to all people on the planet, I never was drawn to the idea of being a world citizen as citizenship without community is an empty shell, and its affirmation given world conditions today seems silly and inconsequential.[8]

My transformational shift became evident later when I began to speak about crimes of war associated with American policies in Vietnam. In this context, I had several friendly debates with General Telford Taylor, a law professor and former Nuremberg prosecutor. Taylor, a highly intelligent patrician humanist, adopted the liberal antiwar view that Vietnam was worse than a crime; it was a mistake. But in the course of doing so, he acknowledged a sharp contradiction between the American demands of Nazi accountability for violating international law in the context of World War II and American claims of impunity in relation to willful violations of legal constraints on the use of force in the course of the Vietnam War.[9]

In these discussions with Taylor, I took the opposite orientation: what was done in Vietnam was far worse than a serious mistake; it was a criminal activity. I continue to believe that this distinction is crucial. As David Petraeus's career exemplifies, mistakes can be "corrected," and then the underlying crime of counterinsurgency can be repeated with political enthusiasm and a relatively clear conscience. If American behavior in Vietnam had been repudiated as a crime (as well as a mistake), then it is far less likely to be done over and over again by a country that values its reputation at home and abroad. My opposition to the Iraq War, and after an ill-considered initial endorsement, to the Afghanistan War, reflected this essential point.[10] My impulsive early support for the Afghanistan War was based on the belief that al-Qaeda was operating from Afghanistan, and in the fevered aftermath of the 9/11, attacks posed a severe security threat that needed to be addressed. I am now embarrassed to admit that such a belief was based on a totally misconceived confidence in the Bush presidency that it was providing the public with a truthful account of the attacks and my belief that the US government would not widen the scope of its military objectives and warmaking beyond the removal of the al-Qaeda threat.

In 1970 toward the end of the Vietnam War, I engaged more directly in activism, but within the framework of nonviolent engaged citizenship. I participated in a civil disobedience action in Washington that took the form of presenting a petition for the Redress of Grievances to the Speaker of the House, coupled with a refusal to leave the halls of Congress until the demands in the petition had been met. Those who took part, maybe seventy-five of us, were all adults with some public notoriety in the arts or academia. After being arrested by polite Capitol police, we were taken to the metropolitan jail in Washington to spend the night until arraigned the following morning. Redress was an adult civil disobedience initiative that sought to express solidarity with young people in the country who were facing the draft and involvement in the war. It tried to draw public attention to the growing opposition to a war that never could be adequately justified legally or morally and was rapidly losing even its political credibility.

My other action in this period was the acceptance of a copy of the Pentagon Papers, that vast trove of classified government documents narrating American involvement in Vietnam. The Pentagon Papers were given to me by Daniel Ellsberg, a high-level RAND consultant, the Edward Snowden of his day. It was a crime, of course, to release such classified material, and I was willingly complicit by agreeing to take possession and refusing to disclose the source. Not surprisingly, I was visited some days later by two FBI agents intent on questioning me about Ellsberg and the papers. When I told them that I would not cooperate because I agreed with what Ellsberg had done, they left my Princeton home disappointedly but politely. A short time later I received a subpoena to appear before a federal grand jury in Boston investigating the release of the Pentagon Papers, and when I refused to testify after being sworn in as a witness, the judge gave me ten days to change my mind and ten days to the government to bring reassurance that I was not the victim of illegal wiretapping. When the reassurance was not produced, I was spared imprisonment for the remainder of the term of the grand jury, which could have been as long as twenty-four months.

I depict these forms of advocacy and defiance as part of my efforts to combine a continuing commitment to scholarship with this evolving idea of what it meant as a practical matter to act as an engaged citizen. It also exhibits a different set of choices about the nature of engagement than that pursued by the independent expert practitioner who may be seeking comparable goals but by other means. At the foundation of my views was the belief that the social contract that binds persons to the state in a democratic republic includes the right of citizens to act nonviolently in opposition to the state and its laws on the basis of their conscience.

Engaged Citizenship and Scholarship in Relation to the New Earth Agenda

My connection with the New Earth agenda began quite haphazardly as an unexpected diversion. In autumn 1968 I was at the start of a year of research and writing at the Stanford Center for Advanced Study in the Behavioral Sciences when I had a coffee urn conversation with a Stanford physicist about the state of the world. In a few minutes, Pierre Noyes convinced me that the dangers posed by population increase, food limitations, pollution, and unregulated economic growth were inclining the world as currently organized toward terminal disaster. Being still of an impressionable age, I altered my research plans on the spot, explored these themes of planetary risk, and became fully convinced that Noyes was justifiably alarmed. On the basis of a determined effort, I produced a book *This Endangered Planet: Prospects and Proposals for Human Survival*, that did little more than elaborate on that conversation over coffee with Noyes, who later became a valued friend.

For the first and only time in my life, the *New York Times* came to my rescue. Its cultural editor, Israel Shenker, commissioned to write a story on the Stanford Center, after interviewing several of the fellows working on a range of projects, decided to concentrate his report on my project. As soon as the article was published, I was flooded with offers from several leading publishers. For reasons that would later cause me some distress, I accepted an offer from Random House because its president, who happened to be a family acquaintance, promised me William Faulkner's editor, a larger advance than I had ever received before, and a major publicity campaign. The book was published, but only after friction with my distinguished editor, who dogmatically insisted that New Earth's problems were exclusively a result of demographic pressure and too many people on the planet, and he didn't approve of my emphasis on "the war system" as part of the overall problem, which included strong criticism of the global role being played geopolitically and economically by the United States.[11]

At this time also, I had been involved with the World Order Models Project (WOMP), a network of scholars from around the world that was committed to work out diverse proposals for drastic global reform. The project brought together prominent scholars from many parts of the world, yielding diverse "relevant utopias" that were published as a scholarly series.[12] The agreed framework of inquiry affirmed several world order values: minimization of war, maximization of economic and social justice, and promotion of human rights. At periodic meetings, I argued for the addition of a value associated with environmental protection, initially encountering resistance from Third World participants who contended that worries about the environment were essentially motivated by rich countries in the North seeking to keep the rest of the world poor and underdeveloped. In the end, this objection was overcome in the spirit of incorporating into the environmental value the dual ideas that poverty was a form of pollution and that environmental protection was definitely necessary, but should be combined with the establishment of an equitable global economic system that overcame trade and investment patterns tilted to favor the rich and powerful countries.

I considered both of these endeavors, my individual role as a scholar and my participation in the WOMP project, as expressions of my scholarly life, yet at the same time reflecting ethical and normative priorities that were departures from the neutrality of the mainstream academic canon. As such, there existed a natural continuity with an undertaking to take part in a small counterconference at the 1972 Stockholm Conference on the Human Environment that was a protest against the exclusion of war from the formal work of this historic intergovernmental conference devoted to environmental protection. Such an exclusion, which continues to this day in climate change policy settings, confirmed my suspicion that the global intergovernmental mechanisms of problem solving and policymaking were deficient from the perspective of global public interests due to the primacy of national interests and Western-dominated geopolitics. We conveners of this conference were anti-Vietnam academics reacting adversely to the successful US-led effort to keep war off the agenda in Stockholm because of Washington's sensitivity about criticisms of American tactics in Vietnam that included destroying vast stretches of vegetation with humanly harmful Agent Orange and other chemicals. This activism made me aware that governments, even those that purported to be dedicated to positive goals, could not be trusted to protect the environment in accordance with any adequate conception of the global public good. Such awareness remains fundamental to my belief that the New Earth agenda will not be addressed in a satisfactory fashion unless there emerges a powerful transnational grassroots mobilization that is shaped by dedication to sustainable forms of livelihood that are to be realized in a manner that also is responsive to the equal human dignity of all peoples, takes account of the destructive relevance of war and militarism, and links environmental protection to environmental justice.

In the mid-1970s I took part in many public events that were publicizing concerns about New Earth issues, often organized around debates associated with the controversy generated by the publication of the avidly promoted Club of Rome study *Limits to Growth*, as reinforced by such influential publications as Paul Ehrlich's *Population Bomb*, and Barry Commoner's *The Closing Circle*. In 1971 at the founding meeting of Friends of the Earth in Aspen, Colorado, under the leadership of David Brower, I had an encounter with John Ehrlichman, then the point man for environmental policy in the Nixon administration. Ehrlichman instructed us at the meeting that the only political truth was what one said when the TV camera red light was switched on, signaling broadcast, and that such a reality always needed to be deferential to horizons of feasibility. With a tone of contempt in his voice, Ehrlichman went on to complain that this conference venue dramatized the centrality of "the problemsolvers" and the irrelevance of "the problemstaters," identifying me as the embodiment of the irrelevant category. This incident illustrates the wide abyss separating horizons of feasibility and horizons of necessity when it came to ecological policy formation. It also exposed the refusal of those controlling the political domain (as dominated by government bureaucrats and special interest lobbyists) to protect the human interest and global public goods, or even to undertake the more modest and noncontroversial task of upholding national public goods. In these sorts of settings, I suppose my identity was more one of being a public intellectual than an activist in the sense of taking part in events situated in public space, including civil disobedience.[13] The essential feature of such a role is to maintain critical distance from those exercising various forms of power, especially governmental and corporate power, and to speak truthfully without being overly concerned about the prospect of adverse reactions.

My scholarly involvements in recent decades have been less concerned with environment than with being a critic of American foreign policy, especially its recourse to war in the Middle East, and of continuing with my engagement with WOMP activities, which went on until the early 1990s. I also became increasingly involved with the Israel/Palestine conflict, especially after being appointed in 2008 as UN Special Rapporteur for Occupied

Palestine, and with the various issues stemming from America's response to the 9/11 attacks.

During the first decade of the twenty-first century, I did become reengaged with the New Earth Agenda, initially as an invited participant in a Stockholm conference, submitting a paper. "A Second Cycle of Ecological Urgency," in which I argued that there was a new wave of international concern, this time associated with global warming and climate change.[14] This led also to the formation of a four-year academic project that I direct, Climate Change, Human Security, and Democracy, that has been exploring the soft (nontechnical, noneconomic) sides of the climate change policy debate through a series of workshops, panels at professional associations, and publications. It is a scholarly project engaging climate experts and environmentalists from around the world, and has adopted normative goals associated with the interplay between reducing global warming and achieving climate justice with respect to the allocation of burdens in the process. During this period, my experience as a member of the Turkish delegation at the UN annual meetings associated with the UN Climate Change Framework Convention agreed on in 1992 had confirmed the existence of paralyzing gridlock when it came to dealing with intergovernmental diplomacy on New Earth issues. In these settings, global and transnational interest perspectives were represented only by nongovernmental participation, which was confined to the outer margins of the formal events to ensure an avoidance of interaction and displays of dissension.

Overall, my citizen engagement with the New Earth agenda has been more in the line of value-oriented scholarship and advocacy than in the sort of activism that was characteristic of my opposition to the Vietnam War. It provides many opportunities to insist on the adoption of a moral epistemology if we are to develop the knowledge and wisdom to deal with the problems of the age. Such a search for the right solutions is conditioned by a commitment to truthfulness and respect for the uncertainties of scientific inquiry. The New Earth agenda will be addressed only by those who act as citizen pilgrims, dedicated to constructing a political community in the future that is wide enough to encompass the global scope of the challenges being directed at human well-being. My hope is that citizen pilgrims embarked on this journey to the future will gain political traction with respect to New Earth priorities as their interpretation of what is needed and what is desirable becomes so widely accepted that it will generate a broad, yet militant, popular movement dedicated to the coevolution of the human species in attainable harmony with its natural surroundings.

Notes

1. See suggestive ideas along these lines in Brecher, Childs, and Cutler, *Global Visions*.

2. For diverse perspectives see Tarnas, *Cosmos and Psyche*; Küng, *A Global Ethic for Global Politics*; Wapner, *Living through the End of Nature*; Žižek, *Living in the End Time*.

3. For my attempt to address this issue, see Falk, *Predatory Globalization*.

4. For differing responses, see Gill, *Power and Resistance in the New World Order*; Hardt and Negri, *Multitude*; Falk, *Re-Imagining Humane Global Governance*.

5. For discussion of nuclear realities, see Lifton and Falk, *Indefensible Weapons*; Falk and Krieger, *The Path to Zero*. For a more general assessment of the risk environment of late modernity, see Beck, *World at Risk*.

6. Falk, ed., *The Vietnam War and International Law*.

7. Falk, *Vietnam and International Law*.

8. I distinguish my own preferred identity as citizen pilgrim, featuring a moral and spiritual allegiance to the construction of a political community encompassing the whole of humanity.

9. Taylor, *Nuremberg and Vietnam*.

10. Falk, *The Great Terror War*.

11. Falk, *This Endangered Planet*.

12. See the chapters summarizing the various visions of positive future world orders in Mendlovitz, ed., *On the Creation of a Just World Order*; my contribution to the series is published as Falk, *A Study of Future Worlds*.

13. For a probing inquiry, see Said, *Representations of the Intellectual*.

14. In Jonas and Okowa, eds., *Environmental Law and Justice in Context*.

Bibliography

Beck, Ulrich. *World at Risk*. Malden, MA: Polity Press, 2009.

Brecher, Jeremy, John Brown Childs, and Jill Cutler. *Global Visions: Beyond the New World Order*. Boston: South End Press, 1993.

Ebbesson, J., and P. Okowa, eds. *Environmental Law and Justice in Context*. Cambridge: Cambridge University Press, 2009.

Falk, Richard. *The Great Terror War*. New York: Olive Branch Press, 2003.

Falk, Richard. *Predatory Globalization: A Critique*. Cambridge: Polity, 1999.

Falk, Richard. *Re-Imagining Humane Global Governance*. Oxford: Routledge, 2014.

Falk, Richard. *This Endangered Planet: Prospects and Proposals for Human Survival*. New York: Random House, 1971.

Falk, Richard. *Vietnam and International Law: An Analysis of the Legality of U.S. Military Intervention in Vietnam* . New York: Lawyers Committee on American Policy Toward Vietnam, 1967.

Falk, Richard, ed. *The Vietnam War and International Law*. Princeton, NJ: Princeton University Press, 1968–1975.

Falk, Richard, and David Krieger. *The Path to Zero: Dialogues on Nuclear Dangers*. Boulder, CO: Paradigm, 2012.

Gill, Stephen. *Power and Resistance in the New World Order*, 2nd ed. New York: Palgrave, 2008.

Hardt, Michael, and Antonio Negri. *Multitude: War and Democracy in the Age of Empire*. New York: Penguin Press, 2004.

Küng, Hans. *A Global Ethic for Global Politics*. New York: Oxford University Press, 1998.

Lifton, Robert Jay, and Richard Falk. *Indefensible Weapons: The Political and Psychological Case against Nuclearism*. New York: Basic Books, 1982.

Mendlovitz, S. H., ed. *On the Creation of a Just World Order*. New York: Free Press, 1995.

Said, Edward. *Representations of the Intellectual: 1993 Reith Lectures*. New York: Pantheon, 1994.

Tarnas, Richard. *Cosmos and Psyche: Intimations of a New World View*. New York: Viking, 2006.

Taylor, Telford. *Nuremberg and Vietnam: An American Tragedy*. Chicago: Quadrangle Books, 1970.

Wapner, Paul. *Living through the End of Nature: The Future of American Environmentalism*. Cambridge, MA: MIT Press, 2010.

Žižek, Slavoj. *Living in the End Times*. London: Verso, 2010.

Section 3 Pedagogies of Hope

Global environmental politics can be a difficult subject to teach and a difficult subject about which to learn. This is not just because of conceptual and empirical intricacies. It is also because learning about the global environmental condition can be a dark and depressing undertaking. One of our colleagues often quips that his undergraduate course on global environmental politics should be retitled Introduction to Doom for the difficult themes with which he requires his students to grapple.

In this section, Karen Litfin and Michael Maniates consider what it means to teach and learn about the New Earth, and how best to do it. They offer insights born of deep reflection and expert classroom practice.

The section opens with chapter 5, a meditation on what Karen Litfin calls "contemplative pedagogies." She argues that wrestling with the vast challenges of global environmental harm and loss requires that professors and students help one another focus on their inner lives. Her journey in this direction in her own teaching has led Litfin to become a pioneer in a burgeoning contemplative pedagogy movement. Here, Litfin outlines the utility of contemplative approaches to teaching and learning, argues for working with (rather than seeking to dismiss) deeply felt emotions, and guides us into consideration of "somatic responses"—the responses of our whole body and individual senses to the world around us. Along the way, she offers a string of extraordinary exercises that have enlivened her own teaching, from "taking the classroom pulse," whereby students simply offer, one after another, a single-word response to the material being tackled in class, to "who am I in a changing climate," a meditation on the nature and meaning of life on the New Earth. These exercises are not any kind of paint-by-numbers to mindfulness; they won't be a good fit for all professors or all students. The exercises, though, and Litfin's chapter, provide clues for the fostering of authentic engagement with the environmental condition.

Michael Maniates follows with a chapter on hope. Many of us enter our learning and teaching about the environmental condition with a desire to find or instill hopefulness. Yet as Maniates argues, an urge to "teach hope," as though there is a step-by-step guide to a hopeful orientation, can be counterproductive. Instead of reaching for trite, rote responses when students ask, "How can I find hope?" Maniates urges his fellow educators to adopt a new pedagogical orientation, focused on exploding what he calls "hope-diverting myths." Maniates' identification and unpacking of a range of myths and misconceptions about the environmental condition, effective social action, human nature, and the possibilities for large-scale change will provide much grist for classroom discussion, in addition to serving as a challenge to all of us to give deep consideration to the assumptions we make about life on the New Earth.

Studying and teaching global environmental politics is, by its nature, a difficult undertaking. *Difficult*, though, does not mean "bad." Litfin and Maniates help us understand that hope ultimately comes not from averting one's gaze from the severity of the challenges that lie ahead, but rather from fully embracing them and working out how to respond in meaningful, effective, and deeply humane ways.

Framing Questions Posed to the Authors in Section 3

- What are our obligations as educators concerned with environmental matters?
- With what intellectual and other tools should our students be equipped?
- What is the current state of environmental education? Is it appropriately oriented to the contemporary environmental condition, or is some course correction called for?

5 Person/Planet Politics: Contemplative Pedagogies for a New Earth

Karen T. Litfin

Stand still. The trees ahead and the bushes beside you

Are not lost. Wherever you are is called Here,

And you must treat it as a powerful stranger,

Must ask permission to know it and be known.
—From David Waggoner, "Lost"

In recent years, those of us who teach Global Environmental Politics have watched enrollment in our courses skyrocket. When I brought this course to the University of Washington in 1991, I was lucky to have 15 students. Enrollment in the same course today is capped at 150, a tenfold increase that is fairly representative of our subfield. While we global environmental politics scholars might feel gratified by the growing popularity of our courses, we must concede that this trend is driven more by the urgency of the issues than our talent and charisma. Given this mounting urgency, it behooves us to consider what we are actually teaching. Any student who completes our courses—and most other environmental studies courses, for that matter— can recite a litany of crises that together comprise an unfolding planetary megacrisis: deforestation, collapsing fisheries, freshwater scarcity, the mass extinction of species, climate change, and more. But what deeper messages—the ones they will remember long after the final exam is over—are they internalizing about how to live on a "new Earth"? As Michael Maniates so cogently prompts us to ask in the next chapter, does the knowledge we convey "make way for hope," or does it elicit fatalism and paralysis?

Over the years, I have come to the conclusion that a purely cognitive approach to global environmental politics tends to engender the latter. Observing my students' faces go blank or glum during my lectures, I realized that I needed to somehow bring the material home for them. Otherwise global problems and international treaties run the risk of seeming too abstract and remote, rendering effective responses seemingly impossible. I also saw that "bringing the material home" required making my 100 to 300 student lectures feel more intimate. At one point in the late 1990s, I learned that a group of my best students was meeting on Thursday nights to get drunk together. According to the student who informed me, "It's just so crushing that we need to put our minds in a different space. We do it together because it's better than being with this stuff alone." I felt simultaneously chastened and intrigued by this extracurricular exercise in emotional catharsis and community building. I soon vowed to teach global environmental politics not only as something happening "out there" but as something happening "in here."

Witnessing my students struggle with fear, anger, grief, despair, and guilt (and, I should add, wrestling with the same dark emotions internally), my first step was to acknowledge their inner lives. In a lecture hall, this might mean simply asking each student to offer a one-word response to the day's material. "Taking the classroom pulse" came to mean a cascade of heartfelt words switchbacking their way down from the top corner to the bottom corner of the room. In three minutes, we could hear two hundred words running the gamut from *overwhelmed* and *hopeless* to *amazed* and *grateful*. Invariably this torrent of words would end with a pregnant pause, a moment of focus far more potent than anything my PowerPoint slides could evoke.

These initial forays into contemplative practice led me to develop a plethora of pedagogical approaches oriented toward the student as a whole person, not simply a disembodied mind. The core question of these in-class exercises is, "Who am I in relation to this?" In some cases, this means having students keep a journal; in others, it means offering guided meditations about course material; in yet others, it means articulating emotional responses to lectures or readings. Some of these experiments were spectacular successes and some awkward failures, but over time I saw the value of this approach and began calling it "person/planet politics." I have even come to suspect that a significant cause of the unfolding planetary megacrisis is the human mind disconnected from the full-hearted and full-bodied life.

Both my confidence and my competence got a big boost in 2009 when faculty from colleges and universities around the Puget Sound came together under the auspices of Curriculum for the Bioregion to study contemplative approaches to sustainability education. Although we hailed from disciplines ranging from poetry to the information sciences, we were united in our commitment to holistic education. This meant engaging our whole selves—mind, heart, body, and soul—not just in our teaching but in our daily lives. From our first meeting at the Whidbey Institute, a conference center working "for Earth and Spirit," we shared our classroom experiences along with good food, poetry, and music. We found common ground in our sense of the profound value of this work alongside experiencing ourselves as iconoclasts in our fields and at our institutions. That core group of about twenty scholars grew into a dynamic learning community that has shared its collaborative work in an online collection of classroom practices (http://serc.carleton.edu/bioregion/index.html), two conferences (2012 and 2014), and a forthcoming book of essays.[1] I have benefited tremendously from the originality and collegiality of our work together.

This chapter draws on my nearly twenty years of teaching person/planet politics as well as what I have learned from my colleagues in the Curriculum for the Bioregion initiative. The first section offers a rationale for contemplative pedagogical approaches to higher education in general and global environmental politics in particular, highlighting the profound and underappreciated value of "the pause" in our harried and distracted culture. The second section, which explores the affective dimension of contemplative pedagogical approaches, makes the case for working consciously with the dark emotions—fear, anger, grief, despair, and guilt—elicited by the subject matter of global environmental politics. The third section focuses on somatic experience as a gateway to a genuinely creative response to living on a new Earth. As literally being of the Earth, our bodies offer a window into the self-awareness, creativity, and sense of sufficiency that may well be the cornerstone of a sustainability culture. In this context, the intersubjective space of the classroom serves as an important counterbalance to the inwardness of contemplative inquiry, which otherwise runs the risk of fostering a tendency toward self-absorption. I conclude by framing each of these domains of contemplative pedagogy—"the pause," the emotions, and the body—in light of the question of personal resilience and how we might assist our students in sustaining themselves for the long haul. The developmental challenge for young people coming of age at the dawn of the Anthropocene is beyond what most of their instructors have had to face. As a consequence, those of us who teach global environmental politics are now called on to step beyond our traditional role as instructors into a more profound quality of mentorship. For this, we must come to see that sustainability is, as much as anything else, an inside job.

"Don't Just Do Something, Sit There"

The mounting socioecological multicrisis looms as the problem of all problems. Consequently our global environmental politics courses tend to focus on the many tentacles of the crisis, lightly seasoned with a few success stories like the ozone treaties. The overarching message of our courses is often one of urgency and alarm, although this message is increasingly tempered by solutions-oriented research and hands-on learning experiences. This makes sense: we certainly want our students to be good problem solvers and, given what they are learning, they are hungry for solutions. Yet, reflecting the larger culture, they gravitate toward individualized solutions. The "solutions" abound: Go vegan! Shorter showers! And for the technophiles: Electric vehicles! Algae biofuels! Geoengineering! For the few with a stronger political bent: Cap and trade! Carbon tax! Reform the World Trade Organization! The strong propensity of the human mind when faced with a problem is to generate solutions—all the more so under great urgency. Yet the problem with acting on a fix-it impulse to the wicked problems that characterize global environmental politics is that many offered solutions are too partial or end up generating more problems. Inadequate solutions follow inexorably when we fail to truly understand the deeper nature of a problem or the unintended consequences of our actions.

Nonetheless, every good teacher wants to help students learn to approach problems in general, including global environmental problems, with self-awareness, focus, patience, discernment, empathy, integrative thinking, and imagination—none of which is likely to be enhanced by a fix-it mentality. Indeed, the rush to solve a problem may well be a defense against the discomfort of not knowing inherent in taking the time to see deeply its genesis and character. Problem solving generally begins with a period of open-ended receptivity in which one simply takes stock of the problem. Seen from this light, contemplation takes on a more practical hue: the more complex the problem, the greater the need for stepping back and taking stock.

In many ways, the Anthropocene presents us with the problem of all problems for the following reasons:

- It was a colossal accident.
- It is a consequence of the everyday life choices of over 7 billion people.
- These choices are strongly driven by an amalgamation of psychological and institutional forces with deep historical and even biological roots.
- The everyday actions of a few of us are far greater drivers than those of most us, but our lower-impact members are quickly adopting the habits of the affluent.

Taken alone, each of these factors presents a conundrum; taken together, they cry out for deep inquiry into the peculiar place of the *anthros* in the scheme of things. The dawning of the Anthropocene seems to compel us to ask ourselves not only, "What on Earth are we doing?" but even more fundamentally, "What on Earth *are* we?" If nothing else, the new geological era highlights our species' paradoxical relationship to the rest of creation. While these questions can be illuminated by the social sciences and humanities, so too can we investigate them through personal and interpersonal introspection. Our complicity in the Anthropocene implies that each of us must answer the question, "Who am I in relation to this?" Whether we as college instructors are sensitive to this implication, we can be sure that if our students are not asking this question of themselves, then they are, along with much of the culture, engaging in some fancy footwork to evade it. The very magnitude of the problem and its undeniable biophysical dimensions tend to transfix our gaze outwardly, yet coming to understand the *anthros* must surely also entail looking within.

Many environmental studies courses, including those focusing on global environmental politics, introduce students to a big-picture formulation of "the problem" by means of "$I = PAT$," where environmental impact (I) is measured as human population (P), their level of affluence (A), and the kinds of technology deployed (T) (see Ken Conca's problematizing of this approach in chapter 1). When students come to see that the average American consumes as much as fifty sub-Saharan Africans and that the acquisition of more energy-efficient technologies typically leads to higher levels of consumption, they soon recognize that the A factor is the crucial variable in the equation. This is not to say that curtailing our numbers and using more environmentally friendly technologies are unimportant; it is only to say that any gains from these measures are likely to be, and currently are being, swamped by the apparently insatiable A factor. If globalized, a process that is well under way, the American (Canadian or Australian) lifestyle would require six Earths.

We might therefore conclude that consumption is the primary problem, but this begs the larger questions of consumption's deeper political, social, economic, and psychological roots. Many global environmental politics courses no doubt delve into these larger questions, but they tend to approach $I = PAT$ as if the variables and their product were occurring solely "out there" in the material world or in abstract intersubjective cultural or institutional arenas. As important as these arenas are, they leave out the inner dimension of the myriad everyday choices that permeate consumer society. Most crucial from a pedagogical perspective, they leave out the vitality and intimacy of the lived experiences of our students, who are on the cusp of becoming full-fledged members of consumer society. Indeed, a primary function of a college degree is to improve their prospects on the job market. Our global environmental politics courses therefore place our students in a highly awkward relationship with their own lives. In the context of the New Earth, the not-so-subtle message is that our students themselves, along with the rest of us in the affluent world, are the problem. The natural response is guilt or, for those with a low tolerance for guilt, evasion. This dead-end of a conclusion—that we are the problem—is certainly one way of bringing the material home but not one that most of us would actively choose. Yet if we are not sensitive to our students' lived experience, this is exactly where our courses will land.

There is a powerful truth to the recognition that we are the problem, one that need not end with guilt and evasion, for this recognition is simply an awareness that our soft-skinned brainy species has unwittingly begun to unravel its own life-support systems. For those of us in the affluent world, this comes with an awareness of being most privileged, most culpable, and most reliant on the ceaseless work of unseen others. Seen from this vantage point, we can view ourselves not so much as a cancerous scourge but as an intriguing puzzle, a riddle whose solution must emerge from a place beyond business as usual. Surely a puzzle of this depth is antithetical to a quick fix; surely it is worthy of earnest contemplation. And surely, since we are (despite our varying levels of privilege and culpability) in the same boat, our reflections should have an intersubjective dimension—all the more so because the truly effective responses will be matters of collective action. As Michael Maniates argues in the next chapter, the challenges of living on a New Earth must be addressed politically and structurally. Contemplative inquiry is therefore the yin to the yang of collective action.

Given these parameters, our global environmental politics classes offer an ideal field of practice. If we have the courage to enter into the space of not knowing and the patience to accompany our students as they take stock of the problems, which includes facing the riddle of ourselves, then their solutions will be far less likely to be the veiled evasions that spring from a fix-it mind-set. As our students grapple with "Who am I in relation to this?" (see box 5.1) they need not lose their capacities for objectivity, analytical thinking, or pragmatic action; they simply add to these an enlivened capacity for introspection and integrative thinking. In so doing, they learn to bring their whole selves to the world's pressing problems.

How do students respond to such an unconventional use of class time? Because most of my teaching is in large lectures, I have little opportunity to interact with students on a one-to-one basis. I therefore do anonymous electronic polling to get their feedback. The following responses are typical:

Box 5.1

Who Am I in a Changing Climate?

This exercise aims to develop students' capacities for self-awareness and integrative learning. I generally offer this fifteen-minute exercise at the end of an eighty-minute class period. This gives students who do not wish to participate the opportunity to leave. Over the years, I have found that a few leave but nearly all choose to participate. If there is time at the end, I bring the exercise into the intersubjective space either by "taking the collective pulse" or inviting students to share something they learned with a neighbor.

Sit in a comfortable yet alert position. You may wish to close your eyes. If you leave them open, please have them downcast so as not to make others feel uncomfortable. Feel yourself in your chair and take a couple of deep breaths as you settle.

We have spent the last two weeks studying climate change and learned that there is a strong scientific consensus that our Earth's climate system is being destabilized by human activity. Take a moment to let this information sink in. Notice what happens in your body as you sit with this information. Simply observe.

We also learned that people in developing countries, people who are already living on the edge but whose greenhouse gas emissions are minimal, will bear the brunt of the impacts. Again, notice your sensations and emotions as you sit with this information. Just notice. If your mind wants to run in another direction, just notice and breathe.

We've also learned that some people's lifestyles are responsible for emitting far more greenhouse gases than others. As Americans, we emit (on average) about four times the global average. Again, sit and watch whatever arises.

Now breathe into your belly and simply relax. There's nothing you need to do, nowhere to go. This is your time to simply be. [Pause] Into this empty space, allow yourself to return to these big issues around climate change, and introduce this question very gently but with a clear focus: Who am I in relation to all of this? Introduce this question into the silence: Who am I in relation to global climate change? And simply observe what arises, and take note. [Repeat this a few times]

Consider that the world you are entering as a young adult is very different from the world of any previous generation. Our species has embarked on a planetary experiment, and you will be living in the results of that experiment. Who are you as you enter this world? [Pause] Just welcome whatever comes as a guest: images, emotions, ideas, sensations. Simply be an open field of perception, asking yourself who you are in a changing climate. [Silence]

As you prepare to bring your focus back to the classroom, take note of what has transpired. [Pause] Now take a breath and open your eyes slowly. Take a few minutes to gather the harvest by writing some notes to yourself.

1. This exercise was not a good use of my time. 4 percent
2. I feel neutral about the exercise. 2 percent
3. I was grateful for the respite from my harried life. 60 percent
4. I gained significant insights into myself in a changing climate. 34 percent

Even more gratifying are the personal responses. One student who had never spoken in class told me after "Who Am I in a Changing Climate?" that he now knew that his calling was to teach environmental science to children in the primary grades. Another told me that he recalled early childhood memories of living in a Mexican village before his family moved to the United States and that he now knew that something in him knows how to live sustainably. Perhaps the most predictable result of these practices is that I am always surprised.

Human Dimensions of Global Change

A good communicator must take into account the context of her audience, a requirement no less necessary for university instructors than other public speakers. We might therefore consider that our students have grown up during the warmest two decades in recorded history, a time that represents the hinge-point when our home planet left behind the 10,000-year sweet spot in which human civilization emerged and eventually became a geophysical force. For our students, who literally inhabit a different planet from the one on which their elders came of age, the question of who they are in a changing climate is a vital one—even if the dominant culture would have them ignore it. Yet when teaching about topics like climate disruption or species extinction, our scholarly proclivity is to present abstract data about these ominous trends without acknowledging the existential challenges they present. Indeed most graduate training prepares us for little else, potentially rendering us technically competent in the classroom but emotionally inept. If we fail to accompany our students as they walk through the anguish that arises in the face of an honest assessment of the facts, we do our students and ourselves a disservice. As global environmental politics instructors, we are called on to balance cognitive learning with more spacious and open-ended modes of inquiry that foster emotional intelligence and more reflective forms of self-awareness. In my experience, the personal rewards of responding to this call are tremendous, not least of which is a sense of coming home to our own basic humanity.

Having watched my students struggle with fear, anger, grief, guilt, and despair—and having personally grappled with them for decades—I have learned to value these dark emotions as potentially powerful catalysts. Without turning the classroom into a group therapy session, I like to end my lectures with a few minutes of personal reflection and sharing. The overwhelmingly positive response from the students confirms what most of us already know: in the absence of emotional engagement, cognition alone can be a dry and disempowering exercise. According to public opinion polls, most people know that the climate is changing, but do we allow ourselves to truly feel it? Or do we tend to distract ourselves, much as we avert our attention from our own mortality? If we truly felt the magnitude of the facts, would we continue with business as usual? Even putting aside our responsibility to the external world, what of our inner life? What does our psychic numbing desecrate within ourselves? In repressing our anguish, which, after all, is rooted in our care for the world, we simultaneously undermine our capacity for effective action and deaden our own hearts. While apathy is typically taken to mean a failure to act, the term actually denotes a failure to feel. Given that a crucial role of emotions is to generate motion, a failure to act may follow as a natural consequence the failure to feel.

As we all know, though, action impelled solely by emotion tends to be reactive and counterproductive, and our cognitive capacities alone do not necessarily supply the missing ingredients. Appropriate action does not follow from simply adding a dollop—or even a generous helping—of reasoning, critique, and analysis to feeling. Rather, effective action in the face of thorny problems requires a willingness to just sit there with uncomfortable facts and emotions rather than cogitating on a solution or rushing into action. In our extroverted and action-addicted culture, this pause may seem like a waste of valuable class time. As instructors, our information-laden minds may have to fight the impulse to fill up the space. Yet our willingness to allow the students to "just sit there" and observe their emotional reactions to the course material sends a host of subtle but powerful messages.

First, by acknowledging our students' subjective reactions to our course material, we convey a sense of empathy and an attitude of respect for their wholeness, thereby fostering these qualities within and among themselves. Since we cannot base their grades on their emotional authenticity or capacity for inner silence, we send a discreet message that we value something about our students beyond their academic performance. In my experience, as students tend to engage more wholeheartedly with the material, they release their obsession with grades. Without ever saying as much, we are communicating in a visceral way that something far more important than their GPA is at stake. For those of us whose training was solely cognitive, bringing our empathic and intuitive qualities more directly into our teaching can also contribute to our own sense of wholeness.

Second, as our students learn to acknowledge and bear their own anxiety, sadness, fear, and confusion, they operate with greater ease and confidence in the world. Paradoxically, sitting with uncomfortable facts and emotions tends to generate insight, resolve, and empowerment. Or perhaps this outcome is not so paradoxical, for any psychologist worth his or her salt will tell us that the dark emotions are most harmful when they are ignored.[2] Is it any wonder, then, that in a culture dedicated to "the pursuit of happiness" (very often through consumption) we have an epidemic of depression? Most of us are—and quite literally so in a car culture—driven to distraction. Yet if we peel away the veneer of so many of our pursuits of happiness and observe ourselves carefully, we see that most of us are perpetually running from the present moment. Turning a blind eye to the existential questions that arise in response to global environmental problems is just one strand in this vast machinery of evasion and complicity. The denial of our feelings about our perilous entry into the Anthropocene may be just as problematic as the climate-denial movement. Is not the majority who passively accepts the reality of climate change and goes about its business as disconcerting as the minority who actively denies it? Or perhaps these two seemingly antithetical positions are rooted in a common aversion to painful emotions—in one case through denying their factual basis and in the other through approaching the facts through cognition alone. In this context, to "just sit there" and steep in self-awareness in the face of world awareness becomes a radical act. When we reconnect with life by willingly enduring our pain for it, the mind regains its clarity and generates new possibilities for relational living and creative action. As Michael Maniates argues in the following chapter, exiting the place of hopelessness is not difficult once we know we are in it. I would add that when we encourage our students to not only know that they are in a state of despair, fear, anger, or guilt but to actually experience and name these emotions in the classroom, we erode some of the psychological and cultural structures that foster hopelessness.

Third, we send a subtle but powerful message by having the courage to set aside our expert personas and enter into the empty space of the pause. In essence, we are modeling a willingness to not know. From the standpoint of our professional training and our students' grades, this state of not knowing might appear as dangerous or absurd. Yet if we are honest with ourselves, we must acknowledge that this state is likely to become increasingly relevant—for better or for worse—as we move more deeply into the terra incognito of the Anthropocene. As valuable as our climate models, UN forecasts, and other predictive tools are, the stark reality is that we live in a mind-bogglingly complex world that defies prediction. We know the climate is changing, but the specifics (which are, after all, where life is lived) are unknowable. We know that climate surprises are inevitable, but surprises are by definition unpredictable. We know that many creatures that constitute the web of life will be extinct in a few decades, but we don't what this will mean for ourselves individually or collectively. Nor do we know what it means to live in the Anthropocene: Will humans take charge of the planet, or is this a hubristic fantasy? In the face of all of this, one of our primary jobs as global environmental politics faculty is to model not knowing not merely as a vacuous respite from the hard facts but as an earnest dive into self-awareness and focus. As Aldo Leopold observed decades ago (and as Simon Nicholson and Sikina Jinnah repeat in this book's Introduction), "One of the penalties of an ecological education is that one lives alone in a world of wounds," and the wounds have only deepened since. The future is dark—in both the sense of unknown and most likely undesirable. We cannot retrieve what has been lost, but we can bring our whole selves to what is here.

Coming to Our Senses

The human animal is a splendid oddity: the species with the capacity of separating itself from whole—at least in our own minds. The very term *environment* assumes that separation. In just a blink of geological time, industrialized societies have enacted a story of separation, altered the face of the Earth, and brought the Cenozoic age (from the Greek, the age of "new life") to an abrupt close. Barring a drastic change, of course, the Anthropocene looms as an age of the impoverishment of life. Ironically, however, the story of separation carries within itself the seeds of its own demise, for the message of collapsing ice shelves and the unraveling web of life is that we are decidedly not separate. Oddly enough, this is also the message of modern science: that we are the astonishing result of nearly 15 billion years of cosmological evolution and 5 billion years of terrestrial evolution. The so-called autonomous individual is inextricably reliant on a vast web of external ecosystems and internal microbial networks. Yet as much as we might know this, for most of us, our everyday lives are radically out of harmony with the community of life. If our lives are out of sync with reality, then practices that allow us to step outside our habitual grooves become all the more important.

Fortunately, we have available at every moment a window into present-moment awareness: our own sensory perception. Mindfulness practices like observing the breath enable us to shift from doing mode to being mode and, in the process, potentially witness our mind's compulsive activity rather than being swept up in it.[3] When my students walk mindfully through a shopping mall, for instance, their sensory awareness serves as an anchor that enables them to become aware of their impulses without acting on them (see box 5.2). Their internal experience often becomes more compelling than the consumer goods. As they walk through the mall, the students frequently report a surprising sense of calm. This confirms psychologists' finding that "mindful attention prevents mindless impulses."[4] Physiologically, mindfulness practices elevate the responsiveness of the parasympathetic and sympathetic nervous systems, thereby generating a simultaneous sense of calm and heightened attention. This state is proving to be of great value in reducing stress and healing a range of psychological problems, including addiction, trauma, and depression.[5] This state of relaxed attentiveness also turns out to facilitate learning, including in college classrooms. The Association for the Contemplative Mind in Higher Education has assembled a rich collection of practices in disciplines from architecture to astrophysics—including global environmental politics. Paul Wapner's webinar, "Contemplative Environmental Studies: Pedagogy for Self and Planet," offers a straightforward rationale for integrating contemplative practices into the global environmental politics classroom.[6]

Sustainability education is particularly amenable to contemplative inquiry. Its implicit critique of the growth imperative invites both a stepping back from impulsive consumption and a deep inquiry into the *anthros*. The special role of somatic experience in contemplative inquiry points to another connection: as organs of perception, our bodies are our intermediaries between Earth and mind, just as they are literally of the Earth. While science tells us this, few of us deeply consider it, much less translate it into lived experience.

The breath, for instance, can be a gateway to a profound experience of interdependence. At the end of a three-week study of global atmospheric politics, for instance, I lead a guided meditation called Living in E*air*th. As David Abram notes, we do not so much live on Earth as within its atmospheric membrane.[7] With each breath, we inhale molecules that have been

Box 5.2

Mindful Mall Walking

Given consumer culture's deep reach into our psyches, a ready channel for person/planet politics involves working with the impulse toward acquisition. In this out-of-class exercise, I ask students to take a solitary thirty-minute stroll through a shopping mall while attending to their emotional and somatic experience, followed by twenty minutes of journaling. Below is a rough sketch of the assignment.

Please block out an hour (not including travel time) for this exercise. Go to a shopping mall alone with no intention of buying anything. Bring a timekeeping device and set it for thirty minutes. Then simply walk slowly enough to be able to attend to whatever draws your attention and your own reactions. If you find yourself walking slowly and aimlessly, you're probably getting it right; the point is to have no agenda beyond observation. The following prompts can serve as anchor points:

- Notice not only what you see but also smells and sounds.
- Notice what you like and what you don't like, including your perceptions and judgments about the people around you.
- Notice which shops draw you in, which items attract your attention, and whether it is difficult to shift your attention elsewhere. What happens in your body?
- Notice your breath. Is it shallow or deep? Notice your body. Are you comfortable or uncomfortable?
- Notice when your mind wanders to outside your immediate experience. Where does it go?

At the end of thirty minutes, find a place to sit down and write about your experience. Write spontaneously about your immediate experience and any insights about yourself or the world, or both. This writing will not be graded; it is for yourself.

The students later share their experiences in small-group discussions and, depending on the course, draw on those experiences in a short paper on the politics of consumption. Students report a range of reactions to this combination of acute visceral experience and the sharing of these experiences in peer groups: insight, embarrassment, empathy, frustration, guilt, gratitude, and so on. All of them report learning something important about themselves or the world, or both. From the intensity of their papers and conversations, I see that the exercise helps them to come alive.

breathed by countless creatures, and with each exhalation, we emit a minute quantity of carbon dioxide to taken up by plants and minerals. The simple act of conscious breathing invites each of us into a visceral experience of living in the circle of life. As important as it is to understand the logic of sufficiency,[8] having the flesh-and-blood experience of sufficiency is of a different order.

Food offers another such opportunity. Integrative thinking is a key learning objective in my upper-level lecture course, Political Ecology of the World Food System. Much of the course is designed to reveal the hidden in the world food system: hidden costs, hidden ecological impacts, hidden relations of power and authority, and hidden surprises. Contemplative practices help the students step back from the facts and analysis into a more spacious and connective approach to the material, and the visceral experience of food facilitates this experience. Students are far less likely to forget the commodity chain of cocoa or corn, for instance, if they are holding a piece of chocolate or popcorn in their hands as they learn. Equally important, the experience of eating food mindfully is inherently valuable. Students have told me that they had never really tasted a raisin or a strawberry before (see box 5.3).

Time spent in contemplative inquiry makes for shorter lectures, which means there are important trade-offs to consider. Were the twelve minutes exploring the hidden life of a strawberry an effective use of classroom time? Were I primarily interested in conveying information, probably not. From a conventional pedagogical perspective, jumping from farmworker justice to soil fungus to the stratosphere is a confusing and scattered approach to world food politics. But I was more concerned with my students' capacities to think systemically and sit with uncomfortable emotions—not the least of which was the temptation to eat the strawberry—than their ability to memorize facts and concepts. I was betting that the visceral experience of the strawberry along with sharing one well-chosen word would enhance these capacities.

Make a Creative Response

When asked how to meet the mounting global environmental crisis without succumbing to despair, cultural historian Thomas Berry reputedly replied, "Make a creative response." A truly creative response to the Anthropocene would be one that moves beyond our habitual patterns of thought and action—beyond clichés, short-term remedies, and technological fixes. Neuroscientists and cognitive psychologists increasingly point to "the

Box 5.3

The Hidden Life of a Strawberry

This exercise illustrates some key concepts from my world food politics course—food justice, food webs, complexity, and unintended consequences. I ask the students to refrain from eating the freshly picked organic strawberries my teaching assistants distribute as I show a few photographs. *El cortito*, the infamous short-handled hoe now outlawed in California, highlights food justice. A gray, fuzzy strawberry shows the fruit's vulnerability to fungus. A graph of the global use of methyl bromide, a powerful ozone-depleting antifumigant used by the strawberry industry, reveals a huge unintended consequence of conventional strawberry production. If soil fungus is the problem, then perhaps farmers should put plastic bubble-wrap over their soil and install powerful electric fans to circulate air between the plants. It sounds far-fetched but a photo of a high-tech wind tunnel demonstrates the practice. It is an ingenious technological fix, I note, but what about the hidden energy costs? One last photo: the local organic farm where I purchased the berries that morning.

By now, the students are primed for a contemplative experience. I invite them to perceive the color, shape, texture of the strawberry—to get curious about their berry, to wonder how it was grown, by whom, with what consequences. I then invite them to eat the berry, noticing whatever arises. After a couple of very quiet minutes, I raise the lights and take the collective pulse. The single-word responses come flowing down the room: *overwhelmed, delicious, guilty, amazed, confused, connected, disconnected, grateful.*

In one class that met just before the lunch hour, the final one-word response, *hungry*, made the room erupt in laughter. In such a moment, I had to make a quick choice: to let the energy dissipate or bring it back into focus. I opted for the latter by asking who heard their own experience in someone else's words. As always, nearly every hand went up. I then invited them to take two deep breaths to help digest the experience, restoring the sense of calm focus before the end of class.

pause" as an essential ingredient in the creative, imaginative process. Perhaps the most obvious example from everyday life is the regenerative value of sleep, a prerequisite to our sanity and our survival. In a sense, contemplative practices offer a form of conscious rest. By disengaging the mind from its habitual grooves through attending closely to the present, contemplative inquiry reorients the mind to the freshness of the moment, thereby opening the imagination to that which has not yet been imagined. By fostering personally relevant understandings of how everyday experience is rooted in global ecological and human systems, instructors can literally bring the curriculum home and open up new possibilities for introspection and moral responsibility.

The inwardness of contemplative inquiry, however, is most likely to generate a truly creative response when it is carefully balanced with a return to the intersubjective space of dialogue with others. Otherwise the subjective pedagogical turn runs the risk of reinforcing a highly problematic tendency toward the individualization of environmental responsibility.[9] In the example above, the strawberry in hand helps to turn the students' attention back to their own experience. Yet the challenges raised (How are most berries grown for market? What about the use of methyl bromide and bubble-wrap wind tunnels?) cannot be resolved at the level of individual action and lifestyle choices. Each of these systemic questions must ultimately be answered in the polis, the interhuman arena of collective action, and not merely at the checkout counter or in the household. It is therefore crucial that classroom practices transcend individual subjective experience; otherwise, they run the risk of reinforcing the solipsistic proclivity of an individualistic culture. Meeting the challenges of the New Earth will likely require new modalities of both individual and collective wisdom.

A first step in making a creative response, for the individual and the collective, is to envision new possibilities. If we cannot imagine a viable future, then we are unlikely to create one. As the economist Kenneth Boulding said:

The image of the future ... is the key to all choice-oriented behavior. The general character and quality of the images of the future which prevail in a society is therefore the most important clue to its overall dynamics. The individual's image of the future is likewise the most significant determinant of ... personal behavior.[10]

Contemplative inquiry opens up the space for envisioning new possibilities—not by rushing to fix the problem or projecting one's conditioned thinking into the future, but rather by being fully present to the fecundity of not knowing and thereby opening oneself to fresh perceptions and insights.

The Self as Seed exercise is designed to help students in my food politics course develop the sustained attention and basic confidence that make for a genuinely creative response. This inquiry serves much the same function that Who Am I in a Changing Climate? serves in my global environmental politics course: to encourage my students to contemplate their entry into full adulthood in a complex world. Although I never say so explicitly,

Box 5.4

Self as Seed

Toward the end of my world food politics course, I guide the students through a number of contemplative exercises around food as metaphor. At the end of my lecture on the global politics of seeds, I guide them through a somatic experience of themselves as seeds.

I first point out that in some languages, the word for "seed" is the same as the word for "intention." This being an upper-level course at the end of spring quarter, I then ask who will graduate either this year or next. Nearly every hand goes up. I ask them to keep their hands up if what they will do after graduation is on their minds. Nearly every hand stays up. I offer them Frederick Buechner's words to the effect that one's calling is the place where one's deep joy meets the world's great hunger, a place we might consider as our core intention that we plant in the world's soil. I then darken the room and ask the students to stand with their eyes closed or downcast in order to attend to their inner experience.

"Consciously plant your feet on the ground. Feeling your weight evenly distributed across the balls of your feet and heels, observe the effect of gravity on your body. Feel the weight of your tailbone and your center of gravity somewhere in your lower abdomen. Notice what happens if you imagine yourself as sending your roots downward. Standing with relaxed yet alert attention, notice the sensations.

"Now imagine the top of your head lifting subtly towards the sun. Relax your breath. Notice the simultaneous downward pull of gravity and the upward attraction to light, much like a germinating seed. Enjoy the simplicity of consciously planting yourself on the Earth.

"Without losing your focus, take your seat. As you plant your butt on the seat, notice the sense of relaxation downward. Again, imagine your roots reaching down from your feet and tailbone. Consider that the Earth's gravitational field determines your roots' directionality. Astronauts report that a seed germinated in outer space sends its roots out in all directions. So from the moment of your birth until the moment of your death, gravity orients you. And by telling you which way is down, gravity also tells you which way is up. With relaxed yet alert attention, notice the feelings in your body.

"Once again imagine the top of your head lifting subtly towards the sun. Relax the breath. Notice the downward pull of gravity and upward attraction to light. Enjoy the simplicity of the sensations. Into the silence, ask the questions: 'What is my intention? What am I seeding? Where am I planting myself?' Observe what arises without judgment and without getting lost in any stories that might come up: simply listen and feel.

"Now slowly open your eyes and take a few minutes to gather the harvest by reflecting quietly or writing." A natural way of reestablishing the cohesiveness of the group is to "take the classroom pulse."

because I want them to trust their own experience over my interpretations, this particular somatic exercise can also elicit a visceral sense of being "of the Earth" and therefore being capable of accessing one's innate earthly intelligence.

Conclusion

According to developmental leadership researcher Sharon Parks,[11] the threshold of emerging adulthood is marked by the cultivation of critical thought and a corresponding recasting of one's relationships, including one's relationship to authority. This entails an intellectual and emotional journey from dependence on assumed sources of authority, which in turn entails relentless inquiry and discernment: What is true and worthy of trust? Who am I really? What matters? In what and with whom can I invest my life? By what narratives do we live and die? In taking responsibility for her own thinking, an emerging adult ripens to the task of composing "a worthy dream" for her life. For Parks, emerging adulthood is a "stem-cell moment in human becoming." At this critical juncture between conventional knowing and critical-connective thought, a strong mentor can serve as a "developmental lure."

But what does it mean to come of age when it is increasingly evident that prevailing institutions, practices, and values are unraveling the tapestry of life? And what does it mean to serve as a mentor under these conditions? No doubt, we as global environmental politics instructors have a responsibility to teach the relevant facts, concepts, and theories, but in our capacity as mentors, we are also called on to attend to their larger experience at the threshold of adulthood. In the arena of contemplative inquiry, the point is not so much to have the right answers but to have the courage to not know, the skillfulness to help guide our students into the depths of their own experience, and the compassion to abide with them there as their native wisdom unfolds.

Notes

1. Eaton, Hughes, and MacGregor, eds., *Contemplative Inquiry for Sustainability Education.*

2. Greenspan, *Healing through the Dark Emotions.*

3. Sega, Williams, and Teasdale, *Mindfulness-Based Cognitive Therapy for Depression.*

4. Barsalou, "Mindful Attention Prevents Mindless Impulses."

5. Sega, Williams, and Teasdale, *Mindfulness-Based Cognitive Therapy for Depression*.

6. Wapner, "Contemplative Environmental Studies."

7. Abram, *Becoming Animal*.

8. Princen, *The Logic of Sufficiency*.

9. Maniates. "Individualization."

10. Boulding, Foreword.

11. Parks, "Human Development and the Power of Pause."

Bibliography

Abram, David. Becoming Animal: An Earthly Cosmology. New York: Vintage, 2011.

Barsalou, Lawrence. "Mindful Attention Prevents Mindless Impulses." In *Proceedings of the International Symposia for Contemplative Studies*. 2012. http://contemplativeresearch.org/proposals/presentation-abstracts.

Boulding, K. Foreword. In *The Image of the Future*, edited by Fred Polak and Elise Boulding. Amsterdam: Elsevier, 1973.

Eaton, Marie, Kate Davies, Sarah Williams, and Jean MacGregor. "Why Sustainability Education Needs Pedagogies of Reflection and Contemplation." In *Contemplative Inquiry for Sustainability Education: Teaching the World Whole*, edited by Marie Eaton, Holly Hughes, and Jean MacGregor. Forthcoming.

Eaton, Marie, Holly Hughes, and Jean MacGregor, eds. *Contemplative Inquiry for Sustainability Education: Teaching the World Whole* . London: Routledge, forthcoming.

Greenspan, Miriam. *Healing through the Dark Emotions: The Wisdom of Grief, Fear, and Despair*. Boston: Shambhala, 2004.

Kabat-Zinn, Jon. *Full Catastrophe Living: Using the Wisdom of Your Body and Mind to Face Stress, Pain and Illness*. New York: Delta, 2009.

Maniates, Michael. "Individualization: Plant a Tree, Buy a Bike, Save the World?" *Global Environmental Politics* 1, no. 3 (2001): 31–52.

Parks, Sharon. "Human Development and the Power of Pause." In *Contemplative Inquiry for Sustainability Education: Teaching the World Whole* edited by Marie Eaton, Holly Hughes, and Jean MacGregor. Forthcoming . (forthcoming).

Princen, Thomas. *The Logic of Sufficiency*. Cambridge, MA: MIT Press, 2005.

Schmidt, S., and H. Walach, eds. *Meditation: Neuroscientific Approaches and Philosophical Implications*. New York: Springer, 2013.

Sega, Zindel V. J., Mark G. Williams, and John D. Teasdale. *Mindfulness-Based Cognitive Therapy for Depression*, 2nd ed. New York: Guilford Press, 2012.

Wapner, Paul. "Contemplative Environmental Studies: Pedagogy for Self and Planet." Retrieved June 28, 2015, from http://www.contemplativemind.org/archives/313.

6 Make Way for Hope: A Contrarian View

Michael F. Maniates

Most people are eagerly groping for some medium, some way in which they can bridge the gap between their morals and their practices.

—Saul Alinsky (1969)

Hope. This one small word weighs heavy, like an important obligation unfulfilled, in conversations about teaching and learning on the New Earth—at least it does for me, and I'm surely not alone. For thirty years I've struggled to balance an honest recitation of what ecological economist Herman Daly and theologian John Cobb call the "wild facts" of environmental disaster with a sensitivity to my students' need for hope.[1] It's a vexing Goldilocks problem. Too much classroom focus on these wild facts inevitably produces emotional responses that Karen Litfin documents in chapter 5: feelings of being overwhelmed, cynicism, despair, apathy, and hopelessness. But anything less than straight talk about the enormity of our collective predicament feels cowardly and paternalistic. Soft-pedalling the enormity of the environmental challenges looming on the horizon out of some attempt to keep hope alive violates the obligation, shared by student and teacher alike, to look reality squarely in the eye no matter the cost. Before being booted out by the Bear family, Goldilocks found the porridge, chair, and bed that was "just right," but it's a tougher search for those of us in the global environmental politics classroom—and for activists and policymakers too. As students, professors, and practitioners, we teach, learn, and act with a loose faith that knowledge equals power and that this power will spawn hope. But we are also aware of the more likely outcome of our work, captured some time back by comedian Paula Poundstone when she asked, "What moron said that knowledge is power? Knowledge is power only if it doesn't depress you so much that it leaves you in an immobile heap at the end of your bed."[2]

No one likes the Paula Poundstone scenario, where knowing more about mounting ecological injury produces disempowered or broken students. No doubt that is why a great deal of ink has been spilled on hope in the classroom of the Anthropocene. For example, writers like Oberlin College professor David Orr argue that hope, as opposed to optimism (the latter is what we feel when the odds are with us, while the former is what we marshal when they're not), is essential to a more just and sustainable world.[3] Without hope, all is lost. Others, including environmental activist Derrick Jensen, bristle over all this "hope talk."[4] Looking to others for hope blinds us to our own strengths, says Jensen, and waiting for hope delays the difficult and sometimes dismal work of building a just and sustainable world. Less hoping and more doing, please. Orr and Jensen are but two examples of widening conversation about this thing we call "hope," a conversation critical to education in the Anthropocene.

In light of these contradictory impulses (hope is necessary, but waiting and hoping for hope is disempowering), how should educators of global environmental politics best respond? By engaging in "contemplative education" that Litfin so wonderfully describes in chapter 5? Through real-world projects that expose students to the joys of collective action?[5] By revisiting anew the limits of ecological literacy?[6] By reframing environmental problems as products of domination and injustice and highlighting the many ways in which the oppressed are already fighting back?[7] Or maybe by acknowledging and accepting the coming collapse, and exploring skills and institutions best matched to the hard times ahead?[8]

The answer, it seems, is "it depends"—on the nature of the course, the strengths and temperament of the teacher, the culture of the institution, the intellectual traditions of the field, the expectations of the students, and the vulnerabilities of the faculty member. Some faculty will opt for experiential education to teach hope; others may invoke narratives of "ecowarriors" to inspire. It is all terribly idiosyncratic and personal, but in ways that are utterly expected. After all, as Parker Palmer reminds us in *The Courage to Teach*, teaching is an intensely personal affair.[9] And the best teaching—including teaching that nurtures hope—doesn't flow from some snappy collection of teaching techniques or classroom exercises, but rather from self-knowledge about one's identity and integrity in the classroom—what Palmer calls the inner landscape of teaching. Imagining that this must sound odd to some readers, Palmer offers the following:

My concern for the inner landscape of teaching may seem indulgent, even irrelevant, at a time when many teachers are struggling simply to survive. Wouldn't it be more practical, I am sometimes asked, to offer tips, tricks, and techniques for staying alive in the classroom, things that ordinary teachers can use in everyday life? The question puzzles me, because for twenty years I have … worked with countless teachers, and many of them have confirmed my own experience: as important as methods may be, the most practical thing we can achieve in any kind of work is insight into what is happening inside us as we do it. The more familiar we are with our inner terrain, the more surefooted our teaching—and living—becomes.[10]

Palmer isn't alone in his claim that powerful teaching flows from introspective educators comfortable in their own skin. There is a rich and engaging literature on the subject to which Litfin's chapter now belongs.[11] At a time when professors like me are packing more material into their classes (not, I promise, out of some perverse hatred of students but rather from a misguided desire to do full justice to the complexities of the Anthropocene), Litfin reminds us that surefootedness comes from self-knowledge and that self-knowledge demands contemplative practice.

Indeed, we all need to slow down in the classroom. Quantity does not equal quality, as Litfin's inspiring students so vividly demonstrate. Their easy embrace of her curricular innovations affirms an understanding of human nature advanced by scholars ranging from biologist E. O. Wilson[12] to psychologist Tari Sharot[13] to mathematician Peter Dodds,[14] and employed by political organizers inspired by Saul Alinsky (quoted at the start of this chapter), Miles Horton, or Paulo Freire[15]: we are naturally and inexorably inclined toward hope. Hopefulness is stamped in our genes and prowls our neurology. It permeates language. We can no more be taught to be hopeful than instructed on how to breathe or digest our food. The best our teachers can do (and it's a critically important task, to be sure) is to illuminate the bonds that shackle our innate hopefulness and diminish our creativity and resolve.

Here is where this chapter turns contrarian. Despite the accepted view among my professor colleagues that we must somehow "teach hope" in our courses, and notwithstanding the common student complaint of "I wish the class was more hopeful," the first step toward a pedagogy of hope for the New Earth is to abandon the misplaced, even arrogant belief that educators can or should teach hope in any systematic or enduring way. We already are a naturally hopeful species—and thus there is no need to waste time devising an Anthropocenic pedagogy that strives to instill hope in students. Instead, a pedagogy for the future must be deaf to student complaints that the facts of life in the New Earth are deeply distressing and persistently depressing. It is a pedagogy that will respectfully listen to classroom questions like, "Is there hope?" "How do I find hope?" or "How do I remain hopeful?" But it will offer no answers in return. It is a pedagogy delivered by educators who understand their own inner landscape, seek authenticity in the classroom, and see in their students an inherent hopefulness waiting to burst forth. It is a pedagogy preoccupied with highlighting and dismantling the myths and misperceptions that separate students and teachers alike from their own reservoirs of creative hope.

And so it's worth repeating: the problem we face is not some dearth of hope. It is a set of walls and canals, many of which are unwittingly produced and reproduced in the classroom, that funnel and imprison our hopefulness in cell blocks of immobility and despair. Attack these structures and answers to students' questions about hope will emerge organically and spontaneously. Litfin's mentors did this for her—and her chapter is best read not as a how-to guide for contemplative education (recall Palmer's words above) but as a story of introspection and self-discovery that delivered her to an authentically hopeful place in her work. Perhaps teaching for hope is little more than this, and as much as this.

What, then, are these structures that separate us from our innately creative hopefulness? Alas, much that has been written on this question for global affairs educators[16] has gone unnoticed, and relevant treatments outside environmental studies[17] have been largely ignored. This isn't surprising. My own sense, after facilitating or participating in several "teaching hope" roundtables and panels at professional conferences, is that educators and students quickly plunge into the nuts-and-bolts of teaching techniques for fostering hope. Like moths to a flame, we are drawn to the erroneous notion that a lack of hope is the problem to be solved. The counterformulation—that there are forces afoot that imprison our innate hopefulness—is pushed to the shadows.

To move this argument forward, the remainder of this chapter explores eight myths and misperceptions that stifle hope and then offers one example, the trinity of despair, to illustrate how these myths can interact to shackle hopefulness. The chapter ends with a personal note to those intrepid readers who make it that far.

Myths and Misperceptions

Some subset of the following eight myths and misperceptions lurk in the global environmental affairs classroom (see box 6.1). They either go unnoticed or are accepted as established fact by students and professors, and thus

---

Box 6.1

Eight Hope-Restricting Myths and Misperceptions

1. The state prevails.
2. Complexity makes action impossible.
3. You'll never get people to sacrifice.
4. We just don't have the right values.
5. Things change only in a crisis.
6. If everyone does a few simple things, we can change the world.
7. A good way to mobilize people politically is to start them with small "green" lifestyle changes.
8. Bottom-up change is good; top-down change is bad.

---

remain unchallenged. Expose and question them, and room for hope grows.

1. *The state prevails.* Global environmental change is transnational in character and global in reach. And yet despite the limited utility of a state-centric lens on global environmental affairs, we see what Ken Conca calls "the persistent personification of sovereign states."[18] "The problem," Conca notes, "is not that we pay too much attention to the state but rather that in doing so we allow cartoonish ahistorical personified imagery to shape our view of what a state really is." This personified imagery of "Brazil needs, China wants, or America refuses" miscasts the problem of global injustice, distorts the nature and distribution of power, and hides some of the most empowering responses to global environmental ills. The statist lens reifies the nation-state as the principal agent in environmental affairs and dominates for a variety of reasons: the ubiquity of national data in the field, the weight of intellectual history, the relative ease with which state behavior can be documented and studied, and the ways in which nonstate activity lives on the margins of discourse (per Paul Wapner's chapter 15).

   If left underproblematized, this statist frame stifles hope, for it comes to appear as the only viable lens through which we might see the world. As a result, our attention gravitates to political struggle at the national level, where the price of entry into the conversation seems impossibly high and environmental concerns are too often an afterthought. More promising (and hopeful) domains of political action escape our gaze.

2. *The hegemony of complexity.* On a grand scale, global environmental challenges are understood as a product of complex human systems interacting with complex natural systems, producing a host of "wicked" and "superwicked" problems that defy easy solution.[19] Additionally, specific instances of these problems (e.g., overconsumption or the depletion of water resources) frequently arise from layered political-economic forces interacting at multiple levels over time. At some point, the weight of this complexity sidelines questions of power and agency,[20] making any action seem meaningless. As I suggest elsewhere, "It may come to seem that no single actor has the power to alter [outcomes] arising from the intricate interplay of social, cultural and material forces, and that the notion of power itself, diffused across an expanding set of nearly autonomous practices and norms, is little more than a quaint concept. Agency becomes ephemeral. Social change ... seems unpredictable and episodic."[21]

If the story of complex systems stops at this point, where complexity itself is overwhelming and disempowering, then our inherent hopefulness is challenged. We must remember that complex systems also offer positive feedback loops and thresholds that can transform small and strategic interventions into large and positive system changes—"the punctuated equilibrium of hope," if you will—where social systems and political life suddenly shift for the better.[22] When this aspect of the systems-complexity story goes untold or underanalyzed, as it too often does in the classroom, the hegemony of complexity needlessly marginalizes hope.

3. *The impossibility of sacrifice (a.k.a. "evolutionary wrong turn").* Sacrifice—the giving up of something valuable now for the possibility (but not the promise) of benefits, individual or collective, in the future—is generally assumed to be an impossibility in environmental politics.[23] In this view, we are the products of an "evolutionary wrong turn"[24] that produced clever and nimble bipeds that are inherently shortsighted, selfish, and materially acquisitive. They are destroying the planet and themselves. Although this narrative of defective human nature can be dismantled on any number of fronts, not the least of which is evolutionary,[25] it still holds influence in the global environmental affairs classroom. It may be the most potent impediment to hope, yet one of the easiest claims to creatively interrogate with students. Individual and collective sacrifice, both voluntary and involuntary, surrounds us daily. Rather than simply conclude that "people will never sacrifice for the environment/future generations/sustainability," it is more rewarding, intellectually and

politically, to assess those conditions under which sacrifice occurs, often joyfully and voluntarily, and to consider how these conditions can be reproduced and scaled.

4. *The quicksand of values.* The absence of proenvironment values or "environmental consciousness"[26] is sometimes perceived as a principal driver of global environmental decline. In this formulation, navigating the Anthropocene without destroying the planet, and ourselves, demands fundamental change in cultural software and human perception. For some who hold this view, the problem lies with human nature; for others, "bad" values are the product of other forces that include the weight of history (e.g. an expansionist value set that served us well when environmental space was abundant), industrial capitalism and its creation of consumers, a growing disconnect with nature, long chains of production and consumption that distance us from the impacts of our actions, and educational systems that direct us away from an intense consciousness of the land.[27]

Cultural orientations toward nature and societal value sets are important factors in global environmental affairs, but conversation about them often degrades into wobbly claims about human nature (as in "people just don't care about the environment") and the pace of change (as in "societal values must change, and that is always a long process"). It is also common to assume that individuals lack the values necessary to a sustainable society, as opposed to recognizing that existing "sustainable" values already reside within us, just waiting to be primed.[28] Avoiding the quicksand of this hope-marginalizing trifecta requires careful classroom scrutiny of the connections among values, environmental degradation, and social change. Complicating the meaning and role of values in environmental politics can be helpful here. For instance, investigating the "environmental values-behavior gap,"[29] where strong environmental values fail to yield environmentally sustainable behaviors, can create classroom space for understanding values as just one of many elements in a politics of sustainability, with other, more malleable factors (e.g., structures, habits, and options in everyday life) emerging as equally, if not more, important.

5. *The prime driver: crisis.* Faith in the restorative effect of crisis runs deep in the student psyche.[30] The belief that social change occurs only during crisis is the inevitable result of myths 3 and 4, though it must be the right kind of crisis: not so small as to be ignored but not so devastating as to overwhelm. Such crisis thinking locks our innate hopefulness into a dark and tiny closet by stating as fact the tenuous claim that

individuals and their leaders cannot change absent external coercion. This view is blind to the many important social, political-economic, and technical changes that have occurred in the absence of crisis. It also ignores the unsettling fact that crisis does not typically privilege progressive, thoughtful, longer-term thinking. Agents of social change should never waste a good crisis. But believing that change happens only in the midst of crisis infantilizes our own capacities to alter our world and offers few avenues for meaningful action beyond attempts to accelerate the onset of crisis.

6. *Every little thing helps.* As the Pulitzer Prize–winning journalist Thomas Friedman observes in his "205 Easy Ways to Save the Earth," doing the "small and easy things" to save the environment has become the overarching mantra for contemporary environmental politics.[31] Saving the planet becomes a lifestyle choice rather than a political act. This thinking, familiar to us all and alive and well in the global environmental politics classroom, asserts that small, individual acts of environmental consciousness model good behavior for others, who will be inspired to act accordingly. The aggregation of these millions, if not billions, of small acts (taking shorter showers, eating less meat, reusing containers, and the like) will then translate into significant political and economic change. This understanding of personal agency and social change appears to create room for hopefulness; we can all be productive agents of change without engaging in difficult political struggle. In fact, in ways described in the following section, this view fosters a theory of social change, a politics of guilt, and a growing faith in crisis that is the antithesis of hope.

7. *The escalator theory.* Ever since the backlash against mainstream environmental policymaking in the 1980s, environmental activists and practitioners have embraced the notion that individual acts of green consumption and lifestyle change are ultimately politicizing. The hope, then and now, is that small and easy environmental behaviors activate what US environmental leader Annie Leonard calls our "citizen muscle," and lead to more environmental activism in a variety of political spaces.[32] This is sometimes known as the escalator theory: start people off with something easy, like buying an energy-efficient lightbulb, and before you know it they'll be engaged citizens fighting for better energy policy. Alas, despite recent scholarship sympathetic to the escalator theory,[33] this notion remains more wish than fact: green consumption and environmental activism are at times correlated, but little evidence suggests that this escalator view accurately

describes the connection. (It is most likely that committed environmentalists engage in political action and adopt small lifestyle and consumption changes, without the latter driving the former). This is a version of myth 6 and suffers from the same deficiencies, described in the next section.

8. *Top down versus bottom up*. If there is one common article of faith in the global environmental politics classroom, it may be that necessary change in key institutions will come from mass mobilization from below rather than elite action from above. In this view, elites are too heavily invested in the status quo, and even if they aren't, the concentration of power and wealth typical of most societies—facilitated or accommodated by elites—in and of itself privileges and perpetuates global environmental ruin. And so bottom-up, mass mobilization it is. This binary view of agency and social change so common to the classroom is attractive for its simplicity, but it romanticizes the power and progressivity of local action while taking off the table a host of elite-driven interventions that could foster needed change. More fundamental, it tends toward a lack of engagement with power and privileges a view that social change occurs only when supermajorities are fully engaged around an issue. The ascendancy of this view in the classroom and the policy arena may be the single greatest constraint on the full flowering of hope, as the next section explains.

The Trinity of Despair

While each of these eight elements alone can keep hope at bay, it is the interaction among them that is particularly troublesome. One especially disabling synergism that I observe in the classroom is what I call the trinity of despair (TOD).[34] This section describes this trinity, which appears to me to be pernicious and widespread, operating under the radar of most classroom inquiry. The TOD stands as but one instance of how many of the elements I have described can converge to undermine our innate hopefulness. As teachers and students, we needn't talk explicitly about hope. We must simply recognize and disarm processes like the TOD through careful thinking and honest conversation. If we do that, hope will find its own way.

Consider figure 6.1, with human nature at the apex and environmental strategies and theory of social change at the corners. One can be drawn into the TOD at any of these three points; locating human nature at the apex

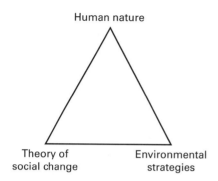

Figure 6.1
The Trinity of Despair

does not mean that the TOD starts there, though for many students it does. Similarly, one can escape the TOD by challenging the assumptions about human nature and social change at any of these three points.

Let's arbitrarily begin with human nature at the top of the triangle. The human nature at work here is the narrowly self-interested, short-term thinking "I won't sacrifice" caricature of human beings. To subscribe to this view does not mean that one judges people as evil or mean-spirited. Instead, it is to see humans as Garrett Hardin saw them when writing about the tragedy of the commons many decades ago: rational, calculating, short-term maximizers of immediate benefit.[35] Many of the students who join my global environmental affairs course hold this view—perhaps because of an earlier environmental science or studies course that celebrated Hardin's model, or because of a need to easily explain patterns of environmental simplification and decline. Blaming human nature is an easy and perhaps natural thing to do.

If one believes humans to be as Hardin describes, and if one is also attached to a bottom-up view of social change, then the best way of "saving the planet" is to appeal to humans with environmental strategies that focus on easy, cost-effective individual action—the strategies represented at the bottom right of the triangle. After all, Hardin's rational man isn't going to work hard on behalf of the environment. He won't support legislation that will increase his taxes or disrupt his way of life. He will be motivated by win-win measures that save him money; if these measures shrink his environmental footprint, that's a bonus. The best way to involve this rational man, at least initially, is through environmental strategies that highlight small acts of green consumption. Consuming is something he likes to do.

For those who are drawn into the trinity of despair, getting individuals to adopt small consumer and lifestyle changes is just the beginning. TOD aficionados believe that as small groups of people begin to behave and consume more environmentally, perhaps by riding their bike or buying organic food, others will observe this behavior and jump on board. As this process builds, aided perhaps by the dissemination of information about the benefits of adopting these small measures, even more people will join in, and the cumulative benefits to the environment will become apparent. These environmental benefits will be inspirational, leading to even wider adoption of an array of simple and easy behaviors. Meanwhile, many of those who began with simple acts of green consumption will become politically active, thanks to the escalator effect, and policymakers will begin to feel pressure to change. They won't get much opposition from corporations, because consumers will be voting in the marketplace with their dollars for clean and green products. The result will be a more sustainable and just planet, initiated by small and easy changes that seemed insignificant at first but grew into a force to be reckoned with.

My current students call this the "many drops in the ocean" approach. Others with whom I've worked on campus sustainability issues understand it as "setting an example for social change." Still others think of it as the "starting people off with easy things, after which they'll move on to more difficult tasks" maxim. I find that many accept this to be a good and plausible strategy, especially given the belief that "most people" won't accept inconvenience or sacrifice to increase environmental quality.

This path forward also fits nicely into a narrative of change promoted by industry and government. For example, when the US Environmental Protection Agency many years ago launched its core energy-efficiency initiatives, one of the primary slogans splashed across its web pages was "buy a bulb and save the world" (the bulb being an energy-efficient one). The recycling bins just outside my office door, which are part of a government program, say "Recycle and Save the Planet!" Marketers of green products amplify the claim that we save the world with our small, individual actions of environmental conscientiousness—by buying one of their organic or recyclable or recycled products. For those still unsure of how to proceed, or why, there are seemingly countless books and websites that describe how we can save the planet in 5, 10, 20, or 101 ways.

Advocates of this approach agree that its success depends on a great many things: strong environmental education, good information campaigns, continued technological development that generates even more ways for people to save money and help the environment, and systems that fully communicate to individuals the environmental consequences of their consumption decisions. What these defenders miss, however, is the third corner of the trinity of despair. In their eagerness to make their plan work, they've neglected to fully interrogate the theory of social change that unavoidably flows from the "small things save the world" perspective. And that is their undoing.

This theory, in a nutshell, is that change happens when you get everyone (or almost everyone) on board. Change won't happen, moreover, until you do. Environmental strategies that revolve around small tweaks to lifestyle and consumption choices require mass participation. It's simple math: small things add up to big outcomes only if there are lots of small things happening. Change through mass commitment and participation is also a big part of the larger narrative—environmental advertisements like "If everyone recycled their phone book, we'd save 10,000 trees a year" or "If everyone moved to energy-efficient lighting, we could shut down five coal-fired power plants" are ubiquitous. Corporations won't change their practices unless there is a huge shift in buying patterns. Governments won't change policy unless a whole lot of people get on the escalator that moves them from ecoshopper to noisy citizen. My clueless neighbor won't start composting until all his neighbors do, at which point he'll awkwardly realize that he's the odd man out. There is way no around it: a bottom-up, small-and-easy strategy tailored to shortsighted consumers leads inexorably to a theory of social change that demands dedicated participation by the masses. And this spells trouble.

The "despair" in the TOD arises when this theory of social change is accepted as truth by those who seek to improve the world. In fact, the notion that we change the world through small interventions spread across large populations is wildly inaccurate. During periods of mobilization for change, you *never* get everyone on board—not even close: not with the end of slavery, not with women's suffrage, not with the rise of economic liberalism, and certainly not with any shift toward political and economic structures conducive to environmental sustainability. Change typically happens through the determined and strategic action of small minorities within a population, with the rest being slowly pulled along.

This fact of political life is difficult to see for individuals trapped in the trinity of despair. It challenges their entire view of how change occurs. And that has costs. So, for instance, instead of celebrating that 15 to 20 percent of Americans regularly engage in determined green behavior (a remarkable level, given the structural incentives in the United States to be anything but environmentally sensitive), and strategizing about how to further mobilize this dedicated minority, those caught in the TOD will highlight the other 80 to 85 percent of the population as further proof of the ignorance and selfishness of humans. Those drawn into the TOD have been set up to struggle for an impossible goal of full participation wrapped around a deceptive theory of social change.

When those trapped in the TOD observe that they aren't getting the supermajorities they need to practice environmentally sound behaviors, they logically respond with more environmental education and information. When that doesn't work, their next step is guilt and blame; if we can't reason with people rationally, the thinking goes, we'll shame them into appropriate behavior. To my eye, this is the single most powerful explanation for why the environmental movement, which used to celebrate the human spirit and the potential of the possible, has succumbed to an ineffective politics of guilt. To the extent that this is true, it is not because the environmentally concerned are naturally judgmental or dictatorial. It is because their theory of social change—a theory that says, come hell or high water, we need to get everyone on board doing the little things, and if information won't work, then guilt might—requires them to be this way.

The students, activists, and policymakers I know who stay trapped in the TOD move in one of two dismal directions. Some conclude that human beings are even more shortsighted and narrow-minded than they initially believed, and they start their path around the triangle with more intensity and vigor. They work harder to figure out even easier, more attractive, and economical environmental strategies. They try to come up with snappier ways of communicating environmental information. They struggle and strive to draw even more people to green lifestyles, first through example and then by guilt. They are never effective in getting everyone on board, but they work hard, all the while losing faith in their fellow humans and despairing for the planet.

Others trapped in the TOD simply conclude that people have "bad values" that produce a lack of broad and enduring interest in easy environmental lifestyles. They see no option other than waiting for some ecocalamity to come along that will teach the uncaring the error of their ways, realign environmental values, and move policymakers in the right direction.

Both reactions are antithetical to hope. They are inevitable responses, however, of initially hopeful (even idealistic) individuals who became trapped in an interlocking set of plausible but inaccurate assumptions about how people behave and how social change occurs. These responses explain much about the cynicism and despair I see in many of my students and in some of my activist colleagues.

Escaping the TOD isn't difficult, however, once you know you're in it. Getting out requires entertaining alternate ideas about the nature of humans, how societies change, the kinds of environmental strategies that inspire and mobilize, and the dangers of a dogged commitment to mass mobilization. So, for instance, learning about theories of social change that highlight how small segments of a population can reengineer culture toward sustainable ends has catapulted some of my students out of the TOD and toward creative, hopeful thinking about social change. Other students have escaped through careful inquiry into elite-driven mechanisms of "choice editing" for sustainability, where a small minority structures everyday life to make it natural and normal to behave in environmentally sustainable ways.[36] Still others are intrigued by thinking strategically about human psychology and the propensity for sacrificial behavior. Of course, these strategies are not without their own complications. Just who are these elites doing the cultural engineering and choice editing, for instance, and how will they be accountable to the larger public? And who is doing the sacrificing, and who isn't, and is this fair? But these are complications with creative and hopeful answers, grounded in a more accurate understanding of the fluidity of human behavior and the dynamics of social change.

And to Avoid Any Misunderstanding

Some of you will note that I have neglected the other side of the hope coin, which is the naive hope that "everything will work out fine" that my colleagues and I are increasingly seeing in the classroom. This hope rests on the shaky assumption that when things get bad environmentally, prices for products will shift to drive the development of new technologies that will solve our problems. The interplay between price and innovation can be a powerful force, but the fallacy underlying this sort of hope should be clear to students of environmental systems. Much of the environmental damage we're risking is characterized by irreversible thresholds, like driving a car off a cliff or pushing grandmother's fine china cup off the table and seeing it shatter on the floor. The "rising-prices equals nifty-technologies that solve the problem" dynamic may work for slowly worsening problems with adequate time for innovation, but it's a poor foundation for hope when dealing with rapidly changing systems that can surprise you, and for which there is no easy or immediate technological solution to environmental damage or resource depletion. Too many of my students underappreciate these arguments; their faith in technological innovation driven by the price mechanism seems unassailable. The hope that springs from this naïveté is disconcerting and counterproductive, and deserves far more attention than I've given it in this chapter.

In addition, my reflections here could be read as giving the cold shoulder to hope in the classroom, or perhaps as disparaging techniques for teaching hope developed by others. Neither was my intent.

I have long been a fan of method and technique for inspiring and soothing my global affairs and environmental studies students. I confess to smarting whenever comments like, "Wow, what a depressing class. Why couldn't you have been more hopeful?" pop up on my teaching evaluations. For a few years in one of my classes, I actually scripted one reading or exercise a week that was meant to address the "hope issue." But I confess to having never been satisfied with this response, as diligent as it was.

As I worked through this chapter, I came to conclude that there are no genuine techniques or tools for teaching or learning hope. It is ultimately conceit to think otherwise. As professors, we don't try to teach empathy or love or compassion in the classroom, do we? And as students, we aren't troubled by a class if it fails to teach us courage or thrift or prudence, are we? So why does hope get special billing? Why, to some extent, have students and their teachers been drawn into a codependent relationship where we each expect to have hope in our hearts at the end of the term?

Our job in the academy, as teachers and students, is to expose myth and uncover the truth. Doing that, in ways that obliterate the fraudulent obstacles to hope, is how we best cultivate optimism and action for a New Earth.

Notes

1. Daly and Cobb, *For the Common Good.*

2. Poundstone, "Lean, Green Fighting Machine," 80.

3. Orr, "Optimism and Hope in a Hotter Time" and *Hope Is an Imperative.*

4. Jensen, "Beyond Hope."

5. Maniates, ed., *Encountering Global Environmental Politics*.

6. Hempel, "Ecoliteracy."

7. Di Chiro, "Living Environmentalisms"; Evans, *Occupy Education*.

8. Assadourian, "Building an Enduring Environmental Movement."

9. Palmer, *The Courage to Teach*.

10. Ibid., 5.

11. See, for example, Ayers, "Teaching as an Ethical Enterprise"; Brookfield, *Becoming a Critically Reflective Teacher*; Horton et al., *We Make the Road by Walking*; Horton and Jacobs, *The Miles Horton Reader*.

12. See McDonough and Braungar, "Foreword to the Chinese Edition of Cradle to Cradle."

13. Sharot, *The Optimism Bias*.

14. Dodds et al. "Human Language Reveals a Universal Positivity Bias."

15. See Horton et al., *We Make the Road by Walking*.

16. See, for example, Conca, "Imagining the State."

17. See, for example, Lappe and Lappe, *Hope's Edge*.

18. Conca, "Imagining the State," 77.

19. See, for example, Rittel and Weber, "Dilemmas in a General Theory of Planning"; Balint et al., *Wicked Environmental Problems*; Levin et al. "Overcoming the Tragedy of Super Wicked Problems."

20. See, for example, Sayer's 2012 critique of one way of analyzing overconsumption: "Power, Sustainability and Well-Being."

21. Maniates, "Sustainable Consumption."

22. Baumgartner et al., "Punctuated Equilibrium Theory."

23. Maniates and Meyer, *The Environmental Politics of Sacrifice*.

24. Orr, *Hope Is an Imperative*.

25. Judson, "The Selfless Gene."

26. See, for example, Litfin, *Ecovillages*.

27. Princen, *Treading Softly*.

28. Gunster, "Self-Interest, Sacrifice, and Climate Change."

29. Kennedy et al., "Why We Don't `Walk the Talk.'"

30. Maniates, "Teaching for Turbulence."

31. Friedman, *Hot, Flat, and Crowded*.

32. Leonard, *The Story of Stuff*.

33. See, for example, Lorenzen, "Convincing People to Go Green."

34. I began to suspect there was a trinity of despair (TOD) on my return from international teaching in 2005. My time away sensitized me to what I'd taken to be normal back home. Since then I have gently queried my environmental studies and global affairs students about the fit of the TOD to their experience while serving at three rather different institutions: Allegheny College in Meadville, Pennsylvania; Oberlin College in Oberlin, Ohio; and Yale-NUS College in Singapore. I have also shared the TOD in several guest lectures around the United States and at workshops at international conferences. A large majority of students report that the TOD accurately describes their experience or the experience of others with whom they closely interact around environmental concerns. For many, the TOD is something of an epiphany. But then again, perhaps in some way I primed my audiences for this response. I've sought to build on this anecdotal evidence with more thorough and systematic data gathering to assess the factors underlying the TOD. A national US survey of undergraduate students in environmental studies and science programs in 2009 and 2010 (Rigotti, Environmental Problem Solving) offers tentative support for the TOD. More ambitious survey work, now underway with help of advanced environmental studies undergraduates at Oberlin College and Yale-NUS College, suggests that the TOD is more pronounced across the US undergraduate classroom than I'd initially suspected.

35. Hardin, "Tragedy of the Commons."

36. Maniates, "Editing Out Unsustainable Behavior."

Bibliography

Alinsky, Saul. *Reveille for Radicals*. New York: Vintage Press, 1969.

Assadourian, Erik. "Building an Enduring Environmental Movement." *In State of the World 2013: Is Sustainability Still Possible?* edited by Erik Assadourian, Tom Prugh and Linda Starke, 292–303. Washington, DC: Island Press, 2013.

Ayers, William. "Teaching as an Ethical Enterprise." *Educational Forum* 63, no. 1 (Fall 1998): 52–57.

Balint, Peter, Ronald Stewart, Anand Desai, and Lawrence Walters. *Wicked Environmental Problems: Managing Uncertainty and Conflict*. Washington, DC: Island Press, 2011.

Baumgartner, Franks, Byron Jones, and Peter Mortensen. "Punctuated Equilibrium Theory: Explaining Stability and Change in Public Policymaking." In *Theories of the Policy Process*, 3rd ed., edited by Paul Sabatier and Christopher Weible. 59–103. Boulder, CO: Westview Press, 2014.

Brookfield, Steven. *Becoming a Critically Reflective Teacher*. San Francisco: Jossey-Bass, 1995.

Conca, Ken. "Imagining the State." In *Encountering Global Environmental Politics*, edited by Michael Maniates, 71–86. Lanham, MD: Rowman & Littlefield, 2003.

Daly, Herman, and John Cobb. *For the Common Good*. Boston: Beacon Press, 1989.

Di Chiro, Giovanna. "Living Environmentalisms: Coalition Politics, Social Reproduction, and Environmental Justice." *Environmental Politics* 17 (2008): 276–98.

Dodds, Peter, Eric Clark, Suma Desu, Morgan Frank, Andrew Reagan, Jake Ryland Williams, and Lewis Mitchell. "Human Language Reveals a Universal Positivity Bias." *Proceedings of the National Academy of Sciences of the United States of America* 112 (2015): 2389–2394.

Evans, Tina Lynn. *Occupy Education: Living and Learning Sustainability*. New York: Peter Lang, 2012.

Friedman, Thomas. 2009. *Hot, Flat, and Crowded: Why We Need a Green Revolution—and How It Can Renew America, Release 2.0*. New York: Picador.

Gunster, Shane. "Self-Interest, Sacrifice, and Climate Change: (Re-)Framing the British Columbia Carbon Tax." In *The Environmental Politics of Sacrifice*, edited by Michael Maniates and John Meyer, 187–216. Cambridge, MA: MIT Press, 2010.

Hardin, Garrett. "The Tragedy of the Commons." *Science* 162 (1968): 1243–1248.

Hempel, Monty. "Ecoliteracy: Knowledge Is Not Enough." In *State of the World 2014: Governing for Sustainability*, edited by Tom Prugh and Michael Renner, 75–88. Washington, DC: Island Press, 2014.

Horton, Miles, Paulo Freire, Brenda Bell, and John Gaventa. *We Make the Road by Walking: Conversations on Education and Social Change*. Philadelphia: Temple University Press, 1990.

Horton, Miles, and Dale Jacobs. *The Miles Horton Reader: Education for Social Change*. Knoxville: University of Tennessee Press, 2003.

Jensen, Derrick. "Beyond Hope." *Orion Magazine* (May/June 2006). https://orionmagazine.org/article/beyond-hope.

Judson, Olivia. "The Selfless Gene." *Atlantic* 300, no. 3 (2007): 90–98.

Kennedy, Emily, Thomas Beckley, Bonita McFarlane, and Solange Nadeau. "Why We Don't `Walk the Talk': Understanding the Environmental Values/Behaviour Gap in Canada." *Human Ecology Review* 16 (2009): 151–160.

Lappe, Frances, and Anna Lappe. *Hope's Edge: The Next Diet for a Small Planet.* New York: Jeremy P. Tarcher/Putnam, 2002.

Leonard, Annie. *The Story of Stuff.* New York: Free Press, 2010.

Levin, Kelly, Benjamin Cashore, Steven Bernstein, and Graeme Auld. "Overcoming the Tragedy of Super Wicked Problems: Constraining our Future Selves to Ameliorate Global Climate Change." *Policy Sciences* 45 (2012): 123–152.

Litfin, Karen. *Ecovillages: Lessons for Sustainable Community.* Cambridge: Polity Press, 2013.

Lorenzen, Janet. "Convincing People to Go Green: Managing Strategic Action by Minimising Political Talk." *Environmental Politics* 23 (2014): 454–72.

Maniates, Michael. "Editing Out Unsustainable Behavior." In *State of the World 2010: Transforming Cultures*, edited by Erik Assadourian, Linda Starke, and Lisa Mastny, 119–126. New York: W.W. Norton, 2010.

Maniates, M., ed. *Encountering Global Environmental Politics.* Lanham, MD: Rowman & Littlefield, 2003.

Maniates, Michael. "Sustainable Consumption" Three Paradoxes." *Gaia* 23, Suppl. 1) (2014): 201–208.

Maniates, Michael. "Teaching for Turbulence." In *State of the World 2013: Is Sustainability Still Possible?* edited by Erik Assadourian, Tom Prugh, and Linda Starke, 255–268. Washington, DC: Island Press, 2013.

Maniates, Michael, and John Meyer. *The Environmental Politics of Sacrifice.* Cambridge, MA: MIT Press, 2010.

McDonough, William, and Michael Braungart. 2003. "Foreword to the Chinese Edition of Cradle to Cradle." www.mcdonough.com/speaking-writing/foreword-to-the-chinese-edition-of-cradle-to-cradle/.

Orr, David. *Ecological Literacy: Education and the Transition to a Postmodern World.* Albany: State University of New York Press, 1992.

Orr, David. *Hope Is an Imperative.* Washington, DC: Island Press, 2010.

Orr, David. "Optimism and Hope in a Hotter Time." *Conservation Biology* 21 (2007): 1392–1395.

Palmer, Parker. *The Courage to Teach.* San Francisco: Jossey-Bass, 1998.

Poundstone, Paula. "Lean, Green Fighting Machine." *Mother Jones* (March/April 1997): 80.

Princen, Thomas. *Treading Softly: Paths to Ecological Order.* Cambridge, MA: MIT Press, 2010.

Rigotti, Samuel. *Environmental Problem Solving: How Do We Make the Change?* Meadville, PA: Department of Environmental Science, Allegheny College, 2010.

Rittel, Horst, and Melvin Webber. "Dilemmas in a General Theory of Planning." *Policy Sciences* 4 (1973): 155–169.

Sayer, Andrew. "Power, Sustainability and Well-Being: An Outsider's View." In *Sustainable Practices: Social Theory and Climate Change*, edited by Elizabeth Shove and Nicola Spurling, 292–317. London: Routledge, 2012.

Sharot, Tali. *The Optimism Bias: A Tour of the Irrationally Positive Brain.* New York: Vintage, 2012.

Alongside civil society engagement and science-informed (and sometimes science-based) policymaking, international institutions have been a defining feature of global environmental politics. Thousands of multilateral environmental institutions now govern actions around such issues as acid rain, climate change, ozone depletion, trade in genetically modified organisms, and biodiversity loss. As several chapter authors note, however, the prevailing view is that these institutions have fallen far short of halting the environmental problems they are designed to address (see chapter 1, for example).

The contributors to this section, Kate O'Neill and Maria Ivanova, offer a more optimistic assessment. Each focuses on the achievements of the world's multilateral environmental institutions to date and reflects on how future institutions must adapt to meet the challenges of environmental governance on the New Earth.

O'Neill begins in chapter 7 by outlining the basic institutional architecture of state-led global environmental politics, reflecting on its strengths, summarizing critiques, and charting its evolution over time. She highlights the existing system's fit with geopolitical realities, its flexibility, and the positive behavioral change it has catalyzed in many countries. She also notes the system's shortcomings, including its tendency toward lowest-common-denominator bargaining and its state-centric nature. O'Neill concludes with a critique of global environmental politics scholarship for inadequately accounting for the rapid change that has characterized the international institutional and problem landscapes. She outlines a global environmental politics research agenda surrounding questions pertaining to power and ideas (rather than the nuts and bolts of institutions themselves) and incorporates approaches and insights from other disciplines in the social and natural sciences. Like Conca in chapter 1, she prescribes, for example, a focus on rights and ethics and underscores the importance of understanding complexities and managing uncertainties.

Ivanova's analysis in chapter 8 zooms in on the United Nations Environment Programme (UNEP) as the "anchor institution" for global environmental governance. Drawing on her own experiences as an engaged expert (see Falk, chapter 4, and Young, chapter 3) in this institution's evolution, she highlights its major development milestones. She further explains UNEP's two-decade-long effort at institutional reform, claiming such successes as the UN Environment Assembly and the Sustainable Development Goals. Ivanova concludes with her own vision for the future of global environmental politics scholarship and practice, which includes fostering leadership, reframing the environment-economy dichotomy, animating communication, developing an analytical foundation for evaluating governance, and cultivating shared values and philosophies. She further notes the heavy load borne by global environmental politics scholars to bring forth solutions to New Earth problems and, like O'Neill, underscores the need to reach across disciplinary boundaries to do this.

Framing Questions Posed to the Authors in Section 4

- How have international institutions historically responded to environmental challenges?
- What are the strengths and shortcomings of these institutions in effectively responding to the contemporary environmental challenges? Are radical changes needed, in terms of scholarly analysis or praxis, or can the state-centric model rise to the challenge?
- Under what conditions, and how, do existing institutions change and learn? Are existing institutions a better fit with the old environmental problems? Said differently, do we need to develop new institutions, or work with the existing system of institutions, and if so, how?
- What types of questions should scholars of international institutions be asking in the face of the contemporary environmental condition?

7 Institutional Politics and Reform

Kate O'Neill

In this chapter I examine the institutional responses on the part of the international community to global environmental challenges: their shape, their impacts and effectiveness, and their scope for learning in the face of pressures for change. I outline the basic shape of the dominant state-led system of global environmental governance, its strengths, some of the best-known critiques of that system, and how it has evolved over time. I go on to argue that the problem is not always that the system is failing to change, but that in some cases it *is* changing (and numbers of institutions are expanding) rapidly and perhaps uncontrollably. Along with Ivanova in chapter 8, I do not consider this system an outright failure, especially given the challenges it faced simply to be created in the first place. However, we do need to pay attention to how, and why, this system is evolving in the ways that it is.

Scholarly work in the field of global environmental politics (notably political science) is failing to render these changes and their impacts fully visible. At the end of this chapter, I consider how a scholarly approach can draw on the important questions asked by political scientists—such as who wields power, in whose interests, and how these changes fit with wider conceptions of an international community or social norms. This process may help us understand what sorts of institutional structures might work and how to guide or steer institution building and reform to address the challenges of a New Earth. In particular, given the nature of the crisis we face, we need to create conditions that foster rapid but effective institutional change to respond to ever-changing conditions. Reform itself need not (and perhaps, given global political realities, cannot) be radical, but it must be responsive. We must also pay attention to history. As Ivanova points out, this system has a rich history, shaped not just by broader institutional forces, but also by the roles played by individual leaders and sometimes the coincidences that lead to successful cooperative outcomes.

Focusing at this level reveals much about the whys and wherefores of contemporary global environmental institutions. Our approaches complement each other in important ways.

How International Institutions Have Responded to Environmental Challenges

I came to study global environmental institutions through the lens of international relations (IR) theory and the emerging field of international environmental politics that began gaining strength after the 1992 Rio Earth Summit. IR theorists tend to problematize global environmental problems as ones of collective action in an anarchic international system. This approach differs, for example, from those out of geography or sociology, which see environmental problems as more a function of processes of economic globalization and associated inequities. Over time, and with exposure to a wider range of disciplinary approaches, my perspective has come to reflect this diversity, although questions and perspectives from political science (more broadly) remain dominant in my work.

The term *international institution* has a long genealogy.[1] It may be defined as the "rules of the game," written and unwritten (formal and informal), that mediate and shape the behavior and expectations, and arguably the interests, of actors engaged in confronting environmental change at the global level. They are, as Ivanova points out in the next chapter in her discussion of the work of the United Nations Environment Programme (UNEP), built on, but are far more than, the concrete entities that are international organizations. The international system consists of tightly interconnected web of rules and norms that shape and constrain the behavior of nation-states, international bureaucracies, and nonstate actors. The building blocks of this system are issue-based international regimes—sets of rules, norms, principles, and decision-making procedures around which actors' expectations converge in a given issue area.[2] The actors who coordinate, drive, and shape this system are often international governmental organizations (IGOs), including the United Nations convention secretariats and broader IGOs such as the UN, UNEP, the World Bank, and others.[3]

Different perspectives within IR theory give some idea of the ways in which international institutions work. A mainstream realist account of international institutions suggests that institutions are merely reflective of the power balance or interests of the state actors who created them.

Institutions change in response to shifting interests or power relations.[4] An institutionalist account focuses instead on the mediating role of institutions, particularly in reducing the transaction costs of cooperation and on how institutions endure even as their underlying constellation of interests changes[5] or they become dysfunctional in terms of fulfilling goals.[6] A constructivist account takes one step further and argues that institutional rules and norms themselves can shape actor interests and roles and that institutions (or organizations) in this sense can take on agency themselves.[7] Together, these approaches suggest that institutional change may not always be guided by good intentions and a desire to halt environmental change, a point I return to at the end of this chapter.

In a formal sense, international environmental institutions are embodied by treaties or multilateral environmental agreements—the legal instruments signed by states that take on commitments to obey the rules set out in that treaty and collectively make up a body of international environmental law.[8] There are hundreds, perhaps thousands, of multilateral agreements with environmental intent or components, depending on how one defines them.[9] Some environmental agreements date back to the nineteenth century, but the majority of treaties that define the field of global environmental governance today were negotiated in the years after the 1972 Stockholm Conference. They include flagship framework conventions on climate change, biological diversity, the law of the sea, and ozone-depleting substances, as well as more specific agreements on international trade in endangered species, protecting migratory species and wetlands, hazardous waste trading, long-range transboundary air pollution, the production and use of persistent organic pollutants, and the production and use of mercury.[10]

International environmental law is embedded in a wider global legal-political framework that designates the diplomatic arena as the place states should go to settle disputes or address collective problems peacefully. Various legal instruments set up and uphold the rules of treaty making (such as the 1969 Vienna Convention on the Law of Treaties) and the central role of states in this process. As well as the hard law laid down in treaties and agreements, international institutions also include informal norms and soft law—shared understandings of appropriate behavior—that shape the behavior of actors in global environmental governance and allocate rights and responsibilities around the issue in question.[11] Sustainable development, even with all its different interpretations, is one such example. The notion of the green economy, popularized at Rio+20 in 2012, is a more recent embodiment of a dominant understanding of how economic growth and sustainable development work together. Other global environmental norms include the principle of common but differentiated responsibility, embodied in many agreements to outline respective obligations of northern and southern countries,[12] and the precautionary principle, which adjudicates policy decisions under conditions of scientific uncertainty.[13]

Many IGOs are involved in instigating and supporting international environmental agreements. These include, at a broad level, the United Nations and its main environmental agency, UNEP, which was established at the first global summit to address the environment, held in Stockholm, Sweden, in 1972. These institutions administer a broad array of treaties and their associated secretariats, and they work with crosscutting IGOs, such as the Global Environment Facility, to administer the existing system of state-led global environmental governance.[14] Other international organizations, such as the World Trade Organization and the World Bank, are taking on an influential role in global environmental governance as environmental issues have spilled over or conflicted with global trade and development agendas.[15]

The Strengths and Shortcomings of State-Led Global Environmental Institutions

This system of state-led global environmental institutions—the body of international law and agreements, the organizations that administer them, and the norms and ideas that underpin them—is highly piecemeal. There are few formal connections across the different issue-based governance regimes (at least until recently), and they rarely contain strong enforcement mechanisms. Nonetheless, and despite relying on voluntary participation by nation-states, this system has been in existence for over forty years, proving considerable durability (as well as institutional density). It has, as we shall see, evolved over this time, although it is not clear this is enough to meet contemporary environmental challenges.

The strengths of this system are significant. For one, it is a fit with existing geopolitical realities—or, to be sure, the realities that have characterized the international system since the rise of the sovereign territorial state. When states settle differences or address shared problems through peaceful means, they do so through a process of bargaining and cooperation. There is no global authority with the power to order states to undertake certain actions. Nor was there, in 1972 in Stockholm, any chance of one being established, despite suggestions to the contrary.[16] In many respects, the number, durability, and extent of global environmental institutions far exceed that which a scholar of IR theory might have predicted. This development reflects a global trend that international cooperation is the norm rather than the exception. Global interconnectedness and a desire to avoid cataclysmic conflict have led states to work together to solve problems that they might previously have ignored or allowed to escalate.

This system is also designed, albeit imperfectly, to allow for flexibility and change over time. Many environmental agreements are negotiated using a convention-protocol approach. States start by agreeing to a general framework convention and then negotiate additional commitments over time using a stricter protocol, based on the assumption that if they are already participating, they may be persuaded to take on further commitments. This design reflects a commitment on the part of the UN to maximize state participation in environmental regimes, either by getting them in at the start or allowing them to join later. The convention-protocol model ideally also encompasses incorporating new knowledge or information about a problem, allowing member states to take action. Other features—for example, the principle of common but differentiated responsibility (whereby countries of the Global South are allotted more time or more resources to meet global commitments)—have been institutionalized across different regimes. However, the extent to which individual regimes do in fact change and learn varies substantially.[17] Some, such as the regime addressing substances that deplete the ozone layer have moved progressively, while others, such as the climate regime have stalled or ossified.[18] Other studies examine the forms of learning and assessment mechanisms that exist and the conditions under which they work.[19] Notably, Greene found that in the case of the ozone regime, a strong network of collaborating organizations, including nongovernmental organizations (NGOs), strengthens its capacity to take up new knowledge effectively.

Although overall assessments are mixed, international environmental institutions as they are currently constituted have induced positive behavioral change on the part of their member states. Examples include the ozone regime (including the 1985 Vienna Convention for the Protection of the Ozone Layer and its 1987 Montreal Protocol) and the 1979 Convention on Long Range Transboundary Air Pollution, which has helped ratchet down emissions of acid-rain causing pollutants. Some have had normative impacts despite little legal enforcement: the 1989 Basel Convention on the Control of Transboundary Movements of Hazardous Wastes and Their

Disposal has highlighted and stigmatized dumping of hazardous waste on communities in poorer countries and empowered local NGOs to fight (sometimes their own governments) to stop waste dumping or dangerous recycling practices. Some have made significant steps toward resolving major problems. If steps had not been taken, for example, to halt global production of chlorofluorocarbons (CFCs), the primary substances that deplete the ozone layer, there is substantial evidence that life on the planet's surface would have become difficult, and probably impossible, by the middle of this century.[20] Further, although hard to prove definitively, it is likely that in the absence of existing institutions—which, let us remember, were designed to be as strong as possible while remaining politically feasible—many global environmental problems are likely to have been significantly worse.

Global cooperation through institution building has wider impacts on the international community over and above the environmental impacts. These impacts are often positive demonstrating that environmental cooperation can have impacts over and above the functional. Global cooperation can bring states into the international community (states, for example, emerging from long-term authoritarian regimes), bring in additional resources to strengthen state capacity, and help empower domestic constituencies to pressure their own governments to comply with international rules and norms.[21] Environmental peace-building or peacemaking initiatives, another example of how international institutions work, can help reinforce long-term stability through stabilizing resource bases and establishing fairer rules of access.[22]

This system also has significant shortcomings. First, the convention-protocol method of bargaining is criticized for being too slow, providing too little, too late.[23] It took eight years for the 1997 Kyoto Protocol to receive the right number and combination of ratifications to enter into force. Second, a state-led bargaining model based on reconciliation of national interests (which may reflect only economic interests) leads to lowest-common-denominator bargaining, or a handful of recalcitrant states wielding veto power over the outcome.[24] The 1992 Convention on Biological Diversity (CBD) is often cited as an example of lowest-common-denominator bargaining. Third, the system has been criticized for being too state-centric and not including the different voices and actors with a direct interest in or abilities to effectively address global environmental challenges. [25] Scholars point to the emergence of nonstate governance—initiatives established by NGOs working alone or in tandem with industry actors to encourage sustainable forestry or fisheries[26]—as a more responsive alternative to international environmental diplomacy. Fourth, international environmental regimes and organizations are too piecemeal—too scattered and separated—to function effectively as a whole. They cannot, it is argued, stand up to more integrated global governance arenas, such as the global trade regime.[27] There are so many ongoing environmental negotiations that we face "summit fatigue,"[28] or treaty congestion placing too great a burden on overstretched negotiators.[29] Finally, of course, complex institutions are nearly always accompanied by unintended impacts, inefficiencies, and side effects. The illegal trade in CFCs, for instance, because of differential restrictions on production of ozone-depleting substances, remains a problem.[30]

Despite these critiques, trenchantly made by some notable global environmental politics scholars, the state-led system of global environmental governance has not remained static. A careful analysis of global environmental governance over the forty- plus years since the first global environmental conference in Stockholm demonstrates critical shifts in the underlying framework of global environmental governance.[31] Global environmental norms have shifted from environmental protection to an equity/human development–oriented concept of sustainable development, to a more neoliberal vision that stresses the interconnectedness of economic and environmental institutions and their development, most recently evinced in the Green Economy theme at Rio+20.[32] Actor roles have changed: the South began by taking a more influential role than was expected and is now differentiating itself as countries like Brazil, China, and India take leading roles in the world.[33] NGOs and corporate sector actors are active players at international negotiations, as well as becoming more engaged in developing their own environmental governance initiatives. Global economic regimes and organizations are, despite their reluctance, becoming important sites of global environmental governance. We are seeing the emergence and incorporation, to varying levels of success, of market-based modes of global environmental governance, such as emissions trading schemes[34] or the concept of payment for ecosystems services coming to the fore in the CBD negotiations.[35]

It is still arguably the case that global environmental institutions have to date responded about as well to global environmental challenges as they could within the constraints they faced being negotiated within the existing global political system. This system therefore does not always generate institutions that fit the changing nature of environmental challenges or our changing understanding of necessary responses. Nor does it adjust rapidly enough to changing and escalating challenges.

The Changing Nature of Global Environmental Challenges and Institutional Responses

In 2013, in a review of methods used to study contemporary global environmental governance, my coauthors and I identified four challenges facing contemporary scholars and practitioners of global environmental governance that in turn inform our understandings of institutional change and response.[36] These are "complexity and uncertainty, vertical linkages across multiple scales, horizontal linkages across issue areas, and (often rapidly) evolving problem sets and international institutions."[37] In particular, global environmental politics scholars are operating in a problem field subject to nonlinearities, sudden change, and feedback effects, where past actions and institutional designs are not necessarily a guide for the future. These challenges and changed understandings apply to both the problems we study in our field and to the design, implementation, and functioning of international institutions. This article emerged out of interests on the part of the faculty authors in how to be a global environmental politics scholar in interdisciplinary, applied environmental studies departments, and take into account the needs and approaches of graduate students not trained in a political science, let alone IR, tradition.

Recent global climate politics provide a good illustration. Taking complexity and uncertainty first, Hoppe et al.[38] argue that early global efforts were dominated by a conception of climate change as a global problem, affecting the global atmosphere, not unlike ozone layer depletion.[39] Under such a framing, global political action was deemed a necessity, and achieving scientific consensus seemed the way to bolster global action to reduce greenhouse gas emissions and mitigate climate change. Hence we see the negotiation of the UN Framework Convention on Climate Change (UNFCCC), the Kyoto Protocol, and subsequent road maps, accords, and platforms.

This problem framing, however, obscured the wicked nature of climate change as a political and environmental problem characterized by inherent uncertainties and complexities and, most of all, strong values conflicts.[40] Despite the Fourth and Fifth Assessment Reports of the Intergovernmental Panel on Climate Change (IPCC), which demonstrate the near-universal consensus on the part of the scientific community on the extent of, threat posed by, and human-activity-driven nature of climate change, political resistance remains strong. Public opinion in key industrialized (and some less industrialized) countries demonstrates increased skepticism or perhaps simply an unwillingness to want to deal with the changes that addressing climate change will require.[41] A tiny but well-funded and politically connected group of scientists continues to promote climate denial. In the meantime, despite more certainty over the causes of climate change, uncertainty over the possibility of tipping points, the distribution of rainfall, or temperature changes and other phenomena make it hard to predict the influence of different institutional responses.

Adaptation to climate impacts is becoming the focus of international, national, and local political attention and is calling particular attention to issues of scale and vertical linkages across jurisdictional levels. Global institutions are not necessarily able to develop adaptation plans with the granularity needed to foster resilience or reduce vulnerabilities in coastal communities in Louisiana or mountain communities in the Himalayas. Funding for climate mitigation or adaptation projects is shifting to arenas well beyond the global environment facility or the clean development mechanism of the UNFCCC. Private funds, bilateral funds, carbon markets, secondary markets for carbon reduction credits—all of these are creating an increasingly complex climate funding architecture that changes rapidly and is highly vulnerable to broader economic and political fluctuations.[42]

Climate negotiations are increasingly linked horizontally to other international negotiations. In the ozone regime, negotiations continue over phasing out nonozone depleting chemicals—hydrofluorocarbons (HFCs)— that are potent greenhouse gases. Climate and forest governance regimes are being brought together through the Reducing Emissions through Deforestation and Degradation (REDD+) mechanism designed to increase carbon sequestration and reduce global deforestation through schemes that would pay forest owners and managers not to cut down trees but rather bolster existing stocks.

In climate politics, therefore, problem understandings are rapidly shifting with scientific advances. Priorities are shifting as influential actors realize the need for adaptation as well as mitigation. Even as new modes of governance emerge —for example, through emissions trading systems and financial markets for emissions reductions certificates—and new ideas about slowing climate change in the near future (e.g., REDD+), values conflicts around what to do about climate change remain intractable. This situation has complicated the climate governance field, leading to the emergence of new sites of climate governance, as well as more radical suggestions about dealing with the threat of global warming. In the former category, regional, local, and city-based emissions-reductions schemes have generated optimism about the possibility of enacting bottom-up climate governance as well as some skepticism about their ability to scale up.[43] In the latter, there has been significant interest in—and concern about— climate geoengineering as a way to rapidly reduce the climate impacts of greenhouse gas emissions.[44] While backed by members of the scientific community, there are significant concerns about possible side effects and unintended consequences of geoengineering, as well as its inter- and intra-generational impacts.

What we have seen in the climate arena is, in effect, what looks like an uncontrolled proliferation of state-led and nonstate governance institutions, both competing and complementary. This process has been described in several ways: as a regime complex,[45] regime fragmentation,[46] and policy experimentation.[47] It is practically impossible to see whether all these developments add up to something more than the sum of their parts or, if not, what could be done to make that so. This failure is one not only on the part of actors directly involved in policymaking but also on the part of scholars whose job it is to render these systems more visible.

Some of these same trends can be seen in the biodiversity regime.[48] Its trajectory—from the 1992 Framework Convention on Biological Diversity, to the 2000 Cartagena Protocol, which chiefly addressed biosafety and trade in living modified organisms, to the 2010 Nagoya Protocol, which addressed access to genetic resources and equitable sharing of any benefits arising from their use—was unexpected at best. Although the successful negotiation of the Nagoya Protocol marked a return from what was perceived as a moribund state, its negotiated biodiversity targets (the first in the CBD's history) are not seen as able to combat the unprecedented levels of extinction currently underway. While the CBD has been more successful than most other international environmental regimes at crossing vertical scales, it has not been as successful so far in addressing biodiversity loss on the ground.

Recent attention to biodiversity regime politics has focused on a significant ideational shift within the regime: away from focusing on biodiversity conservation as a prime motivation toward using the concept of ecosystem services as a driving force. Ecosystem services (ESS) are, briefly, the benefits we receive from healthy, functioning ecosystems, including food, and commodities, but also clean air and drinking water and cultural-social benefits.[49] While scientific communities have used the concept of ESS for a long time, it has become more controversial in discussions of valuation and payment for ESS, suggesting a privatization, or commodification, of nature, and a subsequent devaluation of nonmaterial motivations to protect it.[50] Suarez and Corson chart the rapid diffusion of ESS as an idea through the meeting rooms and halls of the Tenth Conference of the Parties to the CBD in Nagoya. Subsequent research from their group suggests, however, that while ESS has become a powerful idea, it has yet to be transformed into an integrated policy mechanism for biodiversity conservation, let alone a market mechanism reflecting "prices" of biodiversity resources. However, this example illustrates the significance of ideas as they move through institutions and shape the behavior and beliefs of critical actors.

Not all environmental regimes are showing evidence of fragmentation. In the chemicals regime, consisting of the Basel Convention, the 2000 Stockholm and 2001 Rotterdam Conventions on persistent organic pollutants (POPs) and the 2014 Minamata Convention on the control and use of mercury are moving toward more integration.[51] Global chemicals governance in general has hewn more closely to the state-centric model of treaty negotiation than other issue areas. However, across most areas of global environmental governance, horizontal linkages—across and within issue areas—have become a critical component of institution building.[52] Such linkage creation (or overlap management) is often informal. In the chemicals regime, it has taken on the most formality, as the Stockholm, Rotterdam and Basel Conventions have held one joint Conference of the Parties and have merged their secretariats into a single body.

Changing Institutional Landscapes: Political and Scholarly Responses

What should the political response be to the problems existing state-led institutions face in meeting environmental challenges? Should we reform existing institutions or replace them with something else? There are many perspectives from which to answer these questions, and here I take up the challenge offered by the editors of this book: How can global environmental politics scholars reflect on the experience with global environmental governance to date and offer thoughts on these issues of pressing concern?

Social scientists have particular responsibilities in responding to complex, real-world issues such as global environmental change. We need to recognize and identify events, trends, and other phenomena. We need to explain these phenomena to the best of our ability or based on our own training or view of the world. We need to problematize, confront, or critically analyze (depending again on one's perspectives) these phenomena, asking questions about effectiveness and impacts, interests, and power. In a field like global environmental politics, we should also be able to recommend analytically grounded courses of action, perhaps not always at a day-to-day level but in ways that guide others to understand or design solutions. This ability to take a step (or a few steps) back from the exigencies of daily politics and policy gives us a particular vantage point when it comes to issues of institutional design. While global environmental politics as a subfield of political science has made many contributions to understanding international institutions, it lags in comprehending and assessing today's rapidly changing institutional and problem landscapes.[53]

Global environmental politics scholarship has provided useful insights on the state of global politics, the role of science, nonstate actors, and North–South politics in governing the global environment and assessing the impacts of international cooperation.[54] Much global environmental politics scholarship has adopted an applied perspective, where scholars are quite explicit about wanting to make global environmental governance more effective and solve these pressing problems while also maintaining a critical perspective.[55] It has, as the examples demonstrate, also done a good job of addressing horizontal linkages and interplay between issue areas and regimes.

In some ways, however, it has yet to address some central issues of governance design, complexity, linkages, and scale—and the drivers of institutional evolution. Bernstein argues that global environmental politics as a subfield has been slow to focus on the importance of ideas and norms in global environmental dynamics.[56] By focusing on the nuts and bolts of interstate cooperation, it has missed the critical role that ideational and normative forces play in shaping responses to global environmental change and understanding the political forces and interests that shape these underlying norms.

Another important point, perhaps arising from a relatively narrow focus on state-led regimes, is that political scientists have been slow to study emerging sites and modes of global environmental governance—such as REDD+, cutting across forests and climate regimes, or carbon markets—that do not immediately appear to fall under a political science purview.[57] In some ways, for example, a multiscalar institution such as REDD+, which in fact does not yet exist as a coherent institution, is hard to see using a standard international relations and global environmental politics lens. Likewise, economists quickly came to dominate literature on emissions trading and other forms of carbon markets, although recent exceptions include Newell and Paterson, Meckling, and Lo and Howes[58] on the global political economy of emissions trading. Various works by Cashore and coauthors have kept pace with the rapid innovations in global forests governance.[59]

So how can global environmental politics scholars, as social scientists, respond to the institutional needs and challenges of the New Earth? We need to respond to, and make visible, institutional proliferation, as well as respond to new knowledge and understanding of complexities, linkages, and scale in both the problem-based and political ones. We should challenge conventional wisdoms and take on a more active (perhaps even activist) role in generating problem-oriented research. We need in particular to foster conditions that promote the sort of rapid institutional learning we will need to meet the challenges of the New Earth. Does, for example, institutional proliferation constitute an effective, rapid response to global challenges, or is it something else? Is it instead a response to other sorts of mandates or interests?

Understanding these questions provides some basis for assessing whether the system needs some kind of full reform or merely adaption. The following points outline, in brief, some of the directions I believe global environmental politics scholarship should take, together with associated questions and themes. Institutionalist approaches have provided (and will continue to provide) many important insights. However, I call for renewed attention to constructivist and realist approaches to study ideas and power and for expanding our field of work out to other disciplines, both social and natural sciences:

1. *Renew focus on the emergence, or selection, circulation, and impact of particular global environmental norms, ideas, and knowledge.* Which of these are selected, how, and why? Is new knowledge taken up effectively into the political process? Into the creation or design of new institutions? This work provides critical clues as to why certain political directions are taken and to the shared norms that might underlie the proliferation of international environmental institutions I have outlined in this chapter. Although perhaps counterintuitive to some, constructivism and constructivist insights play a role in identifying critical dimensions of institutional change and problem solving, as the articles in a special issue of *Global Environmental Politics* on collaborative event ethnography (CEE) demonstrate.[60] The CEE team adopted a methodology that tracks the diffusion of particular ideas around a large international meeting, in this

case, the Tenth Conference of the Parties to the CBD, held in Nagoya, Japan, in 2010. Some of the work in particular demonstrated how particular actors used and translated the idea of ecosystems services in various forums.[61]

2. *Do not ignore the power dynamics that underlie normative and institutional change and are in turn shaped by such change.* Who benefits from a particular set of institutions? How have alliances or constellations of actors (both states and nonstate actors) shifted over time? Are there broader implications for the international system? Although realist approaches, for example, are not often applied in global environmental politics scholarship, they, along with more critical theory approaches, such as the neo-Gramscian framework deployed by Levy and Newell, provide strong tools and concepts to answer these questions.[62]

3. *Focus on ethics, rights, and values.* In the face of challenges such as the deployment of geoengineering strategies or the widespread, and unevenly distributed, human suffering that climate change will cause,[63] how can global environmental institutions protect and be guided by broader human values, rights, and laws? This focus suggests connecting with international legal scholarship on international human rights and distributive justice, some of which is taking on environmental concerns such as climate change.[64]

4. *Embrace complexities and uncertainties and explore ways to understand them.* Scientific, social, and political uncertainties are pervasive on the New Earth. We face outcomes with high probability but lengthy time frames, and ones of low probability that could happen in a very short time frame. This implies embracing techniques such as modeling and scenario analysis.[65] Large-scale models are a critical component of the natural sciences' enterprise to predict patterns of global change, and social scientists, particularly political scientists, need to figure out how to engage with them and contribute valid data and other inputs.[66]

The complexities of the global environment are sociopolitical as well as scientific. This chapter has as its main theme institutional complexity and proliferation, but complexity of actors, ideas, and other social science variables is also significant. This can be unsettling. For instance, we (global environmental politics scholars broadly defined) have been slow to identify the impacts of scale and vertical linkages in international institutions such as how institutions reach down to local levels (and vice versa), and how ideas and actors travel up and down (or across) scales. How well are those linkages articulated and examined?[67]

5. *Consider processes of institutional design, change, and reform.* Debates about what comprise the "best" (however defined) international institutions for the global environment—and how we can create them—have played an important role in the field. Suggestions back and forth about a world environment organization or even ditching the existing system in favor of another reached a height in the first decade of the 2000s.[68] However, I argue that we might best be served at this point in paying more attention to processes of institutional change and reform, which may better help identify and explain goals and why we cannot reach them. Thus, how do we ascribe agency in institutional reform, evolution, or proliferation? Can this process be fully controlled or directed? How can we deploy social science concepts or theories of path dependence, institutional stickiness, and unintended effects? What makes international institutions resilient? What characterizes institutional resilience and learning? How do the past forty or so years of global environmental governance inform today's practice and scholarship?

Studies of institutions such as UNEP have gone some way toward achieving that goal.[69] However, we need to apply concepts used in social science theories of change such as punctuated equilibrium to explain particular forms of change as in, for example, whether fragmentation is a process that involves the breaking up of existing institutions within the same field or the creation of new ones.[70]

6. *Think across disciplines and methodologies.* We continually need more theoretically grounded, applied social science research in this rapidly changing field. This means paying attention to identifying questions and designing appropriate methods to undertake problem-oriented research, which in turn can be applied to understanding or critiquing changing global landscapes. Questions such as, "What are the conditions under which x happens"?—the causal sorts of questions—often have more applicability in this field than the correlational questions do. As we demonstrate, developing answers is not the simplest task and often involves extending across to other disciplines.[71] While standard IR approaches provide some insight into the formation and impacts of international environmental institutions and regimes, they do not easily apply to cross-scale problems and institutions, nonstate actor or market-driven initiatives, or situations of high complexity and uncertainty. Nor does a strictly IR training make it easy to identify relevant questions or gather necessary data. The work cited throughout this chapter demonstrates the effective use of a range of different

methods, often collaborative, in designing and undertaking problem-oriented research.[72]

Conclusion

As someone who has studied the ups and downs and ins and outs of international environmental institutions for over twenty years now, I have learned that nothing stays still in this particular universe. I have also learned to appreciate that environmental institutions are situated in a broader global political context. They are answerable to, and shaped by, a wider set of interests and norms or values that do not always place the environment at the top of the list of global challenges. On occasion, this slows down and frustrates environmental progress. On other occasions, it may be positive, as and if it tempers tendencies to address environmental challenges, as has happened in the creation of REDD+, and will again if moves toward geoengineering deployment continue while ignoring wider norms of justice and human rights. It reminds us that the global community faces many challenges, of which the environment is just one (albeit pervasive). As of now, we have not, as social scientists, begun to assess whether international environmental institutions have helped foster networks of actors, resources and rules that could strengthen resilience in the wake of crisis. There is still not enough global environmental politics work on processes of institutional change and on causes and measurements of learning and response. As a field, we have an imperative to identify new research frontiers or at least to foster those who do. At the same time, we need to keep an eye on the big picture of global (environmental) governance. When academic pressures push scholars to develop expertise in a particular niche, this may come at the expense of understanding broader trends, over and above a particular topic.

One major open question remains: Given the pressing problems faced by the New Earth, are we doomed because of institutional failure? Or can institutions yet be wrangled to provide the needed help?

Notes

1. See Young, *International Governance*.

2. Following Krasner, ed., *International Regimes*, 3.

3. O'Neill, "Architects, Agitators, and Entrepreneurs." See also Ivanova, chapter 8, this volume.

4. It should be noted that there are other realist approaches that are more nuanced with respect to international institutions (e.g., Jervis. "Realism, Neoliberalism, and Cooperation").

5. Keohane, *After Hegemony.*

6. Krasner, "Sovereignty."

7. For more on these approaches, see O'Neill, *The Environment and International Relations.*

8. Bodansky, *The Art and Craft of International Environmental Law.*

9. Ron Mitchell's International Environmental Agreement Database lists 1,225 multilateral environmental agreements; see http://iea.uoregon.edu/page.php?file=home. htm&query=static.

10. See O'Neill, *The Environment and International Relations*, Table 4.1.

11. Bernstein, "Global Environmental Norms," 128.

12. Najam, "The View from the South."

13. O'Riordan and Cameron, eds., *Interpreting the Precautionary Principle*; Aven, "On Different Types of Uncertainties in the Context of the Precautionary Principle."

14. O'Neill, *The Environment and International Relations.*

15. O'Neill, "Architects, Agitators, and Entrepreneurs."

16. Kennan, "To Prevent a World Wasteland: A Proposal."

17. Siebenhüner, "Can Assessments Learn?"

18. Young, "Effectiveness of International Environmental Regime"; Depledge, "The Opposite of Learning: Ossification in the Climate Change Regime."

19. Greene, "The System for Implementation Review in the Ozone Regime."

20. Newman et al., "What Would Happen to the Ozone Layer If Chlorofluorocarbons (CFCs) Had Not Been Regulated?"

21. See, for example, Haas, Keohane, and Levy, eds., *Institutions for the Earth.*

22. E.g., Conca and Dabelko, eds., *Environmental Peacemaking.*

23. Susskind, *Environmental Diplomacy.*

24. Chasek, Downie, and Brown, *Global Environmental Politics.*

25. E.g., Speth, *Red Sky at Morning.*

26. Gulbrandsen, *Transnational Environmental Governance*; Cashore, Auld, and Newsom, *Governing through Markets*.

27. O'Neill and Burns, "Trade Liberalization and Global Environmental Governance."

28. VanDeveer, "Green Fatigue."

29. Muñoz, Thrasher, and Najam, "Measuring the Negotiation Burden of Multilateral Environmental Agreements."

30. Young, *Institutional Dynamics*.

31. O'Neill, "From Stockholm to Johannesburg and Beyond"; O'Neill, *The Environment and International Relations*.

32. Bernstein, "Global Environmental Norms."

33. Hochstetler, "The G-77, Basic, and Global Climate Governance: A New Era in Multilateral Environmental Negotiations."

34. Meckling, *Carbon Coalitions*; Newell and Paterson, *Climate Capitalism*.

35. Gómez-Baggethun and Pérez, "Economic Valuation and the Commodification of Ecosystem Services."

36. O'Neill et al., "Methods and Global Environmental Governance."

37. Ibid., 444.

38. Hoppe, Wesselink, and Carins, "Lost in the Problem."

39. See also Miller and Edwards, eds., *Changing the Atmosphere*.

40. Hoppe et al., "Lost in the Problem," 286.

41. Engels et al., "Public Climate-Change Skepticism, Energy Preferences and Political Participation."

42. See Marcacci, "Why Europe's Carbon Market Collapse Won't Kill Cap and Trade."

43. Bulkeley 2010.

44. Burns and Strauss, eds., *Climate Change Geoengineering*.

45. Keohane and Victor, "The Regime Complex for Climate Change."

46. Biermann et al., "The Fragmentation of Global Governance Architectures; Zelli and van Asselt, "The Institutional Fragmentation of Global Environmental Governance."

47. Hoffman, *Climate Governance at the Crossroads* and "Global Climate Change."

48. Rosendal, "Global Biodiversity Governance."

49. Millennium Ecosystem Assessment, *Living beyond Our Means*.

50. Gómez-Baggethun and Pérez, "Economic Valuation and the Commodification of Ecosystem Services."

51. Selin, "Global Chemicals Politics and Policy" and "Global Environmental Law and Treaty-Making on Hazardous Substances."

52. Jinnah, *Post-Treaty Politics*.

53. Bernstein and Cashore, "Complex Global Governance and Domestic Politics."

54. For recent overviews, see O'Neill., *The Environment and International Relations*; Morin and Orsini, "Insights from Global Environmental Governance"; Axelrod and VanDeveer, eds., The Global Environment.

55. See Wapner,"The Importance of Critical Environmental Studies in the New Environmentalism."

56. Bernstein, "Global Environmental Norms."

57. O'Neill et al., "Methods and Global Environmental Governance."

58. Newell and Paterson, *Climate Capitalism*; Meckling, *Carbon Coalitions*; Lo and Howes, "Powered by the State or Finance?"

59. Cashore, Auld, and Newsom, *Governing through Markets*; Kanowski, McDermott, and Cashore, "Implementing REDD+" ; Cashore and Stone, "Can Legality Verification Rescue Global Forest Governance?"

60. Campbell et al., "Studying Global Environmental Meetings."

61. As discussed above. See Suarez and Corson, "Seizing Center Stage: Ecosystem Services, Live."

62. Levy and Newell, "Business Strategy and International Environmental Governance."

63. Wapner, "Climate Suffering."

64. E.g., Caney. "Cosmopolitan Justice, Rights and Global Climate Change."

65. Following O'Neill et al., "Methods and Global Environmental Governance."

66. E.g., Thompson et al., "A Systems Approach to Evaluating the Air Quality Co-Benefits."

67. Andonova and Mitchell, "The Rescaling of Global Environmental Politics"; O'Neill, "Vertical Scale and Linkages."

68. E.g., Biermann, "The Emerging Debate on the Need for a World Environment Organization"; Speth, *Red Sky at Morning.*

69. See Ivanova, "Moving Forward by Looking Back" and chapter 8, this volume.

70. Cammack, "The New Institutionalism."

71. In O'Neill et al., "Methods and Global Environmental Governance."

72. As well as those in ibid.

Bibliography

Andonova, Liliana B., and Ronald B. Mitchell. "The Rescaling of Global Environmental Politics." *Annual Review of Environment and Resources* 35 (2010): 255–282.

Aven, Terje. "On Different Types of Uncertainties in the Context of the Precautionary Principle." *Risk Analysis* 31 (2011): 1515–1525.

Axelrod, R. S., and S. D. VanDeveer, eds. *The Global Environment: Institutions, Law, and Policy,* 4th ed. Los Angeles: Sage/CQ Press, 2015.

Bernstein, Steven. "Global Environmental Norms." In *The Handbook of Global Climate and Environment Policy,* edited by Robert Falkner. London: Wiley, 2013.

Bernstein, Steven, and Benjamin Cashore. "Complex Global Governance and Domestic Politics: Four Pathways of Influence." *International Affairs* (2012).

Biermann, Frank. "The Emerging Debate on the Need for a World Environment Organization: A Commentary." *Global Environmental Politics* 1 (2001): 45–55.

Biermann, Frank, Philipp Pattberg, Harro van Asselt, and Fariborz Zelli. "The Fragmentation of Global Governance Architectures: A Framework for Analysis." *Global Environmental Politics* 9, no. 4 (2009): 14–40.

Bodansky, Daniel. *The Art and Craft of International Environmental Law.* Cambridge, MA: Harvard University Press, 2009.

Bulkeley, Harriet, Liliana B. Andonova, Michele M. Betsill, Daniel Compagnon, Thomas Hale, Matthew Hoffman, Peter Newell, Matthew Paterson, Charles Rogers, and Stacy VanDeveer. *Transnational Climate Change Governance.* Cambridge: Cambridge University Press, 2014.

Burns, W. C., and A. L. Strauss, eds. *Climate Change Geoengineering: Philosophical Perspectives, Legal Issues, and Governance Frameworks.* Cambridge: Cambridge University Press, 2013.

Cammack, Paul. "The New Institutionalism: Predatory Rule, Institutional Persistence and Macro-Social Change." *Economy and Society* 21 (1992): 397–429.

Campbell, Lisa, Catherine Corson, Noella J. Gray, Kenneth I. MacDonald, and J. Peter Brosius. "Studying Global Environmental Meetings to Understand Global Environmental Governance: Collaborative Event Ethnography at the Tenth Conference of the Parties to the Convention on Biological Diversity." *Global Environmental Politics* 14, no. 3 (2014): 1–20.

Caney, Simon. "Cosmopolitan Justice, Rights and Global Climate Change." *Canadian Journal of Law and Jurisprudence* 19 (2006): 255–278.

Cashore, Benjamin, Graeme Auld, and Deanna Newsom. *Governing through Markets: Forest Certification and the Emergence of Non-State Authority.* New Haven, CT: Yale University Press, 2004.

Cashore, Benjamin, and Michael Stone. "Can Legality Verification Rescue Global Forest Governance? Analyzing the Potential of Public and Private Policy Intersection to Ameliorate Forest Challenges in Southeast Asia." *Forest Policy and Economics* 18 (2012): 13–22.

Chasek, Pamela S., David L. Downie, and Janet Welsh Brown. *Global Environmental Politics*, 6th ed. Boulder, CO: Westview Press, 2014.

Conca, K., and G. D. Dabelko, eds. *Environmental Peacemaking.* Baltimore, MD: Johns Hopkins University Press, 2002.

Depledge, Joanna. "The Opposite of Learning: Ossification in the Climate Change Regime." *Global Environmental Politics* 6, no. 1 (2006): 1–22.

Engels, Anita, Otto Hüther, Mike Schäfer, and Hermann Held. "Public Climate-Change Skepticism, Energy Preferences and Political Participation." *Global Environmental Change* 23 (2013): 1018–27.

Gómez-Baggethun, Erik, and Manuel Ruiz Pérez. "Economic Valuation and the Commodification of Ecosystem Services." *Progress in Physical Geography* 35 (2011): 613–628.

Greene, Owen. "The System for Implementation Review in the Ozone Regime." In *The Implementation and Effectiveness of International Environmental Commitments: Theory and Practice*, edited by David G. Victor, Kal Raustiala, and Eugene B. Skolnikoff. Cambridge, MA: MIT Press, 1998.

Gulbrandsen, Lars H. *Transnational Environmental Governance: The Emergence and Effects of the Certification of Forests and Fisheries.* Northampton, MA: Edward Elgar, 2010.

Haas, P. M., R. O. Keohane, and M. A. Levy, eds. *Institutions for the Earth: Sources of Effective International Environmental Protection.* Cambridge, MA: MIT Press, 1993.

Hochstetler, Kathryn Ann. "The G-77, Basic, and Global Climate Governance: A New Era in Multilateral Environmental Negotiations." *Revista Brasiliera Politica Internacional* 55 (2012): 53–69.

Hoffmann, Matthew J. *Climate Governance at the Crossroads: Experimenting with a Global Response after Kyoto.* Oxford: Oxford University Press, 2011.

Hoffmann, Matthew J. "Global Climate Change." In *The Handbook of Global Climate and Environment Policy*, edited by Robert Falkner. London: Wiley, 2013.

Hoppe, Rob, Anna Wesselink, and Rose Carins. "Lost in the Problem: The Role of Boundary Organizations in the Governance of Climate Change." *WIREs Climate Change* 4 (2013): 283–300.

Ivanova, Maria. "Moving Forward by Looking Back: Learning from UNEP's History." In *Green Planet Blues: Four Decades of Global Environmental Politics*, 4th ed., edited by Ken Conca and Geoffrey D. Dabelko. Boulder, CO: Westview Press, 2010.

Jervis, Robert. "Realism, Neoliberalism, and Cooperation: Understanding the Debate." *International Security* 24 (1) (1999): 42–63.

Jinnah, Sikina. "Singing the Unsung: Secretariats in Global Environmental Politics." In *The Roads from Rio: Lessons Learned from Twenty Years of Multilateral Environmental Negotiations*, edited by Pamela S. Chasek and Lynn M. Wagner. New York: Routledge, 2012.

Jinnah, Sikina. *Post-Treaty Politics: Secretariat Influence in Global Environmental Governance.* Cambridge, MA: MIT Press, 2014.

Kanowski, Peter J., Constance McDermott, and Benjamin Cashore. "Implementing REDD+: Lessons from Analysis of Forest Governance." *Environmental Science and Policy* 14 (2011): 111–117.

Kennan, George F. "To Prevent a World Wasteland: A Proposal." *Foreign Affairs* 48 (1970): 401–13.

Keohane, Robert O. *After Hegemony: Cooperation and Discord in the World Economy.* Princeton, NJ: Princeton University Press, 1984.

Keohane, Robert O., and David G. Victor. "The Regime Complex for Climate Change." *Perspectives on Politics* 9, no. 1 (2011): 7–23.

Krasner, S. D., ed. *International Regimes.* Ithaca, NY: Cornell University Press, 1983.

Krasner, Stephen D., ed. "Sovereignty: An Institutional Perspective." *Comparative Political Studies* 21, no. 1 (1988): 66–94.

Levy, David L., and Peter J. Newell. "Business Strategy and International Environmental Governance: Toward a Neo-Gramscian Synthesis." *Global Environmental Politics* 2 (2002): 84–101.

Lo, Alex Y., and Michael Howes. "Powered by the State or Finance? The Organization of China's Carbon Markets." *Eurasian Geography and Economics* 54 (2013): 386–408.

Marcacci, Silvia. "Why Europe's Carbon Market Collapse Won't Kill Cap and Trade." *Energy Collective Blog Post*, April 22, 2013, http://bit.ly/1gj8BZR.

Meckling, Jonas. *Carbon Coalitions: Business, Climate Politics, and the Rise of Emissions Trading*. Cambridge, MA: MIT Press, 2011.

Millennium Ecosystem Assessment. *Living beyond Our Means: Natural Assets and Human Well-Being*. New York: United Nations, 2005.

Miller, C. A., and P. N. Edwards, eds. *Changing the Atmosphere: Expert Knowledge and Environmental Governance*. Cambridge, MA: MIT Press, 2001.

Morin, Jean-Frédéric, and Amandine Orsini. "Insights from Global Environmental Governance: An Edited Symposium." *International Studies Review* 15 (2014): 562–89.

Muñoz, Miquel, Rachel Thrasher, and Adil Najam. "Measuring the Negotiation Burden of Multilateral Environmental Agreements." *Global Environmental Politics* 9, no. 4 (2009): 1–13.

Najam, Adil. "The View from the South: Developing Countries in Global Environmental Politics." In *The Global Environment: Institutions, Law, and Policy*, 4th ed., ed. Regina S. Axelrod and Stacy D. VanDeveer. Los Angeles: Sage/CQ Press, 2015.

Newell, Peter, and Matthew Paterson. *Climate Capitalism: Global Warming and the Transformation of the Global Economy*. Cambridge: Cambridge University Press, 2010.

Newman, P. A., L. D. Oman, A. R. Douglass, E. L. Fleming, S. M. Frith, M. M. Hurwitz, S. R. Kawa, et al. "What Would Happen to the Ozone Layer If Chlorofluorocarbons (CFCs) Had Not Been Regulated?" *Atmospheric Chemistry and Physics* 9 (2009): 2113–2128.

O'Neill, Kate. "Architects, Agitators, and Entrepreneurs: International and Nongovernmental Organizations in Global Environmental Politics." In *The Global Environment: Institutions, Law, and Policy*, 4th ed., edited by Regina S. Axelrod and Stacy D. VanDeveer. Los Angeles: Sage/CQ Press, 2015.

O'Neill, Kate. *The Environment and International Relations*. Cambridge: Cambridge University Press, 2009.

O'Neill, Kate. "From Stockholm to Johannesburg and Beyond: The Evolving Meta-Regime for Global Environmental Governance." *Amsterdam Conference on the Human Dimensions of Global Environmental Change*. 2007.

O'Neill, Kate. "Vertical Scale and Linkages." *International Studies Review* 15 (2014): 571–73.

O'Neill, Kate, and William C. G. Burns. "Trade Liberalization and Global Environmental Governance: The Potential for Conflict." In *Handbook of Global Environmental Governance*, edited by Peter Dauvergne. Cheltenham: Edward Elgar, 2005.

O'Neill, Kate, Erika Weinthal, Kimberly R. Marion Suiseeya, Steven Bernstein, Avery S. Cohn, Michael W. Stone, and Benjamin Cashore. "Methods and Global Environmental Governance." *Annual Review of Environment and Resources* 38 (2013): 441–471.

O'Riordan, T., and J. Cameron, eds. *Interpreting the Precautionary Principle*. London: Earthscan, 1994.

Rosendal, G. Kristin. "Global Biodiversity Governance: Genetic Resources, Species and Ecosystems." In *The Global Environment: Institutions, Law and Policy*, 4th ed., edited by Regina S. Axelrod and Stacy VanDeveer. Washington, DC: Sage/CQ Press, 2015.

Selin, Henrik. "Global Chemicals Politics and Policy." In *The Handbook of Global Climate and Environment Policy*, edited by Robert Falkner. London: Wiley, 2013.

Selin, Henrik. "Global Environmental Law and Treaty-Making on Hazardous Substances: The Minamata Convention and Mercury Abatement." *Global Environmental Politics* 14, no. 1 (2014): 1–19.

Siebenhüner, Bernd. "Can Assessments Learn, and If So, How? A Study of the IPCC." In *Assessments of Regional and Global Environmental Risks: Designing Processes for the Effective Use of Science in Decisionmaking*, edited by Alexander E. Farrell and Jill Jäger. Cambridge: MA: MIT Press, 2006.

Social Learning Group. *Learning to Manage Global Environmental Risks*, vols. 1 and 2. Cambridge, MA: MIT Press, 2001.

Speth, James Gustave. *Red Sky at Morning: America and the Crisis of the Global Environment*. New Haven, CT: Yale University Press, 2004.

Suarez, Daniel, and Catherine Corson. "Seizing Center Stage: Ecosystem Services, Live, at the Convention on Biological Diversity!" *Human Geographies* 6, no. 1 (2013): 64–79.

Susskind, Lawrence E. *Environmental Diplomacy: Negotiating More Effective Global Environmental Agreements*. New York: Oxford University Press, 1994.

Thompson, Tammy M., Sebastian Rausch, Rebecca K. Saari, and Noelle E. Selin. "A Systems Approach to Evaluating the Air Quality Co-Benefits of US Carbon Policies." *Nature Climate Change* 4 (2014): 917–923.

VanDeveer, Stacy. "Green Fatigue." *Wilson Quarterly* 27 (2003): 55–59.

Vogler, John. "Defense of International Environmental Cooperation." *In The State and the Global Ecological Crisis*, edited by John Barry and Robyn Eckersley. Cambridge, MA: MIT Press, 2005.

Wapner, Paul. "Climate Suffering." *Global Environmental Politics* 14, no. 2 (2014): 1–6.

Wapner, Paul. "The Importance of Critical Environmental Studies in the New Environmentalism." *Global Environmental Politics* 8, no. 1 (2008): 6–13.

Young, Oran R. "Effectiveness of International Environmental Regimes: Existing Knowledge, Cutting Edge Themes, and Research Strategies." *Proceedings of the National Academy of Sciences of the United States of America* 108 (2011): 19853–60.

Young, Oran R. *International Governance: Protecting the Environment in a Stateless Society*. Ithaca, NY: Cornell University Press, 1994.

Young, Oran R. *Institutional Dynamics: Emergent Patterns in International Environmental Governance*. Cambridge, MA: MIT Press, 2010.

Zelli, Fariborz, and Harro van Asselt. "The Institutional Fragmentation of Global Environmental Governance: Causes, Consequences, and Responses." *Global Environmental Politics* 13, no. 3 (2013): 1–13.

8 An Engaged Scholarship Narrative

Maria Ivanova

As the causes and consequences of environmental problems extend beyond national jurisdictions, international environmental institutions have become more prominent and necessary than ever before. Accordingly, their performance has received increased attention, and attempts to reform them have multiplied. The latest United Nations environmental summit, the 2012 UN Conference on Sustainable Development, Rio+20, concluded a decade-long reform process of the institutional frameworks for environment and sustainable development that aimed to curtail institutional proliferation, improve coherence, and enhance delivery of results across scales and geographies.

While many criticized the outcome of the conference as a "colossal failure"[1] and a "missed opportunity"[2] because it did not provide the grand global vision deemed desirable and necessary, the institutional gains that Rio+20 triggered are significant and should not be underestimated. The UN Environment Programme (UNEP) emerged from the process stronger, with an expanded governing body, increased budget, and reconfirmed authority. The Commission on Sustainable Development was abolished and replaced with the new High-Level Political Forum. Governments also agreed to recommit to a new set of global goals—Sustainable Development Goals to replace the expiring Millennium Development Goals in 2015. The decisions taken at Rio+20 illustrate the transformation of the international environmental institutions in a new global political context on the New Earth that this book portrays.

In this chapter, I highlight key historical elements of the institutional design and development in global environmental politics, reflect on the close to two decades of reform efforts, and offer a vision for change in the worlds of policy and academia alike. Thus, I take to heart the recommendations Kate O'Neill puts forward in chapter 7 to pay more attention to processes of institutional design, change, and reform. While I discuss international environmental institutions broadly, I zero in on UNEP because much of my scholarship has focused on the creation and performance of what I have called the "anchor institution for the global environment."[3] I employ the term *institution* in the broad sense articulated by sociologist William Graham Sumner over a hundred years ago. He defined institutions as "consisting of a concept (idea, notion, doctrine, interest) and a structure."[4] The concept outlines the goals and functions, the rules of the game, and the structure supplies the instruments through which these rules are put into action. In my analysis, institutions are not only the rules of the game or simply a tool in the hands of the state but a composite entity, an organism that undergoes various stages of development and reacts and adapts to its environment.

The extent, magnitude, and impact of scholarly contributions toward the resolution of global environmental challenges form a core theme of this book. Through this chapter, I seek to provide insights into the past and future of international environmental institutions drawing on my mixed scholarly methods: archival research about the creation of the institutions, direct interaction with their founders and leaders, and engagement in the political process for their reform. The international environmental governance reform process began in earnest in 1997 and formally concludes in 2015. It resulted in the establishment of the UN Environment Assembly as UNEP's new governing organ with universal membership, the creation of the High-Level Political Forum as the new international body for sustainable development, and the articulation of Sustainable Development Goals. Participation in these international environmental governance reform processes has informed much of my analysis and motivated my further scholarship.

I entered this field at the beginning of the reform process, in 1997, when, as a graduate student, I cofounded, with Daniel Esty at Yale, the Global Environmental Governance Project. The project has three core functions: (1) provide a clearinghouse of environmental governance information for scholars, researchers, students, policymakers, and diplomats; (2) serve as a rigorous analyst of available data offering theoretical, empirical, and policy-relevant analysis; and (3) act as an honest broker convening various stakeholders and facilitating dialogue and engagement. As the political debates intensified in the run-up to the Johannesburg Summit in 2002, we held annual dialogues among a group of scholars, practitioners, and politicians seeking to identify reform options. We released an edited volume, *Global Environmental Governance: Options and Opportunities*, in Johannesburg and made it available online for free. [5] This was not standard practice in 2002 and led to thousands of downloads from around the world and to a translation of the book into Portuguese and its publication in Brazil.[6] The authors we convened included renowned academics, policymakers, and activists, people who had not met each other before but whose collective work provided a new and welcome perspective in the environmental governance field.

Since the summit delivered little, the political appetite for reform dampened and funding dried out. Nevertheless, we continued to convene, reflect, write, and engage, and when the reform process rekindled in 2006, the Global Environmental Governance Project had become a trusted partner. I continued to direct the project as I took on a faculty position at the College of William and Mary in 2005, and when I joined the University of Massachusetts Boston in 2010, the project formed the foundation for the Center for Governance and Sustainability, which I now codirect with Craig Murphy. The center took on the three core functions of the Global Environmental Governance Project—to serve as a clearinghouse, a rigorous analyst, and an honest broker—and expanded the focus areas into global development and sustainability concerns. By engaging students from our new PhD program in global governance and human security at the University of Massachusetts Boston in the work of the center, we continue to build a community of global problem solvers across sectors and around the world.

Understanding that solving global environmental problems demands good global environmental governance, which in turn requires an active global public, I began producing short documentaries and have maintained an active analytical online presence. Dubbed the white papers on global environmental governance in images, the documentaries *Quest for Symphony* and *Quest for Leadership* have found their way into classrooms and boardrooms around the world. We have also established an online platform for analysis and communication about key issues in the field that attracts visitors from more than two hundred countries and territories around the world: www.environmentalgovernance.org. We keep an active online presence through regular blog posts about current events in the fields of environment, development, and sustainability that our students author several times a week. This active engagement helps students be aware of the policy and political developments while developing a significant research agenda, connect with interested organizations and individuals, and gain additional expertise across issue areas. It also attracts attention to our scholarship and the educational opportunities we offer at the university. Importantly, it helps us create and maintain an engaged global community around global governance and sustainability.

Indeed, many of the institutional insights this chapter summarizes derive from the collective wisdom of a global community of men and women committed to solving environmental problems and working through international institutions to do so. I sought these individuals out as we convened the Global Environmental Governance Dialogues in the 1990s and first decade of the 2000s, and I sought their help as I researched the history of the institutional architecture. In 2009, this work culminated in a rare gathering of eighty global environmental leaders, including founders and directors of key international environmental institutions and young people ready to take on leadership positions in this field. The Global Environmental Governance Forum in Glion, Switzerland, brought together for the first and only time all five consecutive executive directors of UNEP, former heads of UNDP and the GEF, former and current negotiators, international organization officials, and nongovernmental organization representatives to reflect on the past and put forward a vision for the future.

We began articulating a new historical narrative of institution building,[7] and the role of individuals as the creators, shapers, and leaders of institutions emerged as a core theme. As John Scanlon, policy advisor to UNEP's executive director at the time and currently secretary-general of CITES,[8] exclaimed, "As far as I've heard from the leaders of the past, this work has never been easy. But it happened against the odds. It happened through the strength of leadership; it happened through the strength of passion; it happened through the strength of commitment to purpose."[9] Ultimately the narrative about the creation and performance of international environmental institutions revealed through empirical work and personal interaction with the people who created and led these institutions reaffirms agency, influence, and impact and empowers us as scholars and citizens on a New Earth.

The Bold and Ambitious Original Vision for International Environmental Institutions

As Kate O'Neill illustrates in chapter 7, the system of global environmental governance was formalized as a result of the 1972 Stockholm Conference on the Human Environment and the creation of UNEP. States created an institutional framework for environmental governance to foster collaboration toward solving problems that compromised environmental integrity and economic development. They established UNEP as the core anchor institution for the global environment to catalyze and coordinate environmental action of intergovernmental agencies that already possessed environmental mandates across the UN system. Over time, however, environmental responsibilities have spread even wider across multiple institutions, including numerous multilateral environmental conventions, various UN bodies, development agencies, and the financing and trade institutions. Some analysts consider this proliferation a significant achievement for the environmental movement,[10] and others regard it as "treaty congestion"[11] resulting in unproductive duplication, competition, and waste of scarce resources.[12] Indeed, the number and severity of international environmental problems has continued to increase, leading to a serious questioning of the effectiveness and relevance of these institutions. Both scholars and policymakers have argued passionately that the system of global environmental governance has not lived up to the global needs.[13]

In the policy world, a key assumption is that the root cause of these persistent problems is the fact that the international institutions charged with solving global problems are too weak. They have big mandates, little money, and weak authority. They also compete with many other institutions and nonstate actors for political attention, priority, and, ultimately, funding from the same few states. The key problems articulated in most of the reports that these institutions issue therefore include fragmentation, lack of authority, lack of legitimacy, and lack of funding. The proposed solutions include institutional reform, consolidation of functions, changes in institutional form, and greater financial contributions.

Many scholars assume that the root cause of global environmental problems is the inability or unwillingness of states to prioritize the necessary actions themselves or to delegate appropriate authority to the international institutions. The key premises for this explanation derive from the assumptions that "governments are naturally and properly reluctant to empower an international organization to make, or even to significantly constrain, their national environmental and economic policy choices,"[14] that the objective of the creation of institutions is control,[15] and that failure to accomplish anything of significance in terms of governance reform arises out of a lack of political will among states.[16] Based on this premise, the core thesis and dominant narrative is that international environmental institutions are deficient by design because nation-states have no interest in creating powerful international bodies that might jeopardize national self-interest and would therefore deliberately design such agencies to be weak.

Archival materials of the intergovernmental discussions and the accounts of the founding architects, however, reveal a surprising and compelling story about institutional design for the environment. Governments created a new international environmental body with a clear vision for an agile and able intergovernmental agency that would bring coherence, competence, and connectivity in an institutional landscape of independent agencies with existing priorities. Contrary to conventional wisdom, UNEP was not created to be weak. Its mandate was ambitious, its institutional form flexible, and its funding mechanism solid and envisioned to grow over time. Indeed, there is no historical evidence that governments purposefully created a weak international environmental institution. As O'Neill argues in chapter 7, "existing institutions ... were designed to be as strong as possible while remaining practically feasible." This presents us scholars with a new challenge: to explain the evolution of the international environmental institutions using empirical evidence.

I present a shortened version of the history of UNEP's creation to illustrate key historical facts and begin to challenge some of the mythology that we have inadvertently created in the academic literature. I show that UNEP's mandate was ambitious but feasible, its institutional form suitable and flexible, and its financing appropriate and adequate. Indeed, the core design principle for the new institutional machinery was that "form should follow function." The consensus was that there was a need to provide broad and continuous policy direction for international cooperation in the field of the environment and that the function of the institutional arrangements was to be normative and catalytic. A principal task would be to "review the environmental activities of the UN system and of other international organizations which perform functions in that field with a view to achieving well-coordinated and concerted action."[17] The creators of the new UN body[18] therefore saw it as a "brain,"[19] not a bureaucracy, that would ensure coherent collective environmental efforts. The new institution—what would come to be known as UNEP—would inform, guide, regulate, coordinate, and support governments and UN organizations in developing an environmental focus.

UNEP was clearly designed with an eye to the UN system's limited resources and tendency toward interagency competition. It was given a clear and specific mandate and key financial tools to perform it and was expected to grow and receive increased support as it demonstrated its competence. A key goal was to ensure that the institutional arrangements would enable governments to agree on the periodic assessment of new issues and problems requiring multilateral cooperation and to take the necessary initiatives. It was generally agreed that this did not require the establishment of a new specialized agency. The intergovernmental body would be set up as a subsidiary organ of the General Assembly as a means of enabling the Assembly, and thus the whole membership of the organization, to consider environmental problems in a broader context.

Subsidiary organs are entities created under Article 22 of the UN Charter to address emerging problems and issues in international economic, social, and humanitarian fields. They can have many different formal designations—programs, funds, boards, committees, commissions, councils, panels, and working groups—and governance structures. A UN General Assembly resolution is the instrument through which governments create subsidiary organs. Subsidiary organs work directly through the United Nations, which gives them access to UN administrative and security services as well as a direct relationship with a number of UN offices and other subsidiary organs. UN specialized agencies are autonomous organizations set up independently and linked to the United Nations through special agreements in accordance with Articles 57 and 63 of the UN Charter. They are usually set up around a particular issue or "sector." Governments establish specialized agencies through the adoption and ratification of intergovernmental treaties. The UN General Assembly has no direct administrative, programmatic, or financial authority over them. UNEP was not created as a specialized agency for three reasons.

First, a new specialized agency would need to assume a wide range of functions already performed by existing agencies, including the World Organization (WHO), the International Labour Organization (ILO), the International Maritime Organization (IMO), and the UN Educational, Scientific and Cultural Organization (UNESCO), among others. None of these organizations could or should relinquish their environmental functions. The scope of work for a new specialized agency therefore would be difficult to define short of an all-inclusive mandate. Moreover, as a US delegate observed, "Problems of environment are all-pervasive, and to remove environmental responsibility from existing bodies would not only weaken current efforts but deny the basic concept of the complex dependence of man's surroundings on all of his activities."[20] Second, the environment could not become another "sector." As Maurice Strong recalled during the 2009 Glion Forum, "Right from the beginning, it was recognized that UNEP could not be sectoralized, that the worst thing you could do is sectoralize the environment; because inherently the decisions and the actions that affect the environment are taken largely through the economy. They have social impacts, they have economic impacts, and they have environmental impacts."[21] The status of a specialized agency would isolate the environment on the periphery of the UN; a subsidiary body would put the environment at the center of the United Nations—in its General Assembly rather than in an autonomous, separate agency.[22] Third, a subsidiary body status would allow governments to move quickly and create the institution almost immediately. Creating a specialized agency in the UN system would have required an international treaty that could take many years for ratification by member states, whereas a subsidiary organ could be created right away through a resolution of the General Assembly under Article 22 of the UN Charter.

Financing of the new environmental body was deemed critical from the start, and the United States led the effort to create solid financial footing. In suggesting the establishment of a $100 million Environment Fund to support the new agency, President Nixon explained in a proposal to the US Congress that efforts to improve the global environment without financial means would accomplish nothing and that his proposed level of support would "provide start-up assistance" and would "help to stimulate international cooperation on environmental problems by supporting a centralized coordination point for United Nations activities in this field."[23] Importantly, the initial vision for the Environment Fund emphasized the expectation that its resources would increase as the environmental agenda expanded. An advisory committee to the US secretary of state on the Stockholm Conference wrote about the fund:[24]

We believe that $100 million is a beginning. However, this amount should be viewed as a minimum, a starting figure. It is not yet clear how much money will be required for adequate environmental action. The Voluntary Fund should be of such size as to guarantee that financing will not be a limiting factor to all necessary action. United States participation in this Fund should be exemplary and a reflection of the fact that we are the world's major polluter.

The fund was deliberately created to comprise voluntary rather than assessed contributions because a voluntary setup held distinct advantages. First, it tapped into generous American financial support, which would have remained inaccessible under a mandatory assessment regime. Already in arrears in its assessed contributions to the UN, the US Congress had just cut future payments to the UN by over 20 percent in 1972.[25] Since contributions to the voluntary fund were to be allocated by the president, however, they were not subject to the same congressional oversight as assessed contributions and the president could commit the funds directly. Second, it was unclear what amount of funding was necessary to address the growing environmental agenda. Assessed contributions are set at a certain percentage from the start and difficult to change. Voluntary contributions, however, would allow an increase in funding over the years as new environmental needs appeared and the new organization for the environment proved its effectiveness in addressing them. Third, a budget dependent on assessed contributions would have mandated all member states, including developing countries, to make contributions to the Environment Fund, an unacceptable proposition in 1972 when environmental problems were often cast as a consequence of industrial pollution. All of these arrangements served to solidify the support of the United States, which was interested in ensuring a sufficient level of financing and aware it would not come from the cash-poor United Nations at the time.[26]

The clearest testament to the US commitment to a solid financing scheme for the future organization was the neglected proposal for contributions along an "energy consumption formula." Acknowledging that industrialized countries held a responsibility to improve environmental conditions and should provide the bulk of the new organization's financing, the US secretary of state's advisory committee on the Stockholm Conference proposed a concept akin to assessed contributions: the largest consumers of energy, and thus the largest polluters, were to contribute to the fund on an escalating curve. "A formula derived from each nation's consumption of energy," the committee wrote, "could provide the basis for the suggested participation in the United Nations Voluntary Fund for the Environment. Or, it might provide the basis for a long-range system of funding, which could be a matter of assessment rather than voluntary participation."[27] Participation in the fund by smaller nations was encouraged as a means of emphasizing that all have a stake in international environmental protection—even by symbolic annual contributions of $1,000 ($5,600 in 2014 dollars). This proposal, however, did not find sufficient support to be implemented in practice. Indeed, UNEP has found it difficult to garner financial contributions, especially from developing countries. While the number of countries pledging to the Environment Fund has increased to 108 countries, in 2012, 32 of them, or 30 percent, did not contribute at all, and 40 countries (37 percent) pledged less than $5,000. In practice, 54 countries, or 50 percent, of UNEP's contributors, gave between $0 and $5,000, less than the symbolic contributions envisioned in 1972.[28]

In essence, UNEP was developed by men and women with clear priorities and sharp instincts. They knew which functions they wanted the new institution to perform and devised a mechanism appropriate to the task despite opposition from some governments and many of the specialized agencies. John W. McDonald, was director of economic and social affairs at the Bureau of International Organization Affairs at the US State Department. He had been instrumental in the creation of several UN offices previously, including the UN Fund for Population Activities, UN Volunteers, and the post of UN disaster relief coordinator and recognized the need for a central structure for all environmental efforts. As he told the participants in the 2009 Glion Forum:

As we began to move into 1971 we began to design that particular agency, and so I sat down and I wrote out four resolutions. The first resolution set up the terms of reference of the governing body. The second resolution set up the terms of reference of the Secretariat. The third resolution set up a special fund that was designed along the lines of the UNDP fund, it was outside of the regular budget and it was designed to attract government support for special projects in the whole field of the environment. And the fourth resolution was a coordinating committee chaired by the Head of UNEP with all of the other agencies in the UN system who had a piece of the serious action of the environment, to sit together and ensure that there was no overlap and duplication. So those four resolutions were the basis of what we were trying to achieve, and then we had to convince the US Government and the establishment that this was worthwhile. I used the argument I had used earlier for the creation of the UN Population Fund. I had said that population had never been focused on in the UN system, it was a critical issue that the world should face and so we needed something separate and different to make that happen. I said the same thing about the environment: there is a growing movement across the world, particularly in the United States, and if we want anything to happen in this global system, we have to have a new agency. And that became my mantra—you had to have a new agency to actually make this happen.[29]

By "agency," McDonald meant a new UN body, not a specialized agency. The report of the Committee on International Environmental Programs of the National Academy of Sciences, commissioned by the US State Department in preparation for the Stockholm Conference, arrived at the same conclusion: "We recommend the establishment of a unit in the United Nations system to provide central leadership, to assure a comprehensive and integrated overview of environmental problems, and to develop stronger linkages among environmental institutions and the constituencies they serve."[30]

A contemporary UNEP official exclaimed at the Global Environmental Governance Forum in Glion, "For some reason something happened to create in 1972 the UN Environment Programme with possibly a stronger mandate than we have today, with an Environment Fund, a Coordination Board and a system-wide programmatic approach."[31] The vision was indeed ambitious but necessary and practical. Over time, UNEP delivered on some aspects but faced many challenges. Forty years after its creation, a serious political effort to reform the system of international environmental institutions took place and culminated in the decisions adopted at the Rio+20 conference in 2012. While reformers sought novel ideas for a new environmental order, they recognized that the initial vision for the anchor institution provided a compelling blueprint. What required reform was the set of tools the institution possessed to enact its mandate in a more crowded landscape, a new geopolitical order and economic paradigm, and a new world of instant and immediate connectivity.

The Reform of International Environmental Institutions

Efforts to design and reform the institutional structure for the environment coalesce around global conferences. Such gatherings provide the political impetus and the collective forum for intergovernmental deliberation and decision making and offer the requisite political opportunity, legitimacy, and new resources. The core international environmental institutions were created during the first two of the four major global conferences over the past four decades: the 1972 Stockholm Conference and the 1992 Rio Earth Summit. Reform initiatives for these institutions in turn crystallized during the latter two conferences: the 2002 Johannesburg World Summit on Sustainable Development and the 2012 Rio+20 Conference.

The International Environmental Governance reform process, often known as IEG reform, began in 1997 when four governments—Germany, Brazil, Singapore, and South Africa—expressed concern with the perceived inability of the UN system to tackle global challenges in the environmental field calling for a comprehensive and radical institutional reform and proposing the creation of a World Environment Organization. At the first Global Ministerial Environment Forum that UNEP convened in Malmö in 2000, over one hundred environmental ministers urged an improved institutional architecture to address global environmental problems.[32] As governments were beginning to prepare the 2002 Johannesburg Summit, the activism of environment ministers provided the political impetus for reform efforts and elicited spirited calls for a World Environment Organization from world leaders, including the French president at the time, Jacques Chirac who exclaimed, "our house is burning down and we're blind to it," and proposed the creation of an Economic and Social Security Council and a World Environment Organization.[33] However, without an explicit political process deliberating the functions, form, and financing of the institutions to be reformed, the Johannesburg Summit offered no concrete political outcomes for the international environmental and sustainable development architecture.

Reform deliberations continued haphazardly over subsequent years until the 2005 UN World Summit. Under the rubric of UN reform, the summit stimulated a structured political effort to reform the architecture for international environmental governance.[34] In early 2006, the president of the UN General Assembly, Jan Eliasson, launched an informal consultation process to reform international environmental governance; selected its leadership, the ambassadors of Mexico and Switzerland; and set up the foundation for knowledge creation and accumulation within three months. The highly transparent, analytical approach he put in place became the norm for the consultations within the UN General Assembly and subsequently under the aegis of UNEP. The cochairs produced substantive documents outlining the possible building blocks of a new architecture and engaged with both the policy and academic worlds. Their overview and analysis of the reform process published in an edited volume on global environmental governance in 2006 provided a bridge between the often insulated intergovernmental negotiations and the often cloistered academics.[35] Other UN bodies also contributed to the analytical process. In 2008, the Joint Inspection Unit of the United Nations carried out an independent assessment of the UN system for international environmental governance mapping out the complex institutional landscape and affirmed the reform imperative. The report stressed the negative impacts of fragmentation and high level of specialization in the institutional framework of the United Nations caused by lack of division of labor and common vision and leading to a deficient international environmental governance system.[36]

In 2009, at its twenty-fifth session, UNEP's Governing Council launched the Consultative Group of Ministers or High Level Representatives to "present a set of options for improving international environmental governance."[37] The chair of UNEP's Governing Council at that time, the environmental minister of Serbia, hosted the first meeting in this new series in Belgrade (hence, this was dubbed the Belgrade process), with the negotiations spanning two years. The process concluded with the Nairobi-Helsinki Outcome Document in 2010 with a clear purpose to shape the discussions in the run-up to Rio+20. The document proposed a set of functional responses focusing on issues such as the science-policy interface, system-wide strategy for environment in the United Nations, synergies among the environmental conventions, capacity building, and financing. The institutional options suggested included:[38]

- Enhance UNEP.
- Establish a new umbrella organization for sustainable development.
- Establish a specialized agency such as a world environment organization.
- Reform the Economic and Social Council (ECOSOC) and the Commission on Sustainable Development (CSD).
- Enhance institutional reforms and streamline existing structures.

As the negotiations progressed, two institutional options emerged as the main alternatives: enhancing UNEP and creating a specialized agency. The first option assumed the continuation of UNEP as a subsidiary body of the UN General Assembly, with improvements to its ability to deliver on its mandate; the second was that UNEP would be transformed into and superseded by a specialized agency.

The EU was the longest-standing and most consistent proponent of creating a UN specialized agency for the environment and argued that a specialized agency would "be recognized as the leader on matters relevant to the environment and would perform a coordination function with regard to other UN bodies."[39] It would also serve as "the UN voice for the Environment" and would have "a strong mandate so that the UN response to the outstanding issues in the area of environment reflects the size of the challenges."[40] Other proposed functions included public education, unified monitoring, and the coordination of financing and technology transfer efforts.[41] The African Union (AU) adopted a similar position, urging Africa to "consider the creation of an international environmental organization from UNEP, with a transparent and functioning structure, with means and adequate powers, with universal membership [which would] be the first specialized UN agency to be located in Nairobi, Africa."[42]

Other governments, however, argued that changing UNEP's institutional design would not necessarily lead to improved international environmental governance because it would not directly address the root causes of ineffectiveness; they advocated the alternative option of "enhancing UNEP."[43] This option could be fulfilled through multiple avenues, involving various levels of institutional change. Few analyses, however, presented detailed recommendations that would deliver the functions governments deemed necessary in a politically expedient manner. Through various channels—publications, presentations, informal and formal discussions with governments—I emphasized that UNEP's mandate was already ambitious and covered most of the functions governments wanted performed, that its institutional status as a program was not a significant impediment, and that UNEP could be enhanced by carrying out a few politically significant yet practically possible steps. In articles in the *State of the World Report* and *International Affairs* in 2012, I outlined several such options (see box 8.1).[44]

Box 8.1
Actions Needed to Fulfill UNEP's Mandate

1. *Expand Governing Council Membership.* Universal membership in UNEP's Governing Council could enhance the organization's legitimacy vis-à-vis states and the UN system because all governments will be members. It could also enhance UNEP's authority with regard to multilateral environmental agreements many of which have near-universal membership. Universal membership, however, should be considered more broadly than just expanding the representation to all nation-states. Creating new and innovative mechanisms for engagement of civil society, the private sector, and academic institutions will be imperative to effective global problem solving.

2. *Create an Executive Board.* UNEP's Governing Council/Global Ministerial Environmental Forum (GC/GMEF) performed both of the organization's governance functions: providing leadership to international environmental governance and overseeing UNEP's program and budget. Performing both roles leads to circumscribed leadership and circular decision making, in which programs and budget, rather than global needs, drive priorities and strategies. The large and inclusive UN Environment Assembly, UNEP's new governing body with universal membership, can review global issues, assess needs and identify gaps, identify priorities, and develop strategies to address them. The internal oversight role, however, would be best performed by a smaller body with greater discipline and focus on the program of work, budget, management oversight, and program evaluation. An executive board of twenty to thirty members, with representatives of both member states and civil society (at least as observers), could perform this role.

3. *Review the Need for Implementation Mandate.* Analysts and policymakers have identified an implementation gap in international environmental governance. While many international institutions dictate policy and even provide incentives for implementation, there is no clear line of responsibility and accountability for implementation of multilateral environmental agreements or other internationally agreed goals. An independent external review of existing and necessary roles and responsibilities for implementing the myriad international environmental agreements would help clarify the

mandates of other UN agencies and programs, reveal their comparative advantage, and provide a vision for reduced competition and a productive division of labor.

4. *Allow for Some Assessed Financial Contributions.* Assessed contributions may not lead to a greater overall budget, but they are likely to bring greater stability and predictability of financial resources. A transition from a voluntary to a mixed financial contributions model might provide the necessary certainty for a core budget and the opportunity to be entrepreneurial and raise program resources.

5. *Create a High Commissioner for the Environment.* The primary function of a high commissioner within the Office of the U.N. Secretary-General would be to stimulate concern for and action on behalf of environmental enhancement and protection. This individual should be empowered to go directly to the people of all nations. In addition, the executive would focus attention on high-priority environmental problems and possible solutions, provide advice and offices for dispute settlement, establish a global monitoring system, and promote public awareness and education.

Source

Adapted from Maria Ivanova, "A New Global Architecture for Sustainability Governance," in *State of the World 2012: Jumpstarting Sustainable Economies* (Washington, DC: Worldwatch Institute, 2012).

Consensus on reform was not attained easily but was the result of sustained and substantive negotiations over several years during which states' positions evolved. At Rio+20, governments decided to retain UNEP's institutional form as a subsidiary body, maintained its ambitious original mandate, and gave additional authority to its governing body through universal membership. They also committed to greater financing from the UN regular budget, an arrangement akin to assessed contributions, contributed additional voluntary financing, and enhanced UNEP's implementation function.[45] An executive board and a high commissioner for the environment remain simply recommendations.

An analysis of official statements delivered at the intergovernmental consultations on international environmental governance from 2006 to 2011 that I carried out in 2012 revealed a significant shift in state preferences about the two main institutional reform options: creating a specialized agency and enhancing UNEP.[46] At the beginning of the process, most countries opposed the creation of a specialized agency. Indeed, they opposed any reform of the international environmental institutions. In 2011, however, 35 percent of the one hundred UN member states that had contributed statements to the Rio+20 preparatory process supported the creation of a specialized agency for the environment. Another 30 percent supported enhancing UNEP, and the remaining 35 percent had not expressed any preference.[47] Importantly, the status quo was no longer an openly supported option. Even Australia and the United States, which had argued very strongly against any reform, expressed support for strengthening UNEP.[48]

Australia's official statements illustrate this evolution rather starkly. In 2007, during the first consultations on international environmental governance under the aegis of the UN General Assembly, Australia noted that it had "not heard a convincing argument that there is something fundamentally wrong with the structure of our current system" and emphasized the need to make better use of existing institutions.[49] During the following consultative process that year, led by UNEP, Australia expressed the view that it would consider reforms if they did "not undermine the legal autonomy of the separate governing bodies of the various multilateral environment agreements and [did] not simply create another layer of bureaucracy, further delaying decisions and wasting resources."[50] In its contribution to the Rio+20 process in 2011, Australia supported the following conference outcomes: "strengthening UNEP, including consideration of expanding it to universal membership; strengthening its governance structures; and strengthening its role in relation to the science–policy interface."[51] Indeed, the majority of states coalesced around these reform options leading to the decisions reflected in paragraph 88 of the outcome document of Rio+20.[52]

Four key features of the international environmental governance reform process determined its success: clear mandate, systematic analysis, sustained leadership, and the time-bound opportunity that Rio+20 presented. A clear political mandate for reform coming from governments through the outcome document of the 2005 World Summit and the UN secretary-general through his High-Level Panel on System-Wide Coherence provided the necessary impetus and backdrop for a continuous political effort. A large body of systematic analysis, as well as sound practices developed over time, was available—from studies on the reasons behind UNEP's challenges to implementation of complaints procedures in the Human Rights Council. Many observers criticized the IEG reform process as slow, ridden by political prejudice, and even pointless. Yet the ultimate outcome—the reform of the form, function, and financing of UNEP—was successful.

In the sustainable development field, there was no such significant political attention for such a prolonged period of time. Rather, reform discussions focused on whether to transform the CSD into a Sustainable Development Council and occurred mainly among scholars and think-tanks rather than in the political space. In a rare institutional reform move, at Rio+20 governments decided to abolish the CSD and replace it with a high-level political forum within the UN General Assembly. The High-Level Political Forum was launched in September 2013 and will meet every four years at the level of heads of state at the UN General Assembly and every year at the ministerial level at ECOSOC. Rio+20's institutional impact on ECOSOC went most unnoticed but is significant. By adding "environmental and related fields" to ECOSOC's functions, governments expanded its mandate and reaffirmed the need to reform the institution.

Reform of the system, however, is far from complete. Gaps in function and delivery persist, and there is no agreement on how to address them. Ultimately, without clear division of labor between the environment and sustainable development institutions, the potential for overlap, duplication, and competition between the new High-Level Political Forum, a reformed ECOSOC, UNEP, and other UN institutions and multilateral environmental agreements (MEAs) remains significant and threatens to perpetuate the dynamics that led to the institutional reform in the first place. Table 8.1 outlines a set of five core functions, based closely on the model system devised by UNEP's founders, which the parts of any future system must perform as a whole: (1) monitoring, assessment, and early warning; (2) policy and norm development; (3) capacity development; (4) enforcement; and (5) coordination. The table identifies some of the main bodies currently performing these functions, outlines the gaps in their activities, and summarizes the areas where the need for augmented function is most urgent. It presents a gap analysis, an important step in the process of institutional reform, which was not formally carried out at the intergovernmental level. We cannot decide the division of labor and institutional arrangements until we have reached a consensus on where there are gaps today. The role of academia will be critical in this process.

Transforming Academia: Engaged Scholars and Teachers, Scholarship, and Training

One of the main functions of international institutions, as Oran Young explains in chapter 3 in this book, is a generative function. They have identified and brought attention to problems, articulated new policies and practices, and promoted change in global and national narratives. This is also one of the main functions of the academy. Scholars—professors and

Table 8.1

Functions	Rationale	Performed by[a]	Gaps	Needs
		Monitoring, Assessment and Early Warning		
Collect and store data	Monitor the state of the environment	FAO, IOC, IPCC, IPBES, OECD, UNCCD, UNDP, UNEP, UNESCO	Despite the existence of numerous initiatives, no systematic and comprehensive data collection takes place. Comparability of data across countries and institutions is inadequate.	High- quality, systematic data with cross-country comparability are necessary to support problem and causal linkages identification. Data quality control and assurance mechanisms are required to generate common understanding of existing and emerging problems. A science-policy interface is required to translate sound scientific analysis into policy options that are responsive to country needs.
		WMO, World Bank, governments, MEA bodies, NGOs and think tanks, scientific research centers and universities		
Develop indicators and analyze data	Track trends, identify problems, and highlight causal linkages	FAO, IOC, IPCC, IPBES, Millennium Ecosystem Assessment, OECD, UNCCD, UNDP	Multiple sets of indicators exist without a common analytical framework.	
		UNEP Global Environmental Outlook, UNESCO, WMO, World Bank, governments, MEA bodies, NGOs and think tanks, scientific research centers and universities		
Manage and disseminate information	Provide early warning and generate momentum for action	FAO Global Information and Early Warning System, IPCC, IPBES, ISDR, OECD, Platform for the Promotion of Early Warning, UNCCD	Uncoordinated management and dissemination of information limit impact on policy. Numerous early warning initiatives are underway. However, developing countries that are the most vulnerable to disasters often lack the capacity to implement the technologically advanced systems.	
		UNDP, UNEP, UNESCO, WMO, World Bank, governments, MEA bodies, NGOs and think tanks, scientific research centers and universities		

Table 8.1 (continued)

Functions	Rationale	Performed by[a]	Gaps	Needs
Policy and Norm Development				
Provide a policy space	Facilitate dialogue, negotiations and bargaining; synthesize a common vision	HLPF, Conference of the Parties of MEAs, SAB	UNEA, international environmental summits	Fragmented policy spaces that are delinked from other political areas (like trade and development) and that do not take sufficiently advantage of the innovation coming from civil society and business.	Common purpose, common objectives, and common concepts are necessary to facilitate the synthesis of a common vision. Political emphasis needs to be on creating capacity and demand for implementation. In this regard, a new moral theory for the environment is required, as ethical principles are ultimately the prime motivator for implementation. Focus on leadership and guidance. A platform for meaningful civil society and private sector participation and for exchange of best practices
Develop policies, rules, and standards	Provide policy guidance and exchange best practices	European Commission's Environment Directorate-General, ISO, UNEP Best Practices and Success Stories Global Network	UNEP Montevideo Programme III, WTO, governments, multinational corporations and nonstate NGOs, nonstate market-driven systems (e.g., Forest Stewardship Council)	Series of agreements and conventions have been developed, but little has been implemented. No organization exists with the authority and ability to set standards in the environmental field. An accessible platform to share best practices is lacking.	
Policy impact evaluation	Adapt to changes in environmental, economic, political and social circumstances	GEF, UNEP Global Environmental Outlook, WBCSD Corporate Ecosystems Services Review	World Bank Independent Evaluation Group, Yale/Columbia Environmental Performance Index, governments, NGOs and think tanks	If at all present, policy impact evaluations are carried out by each agency separately. The lack of coordination limits the capacity for systematic policy revision.	and lessons learned is required. Systematic and coordinated impact evaluations are needed to allow for a fundamental reassessment of existing policies.

Table 8.1 (continued)

Functions	Rationale	Performed by[a]	Gaps	Needs
Foster new leadership	Provide moral guidance and ethical norms	Business associations (e.g., Conservation International Center for Environmental Leadership in Business) NGOs (e.g. LEAD), UNEP environmental leadership programs, universities	In the environmental policy field, too little attention is paid to ethics. An authority that develops ethical norms for environment and sustainable development comparable to UNHCR or UNHCHR is missing. Existing initiatives lack a coherent vision.	
Capacity Building				
Develop institutional capabilities	Enable implementation of environmental policies, norms and standards	UNDP, UNEP, UNESCO, UNITAR NGOs, governments, private companies and consultancies	Developing countries in particular are unable to address all the requirements of the many international treaties, including numerous meetings, cumbersome reporting, and development of national regulatory frameworks. They also lack the institutional capacity to implement. The funding base for capacity building efforts remains insufficient.	Developing countries need assistance to meet their objectives and obligations. Effective capacity building requires coordinated and adequate financial support, institution building, and investment in human capital development. At the same time, clear lines of accountability are necessary, including a standardized financial tracking system in order to ensure the proper use of funds. Existing resources need to be used

Table 8.1 (continued)

Functions	Rationale	Performed by[a]	Gaps	Needs
Generate intellectual capital	Enable implementation of environmental policies, norms and standards	UNDP, UNEP Environmental Education and Training, UNESCO, UNITAR Think tanks, universities	No widely recognized center of gravity for environmental education and intellectual leadership. While environmental education in the North has gained momentum, no comparable development exists in the South.	more efficiently in order to mobilize additional funding. Successful awareness building requires new story lines and communication strategies that effectively take advantage of the media, state-of-the art information technologies, and networks.
Mobilize economic resources	Enable implementation of environmental policies, norms and standards	GEF, Montreal Ozone Fund, UNEP, World Bank Foundations, governments, NGOs, treaty-based funds	Funds for environmental activities are limited (compared to development for example). Financial mechanisms are fragmented and even duplicative. Inefficient use of resources jeopardizes fundraising as money follows success.	

Table 8.1 (continued)

Functions	Rationale	Performed by[a]	Gaps	Needs
Improve communication among stakeholders	Raise awareness, educate and advocate	UNDP, UNEP, UNESCO, SAB	Governments, NGOs, universities	The urgency of environmental problems and the relevance of international environmental governance have not been communicated effectively. A compelling common narrative that could bring about behavioral and attitudinal change is missing.	
Enforcement				
Monitor and verify compliance	Identify leaders and laggards	European Commission's Environment Directorate-General, IAEA, IPCC, UNEP Enforcement and Compliance Unit	World Conservation Monitoring Centre, Yale/Columbia Environmental Performance Index, governments, MEA bodies, NGOs and think tanks	The current system of accountability is failing. Compliance monitoring remains unsystematic. Convention secretariats often lack the authority and resources to verify reported information or to conduct independent assessments.	Reporting requirements need to be streamlined and compliance has to be verified in a comprehensive and systematic manner. Governments have to be held accountable internally and externally (for what they do to their own people and to the global community). Effective enforcement requires incentives, disincentives and penalties for non-compliance. A mechanism for mediation and the settlement of environmental disputes is needed.

Table 8.1 (continued)

Functions	Rationale	Performed by[a]	Gaps	Needs
Provide incentives and disincentives/sanctions	Remove obstacles to effective implementation and reward innovation	UNFCCC, WTO	Governments, MEA bodies (e.g., Montreal Protocol Meeting of the Parties)	International environmental law is soft law. Few if any international environmental agreements contain effective noncompliance provisions.
Resolve conflict and settle disputes	Ensure that justice is done	ICEAC, ICJ, ICSID, Inter-American Court of Human Rights	Law of the Sea Tribunal, NAFTA, PCA, WTO	A system of dispute settlement is lacking. Important environmental decisions are referred to economic institutions like the WTO. Moreover, only states can be sued or can sue in international courts.

Table 8.1 (continued)

Functions	Rationale	Performed by[a]	Coordination	Gaps	Needs
Clarify roles and strengthen connectivity among UN agencies and other international organizations	Reduce redundancy, optimize resource utilization, and reduce response time Streamline policy development, capacity building, and implementation efforts Ensure better integration of environmental concerns into economic policy and strategic planning	CEB, EMG, Predecessors: ECB/ACC/DOEM/IACSD, UN 3 "Delivering as One" Initiative, UNEP, UN Energy, UN Oceans, UN Water		UNEP has the mandate for coordination but lacks the capacity to coordinate the numerous environmental and sustainable development activities of UN agencies, IFIs and MEA bodies. The current economic paradigm prioritizes profit and growth over ethics and sustainability. Environment and development are still perceived as opposites.	A functional environmental coordination mechanism—with adequate capital, competence and connectivity—is necessary. Some institutional clustering, consolidation or elimination might be required. A new appreciation for the environment as the anchor and foundation for economic activity is necessary in order to develop an economy dedicated to sustaining people, to sustaining communities, to sustaining nature rather than to sustaining itself.

[a]The lists of organizations performing a particular function are not comprehensive but indicate select actors.

students alike—identify problems, analyze their characteristics, search for patterns, and instigate change. "Empower people with the truth," UNEP's executive director, Achim Steiner, urged during the 2009 Global Environmental Governance Forum in Glion. "The truth is the most powerful political force of change in the environmental domain." In the academy, our search for the truth leads to change in understanding and motivation, and even to a change in values and philosophy.

More often than not, however, this search is undertaken in isolation, and the results are communicated only to a limited audience. Yet academic institutions are best positioned to connect people across sectors, scales, and geographies. Through the Global Environmental Governance Project and the dialogues we convened over the years from Yale, William and Mary, and UMass Boston, we sought to expand the community of scholars and inspire the desire for knowledge and change in researchers and policymakers alike. The community we created has become larger and stronger because it was based on communion that only an impartial university environment could provide. When no government or foundation would fund work on global environmental governance in the 1990s, only a few scholars within a few universities persisted with their analyses and outreach to people beyond academia. Many of them are authors in this book who continue to reflect on, imagine, and work toward new institutions on a New Earth.

The 2009 Glion Forum was a pivotal moment in our work of bridging the worlds of academia, policy, and practice. The interactions among scholars of institutions, the founders of institutions, the leaders of institutions, the negotiators of institutional arrangements, and the young talent committed to working in this field had significant impact on scholarship, policy, and programs as well as at a deeply personal level. A set of core ideas emerged as steps essential to living on a New Earth responsibly. The role of academic institutions in all of those is critical and essential;

Foster leadership. Leadership is vital for success in any enterprise and will have to be present at all levels, from community organizers to national executives, to elevate the political status of the environment, generate media attention, and motivate action. Academic institutions can help identify champions for environmental governance among prominent thinkers, political leaders, economic leaders, and cultural leaders, be they individuals or groups and organizations. It is academia that can establish and maintain a network of environmental leaders to generate ideas, muster support for action, and develop capacity. And it is academia that can connect generations of leaders at the national, regional and global levels through formal and informal programs and events.

Reframe the environment-economy dichotomy. Redefining the connection between the environment and the economy in a new paradigm for human progress is essential. Sustainable development, the paradigm for understanding the relationship between economic growth, social welfare, and environmental protection, has largely failed to reform economic decision making in the way originally intended. Rio+20 redefined the traditional three pillars of sustainable development as the three dimensions that need to be interwoven but stopped short of clearly stating that the environmental dimension forms the foundation on which the economic and social structures depend. A new vision of an economy focused less on short-term rewards and externalized risk and more on long-term values of sustainability and social justice is needed. To this end, academia could spearhead the development of new knowledge, a new narrative, and new policies.

Animate communication. The institutional structures of the United Nations and tangible, backyard environmental problems are disconnected issues for most people. Environmental governance academics could establish this connection and facilitate communication to generate strong grassroots demand and support for improved environmental governance. They could conceptualize and create a global environmental governance communication hub, which harnesses existing information tools and resources through new communication technologies and provides a platform, a clearinghouse for up-to-date information on the state of the global environment, governance structures, policy mechanisms, projects, best practices, and so on. They can reframe the narrative, in institutional accounts and in scholarly and published accounts, to place the intellectual and scientific focus of international environmental institutions in the context of a more engaging and gripping story illustrating the connections between the local and the global, between planet and prosperity, and between governance and survival.

Develop an analytical foundation for evaluating governance. A sound analytical foundation for global environmental governance reform would require serious research of the successes, failures, and potential of existing structures as well as scenario development for immediate and longer-term change. Scholars could review and rethink mandates and division of labor among core international organizations in the context of sustainable development; identify aspects of the existing structures that function well; and compile explanatory analyses. They can devise performance metrics, assessment methodologies, and communication methods or create environmental governance scorecards allowing for comparability of individual government efforts, capacities, and performance, as well as for identifying priorities for investment where serious capacity gaps exist. Indeed, academic institutions are best positioned to provide dispassionate analysis and ratings of national performance.

Cultivate shared values and philosophies. Ultimately, the failure of the economic system to incorporate environmental concerns reflects a failure of values. Reorienting our moral and ethical values will be a necessary condition for change in our behavior toward the environment. A new ethic of global citizenship is also essential for effective, legitimate, and equitable global environmental governance. While many academics are wary of the proposition that they shape shared values, the ideas and knowledge we generate cannot but influence the ethics of new generations of scholars and practitioners. As Abraham Lincoln noted, "The philosophy of the classroom of one generation is the philosophy of the government of the next generation."

As scholars on a New Earth, we have significant responsibility, as Kate O'Neill underlines, to identify, confront, and explain global environmental change as well as recommend possible courses of action. Indeed, in the contemporary classroom, students seek a clearinghouse of information and a source of skills for rigorous analysis as well as the empowerment to create new knowledge and realize their ambitions of solving real-world problems. Academia's primary focus has traditionally been on what is and why, that is, on the state of the world and the reasons behind it. In the New Earth classroom, however, students come with aspirations to instigate change in the world, and we are compelled to seriously explore what ought to be. Yet the ultimate challenge in the classroom is to reflect on how to get there, a question that demands serious and humble understanding of causal mechanisms in natural and human systems. Knowledge of such pathways often comes from beyond academia, making engagement with policymakers a valuable learning tool.

Importantly, we have to recognize the sources of such knowledge. The role of individuals in institutions is often neglected in high-level academic analyses of systemic forces. Yet it is individuals who imagine and instigate institutional change. And it is academia that has the capacity to honor such contributions. Recognizing the extraordinary role Ambassador John W. McDonald, director of economic and social affairs at the Bureau of

International Organization Affairs at the US State Department in the 1970s, played in the creation of UNEP and subsequently in global governance at large, our Department of Conflict Resolution, Human Security and Global Governance at UMass Boston created an award in his honor in 2011. Every year, a graduating student receives the Ambassador John W. McDonald Award for showing leadership and innovation in global governance and conflict resolution. Through this award, we celebrate the life and work of Ambassador McDonald and his ambition to integrate thought and action in solving global challenges through innovative means at all levels of governance.

Ultimately, effective tackling of the questions of global governance will require overcoming disciplinary blinders and will demand exceptional imagination, intellectual curiosity, and academic audacity. Through teaching inside and outside the classroom and engagement of students in research work, academics can create a stimulating intellectual climate that enables students to transcend disciplinary divides and empowers them to engage in solving global problems as scholars and professionals. Our classrooms are already global: the people we educate come from all over the globe, are likely to work all over the globe, and are already connected to communities all over the globe. The philosophy of our classrooms today is therefore likely to be propagated across the world in the immediate and the very near future, one person at a time. To begin resolving the environmental problems on a New Earth, we will need bold, unflinching leadership to shatter stereotypes, create a climate of cooperation, and devise an analytically sound and morally grounded agenda for action. Such leadership would draw on the talent, enthusiasm, and energy of the new generations of environmental scholars and activists who are now entering our classrooms.

Notes

1. Jim Leape, WWF (World Wide Fund for Nature), *Statement to the United Nations Conference on Sustainable Development* (Rio de Janeiro, Brazil 2012). http://wwf.panda.org/?205343/WWF-Rio20-closing-statement.

2. Frank Biermann, "Curtain Down and Nothing Settled."

3. Ivanova, *Can the Anchor Hold?*

4. Sumner, *Folkways*, 53.

5. Esty and Ivanova, *Global Environmental Governance.*

6. Esty and Ivanova, *Governança Ambiental Global.*

7. For information about the Global Environmental Governance Forum: Reflecting on the Past, Moving into the Future, the participants, and outcomes, see http://environmentalgovernance.org/events/gegforum2009/.

8. *Convention on International Trade in Endangered Species of Wild Flora and Fauna,* Washington, 3 March 1973, United Nations Treaty Series, vol. 993, No. 14537, p. 243, available from https://treaties.un.org/doc/Publication/UNTS/Volume%20993/volume-993-I-14537-English.pdf.

9. Scanlon, "Global Environmental Governance Forum."

10. See Haas, "Environment: Pollution"; Najam, "The Case against a New International Environmental Organization."

11. Weiss, "International Environmental Law."

12. See Hicks, "Treaty Congestion in International Environmental Law"; Young, "Institutional Linkages in International Society"; Rosendal, "Impacts of Overlapping International Regimes"; Speth, "A Memorandum in Favor of a World Environment Organization."

13. Speth and Haas, *Global Environmental Governance;* (Najam and Selin, "Institutions for a Green Economy"; Indonesia, 'Submission by the Government of the Republic of Indonesia to the zero draft of UNCSD 2012 outcome document', 1 Nov. 2011, http://www.uncsd2012.org/rio20/content/documents/358Submission%20Indonesia%20for%20Rio20.pdf.

14. Gaines, "The Problem of Enforcing Environmental Norms."

15. Moe, "The Politics of Bureaucratic Structure"; Zegart, *Flawed by Design.*

16. Gaines, "The Problem of Enforcing Environmental Norms."

17. United Nations, *International Organizational Implications of Action Proposals.*

18. While national governments are the official creators of UNEP, several individuals in different states, in several institutions, or in their personal capacity played particularly important roles. Christian A. Herter Jr., Russell Train, Gordon MacDonald, and John W. McDonald were among the representatives of the US government who engaged most actively in the institutional deliberations and decisions. They were advised by panels of scientists convened by the State Department. The representatives of Sweden also played a key role as the support of the host government was critical to the outcomes of the Stockholm Conference. Maurice Strong was also a key figure in UNEP's creation and enlisted the help of a number of advisors. Scholars David Wightman of the United Kingdom and Richard Gardner of the United States, for example, were critical in UNEP's creation as they shaped the core questions and provided policy options.

19. Maurice F. Strong, "Development, Environment and the New Global Imperatives: The Future of International Co-operation" (speech at Carlton University, Ottawa, Canada, 1971).

20. Gordon J. MacDonald, "International Institutions for Environmental Management," 373.

21. Ivanova, "Global Environmental Governance in the 21st Century."

22. In the case of international forest governance, the question of institutional design and stature within the UN system emerged in the 1990s. Arguing that forest negotiations need to be central within the United Nations and take place in a setting that would ensure that they were not marginalized, states decided that international negotiations on forests should be within the Commission on Sustainable Development and then become part of the ECOSOC rather than of a specialized agency, the Food and Agriculture Organization (FAO). See Humphreys, *Logjam*. Negotiations eventually led to the creation of the United Nations Forum on Forests (UNFF), a subsidiary body of ECOSOC, located at the UN headquarters in New York City, even though the FAO offered to host the UNFF Secretariat. UNFF, *Report on the Organizational and First Sessions*.

23. US Information Service, "President Proposes Voluntary U.N. Environment Fund," press release, Geneva. February 9, 1972.

24. United States, *Stockholm and Beyond*, 132.

25. In 1973, the United States decreased its contributions to a commitment to supply 25 percent of the general budget for the United Nations, prompting the UN to offset its budget by 6.52 percent. US Congress House of Representatives, *Participation by the United States in the United Nations Environment Program*, 57. In a meeting with Ambassador Bush, UN Secretary-General Waldheim expressed concern over lack of US support. Bush, "Telegram from the Mission to the United Nations to the Department of State," 1972.

26. Ambassador Bush communicated concern over UN financial crisis to US State Department. Bush, "Telegram from the Mission to the United Nations to the Department of State," 1971.

27. US Congress, House, Committee on Foreign Affairs, *International Cooperation in the Human Environment through the United Nations: Hearing on H.R. 13116.* 92d Cong., 2d sess., March 15 and 16, 1972), 132).

28. UNEP, *Annual Report 2012*.

29. McDonald, 2009.

30. Environmental Studies Board, *Institutional Arrangements for International Environmental Cooperation*.

31. Ivanova, "Global Environmental Governance in the 21st Century."

32. UNEP, "Malmö Ministerial Declaration."

33. Chirac, "Statement of the French Republic to the World Summit on Sustainable Development."

34. The mandate for the institutional reform in the environmental field derives from paragraph 169 of the World Summit Outcome Document: "Recognizing the need for more efficient environmental activities in the United Nations system, with enhanced coordination, improved policy advice and guidance, strengthened scientific knowledge, assessment and cooperation, better treaty compliance, while respecting the legal autonomy of the treaties, and better integration of environmental activities in the broader sustainable development framework at the operational level, including through capacity building, we agree to explore the possibility of a more coherent institutional framework to address this need, including a more integrated structure, building on existing institutions and internationally agreed instruments, as well as the treaty bodies and the specialized agencies." United Nations, *A/RES/60/1 2005 World Summit Outcome* (New York: United Nations, 2005).

35. Berruga and Maurer, "The Informal Consultative Process."

36. Inomata, "Management Review of Environmental Governance."

37. UNEP, "UNEP/GC.25/4 International Environmental Governance," United Nations, Nairobi, Kenya, 2005.

38. UNEP, *Consultative Group of Ministers or High-Level Representatives on International Environmental Governance.*

39. European Union, Contribution of the European Union and Its Member States."

40. Ibid.

41. Biermann, "Reforming Global Environmental Governance."

42. African Union, "Mobilizing African Leadership."

43. United States, "Statement to the first meeting of the Consultative Group' and 'Comments to the second meeting of the Consultative Group'; Ivanova, "A New Global Architecture for Sustainability Governance."

44. Ivanova, "Institutional Design and UNEP Reform."

45. United Nations, "The Future We Want."

46. Documents from the following consultations were analyzed: (1) the international environmental governance consultations that took place in the UN General

Assembly from 2006 to 2008 and in UNEP's Governing Council in 2009 and 2010; and (2) the Rio+20 preparatory discussions that took place in 2010 and 2011. In the first group, fifty-one countries submitted statements for the consultations. In some cases, multiple statements from one country were present. In the second group, one hundred countries submitted statements. In the first sample, 41 percent are developed countries and 59 percent are developing. In the second sample, 42 percent of countries are developed and 58 percent are developing.

47. See table 1 in Maria Ivanova, "Institutional Design and UNEP Reform," 571.

48. United States, "U.S. Input to the Belgrade Process," August 8, 2009, copy on file with author; United States, "Sustainable Development for the Next Twenty Years," input for the 2012 UNCSD Rio+20 compilation document, November 1, 2011, http://www.uncsd2012.org/content/documents/compilationdocument/UNandIGOs.pdf.

49. Australia, "Statement to the Informal Consultative Process on the Institutional Framework for the United Nations' Environmental Activities," September 10, 2007, copy on file with author.

50. Australia, 'Comments to the Second Meeting of the Consultative Group of Ministers or High-Level Representatives on International Environmental Governance," August 14, 2009, copy on file with author.

51. Australian Government, "Submission to the Rio+20 Compilation Document."

52. Paragraph 88 is under title C on the environmental pillar in the context of sustainable development. The paragraph encourages member states to adopt a resolution to strengthen UNEP by establishing universal membership; ensuring secure, stable financing; and ensuring active participation of other stakeholders, among others.

Bibliography

African Union. "Mobilizing African Leadership for an Effective Regional Preparatory Process for the United Nations Conference on Sustainable Development Rio+20." June 29, 2011. http://www.unep.org/roa/Portals/137/Docs/pdf/Rio+20_Report.pdf.

Australian Government. "Submission to the Rio+20 Compilation Document." http://www.uncsd2012.org/content/documents/692Australian%20National%20Submission%20to%20Rio20%20Compilation%20Draft.

Berruga, Enrique, and Peter Maurer. "The Informal Consultative Process on the Institutional Framework for the UN's Environmental Activities—Co-Chairs Summary." In *Global Environmental Governance: Perspectives on the Current Debate*, edited by Lydia Swart and Estelle Perry, 16–25. New York: Center for UN Reform Education, 2007.

Biermann, Frank. "Curtain Down and Nothing Settled. Global Sustainability Governance after the 'Rio+20' Earth Summit," *Earth System Governance Working Paper* no. 26 (2012).

Biermann, Frank. "Reforming Global Environmental Governance: From UNEP Towards a World Environment Organization." In *Global Environmental Governance: Perspectives on the Current Debate*, edited by Lydia Swart and Estelle Perry. New York: Center for UN Reform Education, 2007.

Bush, George H. W. "Telegram from the Mission to the United Nations to the Department of State," New York, May 31, 1972." In *Foreign Relations of the United States, United Nations 1969–1976*, edited by Evan M. Duncan. 334–35. Washington, DC: Government Printing Office, 1972.

Bush, George H. W. "Telegram from the Mission to the United Nations to the Department of State," New York, September 15, 1971." In *Foreign Relations of the United States, 1969–1976*, edited by Evan M. Duncan, 307–308. Washington, DC: Government Printing Office, 1971.

Chirac, Jacques. "Statement of the French Republic to the World Summit on Sustainable Development," Johannesburg September 2, 2002, http://www.un.org/events/wssd/statements/franceE.htm.

CITES. *Convention on International Trade in Endangered Species of Wild Flora and Fauna*. United Nations Treaty Series, vol. 993, no. 14537. Washington, DC: March 3, 1973, March 3, 1973. https://treaties.un.org/doc/Publication/UNTS/Volume%20993/volume-993-I-14537-English.pdf.

Environmental Studies Board. *Institutional Arrangements for International Environmental Cooperation: A Report to the Department of State by the Committee for International Environmental Programs*. Washington, DC: National Academy of Sciences, 1972.

Esty, Daniel, and Maria Ivanova. *Global Environmental Governance: Options and Opportunities*. New Haven, CT: Yale School of Forestry and Environmental Studies, 2002.

Esty, Daniel, and Maria Ivanova. *Governança Ambiental Global: Opções & Oportunidades*. São Paulo: Editora Senac, 2005.

European Union. "Contribution of the European Union and Its Member States to the UN Department of Economic and Social Affairs," Input for the 2012 UNCSD Rio+20 compilation document, November 1, 2011. http://www.uncsd2012.org/index.php?page=view&type=510&nr=240&menu=20.

Gaines, Sanford E. "The Problem of Enforcing Environmental Norms in the WTO and What to Do about It." *Hastings International and Comparative Law Review* 26 (2003): 321–85.

Haas, Peter M. "Environment: Pollution." In *Managing Global Issues: Lessons Learned,* edited by P. J. Simmons and Chantal de Jonge Oudraat, 573–601. Washington, DC: Carnegie Endowment for International Peace, 2001.

Hicks, Bethany Lukitsch. "Treaty Congestion in International Environmental Law: The Need for Greater Institutional Coordination." *University of Richmond Law Review* 32 (1999): 1643–74.

Humphreys, David. *Logjam: Deforestation and the Crisis of Global Governance.* London: Earthscan, 2006.

Inomata, Tadanori. "Management Review of Environmental Governance within the United Nations System." JIU/REP/2008/3. Geneva: Joint Inspection Unit, 2008. https://www.unjiu.org/en/reports-notes/archive/JIU_REP_2008_3_English.pdf.

Ivanova, Maria. *Can the Anchor Hold? Rethinking the United Nations Environment Programme for the 21st Century.* New Haven, CT: Yale School of Forestry and Environmental Studies, 2005.

Ivanova, Maria. "Global Environmental Governance in the 21st Century: Way Ahead Wide Open." Report from the Global Environmental Governance Forum: Reflecting on the Past, Moving into the Future," Glion, Switzerland, June 28–July 2, 2009. http://dev.environmentalgovernance.org/cms/wp-content/uploads/2009/10/GEG-Forum-Report_Final.pdf.

Ivanova, Maria. "Institutional Design and UNEP Reform: Historical Insights on Form, Function and Financing." *International Affairs* 88 (2012): 565–84.

Ivanova, Maria. "A New Global Architecture for Sustainability Governance." In *State of the World 2012: Jumpstarting Sustainable Economies,* 565–84. Washington, DC: Worldwatch Institute, 2012.

MacDonald, Gordon J. "International Institutions for Environmental Management." *International Organization* 26 (1972): 372–400.

McDonald, John W. 2009. Presentation at Global Environmental Governance Forum: Reflecting on the Past, Moving into the Future, Glion, Switzerland, June 28–July 2, 2009. www.environmentalgovernance.org.

Moe, Terry. "The Politics of Bureaucratic Structure." In *Can the Government Govern?* edited by J. E. Chubb and P. E. Peterson, 451–94. Washington, DC: Brookings Institution, 1989.

Najam, Adil. "The Case against a New International Environmental Organization." *Global Governance* 9 (2003): 367–84.

Najam, Adil, and Henrik Selin. "Institutions for a Green Economy." *Review of Policy Research* 28 (2011): 451–57.

Rosendal, Kristin. "Impacts of Overlapping International Regimes: The Case of Biodiversity." *Global Governance* 7 (2001): 95–117.

Scanlon, John. Global Environmental Governance Forum: Reflecting on the Past, Moving into the Future, Glion, Switzerland, 2009.

Speth, James Gustave. "A Memorandum in Favor of a World Environment Organization." In *Uneo: Towards an International Environment Organization*, edited by Andreas Rechkemmer. Baden-Baden: Nomos Verlagsgesellschaft, 2005.

Speth, James Gustave, and Peter M. Haas. *Global Environmental Governance*. Washington, DC: Island Press, 2006.

Sumner, William Graham. *Folkways: A Study of the Sociological Importance of Usages, Manners, Customs, Mores, and Morals*. Boston: Ginn, 1906.

US Congress House Committee on Foreign Affairs. *International Cooperation in the Human Environment through the United Nations: Hearing on H.R. 13116*. 92d Cong., 2d sess., March 15 and 16, 1972.

US Information Service. "President Proposes Voluntary U.N. Environment Fund." Press release, Geneva, February 9, 1972.

UNEP. 'Malmö Ministerial Declaration', GMEF/UNEP GCSS-6 UNEP/ GCSS-VI/L.3, (31 May, 2000). Available at: http://www.unep.org/malmo/malmo_ministerial.htm.

UNEP. *UNEP/GC.25/4 International Environmental Governance*. Nairobi, Kenya: United Nations, 2005.

UNEP. *Annual Report 2012*. Nairobi: United Nations Environmental Programme, 2013.

UNEP. *Consultative Group of Ministers or High-Level Representatives on International Environmental Governance/Nairobi-Helsinki Outcome*, 2010. http://www.unep.org/environmentalgovernance/Portals/8/NairobiHelsinkifinaloutcome.pdf.

UNFF. *Report on the Organizational and First Sessions*. United Nations Forum on Forests Secretariat E/2001/42/Rev.1 and E/CN.18/2001/3/Rev.1. 2001.

United Nations. *International Organizational Implications of Action Proposals: Conference on the Human Environment: Report by the Secretary-General*, A/CONF.48/11/Add.1. January 10, 1972.

United Nations. "The Future We Want: Outcome Document from Rio+2." *United Nations Conference on Sustainable Development*, A/RES/66/288, Rio de Janeiro, June 20–22, 2012.

United Nations. *A/RES/60/1 2005 World Summit Outcome*. New York: United Nations, 2005.

United States. *Stockholm and Beyond: Report*. Edited by Secretary of State's Advisory Committee on the 1972 United Nations Conference on the Human Environment. Washington, DC: Government Printing Office, 1972.

United States. "Sustainable Development for the Next Twenty Years," Input for the 2012 UNCSD Rio+20 compilation document. November 1, 2011. http://www.state .gov/e/oes/sus/releases/176863.htm.

US Congress House of Representatives. *Participation by the United States in the United Nations Environment Program*. Committee on Foreign Affairs: Subcommittee on International Organizations and Movements. Washington, DC: Government Printing Office, 1973.

Weiss, Edith Brown. "International Environmental Law: Contemporary Issues and the Emergence of a New World Order." *Georgetown Law Journal* 81 (1995): 675–93.

WWF (World Wide Fund for Nature). *Statement to the United Nations Conference on Sustainable Development*. Rio de Janeiro, Brazil 2012. http://wwf.panda.org/?205343/ WWF-Rio20-closing-statement.

Young, Oran R. "Institutional Linkages in International Society: Polar Perspectives." *Global Governance* 2, no. 1 (1996): 1–24.

Zegart, Amy B. *Flawed by Design: The Evolution of the CIA, JCS, and NSC*. Stanford: Stanford University Press, 1999.

Section 5   Social Movements and Civil Society

One way in which political theorists make sense of the world is to distinguish among three different domains of action: the state, the market, and civil society. In chapter 1, Conca considered the impact of market-based actors on environmental well-being, and in section 4, O'Neill and Ivanova looked at the gains and shortcomings of the interstate institutions that have been developed to respond to environmental harm. In this section, Peter Jacques (chapter 9) and Erik Assadourian (chapter 10) turn our attention to civil society and the broader late-twentieth-century effort to build an environmental social movement (or social movements).

Peter Jacques offers a critical assessment of civil society efforts: "Despite important impacts, environmental civil society ... has not had the impact necessary for humanity to live on this New Earth well or sustainably." Part of the blame for this lack of success, he argues, lies with scholars of global environmental politics for paying too much attention to the positive impacts the environmental movement has had in a few circumscribed areas and too little attention to the inability of civil society to tackle what he sees as the more basic drivers of environmental harm. Jacques makes the case, as a corrective, for a sustained focus on the "counterrevolutionary forces" that hold in place the status quo and for a refinement of long-held theories of social change and civil society.

Erik Assadourian turns from theorizing to strategizing in chapter 10. He argues that the environmental movement has been largely and effectively co-opted by the very forces that it should be opposing. His critique leads him to propose a new model for environmental action, based on features of missionary religions. Missionary religions, he suggests, have in common a compelling and unified philosophy that gives rise to an ethical code, an understanding of the worth and nature of suffering, and rituals of community building. He acknowledges that the work of developing something akin to a missionary religion is a slow, long-term proposition, and so his ideas may be dismissed by those who believe that the current environmental situation calls for swift action. Perhaps, he says, building a new environmental movement today may mean that there are institutions in place to help pick up the pieces should a declining environmental condition lead to large-scale social collapse.

The issues and ideas that Jacques and Assadourian raise are uncomfortable ones to consider. They force us all to challenge established views and confront the potential shortcomings in current forms of response to environmental harm. Such is the quality of thinking demanded by the New Earth.

Framing Questions Posed to the Authors in Section 5

- What is the "environmental movement"? What has it accomplished thus far?
- How has the environmental movement changed over time? What accounts for this evolution?
- How should civil society engage in contemporary global environmental politics? How should we be thinking about the tension between democracy/sovereignty/varied national interests, on the one hand, with the urgent need to solve environmental problems, on the other hand?
- Is the movement up to the challenge of addressing environmental problems on a New Earth, or does the New Earth demand new ways of thinking about social movements?

9 Autonomy and Activism in Civil Society

Peter J. Jacques

All of us who are chapter authors agree that we are now living on a New Earth despite decades of warnings against such a wild experiment. In this section on civil society, we agree on at least one remedy based on the Socratic truism: "Public, know thyself." In chapter 10, Erik Assadourian speaks in terms of public soul searching, and in this chapter, I speak more in terms of political economic battlefields. However, we both find the trajectory of our species on a suicidal course, and we both think that massive social change will either be purposeful or thrust on us through social destruction. To be purposeful, the public must know its own interests and not confuse them for the interests of planetary Sirens that wish to feed on the remains of our earthly ship.

The battles I speak of are won or lost in what Mahatma Gandhi described as an intimate knowledge and mastery of the self, because it was only with this understanding of both the self and through right action that the brutality experienced in noncooperation and civil disobedience was sustainable. In this case, Gandhi serves as an icon of not only nonviolent resistance but successful social change, and part of that success was from the Indian people knowing their own interests enough to oppose vicious and predatory European elites. Beware that none of this resolves the core politics of "who" is the public or how to negotiate legitimate differences (let alone differences between publics), but it does assume that in a public, it is possible to think of big picture plans that secure a public well-being and a path that is destructive of that well-being. So long as Indian civil society accepted the interests of the empire as their own, there was no powerful opposition, no independence, and no home rule. One final clarification on my assumptions is that there need not be overwhelming support from the public for something to truly be in the public interest, but it does require political thinking and action to assert the public interest. In fact, here we will see that many people in the public may buy into conditions that are contrary to the larger public good and that a small but politically educated minority can lead the charge to find cracks in the walls of abusive social power.

In this chapter, the dynamics of civil society on a New Earth are interrogated and related to the following questions: How should civil society engage in contemporary global environmental politics?[1] How should we be thinking about the tension between democracy/the state/firms, on the one hand, and the urgent need to solve environmental problems, on the other hand? Is the movement up to the challenge of addressing environmental problems on a New Earth, or does the New Earth demand new ways of thinking about social movements? Overall, my take on these questions is that the global environmental movement needs to take a much more critical but strategic position to destabilize more dominant and hostile social forces.

Despite important impacts, environmental civil society—the transnational network of environmental nongovernmental organizations (ENGOs) and other components of the global environmental movement—has not had the impact necessary for humanity to live on this New Earth well or sustainably. Scholars of global environmental politics shoulder some of this responsibility because we have focused with too much optimism on (1) the efforts of the global environmental movement to make a difference in (2) facilitating international problem-solving regimes with less attention to the larger political and economic architecture that shape both regimes and civil society, and this has left vast networks of power outside our normal view. In short, we need more Gramsci and less de Tocqueville. Gramsci believed that civil society was too easily convinced that the interests of the ruling elite were the interests of the public, while de Tocqueville saw the public as easily knowing and getting what it wanted from a responsive government that treated varied interests with equity.

To be clear, my comments here are not to detract from these important bodies of work. Research of problem-solving environmental regimes has been nothing less than foundational to global environmental politics. Very little of this literature is Pollyannaish, and the bulk of this work indicates that the effectiveness of regimes is complex and not easily discerned.[2] In this chapter, when I speak of regimes, I am referring not only to formal treaties but the broad network of norms, rules, and decision-making procedures that establish a specific order in the same way that Dauvergne discusses the "international forests regime" that is made up of a patchwork of standards and operating procedures from multiple sources of authority but has no core treaty.[3] The idea of a regime as a political order implies a stability that is formed and can change. For example, after 1944, the global economic regime was an embedded liberal capitalism that changed, starting in 1971–1979, to a neoliberal capitalism, and both of these regimes required legitimation from global civil society. This is the power of civil society: it confers consent to regimes, and under some circumstances, it can also drive the direction of these regimes in a way that democratic ideals might expect. However, as this chapter will explain, we must be very careful about simply assuming civil society gets what it really wants.

Research in global environmental politics on environmental civil society has been quite profound. This body of work has shown the power of the global environmental movement to affect policy through networks, changes to wide-ranging sentiments, the spread knowledge to solve problems, and even the governance of limited relationships between humans and nature.[4] The global environmental politics literature on civil society has moved beyond a simplistic pluralist model where environmental groups or movements simply pressure governments with demands and then governments respond. To be sure, pluralists do not argue that environmental groups will always get what they demand, but rather that ENGOs operate on a relatively open and even political field that treats each specific group or interest evenly, allowing for unbiased competition for policy change. The global environmental politics community writ large has added real-world complexity and nuance to our understanding the politics of the Earth, and few scholars believe that there is an even political field for ENGOs when they compete against the likes of Walmart or the auto industry.

Still, there is room for some critical reflection. For example, much current work on environmental civil society is centered on the changing worldviews of people to affect the way that we live together with nature absent the larger tilt of the political field. For some time now, critical international relations (IR) scholars have warned that overly statist thinking will neglect important power centers controlled by business. In particular, there has been specific neglect of counterrevolutionary forces organized from "market civilization,"[5] or business interests that arguably govern the basic moral order of the most important structural fields of politics. Simply put, IR has not paid enough attention to the way business and industry shape not only policy but the moral environment in which their policy priorities make sense.

Here, the term *counterrevolutionary forces* refers to forces that defend and reproduce elite interests in global capitalism. These interests reproduce deep inequalities that emerge from unequal positions of power in the world economy while organizing global markets that pursue and (try to) consume every last fish in the ocean, old-growth tree in the forest, and predator species that walks the Earth. Counterrevolutionary forces defend the flow of value (e.g., financial capital) to global elites, such as heads of financial firms in urban centers. Counterrevolutionary forces guard this surplus value by anticipating social movements that challenge the elitist arrangements. The counterrevolutionary efforts then work to discredit, undermine, or co-opt the efforts to change the system.

In the larger political arenas, such as security, financial, and trade practices, there is a material, ideological, and organizational supremacy, or hegemony, of economistic interests vested in asymmetrical growth. David Harvey warns too that scholarship, theory, knowledge, and science are crucial counterrevolutionary sources that legitimate the manipulation of and profit from nature:

Far more important, however, is the harnessing of scientific activity, by a process of patronage and funded research, to the special interests of those who are in control of the means of production. The coalition of industry and government heavily directs scientific activity. Thus manipulation and control mean manipulation and control in the interests of a particular group in society rather than in the interests of society as a whole.[6]

Even critical "liberal" academics participate in counterrevolutionary thought inasmuch as we offer "'mere apologetics' for the dominant force in our society: the capitalist market system and all its concomitant institutions."[7]

Under this frame, international environmental regimes have provided a "thin regulatory context for the smooth operation of global capitalism," which "must pretend" to reconcile growth and environmental destruction, "Yet all global institutions are now dominated by neoliberal, trade-oriented, growth-based policy regimes" that contradict sustainability.[8] Economic growth is centrally important. Economic growth comes from multiple global sectors: actual commodities, financial markets, government bond markets, credit markets, insurance and hedge funds, agonistic redistribution from workers through wage suppression, enclosure and accumulation of frontiers and commons, and other forms of moving wealth from common people to wealthy elites through globally unequal exchange arrangements. The vast majority of this activity produces enormous and growing surplus value and reproduces the power of a tangible economic and managerial elite while it erodes social equity, simplifies and consumes ecological systems, and narrows our chances to check the practice of general and specific exploitation that has dominated institutions and norms that guide mass behavior.

In order to have a chance on the New Earth, civil society must intervene with the structural components of global political economy driving this planetary death march. However, thus far the global environmental movement has been limited from arenas having to do with rules of trade and finance, inequality, deepening multitiered alienation, and growth. It is this last condition that may be most important because economic growth provides the material conditions for the way so many people live their lives and directly links to deepening social and ecological crises. Michael Parenti puts it this way: "What is called 'growth' in today's transnational corporate world means ever-expanding, multi-trillion-dollar accumulations for the 1% along with the social impoverishment and environmental devastation for the 99% of us."[9] Growth is the ubiquitous goal of (nearly?) all mainstream corporations and all states and is a defining feature of modern political economy and governance. This growth causes innumerable invisible casualties, and the radical necessity of true sustainability is to challenge the processes of growth and inequality to create something faithful to the public interest.

True sustainability requires that we change the basic operating principles of world civilization.

I begin this chapter by explaining two main theories of social change and civil society, and then I explain important counterrevolutionary forces that defend an increasingly maladaptive and destructive neoliberal moral order that governs key structural processes. Finally, I explore how civil society can govern a more sustainable New Earth by taking the success had in other arenas to more structural ones.

Theories of Social Change and Civil Society

Living on a New Earth means that real public interests must matter more, in a way quite like Peter Dauvergne argues chapter 16. Advancing public interests will require challenging and penetrating structural forces that cause economic inequality, alienation, and growth and changing them to suit the interests of global civilization.

What do I mean by *structure* and *structural forces*? Structural forces are the durable systems across communities that guide the ideals, behavior, and organization of large numbers of actors. Actors can be businesses or industrial actors, governmental and nongovernmental actors, and sometimes hybrids of each. For analytical clarity, but not necessarily accuracy, *civil society* here will refer to the social association of people and does not include corporations or states, or individuals on their own for that matter—because "society" must be part of civil society. Probably the most accurate vision of civil society, the state, and the firm is of a web of mutually constitutive and tangled intersections and intensities that have less clear divisions between public and private interests and a diversity of origins. In other words, in real life there are many hybrid actors who work in multiple sectors. Still, for this chapter, I refer to these areas as more cleanly divided than they really are: civil society, political society (the systems of states and their apparatuses), and economic society (firms and their relations).

In order to do this, we must grapple with one of the most important but complex issues in modern politics: the mechanisms for social change, including obstacles to change. Much work has been done on the impact and processes of a global environmental movement that has affected the general sensibilities of people around the world; however, there is much less work on counterrevolutionary and countermovement projects that help explain the fact that global civilization continues to lurch toward multiple overlapping sustainability crises.

Theories of Civil Society

Theories of social change depend on how civil, political, and economic societies interact. In particular, political philosophers disagree about how independent civil society is from other societies. This level of independence is referred to as autonomy. Philosophers and political economists also disagree about how much this potential autonomy guides and informs government and the formation of institutions and regimes. The more that civil society informs institutions, the more it is thought to have popular sovereignty. Furthermore, to the extent that civil society is generated by the authentic interests of citizens, instead of the interests of the state or interests of business, it is semiautonomous.

Wapner[10] notes that civil society theories emanate from two main competing theories of civil society found in de Tocqueville's *Democracy in America*,[11] first published in 1835, and Gramsci's *Prison Notebooks* (1891–1937). We briefly explore each of these theories in order to better understand the problem of social change more thoroughly.

The context for the original content of both the *Prison Notebooks*, written in fragmented pieces in a fascist Italian prison, and *Democracy in America*, written when the United States maintained legal protections for a slave-based economic system, have changed. However, the conceptual foundations for both provide analytical building blocks are relevant today at multiple political scales, including international governance. For global politics, the relevant dynamics are those between transnational movements and NGOs as civil society organizations, firms and industry coalitions as economic society organizations, and states and state-led organizations in the international system as political society organizations.

Alexis de Tocqueville, a French aristocrat who toured the United States in 1831–1832, observed that the United States enjoyed an unusually high degree of civic involvement. Usually his vision of civil society is used to explain to explain US democratic pluralism; however, we can see that the pluralist vision of international civil society reflects his perspective as well. De Tocqueville was ambivalent about American democracy, but he believed it relied on a rich US civil society of numerous groups that were operating at the time he toured the United States. He believed that this involvement was both autonomous and sovereign. He describes US voters approving legislative representatives and these representatives being responsive to the opinions of the people. De Tocqueville writes, after describing elections for representatives, that "therefore, in reality, it is the people who rule. Although they have a representative government, it is quite clear that the opinions, bias, concerns, and even the passions of the people can encounter no lasting obstacles preventing them from exercising a day-to-day influence upon the conduct of society."[12] Even more impressive is that in this approach, the opinions of the people are guided by concern for the overall welfare of the republic and less concerned about their own individual agendas: "In the United States, as in any country ruled by the people, the majority governs in the name of the people. The majority is chiefly made up of peaceable citizens who, out of inclination or self-interest, sincerely seek the good of the country."[13]

In the end, de Tocqueville believed the people wielded enormous power and that the government was responsive to these influences, and he went so far as to say, "The people reign in the American political world like God over the universe. It is the cause and aim of all things, everything comes from them and everything is absorbed in them."[14]

Today, scholars like Robert Putnam find that when people go out of their homes and get involved in groups, often informal ones, in public, they build networks of knowledge, trust, and reciprocity that can be used to solve problems and come to collective decisions for the collective good.[15] In addition, in a world with a semiautonomous and sovereign civil society, naked power grabs for narrow private interests are counterbalanced by transnational citizens deliberating with each other while they meet in public and make demands as both domestic and cosmopolitan constituents. Thus, the formation of vital social worlds involves knowledge, such as through skills people possess but also through active monitoring of current events reported by an independent media.

Furthermore, as citizens are more involved and personally learn about the lives of their domestic and transnational neighbors, deep inequality is less tolerable. It is assumed that a deeply connected transnational civil society will demand a more egalitarian distribution of goods (opportunities, rights, and wealth) and bads (pollution, disease, and barriers) and work against discrimination as well as unearned privilege. In this way, the de Tocqueville school of thought sees civil society as a critical link for citizens and government to attend to the public good, as opposed to neighbors who serve only themselves and a government that serves only elites. If civil society is robust, social capital will be strong, deep inequalities will be addressed, and governance will serve the larger welfare of a national community. Civil society will have groups that disagree, but this school of thought does posit that a more active civil society will provide stronger social capacity to solve problems accountably and serve justice, and this will always serve the interests of stronger and more equitable democratic regimes. If civil society is weak and social capital wanting, we can isolate ourselves from our neighbor's suffering and will not be forced to care about the problem, and we will have fewer resources to solve the problem anyway. In particular, if civil society is not strong, the fields of politics will be unchecked and despotism can operate with impunity. Quite simply, our Tocquevillian answer to global environmental problems, in the literature and I presume in many of our classrooms, is "Build a social movement!"[16]

However, if Gramsci was right, civil society is not so nearly independent or influential as Tocquevillians presume if civil actors internalize the interests of ruling elites or industry as their own, which occurs through hegemony. Instead of blunt coercive power, hegemony occurs through the consent of civil society, but this consent is often manipulated through long historical arrangements of the state and economic powers rarely in the true interests of the general public good. Hegemonic power "educates" the educators about what to teach, and citizens voluntarily submit to hegemonic power because this influence is adequately mundane and ubiquitous as to be invisible. In other words, the ideas of the ruling class infuse the everyday lives of working-class citizens through civil associations like parties, unions, churches, schools, and environmental groups in such a way that the work-ing class confuses these ideas and interests for their own.

This means that governing arrangements must include the voluntarism and consent of the masses, but that this consent and voluntarism can be produced in ways consistent with the status quo—and rather than being revolutionary, civil society participates in its own suppression through obe-dience to a mundane set of unquestioned norms. Paul Robbins, in his bril-liant exploration of the coercive lawn economy in the United States, makes a good example.[17] Robbins notes that the lawn, an actor that we must respond to, has rather costly needs. Rather than ask, "Why a turf grass lawn for my front yard?" we tend to obey the norms—deeply civic ones that imply we are a poor citizen if we neglect our lawns—which means we deploy enormous resources and labor to maintain a false ecology of typi-cally nonnative vegetation. The very mundane nature of lawns allows for their continuity because they are a "normal" function of our everyday lives. Yet should we break from this hegemonic ensemble of civic norms, county and city ordinances, homeowner association rules, and social governance by refusing to add necessary fertilizers, poisons, and water or cut it regularly so that it is perpetually green (impossible), we will feel the coercive arm of this arrangement through fines. In some cases, neighbors or cities will invade the turf and cut the lawn despite you. These norms were not created by accident; they were facilitated and grown in part by class-based fantasies of mini-British estates and a politically active turf grass industry that built demand, so the turf grass economy only appears to be a "free" market on the surface. As in Gramsci's hegemony, the turf grass economy is founded within the larger coalition of historical arrangements, or historical blocs, which coordinate the political, economic, and civil societies to stabilize not only economic forces like production but social meaning.

Historical blocs allow for capitalist forces, such as big agriculture or big pharma, to rule as the goals of capitalist forces are incorporated into the state and civil society as partners. Thus, the historical bloc is more than just a political alliance; it is, rather, the profound integration of a variety of class interests propagated throughout society in a way that promotes not just a harmony of political and economic aims but also a wider cultural and moral unity. As activists internalize the moral unity of capitalist interests into something like corporate sustainability, the power of environmental activists is used to support capitalism more than challenge it. Unfortu-nately, it appears that global environmental efforts are subsumed under this kind of hegemony; Dauvergne and LaBaron note that activists themselves have not lost their enthusiasm or earnest desire for a better world, but certainly since the 1980s, they argue that activists have internalized corporate interests, where now there are far fewer radicals calling for deep structural change.[18] Note here the concurrence with Erik Assadourian's observation in the next chapter that the environmental movement has lost an important edge: its autonomy. Where Assadourian calls for a missionary-like project that can make sense of loss and grief and instill a sense of purpose, I call for public autonomy that understands its own interests.

Civic power may be won or lost in conflict, usually conflict about public opinion about the material facts of life and the forces of economic production:

Public opinion is the political content of the public's political will that can be dissentient; therefore, there is a struggle for the monopoly of the organs of public opinion—newspapers, political parties, parliament—so that only one force will mold public opinion and hence the will of the nation, while reducing dissenters to individual and disconnected specks of dust.[19]

In Western democracies, we inherit the notion that civil society is made up of a plurality of voices with many agendas competing for episodic political influence over policy that play out on an even battle field. However, this inheritance may neglect important possibilities that the state or corporate spheres are behind what appear to be a plurality. We can represent these as intensities along a grid, as in figure 9.1.

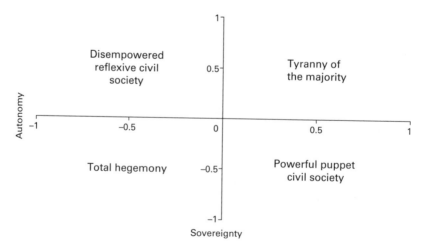

Figure 9.1
Power Intensities of Civil Society

Arenas of Domination

At its most basic form, politics is the intersection of power in the public sphere and the forces that guide, persuade, and coerce how we live together. At this point in history, civil associations extend well beyond domestic politics to create a global civil society that works across boundaries.

In thinking how we live together globally, Paul Wapner has established that civil society can affect global politics by changing the conditions below, above, and around the state and the state system through campaigns that affect our sensibilities, empower local people and groups, or alter the interdependent interests of states.[20]

Sensibilities are formed in a political space, described by political scientist Joel Migdal as "arenas of domination and opposition." These arenas are "not necessarily spatially limited but ... a conceptual locus where significant struggles and accommodations occur among social forces."[21] What is at stake in the arenas of domination goes far beyond state-led policy compromises to the struggle for "the basic moral order and the very structure within which the rights and wrongs of everyday social behavior should be determined."[22] This is the soil from which institutions grow, shaped by the basic moral order of the time produced through the power of the dominant historical bloc. These arenas are found in at least the world markets, mass media, science, education, corporate boardrooms, and the halls of policymakers.

Here, certain social paradigms become dominant, and the core, mundane conditions of ways of thinking and being become institutionalized, acted on, and made real. Many political theorists see the formation of these mundane expressions as formative conditions to the lived rules of society. These are the arenas where domination forms and the limits to social change are bounded by the broad moral order. This order is neither liberatory nor oppressive on its own; where lives are governed in the broadest terms, there is governmentality and it is a goal of the global environmental movement to alter the way global civilization governs its relations with Earth's cycles and systems, as well as nonhuman life. To do this, the global environmental movement must alter the moral order that governs the key arenas, like the financial markets, commodities, resource use, and firms that operate in each area.

Civil society has access to and is subject to these instruments of power, and it is here that Wapner, and many others (myself included), believe the stakes are high:

Unfortunately, the problems of the globe do not turn merely on academic debate or the refinement of intellectual categories. The world faces dangers that threaten all living beings on earth. The greenhouse effect, ozone depletion, species extinction, and so forth are threats to the very infrastructure that supports life on earth. Addressing them properly is one of the most considerable responsibilities currently facing human beings. *The task at hand involves changing widespread behavior. It is a first order of politics.*[23]

The global environmental movement has affected the way lives are governed, but what remains unanswered is this: At what scale and to what effect on a New Earth? Migdal makes an important distinction relevant to my argument:

Some social forces gain paltry sorts of power over limited numbers of people on only a narrow range of issues, while finding themselves substantially transformed by their engagement with other social forces. Others, through an adept mix of sanctions, rewards, and meaningful symbols, can experience power more broadly without giving up too much in terms of their original aims.[24]

Activist networks can circumvent local oppression and multiply resources, voices, and alternative ideas that may otherwise be suppressed locally. Transnational environmental NGOs and the larger global environmental movements have had varied impacts on reconstructing discourses and meaning, exploit windows of opportunity in state imperatives, and have successfully used pressure tactics to make progress on environmental protection by overturning centuries of cornucopian perceptions. The global environmental movement has gained important inroads, but not in the arenas of domination that bound the moral order of economic life. While the global environmental movement has affected issue areas in some regions, such as recycling and air quality in the global North or the protection of some of the very last living representatives of Earth's endangered species in some regions, it has not had the expansive impact on other issue areas like the rules for financial credit, bonds, or the formation of commodity chains, with the scale that the dominant economic values have directed institutions and other macroconditions. I propose that this limit explains why environmentalism and environmental laws continue to expand but major boundaries for a habitable Earth continue to be violated. And even as the scale of environmentalism as a sentiment has increased to cover more people in the world, social change has been limited to individual consumption options and other individual actions that do not affect the moral order of the world economics. Ironically, because the dominant ideology of liberalism is individualistic, it assumes a greater agency of individuals and thereby favors a Tocquevillian notion of civil society, while the ideology also promotes counterrevolutionary forces that narrow this very agency to make a difference at larger societal scales.

The Moral Order of Growth: Enlightenment Liberalism and Its Evolution

Growth, especially economic growth, is the goal of all states and firms. If there are states and firms that do not want to generate growing revenues, I don't know about them. Vastly different regime types and political economies have pursued an industrial growth with enthusiasm, where Western states and the former Soviet Union were equally committed to industrialized growth. The argument here is not that only liberal and neoliberal world orders pursue growth but rather the ways the moral order has shifted to permit the conditions and rules of growth.

Embedded Liberalism

The classical form of liberalism is centered on individual rights, particular to private property, limited government power, a preference for certain forms of science and engineering, a fear of planning. and other elements of what is now called the dominant social paradigm (DSP).[25] In the post–World War II period, the Bretton Woods Accord of 1944 established what Ruggie called "embedded liberalism,"[26] where "international market liberalization hinged on a *compact between state and society* to mediate its most deleterious effects"[27] operating largely through Keynesian macroeconomic policies until 1970. Importantly, markets are central arenas of domination: "In the organization of a liberal order, pride of place is given to market rationality."[28] However, exposed to the volatility and danger of market forces, domestic workers demanded social insurance via the welfare state, and some in the form of capital controls to suppress economic swings of the boom and bust business cycle, all to attenuate the crises and social disorganization that capitalism causes. This form of liberalism saw the state as an essential counterbalance to market forces, a critical protector of civil rights, and a guide for capital controls affected by International Monetary Fund requirements for real value to anchor currencies through the gold standard. Development and protection of the middle class is particularly important, as is avoiding the worst economic and social inequalities and disruptions, and this provided the conditions for public support of the embedded liberal compact.

These expectations of an interventionist state also form the foundation of most modern environmental laws that are now deemed an essential role of the modern state. US environmental policies developed during this time were made as part of the social contract to allow for economic growth. However, embedded liberalism has now given way to a new form, neoliberalism, which moves away from the social compact and pursues a rather more violent form of international market capitalism.

Neoliberalism

Neoliberalism began when President Nixon abandoned the gold standard in 1971, thereby releasing important limits to capital movement, and was fully developed by the 1978–1980 period when Deng Xiaoping began to liberalize China and Prime Minister Margaret Thatcher and President Ronald Reagan took office in 1979 and 1980 to create a remarkable alliance against state intervention, unions, social safety nets, and capital controls. Under the Reagan-Thatcher alliance, the social contract of embedded liberalism was abandoned for deregulation, privatization, and the removal of social controls over capital flows with the singular goal of capital growth and accumulation regardless of the consequences.

Led by the United States and United Kingdom, neoliberalism has spread nearly everywhere with a firm presence in Latin America and the Anglo-American states, and even China demonstrates important neoliberal tendencies under a state-controlled capitalism:

Almost all states, from those newly minted after the collapse of the Soviet Union to old-style social democracies and welfare states such as New Zealand and Sweden, have embraced, sometimes voluntarily and in other instances in response to coercive pressures, some version of neoliberal theory and adjusted at least some policies and practices accordingly.[29]

Neoliberalism holds sway among the core arenas of domination in international financial institutions, education, corporate boardrooms, media, and state administrative and financial units as the historical bloc of our time: "Neoliberalism has, in short, become hegemonic as a mode of discourse. It has pervasive effects on ways of thought to the point where it has become incorporated into the *common-sense* way many of us interpret, live in, and understand the world."[30]

That neoliberalism has succeeded in the most important arenas of domination to control the basic moral order and determines the most important structures of global political economy is a key driver of New Earth crises. In addition, neoliberalism concentrates power and wealth in a specific transnational business elite because it moves global surplus value and income to a very small group of people at the expense of a very large group of people and the Earth. Under a neoliberal moral order, growth has no responsibilities to strengthening equality or public welfare found in ecological safeguards and indeed was founded by economists who were wholly opposed to these social goals.[31]

It is uncontroversial that most of the world needs to consume more to live well, and access to better food, water, energy, and infrastructure, which require growth, are themselves injured in this system that directs increasing wealth and energy to those who need it least. Global inequality between and within countries has grown dramatically, where those in the top 5 percent income control a third of the wealth in the whole world—the same amount as the poorest 80 percent.[32]

Indeed, neoliberalism ascended as the modern global environmental movement matured; meanwhile environmental problems and environmental regimes have continued to grow. In real terms, we are currently accelerating global climate change, the sixth great extinction, and Promethean shifts in atmospheric, marine, and soil chemistry; meanwhile, human efforts control about half of the non-ice land and freshwater, not to mention the vast changes to structure and function of the ocean. At the same time, environmental regulations have grown between and within countries; environmental protection is now presumed to be a role of the modern state, and sustainability is a widely shared goal around the world.

What do these facts mean? I propose that environmental regimes and global environmentalism have been complicit in the "end of nature"[33] and that global civil society efforts have been soundly compromised. Regimes are formed by consenting states on piecemeal problems but will not be formed to curb economic growth or global inequalities, the real causes of the piecemeal problems. In a very real way, we are rearranging the deck chairs on a sinking ship.

Global Civil Society on a New Earth

There's always free cheddar in the mousetrap, Baby.
—From Tom Waits, "God's Away on Business"

Embedded liberalism forged a compromise for social welfare with liberal markets. The motive for states to enter the social contract was to maintain civil consent to legitimize market capitalism in the postwar period. However, once states chose to remove limits to capital, the consent of the governed itself has not taken a notable revolutionary turn. Why?

I propose that the answer lies in counterrevolutionary forces that have established a new common sense in the most important arenas of domination while civil society itself has lost substantial autonomy and sovereignty. The evidence for this proposition is found in three facts:

1. *Stop global whining.* Counterrevolutionary forces have successfully limited access of environmental civil society to the corridors of real power while accumulating billions of dollars in countermovement machinery just in the early years of the new century, laundered as "dark money." These forces have successfully internationalized and spread a populist program.
2. *Plant a tree, buy a bike.* Where environmentalists have been successful in affecting popular sentiments, solutions are narrowed through an individualization of responsibility and commodification of dissent.
3. *And, there's always free cheddar in the mousetrap, Baby.* Environmental groups themselves have changed tactics to coordinate with firms because that is where they see possible gains for protections, and firms take these partnerships on to demonstrate corporate citizenship and legitimacy. This maintains the hegemonic historical bloc of capital elites, NGOs, and state agents—economic society, civil society, and political society.

Stop Global Whining

There is a well-documented and coordinated effort to counter knowledge claims about global environmental changes in order to avoid the civic and ontological problem that is quite obvious if these problems were acknowledged to be indicators for critical life support systems.[34] Early research illustrated the successful tactics of reframing environmental problems as "nonproblems";[35] later work has been able to show how tightly organized these efforts are through pro-market conservative ideology and the conservative movement centered in the United States, and otherwise almost exclusively found in the Anglo-American countries of the former British Empire such as the United Kingdom, Australia, and Canada.[36] If civil society movements typically organize based on resources and opportunities from the grassroots for change in the status quo, those threatened will be beneficiaries of the status quo—elites, who tend to organize countermovements through counterrevolutionary projects like the environmental skepticism and climate denial countermovement that reject the authenticity of global environmental changes and threats to sustainability. Evidence from social science research shows that, perhaps counterintuitively, the efforts to deny environmental problems like human-caused climate change are getting stronger and more successful even as advancing science becomes more certain. Dunlap and Jacques show that the countermovement has successfully spread the seeds of the original elite-led project to a more populist audience of nonelites and more countries.[37] And Robert Brulle[38] has demonstrated that the "denial machine"[39] had accumulated a war chest of $7 billion of capital from corporations donating anonymously through foundations ("dark money") such that the average climate denial counter-movement organizations had an average of $900 million just in the eight years between 2003 and 2010.

In this case, counterrevolutionary forces are those working to preserve the legitimacy of capitalist hegemony that has caused climate and other global environmental changes. Marcuse[40] and Cockett[41] both note *preemptive* and advanced counterrevolutionary forces in civil society: "The Western world has reached a new stage of development: now, the defense of the capitalist system requires the organization of counterrevolution at home and at abroad."[42] We can see the preemptive counters to true sustainability are organized through free market think tanks, nonprofits, and foundations that appear as public interest groups.

Plant a Tree, Buy a Bike …

In a landmark article, Michael Maniates elegantly described a common conclusion we find ourselves facing after coming to terms with the mounting global ecological crisis—this is the "So what do we do about it?" part of so many conversations we have with our students and each other.[43] The easiest answer is to buy green products or even boycott bad ones. However, as Maniates indicates, this makes the very act of dissent a commodity, and the answers are all about what the individual can do. I take this to mean that the global environmental movement has indeed successfully transformed sentiments in many individuals, but the arena of domination is that of a smaller scale and the moral order is to act responsibly as an individual and propose solutions that do not cause a nuisance. Individualization of responsibility and the commodification of dissent conveniently leave unmolested the arenas that govern the structural bases for production, consumption, inequality and other social stratification, and the ultimate drivers for global environmental problems, not to mention the dynamics of global finance, the growth of the bond market, the growth of credit combined with salary suppression, rising commodity prices, and emergent semiperiphery countries as global economic powers.[44]

Meanwhile, civic power has been transformed to a crude arithmetic that reproduces interests of a ruling class through increasing inequality: "Under neoliberalism, citizenship became equity: the more shares or wealth, the more votes or influence. As the bottom 90% had little wealth other than their citizenship claims on states, the greater limitations on these institutions meant that they were also politically poorer.:[45]

Free Cheddar in the Historical Bloc

Gramsci understood historical blocs to be formed dynamically in coalitions of business, civil society, and the state. Under contemporary political economic opportunities, transnational NGOs now organize their efforts more often in collaboration with corporations.[46] One potential reason global environmentalism has failed to penetrate arenas that govern political economic structures is that global environmental civil society has failed to exploit the cracks in the capitalist foundation for embedded, then neoliberal historical blocs, instead actually strengthening them. Under Gramsci's notion of "war of position," a long-term vision of subordinate and subaltern groups coordinate to expose cleavages in the moral order. NGOs in the global environmental movement have largely worked to solidify the historical bloc of elites, providing legitimacy, and missed opportunities for organizing a war of position to the extent that they coordinate with transnational firms and provide a stability for political, economic, and civil societies. And this appears to be one answer to our question, "How do we proceed from here?" Global civil society can create coalitions that expose the cracks within the hegemonic historic coalitions and the moral order, all with a goal of changing the basic operating principles of world civilization that facilitate unequal hoarding of surplus value that drives immiseration, merciless inequality, and our ecological planetary crisis. In other words, one of the basic operating principles of world civilization is economic growth. The current rules of growth funnel resources and power to elites, while impoverishing the least well off and the Earth. This basic operating principle requires our permission, and global environmental activists could work in concert with other revolutionary forces, like the world indigenous and peasant movements,[47] to remove this consent and dislodge the apparent consensus of the neoliberal moral order.

Conclusion

Boyd has convincingly demonstrated an important structural change among the state system, where 178 of 192 countries now have liberal constitutional provisions for the right to live in a healthy environment.[48] In addition, it appears likely that environmental quality is now a nearly universal responsibility of the state. Further, there are now more environmental institutions domestically and internationally than ever before, and the "global society" that is strengthened by these institutions may have a cumulative impact, not just an additive one, on limiting environmental change.[49] In addition, "The environmental movement, which had domestic origins in the West, became institutionalized in the world polity, generating new associations on a global scale."[50] The global environmental movement has grown.

Yet we speed headlong into this New Earth. Concomitant with these moves is the power of neoliberalism that places the interests of capital over the Earth and society facilitated not only by states and firms but civil society as well.

I argue that environmental civil society has not penetrated the deep structures that govern and empower the most important drivers of environmental change in "market civilization" through growth in global finance and the bond market, along with the growth of credit combined with salary suppression, rising commodity prices, emergent semiperiphery countries as global economic powers, and breathtaking global income inequality. These forces are determined in arenas or fields of politics where economism dominates and reproduces historical blocs that provide a stable basic moral order for a violent and rapacious form of growth. Meanwhile, environmental solutions have been narrowed to green consumerism of products that civil society has little control over, not to mention knowledge of, given opaque global commodity chains that unravel ecologies and societies. In order to produce counterhegemonic progress, civil society must assess the long-term field, form enduring autonomous alliances, and strategically demonstrate that markets do not have a universal mandate to chew through the web of life and the critical life supports of world civilization.

Notes

1. *Global* in this chapter does not refer to evenly distributed phenomena around the planet, but uneven transnational networks, effects, and linkages.

2. Young, "Effectiveness of International Environmental Regimes."

3. Dauvergne, "The Environmental Challenge to Loggers in the Asia Pacific."

4. See W. Cox, *Business and the State in International Relations*, 1; Keck and Sikkink, *Activists beyond Borders;*[1] Wapner, *Environmental Activism and World Civic Politics;* Lipschutz and Mayer, *Global Civil Society and Global Environmental Governance.*

5. Gill, "Globalization, Market Civilization, and Disciplinary Neoliberalism."

6. Harvey, "Revolutionary and Counter Revolutionary Theory in Geography."

7. Ibid.

8. Peet and Watts, *Liberation Ecologies.*

9. Boggs, Carl, *Ecology and Revolution.*

10. Wapner, *Environmental Activism and World Civic Politics.*

11. Tocqueville, *Democracy in America.*

12. Ibid.

13. Ibid.

14. Ibid.

15. Putnam, *Bowling Alone.*

16. A social movement is a collective effort organized by civil society actors with a common cause to mobilize others to achieve political and normative changes in the world, including policy changes or changes in political ideals. It is important however, to distinguish between NGOs (individual actors) and movements (coherent organized efforts across and between groups of actors).

17. Robbins, *Lawn People.*

18. Dauvergne and LeBaron, *Protest Inc.*

19. Gramsci, Prison Notebooks..

20. Wapner, *Living through the End of Nature.*

21. Migdal, "The Power and Limits of States."

22. Joel S. Migdal, "The State in Society."

23. Wapner, *Environmental Activism and World Civic Politics.*

24. Migdal, "The Power and Limits of States."

25. Dunlap and Van Liere, "Commitment to the Dominant Social Paradigm."

26. Ruggie, "International Regimes, Transactions, and Change."

27. Ruggie, "Globalization and the Embedded Liberalism Compromise."

28. Ruggie, "International Regimes, Transactions, and Change."

29. Harvey, *A Brief History of Neoliberalism,* 3.

30. Ibid.

31. Cockett, *Thinking the Unthinkable.*

32. Milanovic, *Worlds Apart*.

33. Wapner, *Living through the End of Nature*.

34. Jacques, "The Rearguard of Modernity"; Jacques, *Environmental Skepticism*.

35. McCright and Dunlap, "Challenging Global Warming."

36. Jacques, Dunlap, and Freeman, "The Organization of Denial."

37. Dunlap and Jacques, "Climate Change Denial Books and Conservative Think Tanks"; Dunlap and Jacques. "Manufacturing Uncertainty."

38. Brulle, "Institutionalizing Delay."

39. Begley et al., "The Truth about Denial"; Dunlap and M. McCright, "Organized Climate Change Denial."

40. Marcuse, *Counterrevolution and Revolt*.

41. Cockett, *Thinking the Unthinkable*.

42. Marcuse, *Counterrevolution and Revolt*.

43. Maniates, "Individualization."

44. Clapp and Helleiner, "International Political Economy and the Environment."

45. Centeno and Cohen, "The Arc of Neoliberalism."

46. Corson, "Shifting Environmental Governance in a Neoliberal World."

47. Ridgeway and Jacques, *The Power of the Talking Stick*.

48. Boyd, *The Environmental Rights Revolution*.

49. Schofer and Hironaka, "The Effects of World Society on Environmental Protection Outcomes."

50. Longhofer and Schofer, "National and Global Origins of Environmental Association."

Bibliography

Begley, Sharon, Eve Conant, Sam Stein, Eleanor Clift, and Matthew Philips. "The Truth about Denial." *Newsweek*, August 13, 2007, 20–27, 29.

Boggs, Carl. *Ecology and Revolution: Global Crisis and the Political Challenge*. New York: Palgrave Macmillan, 2012.

Boyd, David R. *The Environmental Rights Revolution: A Global Study of Constitutions, Human Rights, and the Environment*. Vancouver: University of British Columbia Press, 2011.

Brown, Wendy. "American Nightmare: Neoliberalism, Neoconservatism, and De-Democratization." *Political Theory* 34 (2006): 690–714.

Brulle, Robert J. "Institutionalizing Delay: Foundation Funding and the Creation of U.S. Climate Change Counter-Movement Organizations." *Climatic Change* (2013): 1–14. doi:.10.1007/s10584-013-1018-7

Bunker, Stephen G. *Underdeveloping the Amazon: Extraction, Unequal Exchange, and the Failure of the Modern State.* Chicago: University of Chicago Press, 1985.

Bunker, Stephen G., and Paul S. Ciccantell. *Globalization and the Race for Resources.* Baltimore, MD: John Hopkins University Press, 2005.

Carroll, William K. "Transnationalists and National Networkers in the Global Corporate Elite." *Global Networks* 9 (2009): 289–314. doi:.10.1111/j.1471-0374.2008.00255.x

Centeno, Miguel A., and Joseph N. Cohen. "The Arc of Neoliberalism." *Annual Review of Sociology* 38 ((2012): 317–40. doi:.10.1146/annurev-soc-081309-150235

Chotikapanich, Duangkamon, William E. Griffiths, D. S. Prasada Rao, and Vicar Valencia. "Global Income Distributions and Inequality, 1993 and 2000: Incorporating Country-Level Inequality Modeled with Beta Distributions." *Review of Economics and Statistics* 94, no. 1 (2010): 52–73. doi:.10.1162/REST_a_00145

Clapp, Jennifer, and Eric Helleiner. "International Political Economy and the Environment: Back to the Basics?" *International Affairs* 88 (2012): 485–501. doi:.10.1111/j.1468-2346.2012.01085.x

Cockett, Richard. *Thinking the Unthinkable: Think-Tanks and the Economic Counter-Revolution, 1931–83.* Waukegan, IL: Fontana Press, 1995.

Corson, Catherine. "Shifting Environmental Governance in a Neoliberal World: US AID for Conservation." 42 (2010): 576–602.

Cox, Ronald W. *Business and the State in International Relations.* Boulder, CO: Westview Press, 1996.

Dauvergne, Peter. "The Environmental Challenge to Loggers in the Asia Pacific." In *The Business of Global Environmental Governance*, edited by David L. Levy and Peter J. Newell, 169–96. Cambridge, MA: MIT Press, 2005.

Dauvergne, Peter. *The Shadows of Consumption: Consequences for the Global Environment.* Cambridge, MA: MIT Press, 2008.

Dauvergne, Peter, and Genevieve LeBaron. *Protest Inc.: The Corporatization of Activism.* Hoboken, NJ: Wiley, 2014.

de Tocqueville, Alexis. *Democracy in America and Two Essays on America.* Translated by G. E. Bevan. New York: Penguin Classic, 2003.

Deleuze, Gilles, and Félix Guattari. *A Thousand Plateaus: Capitalism and Schizophrenia*. Minneapolis: University of Minnesota Press, 1987.

Dirzo, Rodolfo, and Peter H. Raven. "Global State of Biodiversity and Loss." *Annual Review of Environment and Resources* 28 (2003): 137–67. doi:.10.1146/annurev.energy.28.050302.105532

Dryzek, John, Daid Downs, Christian Hunold, David Schlosberg, and Hans-Kristian Hernes. *Green States and Social Movements: Environmentalism in the United States, United Kingdom, Germany, and Norway*. Oxford: Oxford University Press, 2003.

Dunlap, Riley E., and Peter J. Jacques. "Climate Change Denial Books and Conservative Think Tanks: Exploring the Connection." *American Behavioral Scientist* 57 (2013): 699–731. doi:.10.1177/0002764213477096

Dunlap, Riley E., and Peter J. Jacques. "Manufacturing Uncertainty: Conservative Think Tanks and Climate Change Denial Books." In *Yale Forum on Climate Change and the Media*. New Haven, CT: Yale University, 2013.

Dunlap, Riley E., and Aaron M. McCright. "Organized Climate Change Denial." In *The Oxford Handbook of Climate Change and Society*, edited by John S. Dryzek, Richard B. Norgaard, and David Schlosberg. 144–60. Oxford: Oxford University Press, 2011.

Dunlap, Riley E., and Kent D. Van Liere. "Commitment to the Dominant Social Paradigm and Concern for Environmental Quality." *Social Science Quarterly* 65 (1984): 1013–28.

Foster, John Bellamy, Bret Clark, and Richard York. *The Ecological Rift: Capitalism's War on the Earth*. New York: New York University Press, 2011.

Foucault, Michel. *Society Must Be Defended: Lectures at the Collège de France, 1975–76*. Translated by D. Macey. New York: Picador, 2003.

Frank, David John, Ann Hironaka, and Evan Schofer. "The Nation-State and the Natural Environment over the Twentieth Century." *American Sociological Review* 65 (2000): 96–116.

Gill, Stephen. "Globalization, Market Civilization, and Disciplinary Neoliberalism." *Millennium* 24 (1995): 399–423.

Gramsci, Antonio. *Prison Notebooks*. vols. 1–3. New York: Columbia University Press, 1996.

Guha, Ramachandra. *The Unquiet woods: Ecological Change and Peasant Resistance in the Himalaya*. Berkeley: University of California Press, 2000.

Harvey, David. *A Brief History of Neoliberalism*. Oxford: Oxford University Press, 2005.

Harvey, David. "Revolutionary and Counter Revolutionary Theory in Geography and the Problem of Ghetto Formation." *Antipode* 4 (2) (1972): 1–13. doi:.10.1111/j.1467-8330.1972.tb00486.x

Jackson, Jeremy B. C. "Ecological Extinction and Evolution in the Brave New Ocean." *Proceedings of the National Academy of Sciences of the United States of America* 105 (Supp. 1) (2008): 11458–65. doi:.10.1073/pnas.0802812105

Jacques, Peter J. *Environmental Skepticism: Ecology, Power, and Public Life.* Burlington, VT: Ashgate, 2009.

Jacques, Peter J. "The Rearguard of Modernity: Environmental Skepticism as a Struggle of Citizenship." *Global Environmental Politics* 6 (2006): 76–101.

Jacques, Peter J., Riley E. Dunlap, and Mark Freeman. "The Organization of Denial: Conservative Think Tanks and Environmental Scepticism." *Environmental Politics* 17 (2008): 349–85.

Josephson, Paul. *Industrialized Nature: Brute Force Technology and the Transformation of the Natural World.* Washington, DC: Island Press, 2002.

Keck, Margaret E., and Kathryn Sikkink. *Activists beyond Borders: Advocacy Networks in International Politics.* Cambridge: Cambridge University Press, 1998.

Laxer, Gordon, and Dennis Soron. *Not for Sale: Decommodifying Public Life.* Peterborough, Ontario: Broadview Press, 2006.

Ledeen, Michael A. *Tocqueville on American Character: Why Tocqueville's Brilliant Exploration of the American Spirit Is as Vital and Important Today as It Was Nearly Two Hundred Years Ago.* New York: St. Martin's Press, 2001.

Leiserowitz, Anthony A., Robert W. Kates, and Thomas M. Parris. "Sustainability Values, Attitudes, and Behaviors: A Review of Multinational and Global Trends." *Annual Review of Environment and Resources* 31 (2006): 413–44. doi:.10.1146/annurev.energy.31.102505.133552

Levy, David L., and Peter J. Newell. "A Neo-Gramscian Approach to Business in International Environmental Politics: An Interdisciplinary, Multilevel Framework." In *The Business of Global Environmental Governance,* edited by David L. Levy and Peter J. Newell, 47–69. Cambridge, MA: MIT Press, 2005.

Lipschutz, Ronnie D., and Judith Mayer. *Global Civil Society and Global Environmental Governance: The Politics of Nature from Place to Planet.* Albany, NY: SUNY Press, 1996.

Longhofer, Wesley, and Evan Schofer. "National and Global Origins of Environmental Association." *American Sociological Review* 75 (2010): 505–33. doi:.10.1177/0003122410374084

Maniates, Michael F. "Individualization: Plant a Tree, Buy a Bike, Save the World?" *Global Environmental Politics* 1, no. 3 (2001): 31–52. doi:.10.1162/152638001316881395

Marcuse, Herbert. *Counterrevolution and Revolt*. Boston: Beacon Press, 1972.

McCormick, John. *Reclaiming Paradise: The Global Environmental Movement*. Bloomington: Indiana University Press, 1991.

McCright, Aaron M., and Riley E. Dunlap. "Challenging Global Warming as a Social Problem: An Analysis of the Conservative Movement's Counter Claims." *Social Problems* 47 (2000): 499–522.

Migdal, Joel S. "The Power and Limits of States: Struggles for Domination Between States and Societies." In *Waves, Formations and Values in the World System*, edited by S. Weltgesellschaft, V. Bornschier, and P. Lengyel. 2:213–34. New Brunswick, NJ: Transaction, 1992.

Migdal, Joel S. "The State in Society: An Approach to Struggles for Domination." In *State Power and Social Forces: Domination and Transformation in the Third World*, edited by Joel S. Migdal, Atul Kohli, and Vivienne Shue, 7–34. Cambridge: Cambridge University Press, 1997.

Milanovic, Branco. *Worlds Apart: Measuring International and Global Inequality*. Princeton, NJ: Princeton University Press, 2011.

Miles, Edward L. "On the Increasing Vulnerability of the World Ocean to Multiple Stresses." *Annual Review of Environment and Resources* 34, no. 1 (2009): 17–41. doi:.10.1146/annurev.environ.33.041707.110117

Mitchell, Ronald B. "International Environmental Agreements: A Survey of Their Features, Formation, and Effects." *Annual Review of Environment and Resources* 28 (2003): 429–61. doi:.10.1146/annurev.energy.28.050302.105603

Onaran, Özlem. "From Wage Suppression to Sovereign Debt Crisis in Western Europe: Who Pays for the Costs of the Crisis?" *International Journal of Public Policy* 7 no. 1 (2011): 51–69. doi:.10.1504/ijpp.2011.039575

Peet, Richard, and Michael Watts. *Liberation Ecologies: Environment, Development, Social Movements*, 2nd ed. New York: Routledge, 2002.

Putnam, Robert D. *Bowling Alone: The Collapse and Revival of American Community*. New York: Simon and Schuster, 2000.

Ridgeway, Sharon, and Peter Jacques. *The Power of the Talking Stick: Indigenous Politics and the World Ecological Crisis*. Boulder, CO: Paradigm Publishers, 2013.

Robbins, Paul. *Lawn People: How Grasses, Weeds, and Chemicals Make Us Who We Are*. Philadelphia: Temple University Press, 2007.

Robinson, William I. "Global Capitalism Theory and the Emergence of Transnational Elites." *Critical Sociology* 38 (2012): 349–63. doi:.10.1177/0896920511411592

Ruggie, John G. "Globalization and the Embedded Liberalism Compromise: End of an Era?" In *Internationale Wirtschaft, nationale Demokratie: Herausforderungen für die Demokratietheorie*, edited by W. Streek, 79–97. Frankfurt: Campus Verlag, 1998.

Ruggie, John G. "International Regimes, Transactions, and Change: Embedded Liberalism in the Postwar Economic Order." *International Organization* 36 (1982): 379–415. doi:.10.1017/S0020818300018993

Rupert, Mark. "(Re-)Engaging Gramsci: A Response to Germain and Kenny." *Review of International Studies* 24 (1998): 427–34.

Schofer, Evan, and Ann Hironaka. "The Effects of World Society on Environmental Protection Outcomes." *Social Forces* 8, no. 1 (2005): 25–46.

Steffen, Will, Paul J. Crutzen, and John R. McNeill. "The Anthropocene: Are Humans Now Overwhelming the Great Forces of Nature?" *Ambio: A Journal of the Human Environment* 36, no. 8 (2007): 614–21.

Szasz, Andrew. *Shopping Our Way to Safety: How We Changed from Protecting the Environment to Protecting Ourselves*. Minneapolis: University of Minnesota Press, 2007.

Vitousek, Peter M., Harold A. Mooney, Jane Lubchenco, and Jerry Melillo. "Human Domination of Earth's Ecosystems." *Science* 277 (1997): 494–99.

Wapner, Paul. *Environmental Activism and World Civic Politics* . Cambridge, MA: MIT Press. 1996.

Wapner, Paul. *Living through the End of Nature: The Future of American Environmentalism*. Cambridge, MA: MIT Press, 2010.

Young, Oran R. "Effectiveness of International Environmental Regimes: Existing Knowledge, Cutting-Edge Themes, and Research Strategies." *Proceedings of the National Academy of Sciences of the United States of America* 108 (50) (2011): 19853–60. doi:.10.1073/pnas.1111690108

10 Converting the Environmental Movement into a Missionary Religious Force

Erik Assadourian

"New Earth" is perhaps too generous a way to describe the future planet that the remnants of human civilization will most likely live on. "Venus Junior" may be more accurate. With governments and corporations already working to mine tar sands and oil shale, to drill deep water oil deposits, including under the now-thawing Arctic, and even to capture natural gas from frozen methane hydrates (all while continuing to mine coal and drill current oil and gas reserves), a radically hotter world than civilization developed in seems highly likely. That's a world where average atmospheric temperatures are 4°C,[1] 5°C, even 6°C hotter,[2] where the North Pole is again nearly ice free, where the western Antarctic ice sheet has collapsed,[3] and much of the coastal land where many people now live has been submerged. Yes, that nightmarish reality might take a few centuries to manifest, but it seems clear that this is the future we're choosing for ourselves and that the environmental movement tacitly accepts.

Preventing that future—if that's even possible at this late stage in the game—will require a radical reformation of the environmental movement, as either a bolder political force as Peter Jacques discusses in chapter 9, or even as a religious missionary force (or ideally both). The movement has taken neither form thus far—at least in any significant way—and might not be able to fill either niche, but in its current "soundly compromised" form where it prioritizes incremental reform, the catastrophic future we're heading for is all but certain (see chapter 9). Yes, the movement is helping to modestly slow down the ecological transition (or "collapse" from a human's perspective), but in the end, this will mean only that the collapse comes a few years or decades later. Until a radical redesign of the movement is orchestrated, we can expect little more than this.

In this chapter, I critique the current form of the environmental movement, which at its best is doing little more than slowing the spread of the global cancer that human civilization currently has become and at its worst is legitimizing the unsustainable growth and consumer culture that the movement is embedded in. I then propose an alternative design of the movement—one that could reintegrate humanity as a functional and healthy part of a larger Earth system. Specifically, I apply the lessons from over 2,000 years of missionary religious organizing to the environmental movement to see how these lessons could lead to more enduring success for the movement. While the speed of this type of change may be too slow to prevent civilizational collapse, it may turn out to be exactly the strategy needed to get humanity through the ecological transition, which at this point appears unstoppable, and rebuild in a manner that prevents further human-triggered collapses in the future.

The Roots of the Environmental Movement

How far back does one go to describe the environmental movement? Can it be pinpointed to the tumultuous 1960s and 1970s when Rachel Carson warned that forever more, springs may be silent of birdsong? When the Club of Rome warned that human civilization had reached the limits to growth? When Paul Ehrlich warned that the future would be plagued by mass starvation unless we slowed population growth? Do we stick to when the United States passed monumental clean air and clean water legislation and the world united around a new understanding of Earth as a borderless entity—facilitated by the first images of the planet taken from space—and came together to celebrate Earth Day?

Or do we have go back further to the conservation movement of the late 1800s and early 1900s when groups like the Sierra Club got their start or earlier in the 1800s when authors like Henry David Thoreau and Ralph Waldo Emerson inspired a transcendental relationship with nature?

Or was it even before that when the thick black smog from industrialization started causing new illness and mortality in cities like London when the first signs of the industrial revolution's ravages became unmistakable?[4] These are battles that have never stopped and often now take the mantle of "environmental justice."

Or maybe we have to go much further back: when first societies created myths, rituals, and taboos to prevent poor stewardship of essential resources—whether sacralizing forests, banning certain foods during certain times of the year, or ritually redistributing wealth to prevent overconsumption, hoarding, and inequity?[5]

All of these could be argued as the starting point of the environmental movement perhaps. In fact, none of these really ever disappeared, continuing to work in parallel—sometimes in unconnected ways, sometimes in symbiosis, sometimes even in conflict—such as when one NIMBY ("not in my back yard") struggle conflicts with a broader global environmental agenda. But if we're talking about today's environmental movement—one deeply associated with charismatic megafauna and global issues like ozone depletion, toxic waste, and, most recently, climate change—I would argue that this movement has existed in its modern form since the first nonprofit environmental organizations created multinational franchises or subsidiaries. This took a series of disparate and relatively unconnected but similar (in biological terms, "convergent") struggles and created a global unifying presence that could direct resources around the world and help set (or even trump) local priorities.

Sometimes this has proved advantageous—shepherding rich country resources to developing country battlegrounds—and other times less so, such as when environmental organizations serve as collaborators with corporations whose local agendas are directly at odds with the goals of long-term environmental stewardship.

In certain cases, this global standardization process led to positive results, including international cooperation on key environmental issues, like phasing out chlorofluorocarbons, preventing cross-border water conflict, and banning toxins like persistent organic pollutants. It has also led to subtler benefits, like creating civil society power where it was relatively weak or suppressed to help orchestrate environmental action and redirect the destructive pursuit of progress. Western nongovernmental organizations entering China (see chapter 12) and post-Soviet states, for example, have helped create a core of environmental energy there and helped to build and fund the movement, creating political space for homegrown activists, support for those activists, and international recognition (which also helped to increase their protection against persecution).[6]

The Corruption of Environmentalism

Sometimes, however, international civil society has had a less beneficial influence. In 2004, conservationist Mac Chapin wrote a critique of the conservation community's work in Latin America and how it often ignored, marginalized, disempowered, even displaced the indigenous community as it worked to protect biodiversity hotspots.[7] And while in theory the movement should have learned that this is not a model for success, the marginalization of essential constituencies and powerful potential partners continues. Similar stories to Chapin's continue to be told about initiatives like the REDD+ (Reducing Emissions from Deforestation and Forest Degradation) mechanism. While designed to slow deforestation and incentivize additional forestation, critics argue that REDD+ is leading to the conversion of forests into monocropped tree plantations, undermining indigenous peoples' conservation efforts, and even propping up extractive industries.[8]

These stories aren't limited to the distant forests of developing countries. Tom Goldtooth, executive director of the Indigenous Environmental Network, noted that even 350.org, often viewed as the new face of the United States (and even the global) climate movement, resisted engagement with indigenous people. "We had to challenge them to bring us to stand with them on the pipeline issue," noted Goldtooth in 2011.[9]

Perhaps as problematic is that many organizations accommodate the political realities of the consumer societies of which they're part—either consciously or unconsciously—and so at best they work to slow ecological decline, not fight to create an entirely new sustainable reality. Some, like Ted Nordhaus of the Breakthrough Institute, defend this position by explaining that development is inevitable: "The question isn't whether Brazil is going to develop the Amazon, it's how. You have to think about how you're going to work with that process as opposed to resist it."[10] When moderating development is the starting point of the struggle, the end point can at best be an "ecodeveloped" Amazon (read: condominiums, malls, factories, stadiums, and farms, built with green materials and running on renewable energy). But considering the global ecological importance of the Amazon to a stable climate and preserving biodiversity, if development is inevitable, so is our eventual collapse.

Worse is that most multinational environmental organizations have fully embraced their part in the industrial-consumer paradigm, even if they self-identify as correctives to this system. From large salaries and posh office buildings, regular global travel junkets, and many of them actively partnering with corporations, to nearly all of them failing to question growth and having investments[11] in the very system that has to be radically changed to have any chance at preventing runaway climate change and other catastrophic disruptions of Earth's systems, these organizations are in no position to foment the scale of change needed to create a sustainable future for the 9.6 billion people the United Nations projects will be inhabiting Earth in 2050.[12]

But even worse is many organizations now suffer from undue influence from corporations—in the research, health advocacy, and environmental communities. With many organizations taking millions of dollars in donations and having corporate leaders on their boards, this has not only weakened the independence of these organizations but provided a vehicle for some of the dirtiest corporations to "greenwash" themselves. Accepting funding from corporations, which have millions of dollars available to invest in public relations efforts, has misdirected organizations from the true challenges facing them. Moreover, it has led some groups to soften their criticism of supportive companies and in some cases has even led to questionable endorsements of polluting companies or their products.[13]

As journalist Christine MacDonald writes in *Green, Inc.*, of those corporations listed in the Political Economy Research Institute's Toxic 100 (a list of the worst corporate air polluters in America), twenty-nine are major contributors to conservation organizations.[14] While it isn't easy to identify how much influence these contributions provide companies, it is hard to imagine that these relationships provide no influence at all. David Morine, a former vice president in charge of land acquisition at the Nature Conservancy, after leaving the organization, discussed with the *Washington Post* that his pioneering effort to bring in corporate funders "was the biggest mistake in my life." "These corporate executives are carnivorous," he explained, "you bring them in, and they just take over."[15]

How does this corporate influence affect organizational priorities and willingness to advocate for the difficult changes necessary—such as economic degrowth and the curtailing or even dismantling of unsustainable industries? And with most groups receiving funding from affluent donors and foundations, both of which depend on a growing economy that allows the wealthy to continue their philanthropy, will these groups really risk alienating their funders and members advocating for the tough remedies the planet needs?

What True Sustainability Will Require

The mainstream environmental movement has made itself into an incremental change agent at best—saving a percentage of forests slotted for logging or habitat to be drilled, stopping a percentage of the new power plants being built, and accelerating the growth of renewables even when the real battle is not shifting to less unsustainable technologies like renewables but curbing energy and material use to a point that makes the consumer lifestyle impossible. After all, renewables also take massive amounts of upfront energy to build and additional energy to maintain.[16] Ultimately the only way we get to a sustainable future is by reining human civilization back within planetary boundaries, and that will require dramatic degrowth of energy and material usage, consumption, and the total population of both humans and its dependent species, including livestock and pets, none of which will be very popular positions to take.[17]

There's a lack of honesty in the movement when we talk about what sustainability is going to require on the New Earth. For any chance at a sustainable future, we are going to have to radically reduce consumption, especially if justice continues to be a priority and we want to provide additional resources to the most impoverished among us to increase their chances of having a decent quality of life. In that context and in the context of a growing population,[18] the only thing that can give is how many of us live the lifestyles of consumers.

The ecological footprint, while not a perfect indicator (for one, it is far too conservative), does offer a rough benchmark of how many people the Earth can sustain. At current consumption levels, for example, humanity is using 1.5 planets worth of biocapacity.[19] In other words, we're undermining planetary stability as we burn through Earth's ecological capital. At our current global average consumption level, the Earth could sustain just 4.4 billion people without undermining the well-being of the Earth's systems. And if everyone consumed like Americans, the Earth could support only a quarter of today's population. On the flip side, if we lived very humbly (at a $3,000 per capita annual income rate, as in low-income countries), the Earth could support nearly double our current population.[20] Naturally, few people would choose such an "impoverished" lifestyle and no mainstream environmental organization would dream of advocating for this. Worse, with global marketers and policymakers pushing growth and increased consumption worldwide—and projections estimating that another 1 billion people will join the ranks of consumers by 2025[21]—this extreme reining in of human consumption probably won't happen unless major ecological changes force us to live like that.

But what about attempting to converge around a one-planet footprint? William E. Rees and Jennifer Moore calculated a one-planet footprint and found that it is dramatically smaller than what high-income consumers take for granted (see table 10.1).[22] Calorie consumption is a third less, meat consumption 80 percent less, living space just a quarter, and air travel just 4 percent of what it is in a high-income country.[23] Most striking is the number of cars per person: while there is one car per 2 people in a high-consumption society, in a one-planet society there is just one

Table 10.1

Comparing Fair Earth-Share, World Average, and High-Consumption Countries

Consumption Measures (per Capita)	Fair Earthshare: 1 Planet	World Average: 1.5 Planets	High Consumption: 3 Planets
Daily calorie supply	2,424	2,809	3,383
Meat consumption (kg/year)	20	40	100
Living space (m2)	8	10	34
People per household	5	4	3
Home energy use (GJ/year)	8.4	12.6	33.5
Home energy use (kWh/year)	2,300	3,500	9,300
Motor vehicle ownership	0.004	0.1	0.5
Motor vehicle travel (km/year)	582	2,600	6,600
Air travel (km/year)	125	564	2,943
Carbon dioxide emissions (tons/year)	2	4	14
Life expectancy (years)	66	67	79

Source: From Moore and Rees, "Getting to One-Planet Living"

car per 250 people.[24] In a city like Washington, DC, with a population of about 620,000, that means a vehicle fleet of just 2,500 cars. Giving priority to emergency vehicles, public transit, and shared cars (taxis, car sharing, and rentals), that means essentially no private car ownership, something Americans will be even more reluctant to do than cutting their meat intake by 80 percent.[25] Of course, there would be some significant health benefits to shifting over to a one-planet lifestyle, such as having far fewer people overweight or obese because they'd be eating less and walking more. After Cuba's transition to a one-planet lifestyle—due to a lack of oil access after the collapse of the Soviet Union, not enlightened environmental consciousness—the country's obesity rate halved, plunging from 14 percent in to 7 percent in just 5 years (1990–1995).[26] While it has since risen to 19 percent, it is still far lower than the 35 percent obesity rate in the United States.[27]

Moore and Rees's one-planet calculations assume today's population, however. Add another 2.4 billion—the UN's medium-growth projection for 2050—and these standards will have to drop even further.[28] So how can a mainstream environmental movement—dependent on donations from consumers, foundations, corporations, and rich individuals who have profited off these consumer trends—advocate for the radical changes necessary? Are organizations blind to the fact that it is the Western consumer culture that has caused the environmental crisis, or is it that organizations' continuing financial stability depends on keeping their eyes willfully shut to that truth? Either way the environmental movement as currently designed is failing to "save the planet" or, more correctly, prevent radical ecological changes that will lead the Earth, in comedian George Carlin's words, to "shake us off like a bad case of fleas."[29]

So where do we go from here? Assuming we don't want to wait patiently for the collapse to wipe out humanity and the Earth to heal and repopulate its biological diversity millions of years from now after the sixth wave of extinction runs its course, how should the environmental movement reform itself? And by "reform itself," I mean in the sense that Martin Luther broke some minority of Christians away from the decadent Catholic church. The majority of environmental groups (i.e., the Catholic church) will continue to be part of the established order committed to minor incremental change (e.g., green growth) while living affluent lifestyles. While they will most likely remain as the dominant player, a new wave of energy and authenticity could come from the Lutheranesque upstarts and over the coming decades bring environmentalism in a radically new direction.

Considering the massive scale of change necessary, I see one strategy as superior to others: the creation of environmentalism as a missionary philosophical movement. While this certainly will be met with ambivalence at first glance, it should be considered a real alternative to the ineffectual strategies currently employed by the mainstream environmental movement. I hope my detailing of this will at least spark a deeper introspection within the movement's membership, leadership, and supporters and perhaps even trigger the hammering of some treatises upon a door or two.

Cultivating an Ecological Philosophical Missionary Movement

What have been the most successful and long-lasting movements in history? Democracy? Capitalism? Expansion of human rights in a variety of forms? Or should we go back far further to the spreading of entire ways of being—religious belief systems that provide codes of ethics, offer an understanding of how the world works, and promise guidance in how to achieve a better life now and in the future, even after death. Religions, over millennia, "changed the basic principles of world civilization," as Peter Jacques points out in chapter 9. This is what a true sustainability movement will need to do too. The fact that Christianity, Islam, Buddhism, and other religions have spread and remained dominant social and cultural forces for the past few thousand years, and across a wide variety of geographic and cultural realities, reveals the power in this type of organizing: for the long term, around a deeper way of being and acting, and not just around a specific short-term campaign goal.

The environmental movement must learn lessons from this—to understand that it needs to espouse a comprehensive philosophy and use its core energy to spread that philosophy first and foremost. That's not to say this shift would mean renouncing working to achieve shorter-term political goals (today's missionary movements are no stranger to political engagement), only that those immediate campaigns are subordinated to longer-term missionary movement building.

By "comprehensive philosophy," I mean the creation of an ethics, cosmology, theodicy, rituals, even stories of redemption that could deeply affect people and change the way they live. There have been some attempts at this already. Arne Naess, in 1973, criticized the anthropocentric "shallow" environmental movement and advocated for "deep ecology," which included eight principles that could be at the heart of people's personal ecological philosophies.[30] One problem with that approach, however, is that it's not easy to organize a missionary philosophical movement if everyone gets to make their own personal "ecosophy."

Vaclav Havel, the Czech writer and political leader, once asked, "What could change the direction of today's civilization?" He answered, "We must develop a new understanding of the true purpose of our existence on this Earth. Only by making such a fundamental shift will we be able to create new models of behavior and a new set of values for the planet."[31] Offering a purpose of life should be the starting point of any philosophy. What is our purpose? Why do we have consciousness and the power to shape the planet's long-term development? While both religion and science have offered different answers to this question, neither has been able to answer in a way that allows humanity to live within the bounds of a flourishing planet. An ecomissionary philosophy could offer a new purpose—one as simple as helping the Earth to flourish and at the very least not developing in a way that impedes Earth's ability to do so. As deep ecology's first principle notes, "The flourishing of human and nonhuman life on Earth has inherent value. The value of nonhuman life-forms is independent of the usefulness of the nonhuman world for human purposes."[32] Ensuring that the nonhuman world thrives may be at the heart of any ecomissionary's creed.

This purpose would also help shape the ethical code that a philosophical system requires. The ethics of an effective ecophilosophy would need to be fully grounded in Earth's ecological realities and should facilitate humanity's Earth-nurturing purpose. As conservationist Aldo Leopold noted over sixty years ago, "A thing is right when it tends to preserve the integrity, stability, and beauty of the biotic community. It is wrong when it tends otherwise."[33] This simple rule could serve as a foundation for a broader ecological ethics. Of course, considering how far we've trespassed beyond Earth's limits, this will not be an easy ethical code to follow. Obeying an Earth ethic will mean tough sacrifices and giving up many modern luxuries—and some things taken today to be fundamental rights (such as the ability to be as "fruitful" as one would like). But better to make sacrifices than to accelerate Earth's decline, and if the movement was organized in a way that provides other life wisdom and communitarian benefits, these might outweigh the tough moral requirements. Look, for example, at the Shakers, who because of their economic success and strong community grew to a peak of 6,000 adherents, even though being a Shaker required celibacy—a far higher bar than having fewer children and giving up air-conditioning would be.[34]

Beyond ethics, this philosophy would need to provide an updated theodicy—or understanding of suffering. Ancient theodicies rely on ancient understandings of the world. God's punishment or testing of faith or karma often serves to explain away bad fortune. But humans are capable of more nuanced understandings of the world now, including why we suffer. Grasping that the Earth is a complex, self-organizing system means certain forms of suffering are natural: prey/predator relationships, for example, or the chaos caused by violent planetary change like volcanic eruptions or earthquakes. But some other forms of suffering stem from imbalance, such as when one population grows unchecked, whether that be populations of homo sapiens or cancer cells. Distinguishing between forms of suffering and minimizing preventable types, while finding mantras and rituals to accept that which isn't preventable, could serve people far better than many theodicies available today.

Having a robust theodicy will be especially important in getting through the next centuries, when, even in the best case, there will be massive life loss and suffering as sea levels rise from thermal expansion and a collapsing western Antarctic wipes cities and even entire countries off the map. God's (or Gaia's) wrath could serve to explain these losses, but a more nuanced understanding of system change may lead to a healthier coping with those changes (e.g., settling on higher land rather than having faith that God will protect us no matter where we settle).

Beyond codes and creeds, any effective philosophy will provide means to bond communities in celebration and mourning. As theologian and environmentalist Martin Palmer notes, "Environmentalists have stolen fear, guilt and sin from religion, but they have left behind celebration, hope and redemption."[35] The problem is that fear without hope, guilt without celebration, and sin without redemption is a model that fails to inspire or motivate. Thus, creating rituals to mark birth, marriage, death, and annual cycles like the coming of a new year that both celebrate human life and our dependence on the planet will play a key role in developing a strong missionary philosophy. If done well, these rituals can also be a restorative ecological force rather than an ecological drain as they often are today. With the average funeral costing over $10,000 in the United States and using massive amounts of resources (concrete, woods, steel, and toxic chemicals) to inter loved ones, it would be hard to design a more unsustainable way to celebrate death if we tried.[36] But redeveloping this ritual, as the green burial movement is doing, could make death into a driving force for ecological restoration, burying the body simply (in just a shroud) in a natural setting that becomes a sacred forest of the future, in the process sequestering carbon, providing community parkland and food, and providing a space for biodiversity and ecosystem services to rebuild themselves (as opposed to the pesticide-laden monocropped cemetery that's typical today). In addition to this, the accompanying funeral ritual could celebrate life, helping mourning friends and loved ones understand that they are part of a larger life cycle, that like the proverbial ocean wave, we should not be afraid of the impending shore as we are actually part of the larger ocean. The body of a loved one will become the food of the forest and eventually the bodies of future generations. While this may not be as satisfying an end as eternal life, it's arguably better than the successful end of the karmic cycle: oblivion.

Could this mix of a hard-edged ethics, new stories, a more nuanced understanding of suffering, and a set of restorative rituals be attractive enough to pull in adherents? Perhaps the whole package could add up to a robust, holistic ecological philosophy that could inspire people across cultures to follow a new ecocentric way of life. If religious systems based on aliens or supernatural beings can spread around the world, it seems that a system based on a living but nonsentient planetary organism—one that science demonstrates we depend completely on for our survival—should absolutely be able to. But the biggest point that Naess misunderstood in promoting his deep ecology is that no philosophies spread without the hard work of missionary organizing, and developing those mechanisms will be at least as important as creating the philosophy itself.

Spreading Philosophies through Social Service Provision

How have missionary religious philosophies been so successful in spreading across cultures, times, and geographies? (Religions, while they are understandably more than this to adherents, are essentially orienting philosophies.) Certainly forced adoption of these philosophies by populations was part of their success (whether driven by converted leaders or invading forces). But more than this was the effective mix of a powerful philosophy combined with a timeless vision, beautiful stories, committed adherents, and perhaps most important, the promise of immediate assistance—the offering of food, clothing, education, livelihoods, medical care, even a supportive community.

As the breakdown of the climate system and other ecosystem services progresses in this century, the need for assistance will only increase—in the most impoverished countries as well as in fully consumerized societies. In places like the United States, for example, few people have retained basic survival skills—whether life skills like food cultivation, carpentry, sewing or repair, or specialized skills like midwifery or basic first aid. As complex societies break down and fewer people can access the fruits of the consumer economy (or depend on it for a livelihood), fewer will have access to medical care, schooling, support during elderly years, or even basic access to food or shelter (something readily visible reading the news about the Great Recession, Spain and Greece's depressions, the breakdown of the Soviet Union, and even the Great Depression of the 1930s). Providing aid, community support, and the skills needed to survive will offer a means to help people in this transition and, as important, provide a means to convert people from the currently dominant ecologically destructive consumer ideology to a more ecocentric and humanistic one.

The Christian socialism movement of the 1800s offers a relevant case study for this transition.[37] Christians, witnessing the destructive effects of rapid urbanization and the poverty that came with it, created social programs, including job training, food pantries, and safe housing for people immigrating to the cities. The goal was not to simply aid those in need but to spread Christianity, capturing the hearts, minds, and labor of the recipients of their aid.[38] This was the time when the Salvation Army and the YMCA were created, which today continue to have a global reach, reaching out to tens of millions of people, and distributing billions of dollars of social services in over 110 countries.[39] Imagine what an environmental movement could do with the same missionary zeal that the Salvation Army exhibited.

Look for example at Kibera, one of the largest slums in Africa. An informal survey of this slum found that of the roughly 250 schools serving the 200,000 to 250,000 Kenyans living there, nearly half are religious in nature.[40] The charitable goal of these religious schools is to provide a basic education to Kiberans, a service the Kenyan government cannot provide enough of. But these schools are also there to save souls and add members to their philosophical communities.

At the same time, there appear to be no schools in Kibera teaching an ecological philosophy. But imagine if there were. Imagine a school that at every turn reinforces the idea that humanity depends completely and utterly on Earth and its complex systems for our well-being; that it is unjust to consume more than your fair share and to have a lifestyle that depends on the exploitation of ecosystems, workers, and communities polluted by factories, mines, and dumps; and that the best life to live is one committed to changing this untenable, inhumane, and unsustainable system in ways that improve the well-being of your local community, your broader philosophical community, and, above all, the planetary community.

This is a philosophy that could be reinforced in every aspect of the school—from what is taught in the classroom (ecology, ethics, activism, and permaculture along with basic math and literacy) to what is served in the lunchroom and everything in between. Some students would walk away just with knowledge, including a better understanding of our dependence on Earth and perhaps basic livelihood and trade skills—skills that will grow in value in a postconsumer future. Others would walk away with a deep commitment to this way of thinking, and perhaps even become missionaries of that ecological philosophy, starting new schools or other social services that could improve people's lives while spreading a way of life that could compete with the seductive consumerist philosophy.[41]

And this model could be applied to a variety of needs. Ecoclinics could provide basic medicine but also focus on prevention that will help both people and the planet. For example, people with adult-onset diabetes might be asked to spend time tending the ecoclinic garden in partial payment for treatment, growing healthy food to replace the toxic, processed fare that contributed to their diabetes and so many other modern ailments. The clinic could also provide cooking and lifestyle courses as well as engaging with the larger community to help patients eat well and regain their health. In the process, their ecological impact would shrink along with their waistlines as they reduced their consumption of meat and processed food, both of which have larger ecological impacts than locally grown vegetables.[42]

Of course, social service provision is expensive, suggesting this new movement may be as dependent on members and foundations as today's movement is. But some of the services provided could be profitable social enterprises that help fund other more costly social services. The Shakers were known for their excellent herbs and craftsmanship. High-quality food production could play a similar role, as could providing key medical services like midwifery. Medicalized birth is expensive, both ecologically and financially, and typically leads to worse outcomes for baby and mother than allowing nature to lead the process.[43] In many countries, including the United States, midwifery is a lost art, and the demand for these services exceeds their supply. Making an ecophilosophy synonymous with high-quality midwifery and doula services could gain adherents through successfully helping mothers to have a healthy pregnancy, birth, and postnatal recovery, including supporting women in the breastfeeding process rather than using less healthy and less sustainable formula. And in the process, they could generate revenue that supports both these practitioners and the broader movement.

Hence social enterprises—like the YMCA's successful gym model and the Salvation Army's secondhand clothing and furniture sales—could play a key role in building a positive feedback cycle to spread this new missionary philosophy. And as the number of lives that these eco-missionaries touch grows, so does the potential for social modeling and friendships to lead to further spreading of the philosophy. As adherents invite friends and neighbors to join a celebration, a wedding, a weekly service, additional people may find their way aligns closer to this worldview than more ancient ones, and thus the movement could grow.

Finally, as numbers grow, some of the energy could be used to bolster immediate political goals—helping mainstream environmentalists in their campaigns, and with their deeper commitment perhaps even playing an outsized role than their small numbers might suggest possible. The Quakers (the Religious Society of Friends) could be an instrumental model for eco-missionaries. This small Christian sect became a dominant economic and political force of Pennsylvania in the 1700s as well as a major force in the abolition movement.[44] Today the Quakers continue to be a powerful voice in international peace and governance processes—far larger than what their total membership of 340,000 would seem to warrant.[45] Eco-missionaries could do the same, engaging in political resistance efforts, and working both inside and outside the system toward the cultural, social, economic, and political change needed (all the while also trying to gather additional adherents to the cause).

The Long Decline and Eventual Rebirth of Civilization

The long decline is on its way—and probably coming much sooner than we think. Climate change alone will prevent human civilization from following a path of more growth, more progress, more "development." It is almost a certainty that there will be major political, social, and economic disruptions; a flood of failing states; the dislocation of millions of people; and wars.[46] As ecosystems unravel, economies falter, and local and national governments go bankrupt or adopt austerity measures to appease lenders, there is a good chance that basic social services will be cut and poverty will grow significantly. Who will fill this vacuum of providing order and basic services? Will it be fundamentalist religious institutions that read the breakdown of ecosystems and society as signs of the end times, or authoritarian governments that offer security in exchange for the last remnants of freedom?

Will either of these forces bring us closer to a sustainable future, or will they bring us further away as they either ignore the ecological restoration needed or, worse, do more damage as they fight over diminishing resources with other imperial governments (fighting, for example, over new resources and lands now available within the Arctic Circle)?

Let's imagine a scenario where instead, adherents of an ecological philosophy come out on top. As sociologist Rodney Stark has found, early Christians survived ancient epidemics in larger numbers because of the mutualistic support members offered each other (made more normal by Christian teachings).[47] More so, their aiding of out-group members (e.g., pagans) ended up helping those fortunate pagans to survive in higher numbers and, often, to convert to Christianity (some, perhaps, out of gratitude or awe, some because their own networks were suddenly much smaller as not-so-fortunate pagans didn't survive the epidemic).[48] Both higher survival rates and high conversion rates helped the rise of Christianity into a dominant religion, even from its tiny starting base.[49]

A strategic mix of essential knowledge retention (particularly in permaculture and essential preventive and medical care), in-group mutual assistance, and missionary aid could play a key role in helping ecophilosophical adherents to both survive the turbulent times ahead in larger numbers and spread their philosophy to many new converts, grateful for the help they received in surviving too.

This in turn could enable these adherents to help redirect the future of humanity to a more ecocentric path as they become a relatively larger, and thus more influential, proportion of surviving humanity. After the dust

settles and new states stabilize, it is possible that this ecomissionary movement (whatever specific name it takes) will have grown large enough to
become a major force in rebuilding civilization and could seed a new harmonious way of relating to the Earth as well as prevent a new growth-
centric/imperial culture taking root.

I can even imagine a day where ecocracies (ecological theocracies)
become the dominant form of state—just as Christian, Islamic, and Bud-
dhist kingdoms guided the world throughout the Middle Ages. Surely these
ecocracies will not be without their problems; no human institution is.
There may even be wars about meaningless nuances of their philosophy or
warring factions of eco-missionaries, as we have seen historically with other
philosophical and religious movements. It is hard to imagine a future where
human conflict is no longer, but if it is waged in a way that neither harms
the planet nor diminishes the prospects of the long-term survival of civilization, perhaps that is a worthy enough outcome to pursue.

Taking the Difficult First Steps on This New Road

While starting a new ecophilosophical missionary movement is surely not
a comfortable discussion topic for most in the environmental movement,
this may offer more hope of saving humanity than the current populist
form of light green environmentalism. While telling middle-class consumers that "you can save the planet in ten easy steps," (with number 10 being
"donate to our organization") makes people feel better, it has shown its
extreme limitations. Clearly that kind of semiuseful or even counterproductive organizing will continue, but perhaps a more enlightened minority
will be enough to bring us a new, deeper environmentalism that can help
us get through the collapse and build a truly sustainable future at the
other end.[50]

The big question is, How do we take the first steps down this road? Does
it require a gathering of committed individuals to hammer out a first draft
of the philosophy to be shaped over the coming decades? Does it require
entrepreneurs to start building social enterprises and social services, embed-
ding philosophical elements within the goods and services provided?
Does it require reformers within the environmental movement working to
ratchet up the role of mainstream environmental movements? Yes, yes, and
yes. All of these and far more is required to get us to a more useful and
enduring environmentalism—one that I hope can push us toward a new
ecocentric future that centuries from now will be built around a billion

or so people living simple, fulfilling lives—lives that will be able to be sustained for millennia by a flourishing Earth, rather than cause a seventh, eighth, then ninth wave of mass extinction, as humans keep repeating the ecocidal growth cycle beyond a scale Earth can sustain.

Notes

1. Potsdam Institute, *Turn Down the Heat.*

2. Lynas, *Six Degrees.*

3. Sumner, "West Antarctic Ice Sheet Is Collapsing."

4. Hanlon. "Pollution and Mortality in the 19th Century."

5. Gardner, "Engaging Religions to Shape Worldviews" and "Ritual and Taboo as Ecological Guardians."

6. Larson, "China's Emerging Environmental Movement." See also, for example, the Global Greengrants Fund and the Goldman Prize for two examples of Western efforts to help support and legitimize the global environmental movement.

7. Chapin, "A Challenge to Conservationists."

8. Cabello, and Gilbertson, *NO REDD: A Reader.*

9. Sharife, "Climate Change, the Big Corrupt Business?"

10. Ted Nordhaus as quoted in Rosner, "Is Conservation Extinct?"

11. Klein, "Time for Big Green to Go Fossil Free."

12. United Nations, "World Population Prospects."

13. MacDonald, *Green, Inc.*

14. Ibid., 25–28.

15. Ibid., 58–60; Ottaway and Stephens, "Nonprofit Land Bank Amasses Billions."

16. Murphy, Jr., "Beyond Fossil Fuels."

17. Moore and Rees. "Getting to One-Planet Living."

18. Due to population momentum, even scenarios with significant expansion of family planning efforts still result in a larger population (albeit not as large as current projections). See, for example. Bradshaw and Brook, "Human Population Reduction Is Not a Quick Fix for Environmental Problems."

19. WWF, *Living Planet Report 2014.*

20. Calculations by author, based on ibid.

21. McKinsey Global Institute, *Urban World.*

22. Moore and Rees, "Getting to One-Planet Living."

23. Ibid.

24. Ibid.

25. Ibid.

26. Murphy and Morgan, "Cuba," and Manuel Franco et al, "Population-Wide Weight Loss and Regain in Relation to Diabetes Burden and Cardiovascular Mortality in Cuba 1980–2010.

27. National Center for Health Statistics, *Health, United States, 2014.*

28. United Nations, "World Population Prospects."

29. *George Carlin: Jammin' in New York*, Cable Stuff Productions, HBO, April 24, 1992.

30. Naess, *The Ecology of Wisdom.*

31. Havel as quoted in Speth, Foreword.

32. Naess, *The Ecology of Wisdom.*

33. Leopold, *A Sand County Almanac.*

34. *Ken Burns' America: The Shakers*, Public Broadcasting System, 1985. This number may have grown far larger; however, the Shakers' economic model of producing high-quality goods was unable to compete with industrialization and the cheap products this brought.

35. Palmer quoted in Grady, "Using Religious Language to Fight Global Warming."

36. Harris, *Grave Matters.*

37. Stewart J. Brown taught an ecclesiastical history course at the University of Edinburgh, "The Social Gospel in Britain, Germany, and the United States, 1870–1920," that explored this topic.

38. Hattersley, *Blood and Fire.*

39. *The YMCA Blue Book*; YMCA, "Mission," at www.ymca.int/who-we-are/mission; Salvation Army USA, *The Salvation Army 2012 Annual Report* (2012); The Salvation Army International, "About Us," at www.salvationarmy.org/ihq/about.

40. Population and area from Karanja, "Myth Shattered," and Maron, "Kibera's Census: Population, Politics, Precision." School calculation based on Map Kibera's

education database at www.mapkibera.org, December 11, 2012, and on Maron, Map Kibera Trust, e-mail to author, December 11, 2012.

41. Erik Assadourian, "The Living Earth Ethical Principles: Life of Service and Prepare for a Changing World," *World Watch Magazine*, May/June 2009, pp. 34–35.

42. Assadourian, "The Living Earth Ethical Principles: Right Diet"; Walpole et al., "The Weight of Nations."

43. Jan Blustein and Jianmeng Liu, "Time to Consider the Risks of Caesarean Delivery for Long Term Child Health," *BMJ* 2015, 350:h2410.

44. Crothers, *Quakers Living in the Lion's Mouth*.

45. Friends World Committee for Consultation, *Finding Quakers Around the World*; see American Friends Service Committee, afsc.org/afsc-history.

46. Potsdam Institute, *Turn Down the Heat*; Welzer, *Climate Wars*.

47. Stark, *The Rise of Christianity*.

48. Ibid.

49. Ibid.

50. Research by Erica Chenoweth and Maria J. Stephan finds that only 3.5 percent of the population is needed to succeed in nonviolent civil resistance (albeit acting in an engaged, active, and sustained manner). If these more deeply engaged adherent-activists were cultivated through deeper, longer-term philosophical organizing, the movement, even with smaller numbers, may be far more effective than one based in a larger number of loosely engaged followers. See Chenoweth, "The Success of Nonviolent Civil Resistance"; and Erica Chenoweth and Maria J. Stephan, *Why Civil Resistance Works*.

Bibliography

Assadourian, Erik. "The Living Earth Ethical Principles: Life of Service and Prepare for a Changing World," *World Watch Magazine* (May/June 2009): 34–35.

Assadourian, Erik. "The Living Earth Ethical Principles: Right Diet and Renewing Life Rituals," *World Watch Magazine* (November/December 2008): 32–33.

Bradshaw, Corey J. A., and Barry W. Brook. "Human Population Reduction Is Not a Quick Fix for Environmental Problems." *Proceedings of the National Academy of Sciences of the United States of America* 111, November 18, 2014, 16610–15. doi:.10.1073/pnas.1410465111

Cabello, J., and Gilbertson eds. *NO REDD: A Reader*. December 2010. http://noredd .makenoise.org.

Chapin, Mac. "A Challenge to Conservationists." *World Watch Magazine* (November/December 2004): 17–31.

Chenoweth, Erica. "The Success of Nonviolent Civil Resistance." *TedX Boulder,* September 21, 2013.

Chenoweth, Erica, and Maria J. Stephan. *Why Civil Resistance Works: The Strategic Logic of Nonviolent Conflict.* New York: Columbia University Press, 2012.

Crothers, A. Glenn. *Quakers Living in the Lion's Mouth.* Gainesville, FL: University Press of Florida, 2012.

Franco, Manuel. "Population-Wide Weight Loss and Regain in Relation to Diabetes Burden and Cardiovascular Mortality in Cuba 1980–2010: Repeated Cross Sectional Surveys and Ecological Comparison of Secular Trends." *BMJ,* April 9, 2013.

Friends World Committee for Consultation. *Finding Quakers around the World.* Philadelphia: Friends World Committee for Consultation, 2007.

Gardner, Gary. "Engaging Religions to Shape Worldviews." In *State of the World 2010,* edited by Linda Starke and Lisa Mastny. New York: Norton, 2010.

Gardner, Gary. "Ritual and Taboo as Ecological Guardians." In *State of the World 2010,* edited by Linda Starke and Lisa Mastny. New York: Norton, 2010.

Grady, Helen. "Using Religious Language to Fight Global Warming." *BBC Radio,* January 25, 2010. http://news.bbc.co.uk/2/hi/sci/tech/8468233.stm.

Hanlon, W. Walker. *"Pollution and Mortality in the 19th Century."* UCLA and NBER, 2015.

Harris, Mark. *Grave Matters: A Journey through the Modern Funeral Industry to a Natural Way of Burial.* New York: Scribner, 2007.

Hattersley, Roy. *Blood and Fire: William and Catherine Booth and Their Salvation Army.* New York: Doubleday, 2000.

Karanja, Muchiri. "Myth Shattered: Kibera Numbers Fail to Add Up." *Daily Nation,* September 3, 2010.

Klein, Naomi. "Time for Big Green to Go Fossil Free." *Nation* (May 2013): 20.

Larson, Christina. "China's Emerging Environmental Movement." *Yale Environment 360,* June 3, 2008.

Leopold, Aldo. *A Sand County Almanac.* New York: Oxford University Press, 1966.

Lynas, Mark. *Six Degrees: Our Future on a Hotter Planet.* Washington, DC: National Geographic, 2008.

MacDonald, Christine. *Green, Inc.* Guilford, CT: Lyons Press, 2008.

Maron, Mikel. "Kibera's Census: Population, Politics, Precision," *Map Kibera* (blog), September 5, 2010.

McKinsey Global Institute. *Urban World: Cities and the Rise of the Consuming Class.* McKinsey & Company, June 2012.

Moore, Jennie, and William E. Rees. "Getting to One-Planet Living." Ed., In *State of the World 2013: Is Sustainability Still Possible?* edited by Linda Starke, 39–50. Washington, DC: Island Press, 2013,

Murphy, Pat, and Faith Morgan. "Cuba: Lessons from a Forced Decline." In *State of the World 2013: Is Sustainability Still Possible?* edited by Linda Starke, 332–42. Washington, DC: Island Press, 2013

Murphy, T. W., Jr. "Beyond Fossil Fuels: Assessing Energy Alternatives." In *State of the World 2013: Is Sustainability Still Possible?* edited by Linda Starke, 172–83. Washington, DC: Island Press, 2013.

Naess, Arne. *The Ecology of Wisdom: Writings by Arne Naess.* Berkeley, CA: Counterpoint, 2010.

National Center for Health Statistics. *Health, United States, 2014: With Special Feature on Adults Aged 55–64,* (Hyattsville, MD: National Center for Health Statistics, 2015.

Ottaway, David B., and Joe Stephens. "Nonprofit Land Bank Amasses Billions: Charity Builds Assets on Corporate Partnerships." *Washington Post*, May 4, 2003.

Potsdam Institute for Climate Impact Research and Climate Analytics. *Turn Down the Heat: Why a 4°C Warmer World Must Be Avoided.* Washington, DC: World Bank, 2012.

Rosner, Hillary. "Is Conservation Extinct?" *Ensia*, July 22, 2013.

Salvation Army USA. *The Salvation Army 2012 Annual Report.* 2012.

Sharife, Khadija. "Climate Change, the Big Corrupt Business?" *Africa Report*, December 5, 2011.

Speth, James Gustave. Foreword to *Toward a New Consciousness: Values to Sustain Human and Natural Communities,* edited by Anthony A. Leiserowitz and Lisa O. Fernandez. New Haven, CT: Yale School of Forestry and Environmental Studies, 2008.

Stark, Rodney. *The Rise of Christianity.* San Francisco: HarperSanFrancisco, 1997.

Sumner, Thomas. "West Antarctic Ice Sheet is Collapsing," *New Science* 12 (May 2014).

United Nations, Department of Economic and Social Affairs, Population Division. "World Population Prospects: The 2012 Revision, Key Findings and Advance Tables." Working Paper. ESA/P/WP.227, 2012.

Walpole, Sarah Catherine, , "The Weight of Nations: An Estimation of Adult Human Biomass," *BMC Public Health* 12 (2012), 439–445.

Welzer, Harald. *Climate Wars: What People Will Be Killed For in the 21st Century*. New York: Polity Press, 2012.

WWF. *Living Planet Report 2014: Species and Spaces, People and Places. McLellan, R.* Ed. L. Iyengar, B. Jeffries and N. Oerlemans. Gland, Switzerland: WWF, 2014.

The YMCA Blue Book. Geneva: World Alliance of YMCAs, 2012.

Joyeeta Gupta explains in this section's opening chapter that geopolitics has historically been a function of the material interests of the most powerful states. Both Gupta and Judith Shapiro argue in this section, however, that geopolitics on the New Earth is changing dramatically. For Gupta, geopolitics can no longer be understood simply as a function of control of material resources, but rather demands attention to how people live together on an ecologically constrained planet. Shapiro, by contrast, explains how changes in the seats of geopolitical power—as traditionally understood—are harming the environment in disastrous ways. Shapiro examines these changes through the lens of China, arguing that China's global quest for resources is catalyzing geopolitical risk.

Gupta develops the concept of ecospace, a notion that refers to the sustainable sharing of abiotic resources—that is, nonliving and nonrenewable resources like minerals and metals—among nations. She explains the three components of ecospace: limited abiotic resources, limited pollution sinks, and fixed resources coupled with increasing demand. She then outlines various options for the equitable sharing of ecospace, along with their geopolitical implications, ultimately arguing that traditional geopolitical theorizing and practice is limited in its capacity to address global ecological degradation on the New Earth. Instead, she advocates for a new governance framework based on "glocal sustainable development," which takes on social, ecological, and economic issues; challenges capitalism through inclusive drivers of development; and promotes a global rule of law and constitutionalism.

In chapter 12, Shapiro highlights the massive impact that China's rise to power is having not only on dominant norms of world politics, such as participation and transparency, but also on ecological systems and the politics surrounding them. Primarily concerned with the latter in this chapter, she argues that China's traditional culture, coupled with its economic rise, is having stunning global impacts through China's approach to the extraction of raw materials to meet not only domestic needs but also global consumption demands. Shapiro spotlights, for example, China's role in trading debt relief for oil extraction rights in Ecuador, buying out mines with dismal environmental records in Peru, and laundering illegal timber from Africa, Asia, and Russia for use by companies like IKEA and Home Depot. Shapiro also discusses how China's resource push is raising geopolitical tensions in, for example, the Arctic, the Tibetan Plateau, and the South China Sea. Echoing Gupta's claims about ecospace, Shapiro argues that geopolitics are now shaped by the "global race to secure resources in a shrinking world."

Framing Questions Posed to the Authors in Section 6

- How are changing distributions of geopolitical power affecting environmental politics?
- How, in turn, is the changing environmental condition affecting geopolitics?
- What are the implications of your analysis for established mechanisms of international cooperation and governance? Are our current efforts up to the task? If not, what needs to change?
- How should we be thinking about the tension between democracy/ sovereignty/varied national interests, on the one hand, and with the urgent need to solve environmental problems, on the other hand? Does the West know best?

11 Toward Sharing Our Ecospace

Joyeeta Gupta

Geopolitics as commonly understood and practiced is about the configuration of world politics around the material power and existential interests of the most powerful states. It has been traditionally about great powers and their economic, energy, and military preoccupations—all issues of high politics.

Geopolitics in a hegemonic setting has often led to the exercise of state power and the suspension of the rule of law to achieve geopolitical goals. Geopolitics in a neoliberal capitalist setting has led to the collusion of market leaders and powerful states to control global resources through pricing public goods and making them subject to private ownership and market power. Geopolitics in a polycentric setting may lead powerful states to use their influence through state-financed and -mandated actors in a diversity of settings to control or influence the diversity of governance processes. While some polycentric processes may challenge state power, this very challenge may lead the state to reassert control as a way to promote national development. This will probably be seen as necessary as politics, fiscal systems, economics, society, and culture tend to be very focused on national identities. This can be demonstrated by the impact of recession in the North on its domestic political and economic strategies: immediately focusing on economic growth and job creation at the cost of other goals.

A series of foresight studies indicate that the New Earth will change rapidly in the coming thirty-five years and geopolitics will evolve with new political entities becoming more dominant. Shapiro argues in chapter 12 that China's role has grown and may well come to dominate on the global stage. In this context, this chapter argues that geopolitics is now facing the challenge of limited ecospace—sometimes in the short term, sometimes in the medium term, and sometimes in the long term—or that ecospace has very specific geopolitical contexts that will make powerful states rethink their strategy toward resources.

This chapter further develops the concept of ecospace, or the resources and ecosystems that humans share, which has been discussed over the last two decades. This makes ecospace a source of growth, conflict, and cooperation in the global arena as states compete to gain control over it. As ecospace is limited and is closely linked to economic growth and the existential interests of states, states will struggle to control technologies, communication, and management systems and the resources and ecospace that underlie these systems. This will not necessarily be done directly; it can be achieved indirectly in hybrid combinations.

These structural changes call for structural changes to our governance patterns. However, our governance systems are mostly reactive and lag behind the needs of the hour, and with every evolutionary change in the system, the governance system tends to fall back even further. This slow governance process is caused by current geopolitics, where powerful states are unwilling to deal with the global nature of the challenges before global society or subject themselves to the global rule of law or constitutionalism.

Against this brief introduction, this chapter addresses the following questions: How will ecospace issues challenge or lead to a reassertion of global geopolitics? Why and how will ecospace sharing in this century affect global geopolitics?[1]

The "Sharing Our Earth" Challenge

We no longer live in a world where great power understandings of geopolitics make sense. The New Earth is marked by a set of emerging ecospace realities that challenge us to reconsider and remake our geopolitical arrangements and define a new social contract. *Ecospace* refers to the environmental utilization space in a sustainable world; it is the space that people can use if they want to sustain the earth's resources and continuously reuse them. If we overuse this space, we run the risk of crossing planetary boundaries. This section argues that ecospace has three elements to it. It then argues that ecospace needs to be shared between humans and between humans and nature, and finally it turns to the geopolitical challenges of sharing our ecospace.

Limited Abiotic Resources

A key element of ecospace is the realization that there are limited abiotic resources. Many of the products people use on a daily basis—such as food and telephones—make use of minerals, metals, and rare earths that have spatial and temporal scarcity patterns.[2] This implies that sometimes these minerals and metals have absolute limits in human timescales; sometimes they are limited in the short term but could be extracted in the medium term; sometimes they are available in the short term but could become unavailable in the medium to long term. Sometimes they are available but are limited to specific countries of the world, and thus there are spatial implications. Availability is a function of cost and access. If the resource is very deep inside the Earth, it becomes too expensive to access; if the resource is located in specific areas, it may be difficult to politically access the resource. The geopolitics of these resources is also affected by the science of resource availability, and this is often monopolized by specific mining and industrial concerns. The prices of these resources keep varying, causing major economic challenges to marginalized economies. Furthermore, the extraction of these resources often leads to serious ecological and social damage, labor troubles, and sometimes civil war.

These resources are thus referred to as strategic resources because of their spatial, temporal, social, and ecological limits. These strategic minerals, metals, and rare earths include zinc, lead, copper, nickel, heavy rare earths, phosphorous, and many others. Many of these resources are concentrated in the poorer countries, giving them more geopolitical power in some ways.

Limited Sinks and the Need to Maintain Ecosystem Services

Human use of resources to generate products and services also leads to outputs. This output, whether solid, liquid, or gaseous, is often in excess of what can be safely absorbed by ecosystems without disrupting their ecosystem functions. Solid wastes can cause major outbreaks of sicknesses and disrupt the socioecological system. Liquid wastes into water systems can cause pollution of the water bodies to an extent that it becomes impossible for ecosystems to flourish in and affect those who directly extract their water resources from these water bodies. And air pollution can cause respiratory disease in humans. Gaseous pollutants such as greenhouse gas emissions are leading to the climate change problem. In general, such use and pollution can disrupt the ecosystem services of the Earth. The Earth can provide continuous services (not resources such as minerals, metals, and rare earths) if we use the ecosystems with care. These ecosystem services include supporting services (recycling nutrients), provisioning services (food, water), regulating services (climate, floods), cultural services (for religious, social, and recreational needs), and miscellaneous services such as natural borders and shipping routes, among others. These services have long been taken for granted by people and countries; we have understood neither the structural and systemic nature of these services nor how vital they are to our personal safety, life, health, and social relations, which empower us to participate in society.[3]

The recognition of the limits of these ecosystem services also raises the issue of stranded resources. For example, if we wish to mitigate climate change, we will have to globally reduce our use of fossil fuels. However, thus far we have used only about 20 percent of the total fossil fuels available. Much of what is left is also available in the nonconventional sectors such as oil sands, shale oil, and offshore production. This raises the problem of stranded resources, resources we should not use. Stranded resources are fast becoming a North–South problem as the issue arises of who is allowed to use fossil fuels and who is not (a point that Shapiro alludes to chapter 12).

Fixed Resources, Unlimited Demand

Finally, there is limited land (including topsoil) and more or less limited freshwater. The demands on land and water keep increasing. Land can be used for multiple purposes—food, meat, biofuel, urbanization, transport, recreation, and ecosystem conservation. The growing global food demands may call for a 60 to 70 percent increase in land for agriculture and animal husbandry by 2050. The growing needs for biofuel may require large tracts of land to be used for this purpose. At the same time, the expected rise in urbanization will lead to large tracts of land being dedicated to city and related infrastructural expansion. Water will be increasingly needed for agricultural production, energy, and the service sector, so much so that there is a strong expectation that by 2050, 50 percent of the world's population will have trouble accessing water.[4]

The limited land and water may lead to large-scale land and water acquisition and grabbing as a way to control production processes. Closely related to this competition will be the competition to control quality seeds and related technologies, as well as the need to control supply chains in vertically integrated markets.

Why Share Ecospace?

The ecospace challenge on the New Earth has three components: a shrinking resource base in the short to medium or long term, or both; a shrinking sink in relation to our growing pollution; and a more or less constant resource base. This implies a shrinking per capita and per use availability ecospace. The ecospace challenge has clear geographical and geopolitical implications. These implications focus on who has physical sovereignty over these resources and sinks and who hasn't; who has physical control over these resources and who hasn't; and who needs these resources and who doesn't. For example, river waters may flow through the physical boundaries of a river and still be claimed by others through the principle of historical use (e.g., Egypt and the former Sudan on the Nile) or privatization (e.g., when an international private company claims rights to the water through its investments in related infrastructure). For example, a country with extensive dependence on solar and wind energy is less dependent on biofuel and fossil fuel imports from other countries.

In an increasingly globalizing world, we all live in one common ecospace. Each ecospace element has its own sharing challenges. First, the component of spatial, temporal, social, and ecological limits to abiotic resources raises a number of questions. Where these resources are vital to survival (e.g., phosphorous needed for food production), it is clear that policies regarding such resources should be made globally and should take sharing aspects into account in a civilized world that respects human rights. But even something like a modern consumer good such as telephones has become vital to the lives of both rich and poor people; it helps the latter engage in the informal economy more effectively. These telephones use rare earth elements, which are also in limited supply. The question is, Should there be global governance on such limited resources because of their close relationship to human economic survival? Perhaps with respect to other resources, such governance of sharing need not be arranged. However, given that mining always has social and ecological impacts (see chapter 12) on the impacts of China's mining activities, rules regarding the sharing of the associated rights, responsibilities, and risks need to be made.

Second, when we talk about shrinking sinks, this has three dimensions that can be illustrated through the case of climate change:

1. Policymakers and lawyers see the ecosystem service of a stable climate as a common concern of humankind calling for protection; economists see it as a global public good—something that is nonexclusive (no one can be excluded from its enjoyment) and nonrival (one person's enjoyment does not impair another's enjoyment). Such public goods cannot be regulated by the market and call for governance.[5] This implies that ecosystemic limits need to be adopted to address the challenge of climate change.

2. These ecosystemic limits imply that net global greenhouse gas emissions must reduce every year until they are no longer permissible. And this

implies in turn that the permissible greenhouse gas emissions shrink annually and this annual shrinking amount has to be shared among countries. This is a problem only as long as societies globally are dependent on a fossil fuel economy. Once they shift to a fossil-fuel-free world and reduce their emissions of greenhouse gases, the issue of sharing becomes less relevant, at least with respect to greenhouse gases.

3. To the extent that climate change is already occurring and countries are suffering from its impacts, it is important to share responsibility with respect to compensating those who have suffered from the impacts for no fault of their own.

Third, in relation to more or less fixed resources on which demands keep increasing, rules for sharing may need to be developed. In the water world, this has led to the calls for hydrosolidarity—an integrated approach to the management of water resources that involves a full range of stakeholders, including affected communities.

This raises the question of how we determine rules of sharing. The concept of sharing focuses not on equality but on equity. I would argue that the survival needs of humans should be guaranteed under human rights law, and this can be subsumed under the topic of access. This would imply, in the case of water, that every human should be guaranteed access to 40 liters of water per day for personal use—whether or not they can pay for it and whether or not such water is physically available near the person. The remaining resources would require the elaboration of specific allocation rules that would allocate the rights, responsibilities, and risks associated with the limited ecospace between peoples and countries.

Ecospace and Its Geopolitical Implications: How Traditional Geopolitics Deals with Shortages

Ecospace has geopolitical implications. The distribution of land, water, minerals, and specific ecosystems tends to have specific spatial characteristics. Because they are in short supply, especially in the context of the Anthropocene, there are three ways in which societies can respond to this shrinking ecospace.

First, societies can adopt the neoliberal capitalist approach. This implies that the ecospace is priced and traded in markets. Those who can afford the price of the scarce ecospace can buy the rights associated with the ecospace. In practical terms, this would mean that landlords would sell or rent their land to the highest bidders and water owners would sell their water to the highest price use. In other words, lands under forests would be converted for biofuel production, which has high returns, and water would move from canals and lakes to golf parks. Only those who could afford to buy greenhouse gas emission rights would be eligible to emit greenhouse gases. The low focus on responsibility toward others would reduce the obligation to actively engage in global norms or global targets. Impact to others would be externalized. For example, most assessments of climate-related costs do not take the costs of compensatingthe impacts that are caused to others in other countries into account. In other words, markets and long-term secretive contracts could be used strategically by dominant geopolitical actors as a way to ensure continued access to the resources they need.

Second, societies may opt for the hegemonic approach. This could have two types of implications. All countries could claim territorial sovereignty over the resources within their boundaries and be unwilling to either share them or take responsibility for the externalized impacts of using these resources. In other words, countries may claim that they will not share transboundary resources or that they will not take responsibility for harm caused to others. This can take the form of deforesting domestically or using domestic fossil fuel, including from fracking. Countries may also make specific rules with respect to accessing strategic resources and are being advised to do so as a way to guarantee security of access. Thus, there are countries with bilateral agreements with other countries to exclusively access their resources or countries that ban the export of certain minerals. A hegemonic geopolitical approach to dealing with ecospace limits will use the concepts of sovereignty and security to ensure access to the resources they wish to control[6] or to avoid responsibilities and the setting of global limits in the confidence that they can deal with their own challenges. A system of nested hegemonies may emerge in such a situation where regional issue-related hegemons may control some resources within the context of hegemonic approaches at the global level.

Third, societies may decide to address the problem through polycentric approaches. An increasing literature argues that states are no longer dominant actors in the global arena and that multinationals, civil society organizations, cities, and transnational networks are becoming more dominant actors in the global arena. They both discuss a phenomenon that they empirically observe as well have a normative position of disliking hierarchic and centralized systems of governance.[7] They argue that polycentric and transnational systems of collective governance may be in a position to allocate scarce resources within each system.

The Limits of Traditional Geopolitics in Dealing with Ecospace

Traditional geopolitics functioned in a world of first-come, first-served politics, which is referred to, for example, in water law as the prior appropriation principle. Traditional geopolitics did not recognize the need for limits, which is also seen as an alien concept in capitalist theory. Traditional geopolitics focused on a core of powerful and rich countries and peoples and a periphery of powerless and possibly poor ones. Traditional geopolitics was interested in the periphery only when it could either provide resource security (e.g., energy security) or when it threatened the security of states (e.g., terrorism).

But in the Anthropocene, these premises of traditional geopolitics stand under pressure. The New Earth is characterized by the need to respect planetary well-being and to recognize that in some cases, this implies recognizing planetary boundaries. On the New Earth, the notion of first-come, first-served stands under challenge from the local to the global level. It is challenged by the recognition of human rights principles that aim to guarantee all people a right to a dignified life and access to minimum resources; as well, it is challenged by the understanding that the ecospace is highly interconnected, there are multiple feedback effects, and it is not something that can be privatized, securitized, and dealt with as it concerns a (glocal) public good. The focus on the core and the perception of others as less important is also challenged on the New Earth, and for a number of reasons. It is not possible for rich and powerful countries to unilaterally force poorer countries to reduce their use of resources in their territory, be it forests or fossil fuels, except in the context of a globally accepted, mutually satisfactory, and fair agreement. The concepts of global limits and global public goods force countries to have to be willing to adopt these limits and share them equitably. Divided, all countries will lose out. It is only in the context of a united vision about the future that we can sustain Earth.

I would argue that today's world is dominated by capitalism concentrating wealth in some key actors and individuals, concentrations of power in some countries, and polycentric systems that may often be controlled by the powerful actors and countries through their long arms in an anarchic system that allows the rich and powerful to hide their transactions in secretive long-term contracts, thereby privatizing increasing elements of the declining ecospace and offshoring their profits and channeling them through tax havens, thereby bypassing distributive responsibilities. But geopolitical strategies that use either the direct strategies of sovereignty and securitization, or the indirect strategies of using capitalist markets and poly-centric approaches may be able to make claims on the ecospace but will not be able to adopt global ecocentric standards or deal with the long-term consequences of such claims on global society. This will lead to a further marginalization of the poor, which may have boomerang impacts in terms of pollution of the global resources and loss of control over the ecosystem services for global society. In other words, short-term geopolitics focused on resource and ecospace control may not be able to deal with the underlying driving forces of long-term global ecological degradation.

I would thus strongly argue for glocal sustainable development gover-nance that takes the ecological, social, and economic issues into account. Within such governance, there is room for markets, hegemonic approaches, and polycentricity. Such sustainable development governance takes into account persistent North–South challenges, the need to counter capitalism through inclusive development, and the need to promote global rule of law and constitutionalism within which fragmented governance takes place.

Persistent North–South and Rich–Poor Challenges in a Changing Geopolitical World

Within the larger context of sharing our earth, traditional geopolitics will be challenged by persistent North–South challenges. Globalization changes global dynamics and geopolitics. However, although North–South relations are changing, persistent challenges remain.

In the twentieth century, North–South relations evolved from a colonial relationship of resource provider and resource user, through a postcolonial phase of tripartite global politics in which the Third World arose also as a reaction to the First and Second Worlds that existed until the 1990s, and hardening North–South relations in the aftermath of the fall of the Berlin Wall during which treaties both recognized and maintained the differences between the two groups, followed by dominant unilateralism by the United States going its own way to an era of current multipolarity.

Changing geopolitics in this century is reflected in five elements. First is the possible and potential role of emerging economies, especially in the context of recession or slowdown in the West. There has been discussion since the turn of the century on the rise of the so-called BRIC countries—Brazil, Russia, India, and China—and their ability to not only grow despite the recession in the West but also to be a formidable competitor to the West in trade and investment (see chapter 12, this volume). It is also argued in the literature that global markets will be located primarily in Asia, where the middle class will tend to be located in the future. Second, while the poor have been mostly located in poor countries, they are increasingly located in middle-income countries. Third, the BRIC countries are also emerging as a possible security threat as Russia flexes its muscles with respect to Ukraine and China builds its military resources. Fourth, the rise of polycentricity and transnational actors leads many to argue that a state-centered approach is passé and new sorts of divisions are arising to replace older divisions. Fifth, new North–South coalitions such as the G20 have developed that might imply that past animosity has given way to current collaboration.

These changes in geopolitics have led to new arguments to add to older ones that North–South approaches are vague and analytically useless; do not reflect the changing realities in terms of national income and power; are increasingly irrelevant fifty years after the end of colonization, the gradual phasing out of aid, and the rise of nonstate actors and the corresponding decline in state power; and is practically problematic because of its polarizing impact. And yet I would argue that although membership in the "North" and membership in the "South" may change and the boundary between North and South may fluctuate, there will be persistent challenges. Clearly there are countries in the margins of the South that no longer belong there (e.g., Qatar, Singapore), and in the future there may be others, including China. However, four interrelated factors will lead to a persistence of North–South politics.

First, there will always be a clear South—a group of countries that are poor, marginalized, and on the periphery of global politics. Today this group includes the majority of the Group of 77. Second, past relations between these groups will cast a long shadow into the future. This leads to a strong us-versus-them belief in both the South and the North, and decades of mutual distrust do not erode overnight. Scholars argue that the West adopts a West-centric approach that frames the "rest" as inferior and needing civilizing, or as an existential threat justifying military force, or as adopting "poor governance" approaches justifying the use of condemnatory language and practices. This is further amplified in the right-to-development debate taking place in the UN General Assembly since the end of colonization. For example, the Third World Approaches to International Law (TWAIL) school argues that developed countries have used international law to protect their interests and institutionalize and reproduce inequality, that it disenfranchises the poorer countries, and that there is a continuing need to call for global justice.[8] In historical terms, post–World War II legal developments promoted hegemonic interest; human rights were promoted but not for the colonized. Subsequently international economic law and international economic organizations promoted rich country interests under the guise of objective and neutral neoliberal theory. Post-9/11 international law is used to promote security interests. In the environmental field, toxic wastes are exported to developing countries justified by economic arguments.

Third, although the UNGA ultimately adopted a declaration on the right to development in 1986, within four years this right was once more under challenge within the context of the climate change negotiations. To the extent that economic growth is linked to the fossil fuel economy, growth will be accompanied by greenhouse gas emissions. Controlling greenhouse gas emissions implies that someone has to reduce these emissions. While initially the leadership paradigm was adopted in the UN Framework Convention on Climate Change, which argued that the developed countries would have to reduce their emissions to make space for the emissions that accompanied the legitimate growth aspirations of the South, it was clear from the start when the United States modified the language on the targets for developed countries that it did not share this view and had in fact actually stated that unequivocally at the Noordwijk Conference on Climate Change in 1989.

This question of who will reduce emissions first and who is the free rider in the climate change negotiations has been the enduring cause of the difficulties in the climate change negotiations. This struggle will be exacerbated as resource and ecospace scarcity sharpens the global competition for resource hunting grounds; as virtual jobs can shift from one territory to another and countries will compete to keep these jobs; as multinationals evade tax payments and seek tax havens; and as the poor in the South are further marginalized by the impacts of climate change. It is not for nothing that the Philippine representative at the climate negotiations in 2013 went on a hunger strike! Climate law too has not adequately taken into account the issues of climate justice for those affected by the impacts of climate change. There is repetitive use of norms and principles such as free trade, the polluter-pays principle, and liability, which are opportunistically applied at the international level. The United States promotes human rights and condemns countries that don't implement these rights, while itself not ratifying or accepting human rights treaties and declarations on women, children, and the human right to water and sanitation. Common standards are promoted to an unequal world, while exceptions are sought on other common standards when they suit hegemonic interests. The adoption of the common but differentiated responsibilities and respective capabilities principle, which was meant to lead to differential standards, has been under fire from US scholars and politicians who argue that it is unjustifiable.

As one commentator has put it, "Mainstream international law scholarship has played a central role in legitimating 'global processes of marginalization and domination.'"[9] TWAIL argues in favor of research "to eliminate underdevelopment in the third world"[10] and "to take the equality of Third World peoples much more seriously: to insist that all thought and action concerning international law and relations should proceed on the assumption that Third World peoples deserve no less dignity, no less security, and no fewer rights or benefits from international action than do citizens of Northern states."[11]

Fourth, although the emerging economies of the South are developing fast, these very economies face the bulk of the rising population growth of 1 billion to 2 billion in the coming decades and growing unemployment, especially in an increasingly mechanized world. The devastating impacts of climate change on their hydrological systems will have major impacts on the agricultural, industrial, and household sectors in these countries and may affect their ability to continuously develop and their ability to develop and maintain a stable political and economic system. Climate change will have serious impacts on the rich: the United Kingdom has seen long-term flooding in recent winters, and the United States was lashed by Superstorm Sandy in 2012. But the poor will become completely devastated. The Philippines has been overwhelmed by a series of unprecedented storms in recent typhoon seasons. Other regions are facing increased water stresses, and agricultural production in Africa may decline by about 50 percent by 2020. Sea level rise will lead to inundations of coastal regions and small island states. The least developed states and the small island countries may be badly affected. The middle-income countries like the Philippines may face major national setbacks as a result. The emerging economies could find their growth prospects severely limited not just because of the need for curtailing the use of fossil fuel, but because water will become the bottleneck that will choke the fossil fuel, industrial, agricultural, and services sectors. Both mitigation and adaptation action have to be mainstreamed into the development story line if these countries want continuing well-being.

It would be a mistake to conflate North–South here for simply rich/poor or powerful/powerless or old powers and new powers. North–South represents an amalgamation of institutional and cultural characteristics that reflect both groups of countries, including past animosities and present competition. The struggle of the North and South is one of those with past wealth and those who want to be the future rich, but how to do that when the ecospace is shrinking is the key question.

It would not be out of place here to briefly reflect on inequality. The issue of who is rich and who is poor is changing. However, the poor are mostly in middle-income countries; older and unemployed people will become more vulnerable, and there remains the problem of inequality. The rich-poor problem is not passé.

At the global level, 82.7 percent of the world income is earned by the richest 20 percent of the population, and 1.4 percent of world income is in the hands of the poorest.[12] But often these poor have access to lands, water, and fish and live above the minerals. Yet even these resources are being expropriated as neoliberal capitalism is institutionalized at a national level and allows for large-scale land, water. and fish grabbing. Fish grabbing takes place when governments sell their fishing rights to other countries. The fisherfolk lose their livelihoods, and the coastal communities lose cheap sources of protein. Land grabbing takes place when the hunt for minerals leads to deforestation at the cost of the locals. Water grabbing takes place in many ways, but private and public bank funding of dams may lead those controlling water infrastructure to rearrange traditional rights and access to water as they choose.

A North–South/rich–poor analysis challenges the idea that changing geopolitics has made this distinction passé. In the context of the New Earth, in fact, changing geopolitics will have to face how paradigms and institutions from global to local level are used to control people and perpetuate inequalities; how a study of the South and/or the poor/new powers must include a study of the relations between the powerful and the powerless; and in a changing geopolitical world, Southern epistemological approaches and beliefs will increasingly have to be taken into account, if only because the center of gravity of global markets may shift to the South.

Inclusive Development Must Counter Dominant Neoliberal Capitalism

Our worldviews are shaped by discourses (see chapters 13, 15, and 16). The dominant discourse is the neoliberal capitalist discourse that underlies global trade and investment in the current geopolitical world. Capitalism that focuses on growth has to continually produce and sell and externalize impacts as a way to cut costs, a key cause of global environmental degradation. Capitalism also leads to a concentration of wealth and is compatible with growing inequalities. This dominant discourse is somewhat countered by the sustainable development discourse.

Sustainable development has emerged in an evolutionary process that first focused on gross domestic product and macroeconomic stability in the 1970s; human development, well-being, and sustainable society in the 1980s; and sustainable development in the 1990s. Sustainable development embodies the ideal process and goal of a world of continuous development for all. Although the concept is vague and open to interpretation, it is seen as inspiring. While sustainable development is a dominant global rhetoric today, as can be seen by its adoption in various national policies and international agreements and the global adoption of the Sustainable Development Goals at the United Nations, it faces fierce competition from the background de facto dominance of neoliberal capitalism and its focus on economic growth and free market politics. This has inevitably led to weak sustainability where there is a trade-off in favor of economic goals at the cost of social and environmental goals. The sustainable development community has split now into two subdiscourses: the green economy and inclusive development.

The green economy discourse follows in the tradition of the green revolution approach; it combines two goals—the environment and the economy—and takes a technocratic, market-oriented, and instrumental approach to ensure that economic growth occurs within environmental boundaries.[13] However, it covers a fairly vast range of options from an incremental approach of internalizing externalities through limited pricing approaches (possibly bordering on ecological modernization) to a structural systemic approach (including industrial transformation, dematerialization, and decarbonization) to combining the goals. However, while these discourses are useful in the way they steer toward sustainable development, they focus on growth at the cost of social issues and work within the system rather than counter the existing distribution of power. They are also seen as not always taking ecological limits into account. Increasingly green economy supporters have tried to add on social inclusion issues, but this could be social wash.

The inclusive development paradigm has normative justifications such as minimizing human indignities; a legal basis in human rights traditions; an economic reasoning that wraps the poor into the market economy to increase overall growth and ensure that inequalities do not undermine economic growth and material, relational, and subjective well-being; political reasons of promoting self-sufficiency, minimizing security risks, and enhancing democratic participation and accountability; and relational justifications that see poverty as resulting from the political system and social relations.

Inclusiveness can relate to growth (increasing people in GNP generation), wealth (including people in the generation of stocks of wealth), and development (including people in well-being).

Inclusive development, as its name suggests, focuses on the marginalized, excluded, and disadvantaged in society; emphasizes contextual support for the mostly informal sectors and areas (periurban and rural) where they work; uses their knowledge and knowledge that is useful for these communities; and tries to provide social support, infrastructure, and amenities, as well as education and related employment opportunities, to engage them in society. However, providing opportunity may not be enough for the most disadvantaged; they need specialized capacity building to avail of these opportunities and explore self-help options. Furthermore, a paternalistic focus on the poor is not enough; inclusive development calls for revisiting the relations between rich and poor and the powerful and powerless in society. Inclusive development thus challenges the neoliberal capitalist drive toward an efficient society with a minimum of state involvement, which makes space for markets. Markets will not redistribute in favor of the most vulnerable; markets will not provide infrastructure and civic amenities to the poorest; capitalism will not redistribute wealth to the unemployed: these are tasks for the state and for politics. In other words, the concept of inclusive development calls for reinventing and reinvigorating the role of the state as provider of the rule of law, amenities, and infrastructure for all and for ensuring a level playing field within which the disadvantaged are gradually included in the processes and profits of development.

Inclusive development is a multilevel concept. At a global level, inclusive development calls for challenging the dominant paradigms that exclusively focus on efficiency and markets and for challenging the dominance of some geopolitical actors that work toward their own interests at the cost of others—for example, where large polluters do not care about or compensate the small island states at the receiving end of climate impacts. At the regional level, inclusive development calls for countering regional hegemony and the domination of regional powers and multinationals and ensuring that resources are shared (e.g., transboundary water resources). At the national level, inclusive development implies a strong and effective role of the state; where decentralization is promoted, it should be complemented by a corresponding shift in responsibilities, mandates, resources, and capacity so that it does not lead to an implicit abdication of state responsibility for public welfare, including the provision of basic services and safety net schemes. None of this means that there is no role for other social actors in inclusive development, merely that few social actors will potentially have the resources, the will, and the objectivity to evenly distribute welfare gains to all.

Global Rule of Law and Constitutionalism Needed to Tame Geopolitics

Geopolitics in an anarchic world leads in several ways to fragmentation in policy. First, it has been in the interests of the most powerful to promote an anarchic system of governance at the global level where power prevails. Second, the substance of economic, ecological, and social issues at the global level is very complex and systemic, and this makes it substantively very difficult to reach for appropriate comprehensive solutions, especially when the most powerful actors are interested only in meeting their own goals. Third, although institutionalists argue that power configurations shift from issue to issue and in this shift in time and space there is room for regime formation, such regimes will never be comprehensive and will be able to achieve only limited goals. Fourth, global negotiations tend to adopt only the highest of the lowest-common-denominator positions and may lead to poor negotiation outcomes. Fifth, in the actual negotiation process, powerful actors may be able to push their perspectives while pacifying the perspectives of the weaker actors, often leading to inappropriate or inadequate policy. Sixth, in the anarchic system, different intergovernmental bodies push different values, and those that are better resourced than others have more influence. For example, the World Trade Organization and the global financial and investment institutions have stronger mandates and are better financed and can thus promote free trade and capitalism. The global legal system protects investments through international contract and investment law, which allows for secrecy and very tough protection of contracts, including secretive arbitration proceedings, leading to policies being made in secret through arbitration precedents. This can lead to policy freezing in developing countries as the contracts take precedence over new environmental laws and often lead to the expropriation of property. Seventh, the inadequacy of the global policymaking system has led many social actors to develop their own systems of governance, leading thus to a proliferation of governance efforts by a multiplicity of actors.

Such fragmentation leads to incoherence. Efforts to deal with incoherence have included concepts and mechanisms such as coordination bodies (e.g., UN Water), coherence policies, integration, and mainstreaming. The newest effort is the nexus approach, which aims to integrate different sectoral approaches, seek individual contradictions, and deal with each separately. All of these individual efforts are limited because they cannot counter the fundamental reason for the incoherence, which is power politics and the systemic difficulties of the challenges before us.

It is clear that on the New Earth, we will have to work together to address common problems. At the same time, the substantive and political issues are such that fragmentation is likely to be inevitable. Hence, I argue in favor of a global system that promotes global constitutionalism and rule of law. This has clearly not been in the interests of the geopolitical hegemons in the past. However, in the Anthropocene, global constitutionalism and rule of law are increasingly becoming an inescapable necessity of modern life. Just as the United States needs China to reduce its rate of growth of greenhouse gas emissions, so does China need a guarantee that the United States will reduce its own emissions. It is not an option for both to opt out. Both have large populations, and both are extremely vulnerable to the impacts of climate change. They will have to come to terms on climate change quite soon. Given that Chinese transnational corporations are heavily investing in oil and gas extraction in Africa and Latin America, the United States and EU need to engage in this discussion quickly. Stranded assets are more expensive than stranded resources, and they will lose their bargaining power the longer they wait. And if both the West and China need to convince the poorer African states that have just discovered oil and gas that they should not recover their fossil fuels, they will have to have something to offer these countries. The issue of ecocentric limits to ensure that we do not cross planetary boundaries is an issue that will force all to reconsider their options.

There are a number of reasons I would argue that global hegemons need to promote the global rule of law and constitutionalism, especially in the context of changing geopolitics and the Anthropocene. First, when hegemons need to control each other, this can lead to an escalation of military investments, but history suggests that the rule of law and constitutionalism is one way to ensure that no hegemon is above the law. It is thus in the interests of different hegemons with different worldviews to invest in global constitutionalism. This has been seen as a necessary condition for stable states; by extension, it is a necessary condition for stability of the global community. Is this possible? It has been seen as possible in most developed countries where the supreme power there has been willing or forced to subject himself or herself to the rule of law. By extension, it is possible, if more difficult, at the global level. Second, substantively we need to adopt planetary boundaries as we are in the Anthropocene and this can backfire on us; we have never faced a similar situation in the past—referred to in the literature as a "no analogue state"[14] at the global level—and this calls for drastic measures; furthermore, neither markets, nor hegemons, nor polycentric governance can solve these global public goods challenges. We clearly have arrived at a stage where we need triple loop transformative learning, which brings us to a constitutional moment in history.[15] Third, such constitutionalization would protect not just procedural rule of law but also substantive rule of law and focus on living within planetary boundaries and promote global equity and inclusive development. One could argue that we are already on the way to such constitutionalization even though the hegemons resist somewhat. After all, we do have an entire system of human rights that offer a basis for protecting humans worldwide. We do have a set of principles on environment and development issues adopted in 1992 at the UN Conference on Environment and Development that together could form key elements of a new global constitution for the New Earth in the Anthropocene. And we have globally adopted Sustainable Development Goals, which brings us closer to the idea of common goals, principles, and rights—key elements of global constitutionalization. The process is inexorably moving forward. Countries that find the green and inclusive approach to enhancing well-being will be the ones that will lead in the future. Resisting such change is suicidal in the long term. Fourth, although there is always the risk that the constitution will protect the powerful at the cost of the powerless[16] in the age of multiple powers in different parts of the world with different worldviews, in the age of global social movements and global social media, the powerless are not entirely alone.

Conclusion

This chapter has argued that one core challenge of the New Earth, the challenge of defining and sharing ecospace between countries, poses new challenges to traditional geopolitics.

In the Anthropocene, human survival in the context of planetary well-being calls on us to be wise enough to respect the short- and medium-term limits of the Earth in order to be able to continually enjoy its ecosystem services. This concept has been translated into a modern version of the ecospace concept. This is the space that we can use and has to be shared between countries and peoples, taking past relations and future trends into account. This is the "sharing our earth" challenge for current geopolitics.

Although we live in a world of changing geopolitics, North–South problems will persist, albeit in a different form and for different reasons. Thus, although some countries may move in and out of both categories, there is a very large periphery of poor countries. Past North–South relations will have a long shadow on future relations. The adoption and sharing of the ecospace will lead to major North–South challenges as dominant Northern countries will not want to give up their space for the South, thus creating and nurturing the resentment of the South to adopting ecospace limits in the first place. Developing countries have been resisting the idea of planetary boundaries at the Sustainable Development Goal negotiations in New York as they fear that the sharing of the space will be inequitable. If the North thus needs to adopt planetary boundaries, the countries will have to find ways to convince the South. Furthermore, the emerging economies may face major challenges to their own development because they will have to find room to accommodate, feed, and provide employment for a population growth of 2 billion people in the coming decades and may also face the brunt of the impacts of climate change—making their role as a prominent geopolitical actor not necessarily a certainty.

This chapter has argued that the dominant discourse of capitalism is to some extent responsible for overusing and polluting resources as well as for the rise in inequalities between and within states even in the developed world. The difference between the ultrarich, their unwillingness to pay taxes and use tax havens instead, and the masses of the poor can be regulated only through global constitutionalism.

Ultimately I conclude that geopolitics in an anarchic world has led to fragmented policy. However, in the context of changing geopolitics in the Anthropocene, it is vital to also argue in favor of developing global constitutionalism and rule of law, although this will not appeal to hegemons that do not wish to see their authority curbed in any way. In a multipolar world, such an approach may help to ensure that no hegemon is above the law. In fact, on the New Earth, hegemons may have no choice but to reconsider their options.

Notes

1. Gupta, "Sharing Our Earth."

2. Lee et al., *Resources Futures*.

3. Chopra et al., *Ecosystem Services and Human Well-Being*.

4. European Commission, *Global Europe 2050 Full Report*.

5. Kaul et al., "Why Do Global Public Goods Matter Today?"

6. Deudney, "The Case against Linking Environmental Degradation and National Security."

7. Ostrom, "Polycentric Systems for Coping with Collective Action and Global Environmental Change."

8. Chimni, "Third World Approaches to International Law."

9. Mickelson, Ibironke, and Pooja, "Situating Third World Approaches to International Law."

10. Khosla, "The TWAIL Discourse."

11. Okafor, "Newness, Imperialism and International Legal Reform in Our Time."

12. Credit Suisse, *Global Wealth Report 2013.*

13. UNEP, *Toward a Green Economy.*

14. Crutzen and Steffen, "How Long Have We Been in the Anthropocene Era?"

15. Biermann et al., "Navigating the Anthropocene"; Koskenniemi, "The Politics of International Law—20 Years Later."

16. Koskenniemi, "The Politics of International Law."

Bibliography

Biermann, Frank, K. Abbott, S. Andresen, K. Bäckstrand, S. Bernstein, M. Betsill, H. Bulkeley, et al. "Navigating the Anthropocene: Improving Earth System Governance." *Science* 335 (2012): 1306–1307.

Chimni, Bhupinder S. "Third World Approaches to International Law: A Manifesto." *International Common Law Review* 8 (2006): 3–27.

Chopra, K., R. Leemans, P. Kumar, and H. Simons, eds. *Ecosystem Services and Human Well-being: Policy-Responses, Millennium Ecosystem Assessment.* Washington, DC: Island Press, 2005.

Credit Suisse. *Global Wealth Report 2013.* October 2013. https://publications.credit-suisse.com/tasks/render/file/?fileID=BCDB1364-A105-0560-1332EC9100FF5C83

Crutzen, P. J., and W. Steffen. "How Long Have We Been in the Anthropocene Era?" *Climatic Change* 61 (2003): 253.

Deudney, Daniel. "The Case against Linking Environmental Degradation and National Security." *Millennium* 19 (1990): 461–76.

European Commission. *Global Europe 2050 Full Report.* Luxembourg: Publications Office of the European Union, 2012.

Gupta, Joyeeta. *Sharing our Earth*. Inaugural address as Professor of Environment and Development in the Global South, University of Amsterdam., June 5, 2014. http://www.oratiereeks.nl/upload/pdf/PDF-3450weboratie_Gupta.pdf.

Kaul, Inge, Pedro Conceica, Katell Le Goulven, and Ronald Mendoza. "Why Do Global Public Goods Matter Today?" In *Providing Global Public Goods*, edited by Inge Kaul, Pedro Conceicao, Katell Le Goulven and Ronald Mendoza, 2–20. New York: Oxford University Press, 2003.

Khosla, Madhav. "The TWAIL Discourse: The Emergence of a New Phase." *International Community Law Review* 9 (2007): 291–304.

Koskenniemi, Martti. "The Politics of International Law—20 Years Later." *European Journal of International Law* 20 (2009): 7–19.

Lee, Bernice, Felix Preston, Jaakko Kooroshy, Rob Bailey, and Glada Lahn. *Resources Futures*. London: Chatham House, 2012.

Mickelson, Karin, Odumosu Ibironke, and Parmar Pooja. "Situating Third World Approaches to International Law (TWAIL): Inspirations, Challenges and Possibilities." *International Common Law Review* 10 (2008): 351.

Okafor, Obiora Chinedu. "Newness, Imperialism and International Legal Reform in Our Time: A TWAIL Perspective." *Osgoode Hall Law Journal* 43 (2005): 171.

Ostrom, Eleanor. "Polycentric Systems for Coping with Collective Action and Global Environmental Change." *Global Environmental Change* 20 (2010): 550–57.

OXFAM. "Working for the Few: Political Capture and Economic Inequality." Oxfam briefing paper 178, January 20, 2014.

UNEP. *Towards a Green Economy: Pathways to Sustainable Development and Poverty Eradication*. November 2, 2011. http://www.unep.org/greeneconomy/Portals/88/documents/ger/ger_final_dec_2011/Green%20EconomyReport_Final_Dec2011.pdf.

12   China on the World Stage*

Judith Shapiro

China's "going-out" policy of the late 1990s, which encourages Chinese state-owned and private enterprises to look overseas to invest and secure resources, is merely a formal iteration of the projection of China's newly found political and economic might on the world stage. In fact, as this chapter argues, China's impact on the planet is so great that the country deserves a major place in any consideration of the future of the global environment. A lengthy but nevertheless incomplete list of such impacts includes the following: climate change; transboundary air and water pollution; watercourse conflicts on rivers that have their headwaters in China; increased deforestation of timber in Asia and Africa since China's 2008 logging ban; biodiversity loss spurred by the growing middle-class market in wildlife and seafood; a catastrophic surge in illegal trade in endangered species, particularly of elephant tusks, tiger bones, rhinoceros horn, and shark fins and other products for use in ivory carvings, traditional Chinese medicine (TCM), or wealth displays; the economic impact of the consumption patterns of the very rich and aspiring rich on products as diverse as luxury goods and infant formula; the implications for global grain supplies and animal welfare of the shift from a plant-based diet to a meat-based diet; the decimation of small-seller livelihoods in the developing world in the face of a flood of inexpensive Chinese products; the flow of new capital from a BRIC (Brazil, Russia, India, and China) multilateral investment bank to fund infrastructure construction in the developing world, likely with weaker social and environmental screens than those required by the World Bank and International Monetary Fund; mining conflicts at some of China's international mines, as well as controversy over China's loans-for-oil programs in Ecuador and elsewhere; illegal and semilegal fishing

---

* Parts of this chapter appear in a different form in Judith Shapiro, *China's Environmental Challenges*, 2nd ed. Cambridge: Polity Books, 2016.

impacts, with an expanded distant-water fishing fleet, China having polluted its own coastal waterways and depleted fish stocks in its exclusive
economic zones (EEZs); contribution to inflated real estate prices worldwide
as Chinese shelter capital overseas; land grabs in developing countries in an
effort to secure grainfields and other resource-rich properties; vigorous territorial claims in the East and South China Seas, energized at least in part by
the presence of fossil fuels and fisheries, as well as shipping corridors; and
active efforts to secure access to the fisheries and transport lanes emerging
from melting Arctic ice.

China's rise has enormous implications for the decline of US hegemony
and the creation of a multipolar world that challenges Western values of
public participation, transparency, and the democratic process even as
China continues to embrace the ethos of global capitalism. To allay global
anxiety at the rapidity and power of its entry into global politics, the country is mounting an intense defense of its motivations, as evidenced by the
government's use of terms like "peaceful rise," "ecological civilization,"
"harmonious society," "China dream," "China consensus," and foreign aid
programs that it claims have no political agenda. Soft power projections
like the Confucius Institutes are promoting the study of Mandarin and Chinese culture in universities worldwide, even as discomfort with the implied
price tag of scholarly censorship seems to build.

This chapter takes no stand on that debate. Rather, it provides an empirical overview of China's environmental impacts, particularly for those who
are not China specialists. It is primarily intended to encourage scholars and
students of global environmental politics, and particularly observers of the
geopolitical implications of life on the New Earth, to pay closer attention
to China's planetary footprint. I hope that readers will join the rich community of scholars and activists who participate in information centers
like chinadialogue.net, monitor global news media with excellent China
coverage, and subscribe to China-based newsfeeds. There are excellent films
that dramatize China's environmental degradation and activism, as well as
excellent books on China's environmental challenges. As Joyeeta Gupta
writes eloquently in chapter 11, we live in a world of limited ecospace. No
scholar of New Earth politics can afford to ignore China.

This chapter is organized into the following sections: China's contribution to climate change and the environmental implications of its efforts to
reduce its carbon dioxide emissions; traditional Chinese cultural practices
relating to the consumption of animals and plants and their impact on
biodiversity; projection of economic clout beyond China's borders; and
geopolitics with resources-securing aspects. These four sections inevitably

overlap but I hope they will be useful ways of organizing our thoughts about a complex situation whose importance is growing by the day.

China and Climate Change

In global negotiations on climate change, China has long claimed that it is a developing country, and in accordance with the principle of "common but differentiated responsibilities" articulated at the Rio Earth Summit in 1992, it should not have to agree to binding targets to reduce its emissions. China argues that the developed world created the problem, enjoys the benefits of a fossil fuel–powered economy, and continues to extract and emit carbon in support of luxury lifestyles.

Indeed, when carbon consumption is considered on a per capita basis, China's position was quite understandable and ethically defensible until recently, if untenable in terms of the endurance of the planet's most basic infrastructure. China has earned itself a reputation as obstructionist in global negotiations, never more dramatically than at the 2009 Copenhagen meeting on climate change, when the Chinese delegation was widely perceived as sabotaging the negotiations, and again in 2010 at Cancun, when it continued obstructionist behavior. In 2002 China's aggregate emissions surpassed those of the United States, making it the largest emitter in the world; in 2014, according to the Global Carbon Project, its per capita emissions surpassed those of the EU, making it the second largest per capita emitter after the United States and rendering its basic position indefensible. Thus, China's 2014 commitments, made through a bilateral agreement with the United States during the November Asia-Pacific Economic Cooperation summit meeting, are a long time in the making and highly welcome. They signal that China is stepping up to its global responsibilities now that it appears that the United States is doing the same.

We will examine the potential environmental impacts of that agreement, but first it must be noted that for a long time, China has been doing more on climate change than is usually recognized. As early as 2009, it started measuring emissions intensity as a factor of economic growth, claiming success in reducing the rate of increase of such intensity. Of course, emissions intensity, a creation of the George W. Bush White House, tends to mask the fact that absolute numbers continue to grow. Nevertheless, unlike the United States, China has consistently acknowledged that anthropogenic climate change is real and dangerous. The major cities of Shanghai, Tianjin, and Guangzhou are at risk from rising sea levels, with a 1 meter rise projected to displace 67 million people; glacier melt promises first to flood, then parch the already water-starved regions of North China, including Beijing; severe storms, droughts, and floods have already ravaged the country with increasing frequency. Thus, it is in China's national interest to control carbon, even independent of any global agreement to do so. At least some of China's reluctance to adopt binding targets under a post-Kyoto treaty may be due more to concerns about sovereignty and equity than about lack of recognition that climate change is an urgent global problem. China is particularly sensitive about its global status and sees itself as reassuming the mantle of greatness that was taken from it during imperialism, Japanese invasion, civil war, and the economic stagnation of the Mao years (the last acknowledged only unofficially). Only when President Obama took unilateral steps to curb power plant emissions and regulate carbon in the United States did China appear assured that making a commitment would not cause the country to lose face by seeming to kowtow to developed country demands.

Another factor that pushes China to curb its carbon emissions is the intensity of its ground-level air pollution, which is so intense that popular discontent promises at times to destabilize, if not the entire country, then certain cities and regions. Pollution is one of the three main issues that drive Chinese anger at the Communist Party, together with government corruption and social inequality. The potential for cobenefits on carbon reduction and particulate air pollution control is thus very attractive to the Chinese government, particularly with respect to coal. Coal burning causes the crippling air pollution that blankets the developed eastern part of the country and, increasingly, cities in the less developed West. The Beijing air was, famously, dubbed "crazy bad" by a US embassy official in a November 2010 tweet. In late 2013, when coal-fired plants were fired up for winter heat, the city of Harbin was completely shut down when bus drivers could not see far enough to navigate the roads. Beijing's "airpocalypse" recurred several times in 2014, the "APEC blue" summit, which saw the government shut down industry and forbid much vehicular travel notwithstanding. For this reason China is already doing a great deal to reduce carbon output. Measures include producing and installing solar and wind energy technologies, constructing dams on rivers throughout the western part of the country, building nuclear power plants, exploring potential for fracking, banning "dirty coal" and increasing fines for polluters, and finding ways to tie government officials' performance not only to economic growth but also to environmental protection. There are already seven pilot emissions-trading schemes in operation, with a plan to launch the largest carbon market in the world sometime in 2016. In the 2011–2015 Twelfth Five-Year Plan, dubbed the greenest in China's history, China committed to further reduce its energy intensity by 16 percent, having already reduced it by 20 percent during the Eleventh Five-Year Plan, and to shift its energy mix to 11.4 percent renewables. The Thirteenth Five-Year Plan is expected to set even more aggressive targets. If everything goes as planned, China's emissions will have peaked, or stopped increasing, by 2030, a remarkable achievement by any standard, albeit insufficient to halt the earth's progression to catastrophic warming absent other actions.

Problems and challenges have already arisen. China's dominance of the low-cost solar panel market, which found its way to the World Trade Organization adjudication panel after accusations of price manipulation, is to be welcomed by environmentalists. But solar panel manufacture is a toxic business, and there have been protests against the pollution created in these plants, as well as problems with distribution on a wide enough scale to make a meaningful contribution to China's energy needs. In sunny Tibet, where many villages are far from any electric grid, it is common to see a small solar-powered kettle in a courtyard. But in the heavily polluted eastern part of the country, the overcast skies interfere with rooftop solar panels' ability to absorb radiation, and their surfaces can become sooty. In wind power, as well, China has become the world's leading manufacturer and a top user, especially in Inner Mongolia, where the flat, open grasslands are a constant source of such energy. But linking the energy to the grid is still largely in the aspirational stages. For now, much of China's renewable technology, particularly solar, is headed for export overseas, with huge investments continuing as China seeks to live up to its path-breaking promises to increase the percentage of renewables in its portfolio.

An epidemic of hydroelectric dam building is making local communities angry at forcible relocations and neighboring countries highly nervous about reductions in river flow. The Three Gorges is only the most famous of the more than one hundred dams under construction in western China, including those on Yangzi River tributaries and along the pristine Nu River (Salween) near the Burma border, a cause célèbre of Chinese environmental groups, as well as on the headwaters of the Lancang (Mekong), and on the Yarlong Tsangpo (Brahmaputra). The recent APEC climate change commitments are likely to put some of the most controversial dams, temporarily shelved because of local and international opposition, back on the table.

The APEC declaration was issued during the "APEC blue" meeting held during two weeks of artificially blue skies as regional industry was shut down and ordinary people were made to curtail their activities and travel.

Those visiting ancestral graves were prohibited from burning traditional paper bank notes and those getting married forbidden to set off firecrackers, sparking widespread resentment even as the people were reminded of the loveliness of a blue sky. China now promises that the country's carbon emissions will peak by 2030, at which time 20 percent of the energy mix will be from renewables. This is remarkable, because it is the first time China has agreed to a non-intensity-based target. To get there, analysts say, China will need not only substantially to shift from coal but also to add 800 to 1,000 gigawatts of energy from solar, wind, and hydro, while building hundreds of new nuclear power plants, a thought that anyone familiar with China's terrible industrial safety record will find quite worrisome. Another element of this program is a plan to shift China from heavy industry toward service industries, a path that the United States and other developed countries followed when they outsourced so much production to China. As a November 19, 2014, an Associated Press headline trumpeted, "Province near Beijing Aims to Move Polluting Industries Overseas." By 2023, Hebei plans to relocate its dirty factories to Africa, Latin America, and Central Asia. For students and scholars of global environmental politics familiar with concepts like displacement of environmental harm, dirty migration, and environmental justice, that would be small comfort indeed. As Joyeeta Gupta reminds us in chapter 11, global ecospace cannot be expanded.

Traditional Chinese Practices, Biodiversity, and Animal Welfare

A classic saying about the people of Guangzhou is that they will eat anything that has four legs except a table. But Cantonese cuisine is just the most obvious example of how traditional Chinese preferences can increase pressure on endangered species. The close association between food and medicine is well established in Chinese culture and deeply rooted in ancient historical study and practice. In addition to the use of herbs, acupuncture, and movement practices like tai qi and qigong that do not have negative environmental impacts, traditional Chinese medicine (TCM) often makes use of the body parts of endangered species, as well as of some plants that are endangered, such as ginseng root, which sometimes resembles the shape of a human being and is considered an aphrodisiac. In TCM, the consumer is often believed to acquire the characteristics of the animal eaten, such as fierceness, sexual prowess, vigor, or longevity. TCM ingredients include tiger bones and claws, rhinoceros horns, shark fins, and the fetuses, scales, and blood of the less-well-known pangolin, a type of scaly anteater whose Southeast Asian population is being decimated for meat and medicine. A broad spectrum of turtle species, including sea turtles, is now disappearing due to the demands of the Chinese market. Other less-well-known endangered species used in TCM include the musk deer, sun bear, and Chinese alligator. In an example of how widespread and arcane this problem can be, an elderly Chinese man from California was convicted in 2014 of smuggling bladders from the International Union for Conservation of Nature red-listed totoaba fish from the Gulf of Mexico. Each bladder is worth $5,000 in the resale Chinese market and is considered a cure for infertility, poor circulation, and skin problems.

Until recently, the high cost of these rare wild animals and plants meant that only the elite could afford them, and their purchase and consumption were often associated with status, luxury wealth display, gift giving, and demonstrations of filial piety (TCM products are often given to revered elders in need of a pick-me-up). But the skyrocketing purchasing power of the Chinese middle class has placed extreme pressure on these species. This is despite China's adherence to the Convention on the International Trade in Endangered Species (CITES), which China joined in 1981 and which it supports with twenty-two branch offices. Although CITES is one of the global community's oldest environmental treaties, it is underfunded, undermonitored, and poorly enforced at borders, where customs officials often lack training to differentiate between permitted and illegal goods; there is far more pressure to screen for drugs and illegal immigrants. However, as is now well documented, the illegal trade in such creatures has a global value estimated to be in the hundreds of millions of dollars a year and is often associated with other, better-known illegal activities.[1]

Not all biodiversity loss associated with traditional Chinese culture is related to food and medicine. Ivory has been a favored medium for Chinese carvings and trinkets since the Ming dynasty, albeit less favored than jade; entire tusks can be seen in museums, carved with elaborate scenes of people and landscapes. The current decimation of African elephant populations is so grave that experts predict the animal's extinction in the wild within decades if the situation is not brought under control. However, the slaughter of elephants is closely tied to organized criminal syndicates run out of China that also deal in human trafficking and drugs and channel funds to rebel armies and rogue militias; about 70 percent of the ivory is destined for China (with the United States and its large Asian population the second largest market). Poaching has increased dramatically in areas where Chinese are building roads and other major infrastructure projects. In effect, elephant tusks have become the "blood diamonds" of this century;

elephant poaching has been tied to the Lord's Resistance Army, where the warlord Joseph Kony has reportedly demanded tusks to help pay for his atrocities, as well as to state-sponsored militias and rebel groups in Congo, Sudan, South Sudan, and Uganda. The situation has gotten so dire that poachers are using helicopters to shoot their prey and chainsaws to remove tusks, and park rangers routinely lose their lives in an effort to defend their charges. Fortunately, Chinese awareness of the threat to the elephant is increasing. In Hong Kong, some public events have recorded the destruction of smuggled and seized ivory products.

Another example of the pressures that traditional Chinese preferences are exerting on biodiversity is in the fishing industry, where aesthetic and cultural values are inadvertently promoting the destruction of coral reefs in Southeast Asia and the Pacific. The Chinese favor fish that are alive and colorful (especially the auspicious red), believing them to be fresher; living fish can fetch five times the price of dead ones. Consumers prefer to purchase living animals in wet markets and select them as they swim in tanks in restaurants; some dishes require the living fish to be placed directly in hot oil. The Chinese market's impact is particularly intense in the Philippines and Indonesia, where poor fishermen often feel they have little choice but to resort to illegal fishing methods so as to harvest as many fish as possible. These include injecting cyanide directly into polyps, which kills the coral and disorients and half-paralyzes the resident fish, making it easy to net them, and placing dynamite on the reef, a process that kills most of the fish but allows the harvest of some living ones. The center of the live fish trade is in Hong Kong, where about 30 percent of the catch is reexported to China.

Sharks, usually harvested by slicing the fins and throwing the animals into the sea to drown (a technique that allows a vessel to magnify its take), are prized for cartilage that is largely tasteless and supplies texture; claims that it has medicinal properties are specious. Yet shark fin soup remains a high-status delicacy at weddings and expensive restaurants wherever there are concentrations of Chinese. So lucrative is the trade that a pound of fin can sell for $300, despite increasingly urgent attention from CITES, which has placed four species on its Appendix II list, and a public education campaign from the environmental nongovernment organization Wild Aid featuring basketball star Yao Ming. With the expansion of Chinese global economic might, shark fishing now has worldwide reach, with coastal Africa particularly vulnerable as poor fishermen see opportunities and new markets. In Tanzania, dolphins are dynamited to use as shark bait, while in Mozambique, the fin trade is frightening off the international reef divers drawn to a nascent ecotourism industry.[2] South Africa is a hub of illegal shark fishing in the region, although Hong Kong is its global center. The Taiwanese mafia is also heavily involved in the shark fin trade, particularly in Latin America. The Yao Ming campaign does seem to have been effective; awareness of the cruelty of the finning practice, as well as of the ecological impact of removing apex predators from the ocean, seems to be spreading among younger Chinese, and important hotel chains are removing the soup from the menus.

We now shift to an example of a terrestrial animal under threat because of traditional beliefs: many species of bears are vulnerable due to their role in CTM. The use of bear bile is mentioned in Chinese medical texts as early as the seventh century. Within China, some 7,000 bears on 200 farms spend their lives in cages, with tubes inserted into their gall bladders to extract bile. Unlike some of the other TCMs that use endangered species parts, it seems that bear bile does have an efficacious effect on some diseases, although synthetic substitutions do just as well. It is difficult to persuade Chinese consumers, however, that chemical replacements work, even as they remain persuaded that bile taken from a wild bear is more effective than that tapped from a captive. Bear bile farming and consumption tends to be a domestic Chinese issue of concern because of its horrific implications for animal welfare, although not only. With the decimation of bear populations in China and nearby countries, hunters have shifted as far away as the United States. There they target American black bears in the mountains of the Shenandoah, Appalachians, Berkshires, and elsewhere; although the US species is not protected under CITES, the export of bear gall bladders is illegal as it is covered under the Lacey Act. Within the United States, bear gall bladders are made into medicine or sold whole, often in New York, California, and other states with large Chinese populations. Smugglers have been caught digging ginseng in North America as well, particularly in the Great Smoky Mountains National Park. Meanwhile, an epidemic of rhino horn thefts associated with an Irish ring active in Asia has struck the museums and private collections of Europe and the United Kingdom, with rhino horn worth as much as $65,000 per kilogram on the black market even though it is made of the same keratin as a human fingernail.

Finally, we would be remiss not to note that the Chinese shift toward a meat-based diet, away from a cuisine where sliced meat was used as a condiment or accent ingredient rather than the main dish, has implications for global croplands conversion, water scarcity, animal welfare, and climate change. We know that every 1 pound of feedlot-produced beef requires 7 pounds of grain. From an environmental point of view, meat consumption is a singularly inefficient use of energy, water, and land; from an animal welfare perspective, it is worse still. China is seeking to "modernize" its meat production system through the introduction of concentrated animal feeding operations (CAFOs) like those common in the developed world; it has also purchased foreign meat and fish suppliers, including the US pork producer Smithfield Foods, as well as rights to some of the offshore fisheries of Peru. These are excellent investments from the Chinese perspective, given the widespread mistrust of domestically produced meats, vegetables, and milk following a long series of scandals and discoveries of heavy metals and pesticides in everything from rice to tea. It is also a way of compensating for China's paucity of arable land and water. As Mark Bittman put it in a *New York Times* opinion piece, "The Smithfield deal is a land and water grab."[3]

As we see from the examples and trends, traditional Chinese belief systems and aesthetic values, coupled with a newly wealthy middle class with adventurous food tastes and a widespread mistrust of domestically produced food, are a toxic combination for global biodiversity. While climate change may eventually become the final blow, habitat loss, pollution, over-harvesting, invasive species, and destructive technologies are already causing a global collapse of life forms.[4] Unfortunately, Chinese consumers are a big part of that story.

Projection of Economic Clout beyond China's Borders

The examples introduced the international impact of China's traditional culture on biodiversity, but China's extraction of raw materials such as fossil fuels and minerals, timber, and grain is, if anything, even more stunning in its effects on the planet (and exerts an indirect impact on nonhuman species through habitat loss, pollution, and carbon emissions). Such extraction provides raw materials for China's domestic consumption needs. But it also provides raw materials for the massive manufacturing project China has undertaken to meet global consumption demands. Control of raw materials is also considered a good business move by Chinese institutions and individuals looking for a place to invest their enormous wealth. The sheer size of China's global environmental footprint in an age of globalization and massive capital flow dwarfs anything the world has heretofore seen.

To ensure a steady supply of primary materials, Chinese state-owned companies have invested heavily in infrastructure like roads and deep ports, often in the name of foreign aid. Some of these projects are funded with private capital, usually with strong government ties; a Chinese telecom magnate with murky connections is building a canal across Nicaragua to rival the Panama, and the Chinese government is building a railroad through the Amazon to link the Peruvian coast with Brazil, with an eye to building a transcontinental railway across the entire continent. In the face of US opposition, China has led the BRIC countries to set up the New Development Bank to counter the influence of the dollar and the World Bank and International Monetary Fund, with the promise of providing credit for infrastructure projects in the developing world (which would facilitate the trade in resources). Other innovative financing mechanisms include the much-criticized loans-for-oil deals signed with the governments of Ecuador and Venezuela. This section examines several examples of the environmental impacts of China's global resources quest.

Ecuador, in a difficult financial position after defaulting on its loans in 2008, began trading oil for Chinese loans in 2009. Heavily dependent on Chinese credit, the Correa government in 2013 concluded an agreement to give drilling rights to Petro China to extract oil from beneath the highly biodiverse and sensitive Yasuni National Park in the Amazon rain forest. This is a UNESCO Biosphere Reserve that is home to the Huaorani as well as other indigenous groups, two of them uncontacted. The deal was widely criticized, not only because the region is a crown jewel of global biodiversity but also because negotiations were conducted while the government claimed to be trying to raise international donations to put the reserve off-limits to drilling. Ecuador will get an initial $1 billion in favorable credit from the China Development Bank, secured by oil to be sold at a fixed price (critics point out that if oil prices rise, Ecuador will be unable to benefit, although recent oil price declines could work in Ecuador's favor). The arrangement is one of the starkest illustrations of China's willingness to step in where other nations, more subject to civil society pressure and public opinion, hold back. The China Development Bank has been active throughout Latin America and Africa, providing generous credit in exchange for guaranteed access to resources, often in regions where corruption or political unrest make them the only game in town.[5]

Mining is one of the world's most conflicted extractive industries, and Chinese mines been associated with social unrest and environmental degradation in Africa and Latin America. In Zambia, the government announced in 2014 that it would take over the strife-ridden Collum copper mine, which had drawn attention from international human rights groups;[6] in Ghana, discontent runs high over small-scale illegal Chinese gold miners.

In the Democratic Republic of the Congo, however, fortune smiles on China: in a variant of the debt-for-oil model, a resources-for-infrastructure project financed by the China Development Bank has revived plans for a huge controversial iron and cobalt mine, Sicomines.[7]

Peru is the Latin American country where Chinese mining interests, particularly in iron ore and copper, are arguably most active. National policies under President Humala actively court foreign mining investment in a sort of new left-wing wave of resource extractivism intended to fund government social programs. Chinese companies seem to be learning from the negative experience of the decades-old Shougang iron ore mine, notorious for strikes and worker discontent. The Chinese are often seen as poor at dealing with local citizens' groups. They assume that a government contract means the project will go forward, since such has been their experience at home in ethnic minority regions like Inner Mongolia, Xinjiang, and Tibet, where mining usually proceeds with little local consultation, sometimes in contravention of indigenous knowledge and spiritual practices. However, Chinalco successfully relocated the town of Morococha at the Toromocho copper mine to make way for an expansion. Activists had expected it would lead to widespread unrest, but the Chinese hired an international consulting firm that gained residents' trust and built a new town better than the old one. In 2014 China purchased Las Bambas, one of Peru's largest copper projects, from Glencore Xstrata, which had been repeatedly fined for environmental violation, in a $7 billion cash deal. Local activists are anxious. How the Chinese consortium, led by state-owned Minmetals, handles construction and community labor relations will show whether it has understood that failure to mitigate environmental impacts and gain community support is ultimately poor business practice. Additional impacts fan out from large projects: In Northern Peru, Chinese buyers of maca, a ground-grown tuber thought to have aphrodisiac properties, have sent prices skyward and brought crime and unexpected wealth to remote highland areas. The tubers are required under Peruvian law to be processed in the country, but smugglers are transporting them overland to Bolivia. Peruvians fear seed stealing and the eventual production of maca in China, with a loss of seed sovereignty.[8]

Timber, too, especially the illegal trade, is often destined for the Chinese market. Liberia, Madagascar, Southeast Asia, Central Asia, and eastern Russia are among the many parts of the world where a global supply chain analysis shows how trees harvested in some of the world's most precious forests are exported over circuitous routes, often relabeled as to wood type and origin along the way. The timber is eventually imported to China, where it is turned into furniture and wood pallets, and thence exported to developed world consumers. Major outlets like IKEA and Home Depot have enormous difficulty verifying the sources of the raw materials that go into their products. Often even Chinese manufacturers have no way to trace the origin of the wood. The timber trade's clear-cutting has devastating impacts on wildlife, as well as the biodiversity of the trees themselves.

One more commodity worth flagging as we survey China's international environmental impact is grain, as China is a major player in the global rush to secure farmland. China is far from the only actor as multinational agribusinesses lead the charge, but China's impact on farmland is felt worldwide, with the Ministry of Agriculture encouraging investors to identify stable, resource-rich, friendly countries as sources for grain, soybeans, corn, and rice. China is particularly sensitive about grain supply; the country has been plagued by famine throughout its history. During the Cultural Revolution, Take Grain as the Key Link was a dominant political campaign, as urban dwellers young and old were sent to the far reaches of the country to try to convert wetlands and fill in lakes to try to increase arable land and secure China's grain supply.[9] Until China's full entry into the global capital system, it was a point of national pride to try to be self-reliant in grain; the loss of arable land domestically to developers and urbanization has been so worrisome to policymakers that a "red line" of 120 million hectares was established in the 2006 Eleventh Five-Year Plan, below which acreage of arable land should not drop. However, given increased attention to heavy-metal soil pollution (cadmium was recently discovered in Hunan's rice) and China's "going out" policy, Chinese investors have seized the opportunity to grow crops overseas. The conversion of forests to grainfields, and the dispossession and displacement of small farmers, is part of a global land grab that groups like the International Land Coalition, GRAIN, and farmlandgrab.org are struggling to document and resist.

A final driver of the expansion of China's environmental footprint overseas is migration: the sheer number of Chinese seeking better economic opportunities (and political freedom) abroad is a testament to an adventurous, entrepreneurial spirit that is far from new (consider, for example, the Chinese construction of America's Transcontinental Railroad). However, the ease with which ordinary Chinese can now get passports (rare, if not impossible, during the Mao period and subsequent decade), and their ability to fund their initial voyage, mean that Chinese small businesses can be found throughout the world, often in unlikely places such as Zambia, where Chinese entrepreneurs are harvesting old-growth redwoods.[10] Although Chinese may be no better or worse than poor people seeking to make a buck from other parts of the world, they seem unusually visible, inexperienced at respecting local customs, and willing to do whatever it takes to turn a profit. Chinese immigrants are not only highly active in industries like mining and fisheries, but they are even cornering the market on obscure commodities like lavender and maca.

China's new economic clout, its enthusiasm for international investment encouraged and enabled by government policy and generous financing, and population outflow are transforming landscapes across the globe. Where others fear to tread, China marches in, often with large numbers of workers and support personnel. Where others hesitate to pursue an opportunity because of high prices or social and environmental concerns, China is ready with an open wallet. At a moment when the environmental transformation of the planet seems to be occurring at warp speed, China's funds, personnel, and investment philosophy act as catalysts and magnifiers. The rest of the world is often preoccupied with other concerns, and countries on the receiving end of so much Chinese attention have little context to understand their new suitor or time to absorb what it all means. Attention to environmental injustice on the global scale sensitizes us to the fact that poor countries are in little position to resist when China comes courting, even when the resources they sell are not renewable or when they give up legal rights to their own land and dispossess their most vulnerable people.

Geopolitics with Resources-Securing Aspects

China's resources push has raised geopolitical tensions. This is particularly evident in four cases: dam building, territorial claims to islands in offshore waters, claims to Arctic resources and shipping lanes projected to become available due to climate change, and oil and gas pipelines from Russia and Central Asia to East Asian ports. This section gives an overview of each of these.

The Tibetan Plateau is home to the headwaters of most of the major rivers of South and Southeast Asia. Particularly contentious are rivers already built or being built on the Mekong (in China, Lancang), Nu (in China, Salween), and Irawaddy Rivers, as well as Chinese sponsorship of dams across the border in Laos and Burma. China has declined full membership in the Mekong River Commission. Domestic campaigns against dam building in the southwest part of China, as well as concerns about risks of dams built in seismically active regions (the 2008 Sichuan earthquake is one such example, some experts arguing that the weight of the water caught above the Zipingbu dam may have caused "reservoir-induced seismicity"), have only sporadically delayed plans to make hydropower a central part of China's renewable energy portfolio. However, the countries of Southeast Asia have little power to resist the gigantic Chinese dam-building machine. An even greater geopolitical flashpoint may be in India's concerns about dams on the Brahmaputra, the first of which, the Zangmu, is already under construction.[11] China and India remain in a contentious geopolitical relationship, with long stretches of the border disputed, while China's cozy relationship with Pakistan and export of nuclear energy technology are another source of tension. China has attempted to reassure India that such dams will not have a significant impact downstream, but India remains suspicious of China's intentions.

The most famous geopolitical flashpoint is doubtless the tensions over the Spratleys, Paracels, and other islands in the South China Sea and the Senkaku (Diaoyu) islands in the Sea of Japan (East China Sea). While some might argue that China's muscular claims have more to do with nationalism and settling historical scores than they do with resources, offshore oil and gas reserves are more accessible than ever before due to new technologies, and China has built an oil rig in the Paracels within an EEZ claimed by Vietnam, accompanied by People's Liberation Army warships, constructed islands out of coastal reefs through dredging, and stepped up deepwater oil and gas exploration in both disputed and undisputed waters. Moreover, the rich fishing grounds and shipping lanes of the region are an important resource, especially now that China has essentially fished out or poisoned the fish stocks near its clearly defined coastal EEZs, with an estimated 30 percent collapsed and another 20 percent severely stressed.[12] Disputes over how EEZ lines should be drawn, which are especially tense with the Philippines and Vietnam, have led China to reject the UN Convention on the Law of the Sea's' efforts to mediate. China claims instead that ancient historical maps prove its ownership of the islands and the extensive EEZ rights that it conveys. Because the United States has traditional security relationships in the region, particularly with the Philippines and Japan, such flashpoints are highly volatile, contentious, and dangerous.

China's 4,000-vessel distant water fleet is often the first projection of military intentions in disputed waters and can be outfitted with sophisticated surveillance and navigation technologies; boats that fish in territorial waters are often sufficient to set off international incidents. South Korea alone has captured almost 4,000 such boats fishing in its waters since 2001.[13] It is alleged that China has threatened to withdraw infrastructure aid programs if developing countries do not provide fisheries access and agree to turn a blind eye to unsustainable fishing practices, particularly in the coastal waters of West Africa, which has the most illegal, unreported, and unregulated fishing vessels on earth. China now lands more wild fish than any other country, with Peru, which sends almost all of its anchovy catch to China, coming in second.

China's role in the Arctic also has potential for conflict. China is not an Arctic nation, yet sheer influence has earned it permanent observer status at the eight-member Arctic Council as of May 2013, together with India and Japan. Although decision making still largely rests with the eight Arctic nations, China has made it clear that it considers itself a player. Access to Arctic shipping lanes will shorten shipping times between Shanghai and Hamburg by 4,000 miles as compared with the usual route via the Suez Canal. Moreover, the rich Arctic fishing grounds are tempting, and China is attempting to keep as much area as possible accessible. There have been contained tensions with Russia over its claims to extended continental shelf rights. China has built an icebreaker and joined Arctic research institutions; Chinese buyers claiming to be interested in building tourist facilities have been strangely active in Stavanger, in Norway's Arctic.[14]

Finally, pipeline disputes are potential geopolitical flashpoints, particularly as China, Japan, and South Korea rival for Russian gas and oil, as well as agents of environmental degradation in and of themselves. For example, the East Siberia–Pacific Ocean oil pipeline was embroiled in accusations that China had underpaid on its obligations; the Gazprom monopoly has repeatedly obstructed China's efforts to gain access to Russian natural gas supplies. Eighty percent of China's gas now comes from the countries of Central Asia via an interlinked Central Asia–China pipeline, even as these countries are prone to territorial disputes among themselves. Moreover, Sino-Japanese relations have reached new lows in recent years, revolving around territory but also around end points for Russian pipelines and the Japanese treatment of World War II in textbooks, Japanese leaders' visits to war dead shrines, and China's withholding of export of the rare earths over which it holds a near monopoly, and that Japan desperately needs for manufacture of electronics, solar panels, and other technological applications.

In sum, China's quest for resources catalyzes geopolitical risk. Contested resources range from hydropower captured on transboundary watercourses, distant fisheries, shipping lanes, and oil and natural gas. While it is well established that resources competition is generally a contributor to conflict rather than a direct cause, China's relationships worldwide are clearly influenced by the global race to secure resources in a shrinking world. The desire to capture resources can be seen in China's relationships with its immediate neighbors, its historical rivals, and its beneficiaries in the developing world. China's environmental footprint is thus not only a matter of supply and demand but one of projection of hard power by a new global superpower.

Conclusion

China's environmental challenges shape broad world politics surrounding the environment and beyond. Its fossil fuel emissions and efforts to curb them have impacts worldwide. Traditional cultural practices related to cuisine and traditional Chinese medicines are having an impact on species around the globe, including both charismatic megafauna and little-known plants and fish. China's drive to secure basic raw materials for its production lines expresses itself through new funding and foreign aid mechanisms in the developing world, as well as direct competition with developed countries on the open market. So rapid and aggressive is China's rise that environmental issues have assumed geopolitical importance. The country's policymakers understand securing resources as part of a legitimate central strategy to which China is entitled by virtue of historical unfairness and its current huge population and vast landmass. While other countries also have a huge "shadow ecology" that extends beyond their borders, none of the others have seen so dramatic a change in such a short time, and none have the global reach to affect the economies and landscapes in the most remote places on earth. The most obscure commodities have changed fortunes when the Chinese spotlight shines, along with the ownership of global brands and extractive projects.

China's global environmental footprint is a moving target. The unimaginable has become possible; the possible has become likely; the likely is already in the past. Scholars of global environmental politics would do well to take heed. China claims to want to play by global rules, but it also claims to want to rewrite them, replacing the Washington Consensus with the China Consensus, supplementing the Bretton Woods Institutions with a developing world bank that will challenge the dominance of the dollar. While Chinese environmentalists are among the world's bravest and most creative, the sheer magnitude of China's global reach limits their influence. It is essential that the world community involve China in the quest for global environmental governance such that the world's largest emerging economy can become a champion of norms of justice and sustainability.

Notes

1. "Wildlife Trade: Background,"n.d.

2. Smith, "Chinese Appetite for Shark Fin Soup Devastating Mozambique Coastline."

3. Bittman, "On Becoming China's Farm Team."

4. Kolbert, *Sixth Extinction.*

5. Sanderson and Forsythe, *China's Superbank.*

6. Human Rights Watch, "You'll Be Fired If You Refuse."

7. Jansson, "The Sicomines Agreement Revisited."

8. Neuman, "Vegetable Spawns Larceny and Luxury in Peru."

9. Shapiro, *Mao's War against Nature.*

10. French, *China's Second Continent.*

11. Chellaney, *Water: Asia's New Battleground.*

12. Blomeyer et al., "The Role of China in World Fisheries."

13. Mallory, "China's Distant Water Fishing Industry."

14. Lewis, "Chinese Investor Eyes Norway's Arctic Islands."

Bibliography

Bittman, Mark. "On Becoming China's Farm Team." *New York Times*, November 5, 2013.

Blomeyer, Roland, Ian Goulding, Daniel Pauly, Antonio Sanz, and Kim Stobberup. *The Role of China in World Fisheries.* Brussels: European Union, Directorate-General for Internal Policies of the Union, 2012.

Carolin, Christopher. "The Dragon as Fisherman." Unpublished course paper. N.d.

Chellaney, Brahma. *Water: Asia's New Battleground.* Washington, DC: Georgetown University, 2013.

French, Howard. *China's Second Continent: How a Million Migrants Are Building a New Empire in Africa.* New York: Knopf, 2014.

Human Rights Watch. *You'll Be Fired If You Refuse: Labor Abuses in Chinese State-Owned Copper Mines.* November 4, 2011. http://www.hrw.org/reports/2011/11/04/you-ll-be-fired-if-you-refuse.

Jansson, Johanna. "The Sicomines Agreement Revisited: Prudent Chinese Banks and Risk-Taking Chinese Companies." *Review of African Political Economy* 40 (2013): 152–62.

Kolbert, Elizabeth. *Sixth Extinction: An Unnatural History*. New York: Holt, 2014.

Lewis, Mark. "Chinese Investor Eyes Norway's Arctic Islands." Associated Press, March 15, 2014.

Mallory, T. G. "China's Distant Water Fishing Industry: Evolving Policies and Implications." *Marine Policy* 38 (2013): 99–108.

Neuman, William. "Vegetable Spawns Larceny and Luxury in Peru." *New York Times*, December 6, 2014.

Osnos, Evan. *Age of Ambition: Chasing Fortune, Truth, and Faith in the New China*. New York: Farrar, Straus & Giroux, 2014.

Sanderson, Henry, and Michael Forsythe. *China's Superbank: Debt, Oil and Influence: How China Development Bank Is Rewriting the Rules of Finance*. Bloomberg, 2013.

Shapiro, Judith. *Mao's War against Nature: Politics and the Environment in Revolutionary China*. Cambridge: Cambridge University Press, 2001.

Smith, David. "Chinese Appetite for Shark Fin Soup Devastating Mozambique Coastline." *Guardian*, February 14, 2013.

"Wildlife Trade: Background." *Traffic: The Wildlife Trade Monitoring Network*. N.d. wwws.traffic.org/trade.

As evident in its making an appearance in nearly all of the chapters in this book, climate change is the quintessential New Earth problem. It cuts across geographical space and political scale in unprecedented ways. Inextricably bound with patterns of energy production and use, climate change transects all sectors of the global economy, from transportation, to agriculture, to construction. The impacts of a warming world have already reached all aspects of life on the New Earth through, for example, increasing the mobility of certain diseases, distorting food supply systems, and forcing adaptive practices in the areas of energy production and infrastructural development. Climate change and the politics of energy production affect everyone, everywhere.

Climate change is therefore the only environmental problem to which we dedicate a stand-alone section in this book. However, rather than focus on its impacts, which are well appreciated and well catalogued elsewhere, the chapter authors in this section take a forward-looking perspective providing critical analyses of possible climate change responses.

Navroz Dubash begins the section in chapter 13 by tackling the thorny issue of energy transformation, an imperative step in combating climate change on the New Earth. Bringing about fundamental shifts in the way regions and the world produce and consume energy is difficult in large part, he argues, because *energy transformation* means different things to different people. He identifies four overarching narratives around energy—climate change, energy security, energy poverty, and local environmental pollution—and explains how each of these narratives shapes and constrains options for energy transformation. He argues that agreement on how each of these narratives should be prioritized at the global level is lacking, which helps to explain why international cooperation on this issue is limited. In contrast, he suggests that political agreement on this issue is more common at the domestic level, allowing the development of policies and programs, even if they are at times disjointed. Therefore, Dubash argues, if energy transformation is to occur, it will be driven by the aggregation of a halting policy landscape in leading economies.

Dubash concludes with a tall order for scholars and practitioners of New Earth politics. He calls for the analytical breaking down of boundaries between domestic and international politics, concurrent policy engagement with multiple narratives leading to multiobjective-based institutions, and the democratization of decision making surrounding energy. Despite the "intellectual mayhem" these changes may create, they are a necessary starting point, he argues, toward energy transformation.

Whereas Dubash focuses on alteration of climate drivers, Burns and Nicholson in chapter 14 grapple with the increasingly prolific debates surrounding technological fixes to climate change that do not, at least on their face, require changes in patterns of energy production and consumption. They do this through the lens of climate engineering (or geoengineering), with its seemingly sci-fi tactics, including sucking carbon dioxide out of the atmosphere with giant artificial trees and reflecting solar radiation back to space with sulfate particles in the upper atmosphere. After giving us a lay of the climate engineering land, Burns and Nicholson consider the unique governance challenges presented by such New Earth technologies. They are acutely skeptical of technofixes, including climate engineering, and caution that if adopted, they must be accompanied by robust rules- and research-based governance structures. They leave us with a reminder that "techno-infatuation" should be tempered by an acknowledgment that such technofixes are merely an indication of our failure to control the preceding technological excesses that got us into the climate change dilemma in the first place.

Framing Questions Posed to the Authors in Section 7

- Is global-scale energy transformation possible or necessary? Will it solve the climate dilemma? Who will be the key actors, and what is demanded of them?
- How do contemporary geopolitics, such as the rise of China, and social movements shape progress in this area?
- What are the limitations of existing institutional structures in grappling with climate change?
- Should we be fatalistic in the face of a laggard US role on these issues? What can, or should, the rest of the world do without meaningful US mitigation commitments and in the face of rising energy demands from the Asian region? Will it be enough?

13 Climate Change through the Lens of Energy Transformation

Navroz K. Dubash

Climate change is emblematic of the pervasive human signature on planetary systems that is the hallmark of a New Earth. While climate change is not only about energy, it is unavoidably so; to address climate change requires transforming energy. But there are also other reasons to transform energy, which start with social and economic rather than environmental concerns and are driven by local rather than global politics. These additional reasons interact in complex ways with climate politics, a key theme of this chapter. Unpacking this complexity is urgent. As Wil Burns and Simon Nicholson remind us in chapter 14, the failure to transform energy will force efforts to engineer the planet's climate, which in turn requires engaging complex governance and ethical challenges.

Bringing about fundamental changes in how we produce and consume energy is hampered by the diversity of views on what this transformation looks like. For some, the economic effects of energy transformation are paramount, while for others, the implications of a transformation for social and environmental objectives are more salient. There is also a divide among those who see potential in how energy is supplied (how we produce) versus those who emphasize the demand side (how we use). And geography matters too; different countries bring different emphases, with a particularly unstable fault line along a surprisingly persistent divide between the North, or the industrialized world, and the South, or developing countries.

In this chapter, I explore existing conversations around energy transformation for a New Earth and put forward ideas toward a conversation that might bridge these divides. I approach the problem by looking at four overarching narrative frames around energy and the implications of each for how energy is institutionalized and how it might be transformed. I use the term *narrative frame* to imply a shared understanding that helps interpret empirical reality and provide a mental map through which to assess new information and ideas (see chapter 15). However, I do not see these as apolitical devices; narratives can be and are deliberately constructed by actors to provide a ready frame of reference as a way of promoting a particular objective.

The four narrative frames I explore are climate change, energy security, energy poverty, and local environmental pollution. Each of these is distinct, although they may, and often do, coexist in particular places and times. In what follows, I examine the prevalence and importance of each of these at a global scale. I argue that the lack of global agreement on how to prioritize among alternative frames is a critical part of understanding why global coordination around an energy transformation is so limited. Instead, I suggest, there is more often (although by no means always) political agreement within countries on what constitutes a driving narrative on energy transformation (or an agreed combination of narratives), at least for a period of time. It is during these periods of agreement that transformational policies and programs can be crafted. Moreover, I argue that explicitly constructing a multiple objectives approach to energy transformation can help bridge differences driven by varying underlying narrative. In practice, therefore, understanding global energy transformation requires understanding the combined effects of several national energy transformations.

Energy Transformation: Multiple Meanings and Processes of Institutionalization

At its most general, energy transformation or transition is "a shift in the nature or pattern of how energy is utilized within a system."[1] More specifically, there may be several drivers of this shift, including technology, energy use practices, carbon reduction, and fuel substitution. These drivers include a mix of normative factors, such as climate change, and positive descriptors, such as technology. Here, I examine four narrative frames, each driven by normative concerns that in practice have been a large part of the global discourse around the need for energy transformation: climate change, energy security, energy poverty, and local environmental sustainability. I then turn to an emerging multiple objectives narrative, which explicitly accounts for interactions between these.

Climate Change

The most strident and urgent global case for an energy transition is driven by concerns about global climate change. This case is articulated in the language of limits—limits to acceptable global average temperature

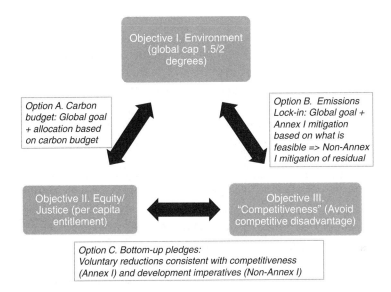

Figure 13.1
The Climate Trilemma

increases, greenhouse gas emission stocks in the atmosphere, and therefore global continued reliance on fossil fuels. This case for energy transformation is implicit or explicit in several global political texts such as G20 documents,[2] international agency reports,[3] and, perhaps most authoritative, reports of the Intergovernmental Panel on Climate Change (IPCC).[4]

However, this language of limits translates immediately into a collective action problem: If climate change is about finite amounts of greenhouse gases that can be held in the atmosphere—a global commons problem—how is that capacity to be divided among nation-states? This is a zero-sum problem, and the competing and inconsistent interests of countries, none of which particularly want to forgo future emissions, are at the heart of the politically contested two-decade-long process of climate negotiations.

A simple heuristic (figure 13.1) of what I call a climate trilemma (a trilemma spells out three objectives of which only two can be achieved at once) illustrates the problem and the politics. To manage the global commons problem requires achieving objective 1: holding temperature increase to 2°C (or 1.5°C). But this can be managed in two different ways, each of which suits a different group of countries.

One approach (option A) rests on a narrative of a global carbon budget that has to be allocated in the fairest possible manner, often expressed as an equal per capita entitlement to the global commons. This narrative, and its corresponding negotiating position, is articulated by large emerging economies,[5] and is reinforced by reference to the UN Framework Convention on Climate Change, Article 3.1, on "equity and common but differentiated responsibilities and respective capabilities," which puts the onus on industrialized countries to act first.[6]

A counternarrative highlights competitiveness concerns of developed countries, arguing that any asymmetric commitments that ask more of the North than the South would undermine developed country economies and is politically untenable. Option B therefore approximately corresponds to the Kyoto Protocol approach of countries putting forward self-selected binding mitigation commitments with some negotiation on the commitments at the margin, but with the addition of a global environmental goal. This was, for example, the proposal advanced by the European Union in the buildup to the Copenhagen climate negotiations in 2009.[7]

Neither of these approaches to allocation of mitigation commitments, however, has been able to pass the test of political acceptability. Under option A, Annex I countries' emission allotments would require steep and immediate emission cuts or substantial financial transfers to cut emissions elsewhere, or both. Under option B, in the absence of an equity-based allocation principle, non–Annex I countries risk being left with the remainder required to achieve the global goal (objective 1) after Annex I countries have set domestic targets based on political acceptability at home (objective 3).[8]

This leaves option C—domestic pledges with no overarching allocation principle—toward which there has been a slow turn due to the incommensurability of options A and B.[9] The desirability of this approach rests, in turn, on another set of narratives. These view the climate problem less as a global commons problem that requires some sort of allocative solution and more explicitly as a narrative of technological transformation—accelerating the expansion of renewable energy sources and downscaling fossil fuel and, particularly, coal-fired electric power.[10] A less dominant but also prevalent theme focuses on behavioral and institutional changes that affect the patterns of energy use (rather than supply) such as shifts in infrastructure patterns, patterns of urbanization, and related behavior changes.[11] Option C focuses attention on discussions of development paths and technological trajectories rather than limits and allocative decisions.

Proponents of a global commons approach are deeply skeptical of option C because it divorces the UN Framework Convention on Climate

Change (UNFCCC) from the global environmental goal—objective 1.[12] For example, initial assessments of the national pledges for greenhouse gas mitigation actions submitted at Copenhagen pledges—a bottom-up approach— suggest a considerable emissions gap.[13] The counterview is that concrete actions on the ground undertaken for a variety of reasons, as long as they have the effect of reducing emissions, are more important than simply articulating national targets arrived at in the unproductive gaming context of the UNFCCC.[14] Somewhat predictably, there is growing convergence on the need for a hybrid mechanism that combines the discipline of a limits narrative with the perceived dynamism of a multiactor experimental approach.[15]

For our purposes here, there is an important larger point about the significant of the role that multiple and incommensurate narratives have played in shaping climate politics. The failure of countries in the UNFCCC process to come to agreement on either version of a solution to the global commons perspective on climate change (options A and B in figure 13.1) has led to option C, an assemblage of bottom-up pledges with only second-ary reference, at best, to the global environmental goal. This political con-vergence is backed by a third narrative, which operates at the national level and rests on the viability and scope of national energy transformations through a mix of technological and behavioral change. While starting as a global issue, the emergent narrative and institutional form of climate gov-ernance is increasingly focused on the national scale.

Energy Security

Energy security provides a second entry point to energy transformation, and one with a much longer track record. While there is a range of possible definitions of energy security, this is an inherently national construction, focused on energy availability and price volatility to meet various domestic needs. However, in a world of interconnected global energy markets, under-standing energy security in any given context requires global-scale analysis. Unsurprisingly, analysis of energy security is often conflated with analysis of energy markets.[16] In this context, energy transformation is often driven by empirical observations that are likely to affect energy security. For a period, concerns about peak oil led to a convergence of energy security and climate change concerns around the desirability of renewable energy adop-tion. More recently, the driving factors have been the effects on global fuel markets of emergent shale gas and tight oil exploitation and the emergence of Asia as a dominant new source of energy demand.[17]

While growing in importance, energy security concerns have led to only partial international institutional mechanisms, organized around specific fuels or specific regions or country groupings.[18] These international institutions tend to be focused on securing the narrow interests of subgroups of countries through coordinating energy markets. The International Energy Agency (IEA), historically a club of industrialized country oil consumers, has stood in counterposition to the Organization of Petroleum Exporting Countries, founded to promote the interests of oil-producing countries. Over time, there have been efforts to institutionalize dialogue between consumers and producers in the form of the International Energy Forum and broaden the membership and engagement of the IEA to include newly industrializing countries.[19] More recently, an intergovernmental organization specifically focused on renewable energy, IRENA, has been established, but it is, as yet, a far smaller presence than the fossil fuel market–focused organizations. Collectively, the emphasis of this landscape of organizations is overwhelmingly on coordination of energy markets rather than on any efforts at transformation, with the minor exception of IRENA.

Energy Poverty and Local Environmental Sustainability

A third narrative focuses on energy poverty and access, while the fourth addresses local environmental sustainability. I discuss them together here because of the many commonalities in how these local issues are addressed globally. As with energy security, energy poverty is a national and regional narrative, but with sufficiently broad global prevalence to also be a global story. As is well known, there is a clear relationship between progress on human development and energy.[20] Increases in energy use are closely associated with increases in measures of human development, such as life expectancy, or the Human Development Index, up to a threshold point, beyond which additional energy consumption has little effect on these social indicators. The importance of energy to improving human development underpins the notion of energy poverty and efforts to address it.

In the broader context of global cooperation on development, as illustrated by the Millennium Development Goals (and notwithstanding the absence of a goal specifically on energy), addressing what is a considerable shortfall in availability and use of energy continues to be an obstacle to improving human development conditions. The energy transformation story, in this case, is one of rapidly ramping up access to energy to many people who currently make do with low energy use levels. While this narrative is at best a subtext in the broader literature on energy transformation, concerns about energy poverty continue to be a central theme for many developing countries and indeed, is the counternarrative they put forward whenever global cooperation is sought on issues such as climate change or energy security.

Local environmental sustainability relates to the negative externalities of existing energy systems. This has historically been a weak driver of change in most countries, and a rash of global summiteering notwithstanding, has resulted in relatively little global coordination. However, one among the suite of environmental issues, air pollution, now looks set to emerge as a significant driver of energy transformation. The leading example is China, where urban air pollution is increasingly cited as the main reason for rethinking domestic energy policy.[21] And this example could proliferate across Asia.

These narratives of energy poverty and local environmental sustainability are minimally institutionalized globally, reflecting, perhaps, that while these are globally prevalent problems, they are locally manifest with limited global externalities. As partial compensation, perhaps for the lack of a Millennium Development Goal on energy, the UN secretary general recently launched the Sustainable Energy for All initiative, seeking to harness political attention on energy poverty.[22] As Bazilian et al. lay out, there is a growing constellation of institutions salient to the question of energy poverty, which the UN initiative seeks to focus into harmonized action.[23] However, to the extent goals of energy poverty and environmental sustainability have been most deeply globally institutionalized over time, it is through a creeping evolution of the mandate of significant public development agencies such as the World Bank.[24]

Despite thin institutionalization, the pursuit of adequate energy access, in particular, continues to play a significant role in debates over global energy, notably acting as a basis for sorting countries on their relative capability to address global climate change. Tensions over the trade-offs between addressing energy poverty and addressing global environmental problems are readily apparent in the internal governance debates of the World Bank. For example, in recent years, the governing board of the World Bank engaged in a public debate over the precedent-setting case of whether it should finance a large coal-fired power plant in South Africa, which the country argued was needed to provide energy access at the lowest possible cost, or whether, in the interests of promoting climate mitigation, it should shift away from financing coal-based power.[25] The battle within the governing board broadly followed a developed and developing world split, mirroring the tensions within the UNFCCC process.

Toward a Multiple Objectives Narrative

As the example of South Africa's power plant illustrates, the challenge of global institution building for energy transformation is hamstrung not only by multiple narratives but also by different combinations of country blocs behind each narrative. These blocs do not neatly break down into old-fashioned North–South categories—recent subdivisions in the climate talks between large emerging economies and small vulnerable nations are an illustration—although the North–South tension continues to have salience. Increasing multipolarity of the global order also means that multiple narratives with multiple backers lead to greater paralysis; in the past, a relatively small group of dominant nations, the G5 or G8, would perhaps have been better placed to muscle their way past conflicting narratives. The relative rise of newly industrializing countries—Brazil, South Africa, China, and India (the BASIC countries)—and their growing coordination on some issues, notably climate negotiations, has led to greater voice for a large proportion of the world's citizens, but necessarily has also led to greater deadlock.[26] The rough compromise reflected in the World Bank's energy strategy is a dual focus on access and clean energy, with an opening to support fossil fuels under certain circumstances.[27]

Reflecting on this uneven institutionalization of global energy coordination, the first two narratives—climate change and energy security—have generated far more robust international institutions than have either energy poverty or environmental sustainability. This is, perhaps because the former two are more clearly global coordination problems. However, strong narratives by no means translate to strong institutions; the politics and split incentives around both of these concerns have limited efforts at designing global coordinating institutions.

It is also important to keep in mind that these narratives are historically contingent and far from invariant. Dubash and Florini posit that global energy governance is highly fragmented in part due to a path-dependent outcome as international institutions are created following the emergence of particular objectives at specific historical moments: energy security in the 1970s, climate change in 1990s, and so on.[28] As climate change has become the dominant global narrative driving energy transformation, much of the recent writing uses climate change as a lens through which to analyze the spectrum of existing institutions. Keohane and Victor describe the existence of multiple loosely coupled specific regimes as a "regime complex" driven in part by a wide distribution of interests and uncertainty over future costs and gains.[29] Colgan, Keohane, and Van de Graaf describe a similar structure for energy, in particular oil.[30] Biermann[31] and van Asselt and Zelli[32] map what they see as a fragmented global climate governance architecture, steering clear of a normative comment about fragmentation, and seeking instead to classify empirical observations into categories of fragmentation, such as the relative tendency toward cooperation versus conflict.

While this fragmentation is arguably an inevitable outcome of the various divisions in energy—between the interests of groups of countries, between different fuel types, and between issue areas around which the narratives described here have been constructed—it seems at least plausible that a larger integrative metanarrative could have facilitated greater coherence in the energy regime complex. There are signs of such a narrative emerging through increasing recognition in the literature that energy concerns are seldom driven by a unitary concern but that these concerns are intersecting and interactive. For example, Sovacool and Mukherjee construct an indicator-based framework for energy security that encompasses environmental and energy access considerations;[33] Sreenivas and Iyer develop a similar effort targeted to India.[34] Using an integrated assessment model, the Global Energy Assessment examines the overlap between objectives of climate mitigation, energy security, and air pollution.[35] The emergent theme from this work, also prominently noted in the recent IPCC Fifth Assessment Report, is that a multidimensional approach to energy and energy transition can be conceptually productive.[36]

At the moment, however, institutions reflect multiplicity of narratives and their ebb and flow over time, leading to three broad conclusions. First, institutions of global energy governance are multiple, fragmented, and in pursuit of overlapping and sometimes contradictory objectives. Second, while they are unlikely to work in a unified fashion toward a single vision of energy transformation, these institutions collectively do have an impact, whether through mobilizing and amplifying bottom-up climate actions or, as the World Bank does, setting trends in national energy investments. Third, institutions of global energy governance are more significant for their role as enablers and influencers of national actions than for their ability to drive national actions through global coordination. With the possible exception of international coordination around fuel markets, national energy governance—whether operating through the climate arena or in service of addressing energy poverty—is relatively unconstrained by efforts at global coordination. The converse of this observation is that international institutions are unlikely to be the primary drivers of energy transformation; understanding the future of energy transformation lies instead in unpacking the trends and drivers in key national economies.

National Energy Governance: Trends and Capabilities

The discussion thus far suggests that global energy transformation depends substantially on the aggregate effects of national energy drivers, policies, and actions. To address this, I shift the analytic terrain from global cooperation to the complexities and specificities of national contexts. As with global energy, national energy politics are shaped by competing narratives, often the domestic counterparts to the global narratives. And as with the global discussions, these frames are malleable, overlapping, and often deliberately shaped by various interests.

To credibly examine a range of national energy contexts and the narratives that shape them is well beyond the scope of this chapter, but I offer some brief reflections on the sorts of questions that need to be posed. First, I describe global trend data to suggest that a relatively few countries and regions loom large in global context. Next, I argue that for each of the major countries, it is useful to understand the energy narrative (or mix of narratives) that is most politically salient in order to understand future policy directions and examine the national institutional context to assess a country's capabilities to achieve a transformation consistent with its narrative. For this latter task, I use the example of India, the country with which I am most familiar, but with some comments on other cases.

Analysis of global energy trends reveals a relatively straightforward story. The Organization of Economic and Cooperation Development (OECD) countries continue to dominate energy demand, but future growth in demand is likely to come disproportionately from the developing (non-OECD) world, and in the next two decades, China will loom extremely large. Unpacking the factors that may influence this trend in the United States, Europe, China, India, and other large emerging economies is central to understanding the scope for future energy transformation. These are, however, complex stories with individual country energy narratives likely to be a complex mix of the various energy sector objectives already described.

Energy Politics and Governance in India

In India, for example, the dominant narrative is one of energy security, driven by considerable anxiety about the availability of energy for future development. The context for this anxiety is a high-energy import bill, low access to domestic energy resources, global fuel price volatility, and pressures to address climate change.[37] To begin, with a Human Development Index (HDI) of about 0.55, India also experiences considerable energy poverty. To add some texture to this number, 29 percent of the population has access to modern energy for heating and cooking, 67 percent has access to electricity for lighting, and about 59 percent has access to at least one television or refrigerator.[38] Those who do have electricity use about one-fifth of the world average.[39] Given this low current baseline of energy use, energy use is likely to increase considerably for both service provision and future infrastructure.

The potential for future growth nevertheless faces a number of constraints. Net energy imports are already 27 percent of total net energy supply, accounting for 61 percent of India's trade deficit.[40] These numbers are likely to grow as demand increases because India has meager energy resources. Coal resources (which are poor in quality) are estimated to last only about thirty to thirty-five years,[41] and much of it is in areas covered by forest protection laws; in addition, oil and gas resources are highly limited. In recent years, oil price volatility has dramatically affected India's macroeconomic situation, and recent decisions by key coal suppliers to increase the price of coal have led to frantic efforts to renegotiate contracts for planned power plants, throwing India's electricity system into turmoil.[42]

Finally, international pressures to address global climate change have led to concern that global mitigation efforts will perversely undermine India's access to cheap energy and, hence, development. The result has been a somewhat defensive international mind-set focused on using concepts of equity as a shield to keep at bay international mitigation commitments, even while domestically a number of progressive efforts that will have the effect of climate mitigation, and designed as multiple-purpose policies, are underway.[43] Even civil society has tended to grapple with dual and somewhat contradictory messages: North–South equity concerns placing responsibility on the North, on one hand, and the need for energy transformation leading to development-focused mitigation in India, on the other.[44]

These forces have combined to yield a broader narrative around the urgency of India's energy security. Interestingly, however, some of the concrete policy measures have come about as a result of the climate narrative. Despite limited domestic support, and indeed active opposition to climate-focused mitigation measures, India has created the National Action Plan on Climate Change in response to international pressures. This plan in turn has spawned eight national "missions," or focused issue-based governmental initiatives, including on solar energy and energy efficiency, which have opened the door to strategic shifts in these areas.[45]

The overarching approach of the National Action Plan is to undertake co-benefits–based actions, which it defines as actions that promote development objectives while also resulting in climate-related gains.[46] Co-benefits are a neat narrative device that allows India to remain true to its historic climate stance based on equity, while allowing the same measures to be packaged as either energy security or climate change, depending on the context and audience. It is a skillful negotiation of the political constraints and opportunities thrown up by potentially competing narratives around Indian energy.

The energy poverty and access narrative has been a long-standing feature of Indian energy politics but for an obvious, and deeply cynical, reason tends not to drive policy: those who lack access remain relatively unmobilized politically. The unelectrified are, however, a latent vote bank, and in recent years, successive governments have created dedicated programs for rural electrification and even succeeded in stringing line to almost all villages. Unfortunately, due to perverse incentives to electricity companies, which would lose money for every unit of low-price electricity provided to rural areas, very little electricity has actually traveled down those lines. Achieving rural electrification in India will require both greater mobilization around the access narrative and larger resolution of India's structurally flawed energy distribution system.

The local environmental narrative, and particularly one around air pollution, is perhaps the best poised to make a difference to policy. Air pollution tends to affect urban India more than rural India and affects the elite among urban Indians just as much (or nearly as much) as average urban dwellers. Although powerful and easily mobilized, this constituency has not internalized the health risks of air pollution. With a flurry of recent studies, by Indian and overseas actors including the World Bank, and unflattering comparisons between Beijing and Indian cities, this nonchalance may give way to more active concern in the coming years and drive shifts in energy policy.[47]

The policies that each of these narratives supports have many complementarities but also some trade-offs. On the latter, for example, low-cost energy access may well increase domestic and global pollution, particularly in the short run, although countervoices argue that access can effectively be achieved through off-grid renewable energy. The larger point is that if India is to avoid the unproductive fragmentation of global energy institutions, a narrative that allows for pursuit of multiple objectives and assessment of complementarities and trade-offs is needed. The co-benefits language, which emerged out of the Indian climate policy debate, provides one such approach. The challenge is winning broad acceptability for this approach and ultimately the formation of relevant institutional mechanisms.

Indeed, the absence of an institutional architecture through which change can be designed, incentivized, and enabled is perhaps the biggest challenge to achieving an energy transformation in India. There are currently five separate ministries or departments dealing with energy-related issues—coal, power, petroleum and natural gas, new and renewable energy, and atomic energy—each with an architecture of public companies, regulatory authorities, advisory bodies, and other agencies.[48] Moreover, under India's constitution, the power sector is a "concurrent," subject to be jointly managed at federal and state levels. There is no mechanism for coordination across sector departments and federal scales.

While the Planning Commission of India, in 2014 abolished and reenvisioned as a longer-term strategic body called Niti Aayog, occasionally does undertake long-range strategic exercises,[49] there is no effective mechanism to translate these into actions; the five-yearly planning exercises tend to devolve back to line ministries with little scope for interministerial coordination. However, the most recent Twelfth Five Year Plan did explicitly articulate a co-benefits–based approach to climate planning as its favored approach, which was reinforced in an expert group report intended to inform India's climate policy.[50]

The benefits of an overarching coordinating body are indicated by the existence for a brief period of an office of the prime minister's special envoy on climate change within the prime minister's office, during which the spate of mission building occurred. An analysis of the institutionalization of climate governance in India suggests that the ability to stand above the ministerial fray and the authority to convene high-level ministerial officials that came with this office was central to pushing through the existing initiatives.[51]

Institutional and political change is, of course, about far more than bureaucratic structures and incentives. While India has a vibrant civil society, multiple industry associations, and some high-level environment and energy analysts in universities and think thanks, this capacity is scattered and has not, as yet, been translated into a cogent transformative vision that has won popular support. Energy debates, including public debates, tend to remain at the level of specific scandals and specific policy actions, such as allocation of coal blocks or tapering off existing subsidies on diesel and kerosene. Indeed, in recent years, a distinct governance narrative around energy, focused on grand corruption around allocation of contracts and resources, and petty corruption around theft and mismanagement, has captured the headlines more than any other narrative.[52] But this is a discourse that is larger than around energy alone. Whether embedded energy in larger governance challenges lends additional political weight to energy transformation, or bogs it down in much broader debates depends on how skillfully civil society groups harness and develop this emergent narrative.

In sum, there are multiple compelling reasons for energy transformation in India, of which energy security and local environmental pollution might be the strongest drivers in coming years. However, the growing salience of governance reform is likely to increasingly form the overarching context for energy policy. Somewhat counterintuitively, climate change plays a facilitative role in these discussions. Despite strong domestic resistance to internalizing low-carbon growth as an objective due to the hold of equity-based narratives around climate change, some of the more far-reaching changes have occurred through the institutionalization of a climate action plan. When packaged within a larger co-benefits framework, climate change could continue to serve as a policy irritant that stimulates, if not drives, institutional change in energy. For this to work, however, India's co-benefits and development-driven approach to climate mitigation must also be recognized as an acceptable part of the global response to climate change.

National Energy Governance Snapshots

In order to obtain a picture of the likelihood and potential for global energy transformation, a similar, if not more detailed, analysis is required of other countries with a large energy footprint as either suppliers or demanders. While such an analysis is beyond the scope of this chapter, I offer some initial reflections on other major regions and countries.

China dominates the present and immediate future when it comes to shifts in energy demand patterns (see chapter 12). While China has relied heavily on domestic coal, imports of oil and gas are likely to rise.[53] With a thirst for imported fuel has come an aggressive effort to lock down equity oil in various parts of the world, notably Africa, as part of a larger package of foreign and economic policy engagement.[54] Concerns of energy security, as reflected in military capabilities to defend energy investments, diplomatic and economic policy to induce energy contracts, bilateral deals such as a major gas contract with Russia, investment in infrastructure, and diplomacy to construct gas networks in Asia are likely to be important themes in Chinese energy policy.

Increasingly, however, there is a counterpoint to the energy security concern in terms of growing domestic political concerns around air quality. At least according to some analysts, domestic political pressures on the government to resolve an air quality crisis in China's cities will drive short-term energy policy more than will energy security or climate change.[55] China already has a significant advantage in developing renewable energy, particularly solar capacity, which may be harnessed to this objective. As the world's largest emitter of greenhouse gases on an annual basis, China is also under great international pressure to signal serious domestic mitigation action, and indeed is experimenting with a slew of approaches from taxes to emission trading systems and strong energy-efficiency regulations. Moreover, China has introduced a strong institutional coordination structure around energy and climate policy housed at the powerful National Development and Reform Commission (NDRC), the Chinese planning body.

Taken collectively, China appears poised for a clean energy transformation for domestic environmental reasons and global signaling motivations, but one that will proceed in parallel with securing fossil fuels for its continued development over the next two decades. This is an agenda that appears to have both political support and institutional foundations.

By comparison to the Asian giants and indeed to other large emerging economies, the OECD countries are relatively stable in their energy demand. However, this stability conceals substantial churning below the surface. The biggest shift with ripple effects on global energy markets is the emergence of shale oil and gas in the United States as a viable industry. Indeed, the United States is expected to flip from being a net importer of energy to a net exporter by 2018,[56] while Asia will account for a growing share of energy imports. As Jones et al. note, this shift provides the United States tremendous geopolitical leverage, but it comes with potentially destabilizing effects.[57]

For example, in the short term, cheap domestic gas was replaced in 2012 by coal-fired power in the United States, making it easier to meet climate obligations, although this trend was reversed in 2013 as the US economy picked up speed. However, displaced coal flooded European markets, undermining renewable energy promotion measures in Europe. Europe, led by Germany's Energiewende, (or "energy transition") has the most pronounced policy efforts aimed at both energy transformation and climate stabilization, but these are under threat not only from global ripples from across the Atlantic, but also from a perception that the rest of the world is not keeping pace, and from short-term higher costs at a time of macroeconomic weakness, leading to a competitive disadvantage for Europe. With instability in eastern Europe and concern about overdependence on Russian gas, energy security concerns have also moved up the agenda.

Taken together, narratives of transformation in the United States are focused on digesting the bonanza of shale oil and gas, which may lead to some short-term improvements in greenhouse gas emissions but may also undermine longer-term lower carbon transformations. President Obama's climate plans, focused on limiting emissions from existing power plants,[58] may have some impact on emissions, but the dominant impression is that long-term transformative changes in the US energy situation is driven by new sources of fossil fuels. In Europe, a deliberately transformative narrative in some trend-setting countries, notably Germany, driven by a mix of climate considerations and energy security is in the balance, faced with the prospects of short-term adjustment costs and uncertain long-term gains in the face of collective global inaction.

There is a growing volume of social science in the comparative politics tradition seeking to unpack domestic energy narratives, politics, and, to a much smaller extent, institutions. These studies are typically driven by climate considerations, with an upsurge after the experience of the Copenhagen climate negotiations in 2009, during which a turn away from a single unitary climate deal and toward a collection of national plans, strategies, and statements became most apparent. That this is a rich area of research is signaled by evidence that there has been an enormous upsurge of domestic climate legislation and nonbinding climate strategies in the period between 2007 and 2012.[59] By 2012, 67 percent of all greenhouse gas emissions were covered by such legislation or strategies, as compared to 45 percent in 2007.[60] The biggest increases were in Asia and Latin America. Given this evidence, it becomes salient to ask: What will drive these domestic actions, how credible are they, and to what will they amount?

In studies of developed countries by Harrison and Sundstrom[61] and Bailey and Compston[62] domestic electoral politics and the costs of compliance are strong considerations in driving the stringency of policies. In developing and newly industrializing countries, factors such as the presence of strong climate co-benefits of the sort discussed earlier—energy security and air pollution—are strong determinants of domestic actions.[63] Yet another line of exploration examines the nature of the state—liberal, corporatist, or developmental—to draw implications for climate policies.[64] Finally, international pressures[65] and ideational factors, including perceptions of equity in climate negotiations, can play a strong role in shaping domestic actions.[66]

This admittedly cursory glance at national narratives, politics, and actions on energy and climate transitions suggests a landscape of considerable ferment. But the emergent narratives are multistranded, sometimes ill formed, backed by shifting politics, and often thinly institutionalized. Climate change is frequently part of the story, but the climate change language of limits is seldom determinative. More frequently, the coalescing of narratives around energy security and climate change, or air pollution and climate change, are more powerful and more domestically salient. Given this complex picture, what is the future for national and global energy transformation, and what can social science contribute to painting a clearer picture?

Toward Integrative Ideas: Energy Transformation for a New Earth

Energy transformation for a New Earth is unlikely to be a smooth process. Instead, it will be driven by halting progress in some leading economies, propelled by multiple and sometimes contradictory narratives, and with drivers operating at multiple scales—national, global, and even subnational. Silver bullets, such as energy transformation driven by a global carbon price or by a global cooperative technology mechanism, are unlikely to materialize.

Working with and seeking to shape this complex reality will require more elastic and creative approaches from scholars of and practitioners and activists engaged in global environmental politics. In particular, it will not be adequate to examine global energy and environmental politics at a purely global scale. For example, the global climate negotiations process has captured a disproportionate amount of intellectual and activist attention, some of which might perhaps have been usefully diverted to the national politics that ultimately has constrained the scope for agreement. At the same time, domestic energy politics do not operate in a vacuum. Technological development and diffusion of solar power globally, for example, have been enabled by the willingness of German consumers to subsidize global solar development and the Chinese government's ability to maintain low-cost labor and an undervalued exchange rate, which keep solar panels cheap.

Ironically, the challenge of exploring an interconnected New Earth may require stepping back from a preoccupation from the international and instead refocusing on politics within domestic borders, and also actively exploring linkages across scales and issue areas in ways that that treat as relatively porous the boundaries between domestic and international politics.[67] In the climate arena, for example, there are likely gains to be had from bringing into conversation three broad groups that each feel they hold the key to the climate problem but seldom seek linkages across arenas: climate negotiators, national climate planners, and organizers in transnational networks, such as the one on cities.[68] In the energy arena, an understanding of global energy markets needs to include significant national patterns, such as the reemergence of national oil companies as major players and the domestic politics in specific countries that make this possible. Linkages to the private sector are also important: efforts by activists to link future climate policy to the valuation of fossil fuel energy companies are an important recent example.[69] The academic language of multilevel governance provides a useful framework to thinking about these linkages.

A second important element of a renewed approach to energy transformation for a New Earth speaks directly to the multiple narratives that I have argued can unproductively lead to dissonance and institutional fragmentation. There is important creative work to be done to build support for an explicitly multiple objective approach to energy and climate, one that recognizes not only complementarities across objectives but also the existence of trade-offs. Such an approach would stem the unproductive competition across narratives and allow for more creative politics. For example, considerable political support for energy efficiency can be built around the simultaneous climate change, energy security, and local air pollution gains that demand measures can bring.

To enable this shift will require scholars to do the work of building and reinforcing this narrative, work that has already begun in the context of the IPCC Fifth Assessment Report Synthesis.[70] Taking this agenda forward required the development of institutions that are explicitly built around consideration of multiple objectives. Single-objective or sector-focused institutions, such as around coal or oil, are ill placed to assess trade-offs across objectives. Moreover, at the moment, the necessary tools and metrics remain underdeveloped.[71] An emergent literature, drawing on more qualitative approaches using multicriteria decision analysis, provides one way in which to make more explicit consideration of multiple objectives.[72] For social scientists, making the case for a multiple objectives approach, documenting instances of its application, categorizing institutional design, and making the linkage to the deliberative and democratic gains are all useful lines of work.

Finally, using a multiple objective approach to policy-making is one small step toward a much larger task: democratizing decision making in energy. Whether public or private, energy sector organizations are among the largest and most powerful entities in national economies and frequently operate in nontransparent ways. They command a system of state support that includes long-entrenched subsidies and the promise of state backing that comes with being perceived as a strategic sector vital to national economic interests.

Both developing an understanding of the various linkages that lock energy into its current patterns and promoting a multiple objective approach are important means to the larger end of democratizing energy. Understanding the linkages helps identify points of leverage and the structures that perpetuate existing patterns, while the multiple objective approach can provide a counterpoint to narratives—particularly energy security—that are frequently used to buttress and perpetuate existing patterns of energy supply and use. Nonetheless, the magnitude of the task should not be underestimated. These are but ways into a large and complex arena.

For scholars of a New Earth, the risk of the approach laid out here is intellectual mayhem, as hitherto separate categories—international and national, climate change and energy access—are forced into conversation in ways that can seem overwhelming. However, the task is precisely to understand and map that complexity by examining linkages and the shaping influence of multiple narratives. Moreover, working within well-defined silos and categories is no longer a viable option. If social science scholars are to shed light on the pathways to energy transformation, and do so in ways that promote engagement with practitioners and activists, engagement with energy systems in all their complexity is a necessary starting point.

Notes

1. Araújo. "The Emerging Field of Energy Transitions."

2. See, for instance, G20 Leaders, "G20 Leaders' Declaration"; G20: Cannes Summit Final Declaration—Building Our Common Future: Renewed Collective Action for the Benefit of All, November 4, 2011, http://www.g20.utoronto.ca/2011/2011 -cannes-declaration-111104-en.html; G8, "Joint Statement by the German G8 Presidency and the Heads of State."

3. See, for instance, International Energy Agency, "Redrawing the Energy-Climate Map"; United Nations Environment Programme, *Emissions Gap Report 2013*.

4. See, for instance, IPCC, "Summary for Policymakers," in *Climate Change 2014: Mitigation of Climate Change*; IPCC, "Summary for Policymakers," in *Climate Change 2014: Synthesis Report*.

5. BASIC Experts, "Equitable Access to Sustainable Development."

6. Ibid.

7. Council of the European Union, *EU Position for the Copenhagen Climate Conference*.

8. Winkler, Vorster, and Marquard. "Who Picks Up the Remainder?"

9. Diringer, "Climate Change"; Dubash and Rajamani, "Beyond Copenhagen."

10. International Energy Agency, *Re-drawing the Energy-Climate Map*; Greenpeace International, European Renewable Energy Council, and Global Wind Energy Council, *Energy [R]Evolution*.

11. GEA, *Global Energy Assessment*.

12. Hare et al., "The Architecture of the Global Climate Regime."

13. United Nations Environment Programme, *The Emissions Gap Report 2013*.

14. Rayner,"How to Eat an Elephant."

15. Dubash and Rajamani, "Beyond Copenhagen."

16. Goldthau and Witte, *Global Energy Governance*:

17. Jones, Steven, and O'Brien, *Fueling a New Order?*

18. Dubash and Florini, "Mapping Global Energy Governance."

19. Florini, "The International Energy Agency in Global Energy Governance"; Van de Graaf, "Obsolete or Resurgent?"

20. Lamb and Rao, "Human Development in a Climate Constrained World."

21. Teng and Gu, "Climate Change."

22. See http://www.se4all.org/about-us.

23. Bazilian, Smita, and Van de Graaf, "Energy Governance and Poverty."

24. Nakhooda, "Asia, the Multilateral Development Banks and Energy Governance."

25. Ibid.

26. Qi, "The Rise of BASIC in UN Climate Change Negotiations."

27. World Bank, "World Bank Group Sets Direction for Energy Sector Investment."

28. Dubash and Florini, "Mapping Global Energy Governance."

29. Keohane and Victor, "The Regime Complex for Climate Change."

30. Colgan, Keohane, and Van de Graaf, "Punctuated Equilibrium in the Energy Regime Complex."

31. Frank Biermann, "The Fragmentation of Global Governance Architectures"; Biermann et al., "Fragmentation of Global Governance Architectures: The Case of Climate Policy."

32. van Asselt and Zelli, "Connect the Dots."

33. Sovacool and Mukherjee, "Conceptualizing and Measuring Energy Security."

34. Sreenivas and Iyer, "A 'Dashboard' for the Indian Energy Sector".

35. GEA, *Global Energy Assessment.*

36. IPCC. "Summary for Policymakers," in *Climate Change 2014: Mitigation of Climate Change;* IPCC, "Summary for Policymakers," in *Climate Change 2014: Synthesis Report.*

37. Dubash, "From Norm Taker to Norm Maker?"

38. Ashok Sreenivas and Rakesh Iyer, "A 'Dashboard' for the Indian Energy Sector" .

39. Rao, Sant, and Rajan, *An Overview of Indian Energy Trends.*

40. Sreenivas and Iyer, *A 'Dashboard' for the Indian Energy Sector*

41. Chand, *The Coal Dilemma.*

42. Supreme Court of India, "Order Dated 25 August 2014,"

43. Dubash, "The Politics of Climate Change in India"; Rajamani. "Deconstructing Durban."

44. Lele, "Climate Change and the Indian Environmental Movement."

45. Dubash.,"The Politics of Climate Change in India"; Rajamani. "Deconstructing Durban."

46. Prime Minister's Council on Climate Change, Government of India, *National Action Plan on Climate Change.*

47. Mani et al., "An Analysis of Physical and Monetary Losses"; Harris, "Beijing's Bad Air Would Be Step Up for Smoggy Delhi."

48. Dubash, "From Norm Taker to Norm Maker?"

49. Planning Commission, Government of India, *Integrated Energy Policy;* Planning Commission, Government of India, *The Final Report of the Expert Group on Low Carbon Strategies for Inclusive Growth.*

50. Planning Commission, Government of India., *Twelfth Five Year Plan*; Planning Commission, Government of India, *The Final Report of the Expert Group on Low Carbon Strategies for Inclusive Growth.*

51. Dubash and Joseph, "The Institutionalisation of Climate Policy in India."

52. Comptroller and Auditor General of India, Government of India, *Performance Audit*; Golden and Min, "Theft and Loss of Electricity in an Indian State."

53. Jones, Steven, and O'Brien, *Fueling a New Order?*

54. Kong, "Governing China's Energy in the Context of Global Governance."

55. Fei, "Presentation at the Centre for Policy Research."

56. British Petroleum, *BP Energy Outlook 2035.*

57. Jones, Steven, and O'Brien, *Fueling a New Order?*

58. Executive Office of the President, *The President's Climate Action Plan.*

59. Dubash et al. , "Developments in National Climate Change Mitigation Legislation and Strategy."

60. Ibid..

61. Harrison and Sundstrom, *Global Commons, Domestic Decisions.*

62. Compston and Bailey, eds., *Turning Down the Heat.*

63. Bailey and Compston, eds., *Feeling the Heat*; Held, Roger, and Nag, eds., *Climate Governance in the Developing World.*

64. Lachapelle and Paterson, "Drivers of National Climate Policy."

65. Held, Roger, and Nag, eds., *Climate Governance in the Developing World.*

66. Harrison and Sundstrom, eds., *Global Commons.*

67. Dubash and Florini, "Mapping Global Energy Governance."

68. Centre for Policy Research, and Mitigation Action Plan and Scenarios Programme, Energy Research Centre, "Building the Hinge."

69. See http://gofossilfree.org.

70. IPCC, "Summary for Policymakers," in *Climate Change 2014: Mitigation of Climate Change*; IPCC, "Summary for Policymakers." in *Climate Change 2014: Synthesis Report.*

71. Urge-Vorsatz et al., "Measuring the Co-benefits of Climate Change Mitigation."

72. See Dubash et al., "Indian Climate Change Policy"; "; United Nations Environment Programme , *MCA4 Climate.*

Bibliography

Araújo, Kathleen. "The Emerging Field of Energy Transitions: Progress, Challenges, and Opportunities." *Energy Research and Social Science* 1 (2014): 112–21.

Bailey, I., and H. Compston, eds. *Feeling the Heat: The Politics of Climate Policy in Rapidly Industrializing Countries*. Basingstoke: Palgrave Macmillan, 2012.

BASIC Experts. *Equitable Access to Sustainable Development: Contribution to the Body of Scientific Knowledge*. Beijingi: BASIC Expert Group, 2011. http://gdrights.org/wp-content/uploads/2011/12/EASD-final.pdf.

Bazilian, Morgan, Smita Nakhooda, and Thijs Van de Graaf. "Energy Governance and Poverty." *Energy Research and Social Science* 1 (2014): 217–25.

Biermann, Frank, Philippe Pattberg, Harro van Asselt, and Fariborz Zelli. "Fragmentation of Global Governance Architectures: The Case of Climate Policy." Global Governance working paper 34. Amsterdam: Global Governance Project, 2007.http://www.glogov.org/images/doc/WP34.pdf.

Biermann, Frank, Philipp Pattberg, Harro van Asselt, and Fariborz Zelli. "The Fragmentation of Global Governance Architectures: A Framework for Analysis." *Global Environmental Politics* 9, no. 4 (2009): 14–40.

British Petroleum (BP). *BP Energy Outlook 2035*. London: BP, 2014. http://www.bp.com/en/global/corporate/about-bp/energy-economics/energy-outlook.html.

Centre for Policy Research, and the Mitigation Action Plan and Scenarios Programme, Energy Research Centre. "Building the Hinge: Reinforcing National and Global Climate Governance Mechanisms." In *Proceedings of a Workshop Held at Neemrana Fort-Palace, Alwar, December 5–7th 2013*. New Delhi: Centre for Policy Research and Energy Research Centre, 2013. http://www.cprindia.org/events/4128.

Chand, S. *The Coal Dilemma*. New Delhi: Energy and Resources Institute and WWF, 2008.

Colgan, Jeff D., Robert O. Keohane, and Thijs Van de Graaf. "Punctuated Equilibrium in the Energy Regime Complex." *Review of International Organizations* 7 (2012): 117–43.

Compston, H., and I. Bailey, eds. *Turning down the Heat: The Politics of Climate Policy in Affluent Democracies*. Basingstoke: Palgrave Macmillan, 2008.

Comptroller and Auditor General of India, Government of India. *Performance Audit of Allocation of Coal Blocks and Augmentation of Coal Production*. Report 7 of 2012–13. New Delhi: Government of India, 2012. http://saiindia.gov.in/english/home/our_products/audit_report/government_wise/union_audit/recent_reports/union_performance/2012_2013/Commercial/Report_No_7/Report_No_7.html.

Council of the European Union. *EU Position for the Copenhagen Climate Conference (7–18 December 2009)–Council Conclusions (14790/09)*. Brussels: Council of the European Union, 2009. http://register.consilium.europa.eu/doc/srv?l=EN&f=ST percent2014790 percent202009 percent20INIT.

Diringer, Elliot. "Climate Change: A Patchwork of Emissions Cuts." *Nature* 501 (7467) (2013): 307–309.

Dubash, Navroz K. "From Norm Taker to Norm Maker? Indian Energy Governance in Global Context." *Global Policy* 2 (2011): 66–79.

Dubash, Navroz K. "The Politics of Climate Change in India: Narratives of Equity and Co-Benefits." *Wiley Interdisciplinary Reviews: Climate Change* 4 (2013): 191–201.

Dubash, Navroz K., and Ann Florini. "Mapping Global Energy Governance." *Global Policy* 2 (2011): 6–18.

Dubash, Navroz K., D. Raghunandan, Girish Sant, and Ashok Sreenivas. "Indian Climate Change Policy: Exploring a Co-Benefits Based Approach." *Economic and Political Weekly* 48, no. 22 (2013): 47–62.

Dubash, Navroz K., and Lavanya Rajamani. "Beyond Copenhagen: Next Steps." *Climate Policy* 10 (2010): 593–99.

Dubash, Navroz K., Markus Hagemann, Niklas Höhne, and Prabhat Upadhyaya. "Developments in National Climate Change Mitigation Legislation and Strategy." *Climate Policy* 13 (2013): 649–64.

Edenhofer, Ottmar, "Technical Summary." In *Climate Change 2014, Mitigation of Climate Change. Contribution of Working Group III to the Fifth Assessment Report of the Intergovernmental Panel on Climate Change*. Cambridge: Cambridge University Press, 2014. http://report.mitigation2014.org/drafts/final-draft-postplenary/ipcc_wg3_ar5_final-draft_postplenary_technical-summary.pdf.

Dubash, Navroz K., and Neha B. Joseph. "The Institutionalisation of Climate Policy in India: Designing a Development-Focused, Co-Benefits Based Approach." Centre for Policy Research, Climate Initiative, working paper. New Delhi: Centre for Policy Research, May 2015.

Executive Office of the President. *The President's Climate Action Plan*. Washington DC: White House, 2013. http://www.whitehouse.gov/sites/default/files/image/president27sclimateactionplan.pdf.

Florini, Ann. "The International Energy Agency in Global Energy Governance." *Global Policy* 2 1 (2011): 40–50.

G8. "Joint Statement by the German G8 Presidency and the Heads of State and/or Government of Brazil, China, India, Mexico and South Africa on the Occasion of the

G8 Summit in Heiligendamm, Germany." June 8, 2007. http://www.g-8.de/Content/
EN/Artikel/__g8-summit/anlagen/o5-erklaerung-en,templateId=raw,property=public
ationFile.pdf/o5-erklaerung-en.pdf.

G20. "Cannes Summit Final Declaration—Building Our Common Future: Renewed
Collective Action for the Benefit of All." November 4, 2011. http://www.g20.
utoronto.ca/2011/2011-cannes-declaration-111104-en.html

G20 Leaders. "G20 Leaders' Declaration." September 6, 2013. http://www.g20.
utoronto.ca/2013/2013-0906-declaration.html.

GEA. *Global Energy Assessment—Toward a Sustainable Future.* Cambridge: Cambridge
University Press and Laxenburg, Austria: International Institute for Applied Systems
Analysis, 2012. http://www.iiasa.ac.at/web/home/research/Flagship-Projects/Global
-Energy-Assessment/GEA-Summary-web.pdf.

Golden, Miriam, and Brian Min. "Theft and Loss of Electricity in an Indian State."
Working paper 12/0060. London: International Growth Centre, 2012. http://www.
theigc.org/wp-content/uploads/2014/09/Golden-Min-2012-Working-Paper.pdf
http://www.theigc.org/sites/default/files/golden_and_min_paper.pdf.

Goldthau, A., and J. M. Witte, eds. *Global Energy Governance: The New Rules of the
Game.* Washington, DC: Brookings Institution Press, 2010.

Greenpeace International, European Renewable Energy Council, and Global Wind
Energy Council. *Energy [R]Evolution: A Sustainable World Energy Outlook.* Amsterdam:
Greenpeace International, EREC and GWEC, 2012. http://www.greenpeace.org/
international/Global/international/publications/climate/2012/Energy
percent20Revolution percent202012/ER2012.pdf.

Hare, William, Claire Stockwell, Christian Flachsland, and Sebastian Oberthür. "The
Architecture of the Global Climate Regime: A Top-Down Perspective." *Climate Policy*
10 (2010): 600–14.

Harris, Gardiner. "Beijing's Bad Air Would Be Step Up for Smoggy Delhi." *New York
Times,* January 25, 2014. http://www.nytimes.com/2014/01/26/world/asia/beijings
-air-would-be-step-up-for-smoggy-delhi.html?_r=0&module=ArrowsNav&contentCo
llection=Asia percent20Pacific&action=keypress&region=FixedLeft&pgtype=article.

Harrison, Kathryn, and Lisa McIntosh Sundstrom, eds. *Global Commons, Domestic
Decisions: The Comparative Politics of Climate Change.* Cambridge, MA: MIT Press,
2010.

Held, D., C. Roger, and E.-M. Nag, eds. *Climate Governance in the Developing World.*
Cambridge: Polity Press, 2013.

IPCC. "Summary for Policymakers." In O. Edenhofer, et al., *Climate Change 2014:
Mitigation of Climate Change. Contribution of Working Group III to the Fifth Assessment*

Report of the Intergovernmental Panel on Climate Change. Cambridge: Cambridge University Press, 2014.

IPCC. "Summary for Policymakers." In O. Edenhofer, et al., *Climate Change 2014: Synthesis Report.* Cambridge: Cambridge University Press, 2014.

International Energy Agency. *Re-drawing the Energy-Climate Map: World Energy Outlook Special Report.* Paris: OECD/IEA, 2013. http://www.iea.org/publications/ freepublications/publication/WEO_Special_Report_2013_Redrawing_the_Energy _Climate_Map.pdf.

Jones, Bruce, David Steven, and Emily O'Brien. *Fueling a New Order? The New Geopolitical and Security Consequences of Energy.* Washington, DC: Brookings Press, 2014. http://www.brookings.edu/~/media/research/files/papers/2014/04/14%20 geopolitical%20security%20consequences%20energy%20jones/14%20 geopolitical%20security%20energy%20jones%20steven_fixed.pdf.

Keohane, Robert O., and David G. Victor. "The Regime Complex for Climate Change." *Perspectives on Politics* 9, no. 01 (2011): 7–23.

Kong, Bo. "Governing China's Energy in the Context of Global Governance." *Global Policy* 2 (2011): 51–65.

Lachapelle, Erick, and Matthew Paterson. "Drivers of National Climate Policy." *Climate Policy* 13 (2013): 547–71.

Lamb, William F., and Narasimha D. Rao. "Human Development in a Climate Constrained World: What the Future Says about the Past." *Global Environmental Change* 33 (2015): 14–22.

Lele, Sharachchandra. "Climate Change and the Indian Environmental Movement." In *Handbook of Climate Change and India: Development, Politics and Governance*, edited by Navroz K. Dubash, 208–17. New Delhi: Oxford University Press, 2011.

Mani, Muthukumara, "An Analysis of Physical and Monetary Losses of Environmental Health and Natural Resources in India." In World Bank Policy Research working paper. Washington, DC: World Bank, 2012. http://elibrary.worldbank.org/ doi/pdf/10.1596/1813-9450-6219.

Nakhooda, Smita. "Asia, the Multilateral Development Banks and Energy Governance." *Global Policy* 2 (2011): 120–32.

Planning Commission, Government of India. *The Final Report of the Expert Group on Low Carbon Strategies for Inclusive Growth.* New Delhi: Government of India, 2014. http://planningcommission.nic.in/reports/genrep/rep_carbon2005.pdf.

Planning Commission, Government of India. *Integrated Energy Policy: Report of the Expert Committee.* New Delhi: Government of India, 2006. http:// planningcommission.nic.in/reports/genrep/rep_intengy.pdf.

Planning Commission, Government of India. *Twelfth Five Year Plan 2012–17.* New Delhi: Government of India, 2013. http://planningcommission.nic.in/plans/planrel/fiveyr/welcome.html.

Prime Minister's Council on Climate Change, Government of India. *National Action Plan on Climate Change.* New Delhi: Government of India, 2008. http://www.moef.nic.in/modules/about-the-ministry/CCD/NAP_E.pdf.

Qi, Xinran. "The Rise of BASIC in UN Climate Change Negotiations." *South African Journal of International Affairs* 18 (2011): 295–318.

Rajamani, Lavanya. "Deconstructing Durban." *Indian Express,* December 15, 2011. http://archive.indianexpress.com/news/deconstructing-durban/887892/0.

Rao, Narasimha, Girish Sant, and Sudhir Chella Rajan. *An Overview of Indian Energy Trends: Low Carbon Growth and Development Challenges.* Pune: Prayas (Energy Group), 2009. http://www.climateworks.org/imo/media/doc/prayas-2009.pdf.

Rayner, Steve. "How to Eat an Elephant: A Bottom-Up Approach to Climate Policy." *Climate Policy* 10 (2010): 615–21.

Sovacool, Benjamin K., and Ishani Mukherjee. "Conceptualizing and Measuring Energy Security: A Synthesized Approach." *Energy* 36 (8) (2011): 5343–55.

Sreenivas, Ashok, and Rakesh Iyer. "A Dashboard for the Indian Energy Sector" *Economic and Political Weekly,* March 14, 2011: 13–16.

Supreme Court of India. "Order Dated 25 August 2014." In *Uttar Haryana BijliVitran Nigam Ltd &Anr. v. Central Electricity Regulatory Commission &Ors.* Civil Appeal No. 7466 of 2014.

Teng, Fei. "The recent development of climate policy in China: Progress in 12th Five Year Plan" Presentation at the Centre for Policy Research, New Delhi, India, August 7, 2013.

Teng, Fei, and Alan Gu. "Climate Change: National and Local Policy Opportunities in China." *Environmental Sciences* 4 (2007): 183–94.

United Nations Environment Programme. *The Emissions Gap Report 2014: A UNEP Synthesis Report.* Nairobi: UNEP, 2014. http://www.unep.org/publications/ebooks/emissionsgapreport2014/ .

United Nations Environment Programme. *MCA4 Climate: A Practical Framework for Planning Pro-Development Climate Policies.* Paris: UNEP, 2011. http://www.mca4climate.info/_assets/files/FINAL_MCA4report_online.pdf.

Urge-Vorsatz, Diana, Sergio Tirado-Herrero, Navroz K. Dubash, and Franck Lecocq. "Measuring the Co-Benefits of Climate Change Mitigation." In *Annual Review of Environment and Resources* 39:20.1–20.35, 2014.

van Asselt, Harro, and Fariborz Zelli. "Connect the Dots: Managing the Fragmentation of Global Climate Governance." Earth System Governance working paper25. Lund and Amsterdam: Earth System Governance Project, 2012. http://papers.ssrn.com/sol3/papers.cfm?abstract_id=2139375 (.

Van de Graaf, Thijs. "Obsolete or Resurgent? The International Energy Agency in a Changing Global Landscape." *Energy Policy* 48 (2012): 233–41.

Winkler, Harald, Shaun Vorster, and Andrew Marquard. "Who Picks Up the Remainder? Mitigation in Developed and Developing Countries." *Climate Policy* 9 (2009): 634–51.

World Bank. "World Bank Group Sets Direction for Energy Sector Investment." *World Bank News,* July 16, 2013. http://www.worldbank.org/en/news/feature/2013/07/16/world-bank-group-direction-for-energy-sector.

14 Governing Climate Engineering

Wil Burns and Simon Nicholson

The real revenge ... is the tendency of the world around us to get even, to twist our cleverness against us.

—Edward Tenner

One of the defining features of the New Earth is humanity's rapidly expanding technological reach. The modern world is filled with marvels. Devices that fit in the palms of our hands can connect us with friends and happenings in all corners of the world. Satellites and sensor arrays can deliver pinpoint information about human activities and the state of Earth systems. Looking forward, the positive potentials of near-future technologies are mind-boggling. In particular, extension of the rapid advances already being seen in genetics, robotics, information technology, and nanotechnology—a suite of developments that social commentator and former *Washington Post* journalist Joel Garreau terms the "GRIN" technologies—offers remarkable promise for the betterment of our lives and our world.[1]

At the same time, though, technology's immense promise comes with peril. Technologies are implicated deeply in the most pressing problems of the New Earth. For example, technological churning within industrialized economies produces an array of disruptive social effects, with each new major technological innovation challenging established patterns of livelihood. It is also now widely appreciated that the patterns of technology-driven economic and social development are at the root of much environmental harm, from localized pollution and resource scarcities to ecological distress on a global scale (see chapter 1). At the extreme, it is one of the intrinsic burdens of living on the New Earth that humanity has developed the technological capacity to destroy the preponderance of life, whether by choice or error, in a number of different ways. Nuclear weapons—deployed in the service of either superpower security or megaterrorism—threaten all living things. Many other innovations similarly contribute to our collective abilities to kill one another, poison ourselves, and, most dramatic, undermine the planet's life-supporting functions. Climate change stands as the most potent example of this reality.

The New Earth, then, is marked by humanity's ability, through the application of technology, to fundamentally shape and reshape all aspects of the world. In a very real sense, the fate of the planet rests on humanity's coming to terms with potent technologies and with effectively steering their development. An important set of questions for scholars and practitioners of global environmental politics then centers around technological governance. Is the shaping of technological development something that is even possible? If it is, by what means can technological development be nudged in productive rather than destructive directions? Other questions follow. Who gets to set the technological agenda, and in pursuit of what ends? What does a realistic and honest conversation about technological futures look like? And so on.

In this chapter, we take on one particular technological governance question: How can the existing tools and techniques of global governance, and in particular the kinds of institutional arrangements that Kate O'Neill and Maria Ivanova explore in, respectively, chapters 7 and 8, to good effect, be used to shape the directions of technological innovation? We examine that question through the emerging technological realm of climate engineering, or geoengineering.

Climate engineering is an umbrella term that encompasses a wide array of speculative technologies and techniques that, proponents contend, could be a bridge to help avoid passing critical temperature thresholds while the global community moves toward the decarbonization of the world economy that Navroz Dubash looks at in chapter 13, or as a response to a climate emergency, such as rapid melting of ice masses or permafrost. A number of climate engineering ideas have been advanced, and the ideas are normally separated into two categories. In the first category are carbon dioxide removal (CDR) proposals, which might draw down carbon (and perhaps other greenhouse gases) from the atmosphere, to be held in long-term storage or put to beneficial use. Examples include seeding the oceans with iron to encourage carbon-inhaling blooms of phytoplankton and the imagined deployment of "artificial draws" that would trap carbon in the open air using a chemical receptor. The second category is known as solar radiation management (SRM), or albedo modification, on the understanding that reflecting some amount of incoming solar radiation back into space before it can warm the earth's atmosphere would suppress global, or perhaps regional, temperatures. The leading SRM proposals include depositing reflective sulfate particles in the upper atmosphere and artificially brightening clouds by spraying saltwater into the cloud layer.

Such ideas have the ring of science fiction, and for many years, they were largely viewed as "a freak show in otherwise serious discussions of climate science and policy."[2] However, climate engineering is rapidly emerging from the fringes of climate policymaking to the realm of serious contemplation.

Both of us have been paying close attention to the scientific, legal, political, and public conversations around climate engineering for many years. We were drawn to an examination of climate engineering initially out of simple intellectual and academic curiosity. Until quite recently, discussions of climate engineering seemed devoid of any practical relevance. Now, though, the push for geoengineering is gathering steam. This is understandable, as we'll explain below, but also potentially troubling.

The Fast-Evolving Climate Engineering Conversation

Many of the ideas we touched on above are not new. In fact, some of them have been floating around for decades. In the United States, the Report of the Environmental Pollution panel of the President's Science Advisory Committee in 1965 included a discussion of the potential impacts of climate change and "the possibilities of deliberately bringing about countervailing climatic changes" by "increasing the albedo of the world's oceans by spreading reflective particles over large portions."[3]

In 1977, the National Academy of Sciences (NAS) released a report, "Energy and Climate," that included in its discussion of "four crucial questions" the issue of "what, if any, countervailing human actions could diminish the climatic changes or mitigate their consequences." Several options were discussed, including ocean fertilization with phosphorus, engineered increases in planetary albedo, and massive afforestation. While the report concluded that mitigation via reliance on renewable energy sources would most likely emerge as a more viable strategy, it also stated that if climate change projections were further substantiated, there might be a need for looking at options under which carbon dioxide can be "controlled" or "compensated" for.

The impulse to control the world around us is hardly a new thing. Our earliest ancestors used the power of mind and muscle, augmented by rudimentary tools, to bend and shape local ecosystems. Since the birth of agriculture around 10,000 years ago, humanity's efforts to alter the world to fit human needs and desires has taken on a new character and force as human populations have settled and expanded, as capital and knowledge have accumulated, and as ever more powerful technologies have been brought forth. One way to read climate engineering proposals is as the logical (and perhaps culminating) expression of this deep urge to control the world around us.

Still, despite some scattered attention in prior times, it is only in the last handful of years that climate engineering proposals have lost the ring of the impossible and have started to receive serious consideration by scientists and policymakers. Talk of climate engineering is now edging from the fringes of the climate conversation for two closely related reasons.

First, there is a growing sense of widespread disillusionment with international and national responses to climate change. The United Nations Framework Convention on Climate Change (UNFCCC)[4] and its Kyoto Protocol,[5] the primary international instruments to address climate change, have proven to be feckless. Greenhouse gas emissions have grown by a third since the UNFCCC was agreed to in 1992,[6] and its parties have failed to commit to meaningful future reductions in greenhouse gas emissions within the requisite time frames to exceed critical temperature thresholds. Moreover, at the national level, major emitters, including the United States, China, and India, remain committed to fossil fuel–based economies. Indeed, a recent assessment by the International Energy Agency concludes that at current rates of greenhouse gas emissions, the "carbon budget" to avoid exceeding temperature increases of 2°C above preindustrial levels could be exceeded in approximately twenty-five years.[7] The Intergovernmental Panel on Climate Change (IPCC) concludes, in its most recent assessment reports, that temperature increases of this magnitude would substantially increase the likelihood of "severe, pervasive and irreversible impacts for people and ecosystems."[8] By the end of the century, temperatures could increase by 3°C to 4°C or more, with potentially catastrophic implications.[9] Moreover, temperatures would not begin to drop substantially for at least a millennium.[10]

As a consequence, a range of voices has begun to call for serious consideration of what some are calling a "plan B" response to climate change, usually as part of a suite of strategies including mitigation and adaptation approaches.[11] One of the most important endorsements of climate engineering research in the past decade was by Paul Crutzen, a recipient of the Nobel Prize in Chemistry. In a 2006 article, Crutzen bemoaned "the grossly disappointing international political response to the required greenhouse gas emissions." Concluding that "drastic results" could occur from projected temperature increases, Crutzen advocated research on the feasibility of using stratospheric sulfur injections to cool the planet.[12] Crutzen's intervention set the stage for the recent burst of scientific activity around climate engineering by helping to dispel the widely-held taboo associated with it that to that point had been held within the scientific community.

Second, a growing number of credible and respected scientists and scientific bodies around the world are now devoting serious attention to climate engineering. Relevant research programs have been established by individual labs and by groups of scientists at national laboratories and universities in the United States, Canada, several European countries, Japan, and India. In addition to work on atmospheric modeling related to climate engineering science and technological logistics, prominent universities in the United States and Europe have established programs focused on geoengineering policy, ethics, and governance. The Fifth Assessment Report of the IPCC, released in 2013 and 2014, surprised many in the climate world by including a quite extensive analysis of climate engineering approaches. The technical work completed to date as a result of these various efforts indicates that, at least in theory, there appear to be some relatively straightforward and cost-effective ways to intervene in the climate system in order to bring about meaningful levels of change. Some strategies, such as the introduction of sulfates into the stratosphere, build from existing technologies and technical knowledge such that they could conceivably be deployed within a handful of years. Other options exist largely as promising lines of inquiry.

These are recent and quite rapid developments. Tellingly, one study from 2013 notes that at that point, there had been more peer-reviewed articles on climate engineering in the prior three years than were seen in the thirty years before that period.[13]

The heightened levels of academic interest in climate engineering are beginning to be echoed in the policy realm. A notable intervention took place in 2009 when John Holdren, President Obama's chief science advisor, stated in an interview with the Associated Press, "It [climate engineering] has got to be looked at. We don't have the luxury of taking any approach off the table."[14] He subsequently emphasized, however, that the focus of the administration was on decarbonizing the economy. That same year and in 2010, the House Science and Technology Committee of the US House of Representatives, under the chairmanship of Bart Gordon, a Democrat from Tennessee, held hearings on geoengineering that examined the "potential environmental risks and benefits of various proposals, associated domestic and international governance issues, evaluation mechanisms and criteria, research and development (R&D) needs, and economic rationales supporting the deployment of geoengineering activities."[15] The United Kingdom's House of Commons Science and Technology Committee also held hearings in 2009 and 2010, culminating in a committee report that recommended public funding of climate engineering research and consideration of potential regulatory architecture for climate engineering research.[16]

The year 2010 ended up being a signal year for the climate engineering discussion in the United States. In March of that year, Margaret Leinen of the Climate Response Fund and Michael MacCracken of the Climate Institute organized and facilitated the Asilomar International Conference on Climate Intervention Technologies, which culminated in the release of a report calling for climate engineering research under a set of prescribed guidelines.[17] Also in 2010, the Bipartisan Policy Center, a nonprofit organization established by several former US Senate majority leaders from both parties, launched the Task Force on Geoengineering, consisting of American scientists, academics, and representatives of various policy communities. The task force's work culminated in the release of a report calling for an international research program on climate engineering options and a dialogue on policy issues.[18]

A final notable occurrence in 2010 was the establishment of the Solar Radiation Management Governance Initiative (SRMGI) by the American-based nongovernmental Environmental Defense Fund, in conjunction with the United Kingdom's Royal Society and the World Academy of Sciences.[19] The purpose of this group has been to meet with and encourage conversation among a wide variety of stakeholders, especially those in the developing world and emerging economies, to ensure more robust and global discussions of SRM research and governance.

Since 2010, the pace of public and policy engagement has, if anything, continued to speed up, with a wider variety of actors showing interest in different aspects of the climate engineering conversation. In 2013, for instance, the American Meteorological Society readopted a policy statement on climate engineering that concluded that "it is prudent to consider geoengineering's potential benefits, to understand its limitations, and to avoid ill-considered deployment," and that climate engineering "could contribute to a comprehensive risk management strategy to slow climate change."[20] Some level of ongoing interest on the part of the US Congress has been signaled by two reports on climate engineering being commissioned from the Congressional Research Service (CRS) in the span of three years, with the second report released in November 2013. The most recent CRS report provided an overview of then-current climate engineering research and funding by government agencies and the current state of international law in the context of climate engineering.[21]

Still, it should be stressed that activity focused on climate engineering within the US government, or public research funded by government agencies, is still very small in scale. Despite a US Department of Energy white paper recommendation in 2001 for a $64 million geoengineering proposal, there was only, by late 2014, approximately $1 million of government money directly funding climate engineering research in the United States, though substantial amounts of research in other areas (e.g., carbon capture and storage and climate modeling) are pertinent. In testimony before the House Committee on Science and Technology, officials from various interagency bodies coordinating the US response to climate change stated that their offices "(1) have not developed a coordinated research strategy [for geoengineering activities], (2) do not have a position on geoengineering, and (3) do not believe it is necessary to coordinate efforts due to the limited federal investment to date."[22]

In retrospect, a potential inflection point may have been the release in early 2015 of a pair of reports by an ad hoc committee on climate engineering established by the National Research Council of the National Academy of Sciences.[23] In the past, reports issued by this body have proven highly influential in guiding national agendas on major technologies.[24] The committee was tasked with both conducting a technical evaluation of climate engineering options and identifying future research needs. The reports' release followed closely on the heels of a meeting in Washington, D.C., convened by dozens of international scientific societies to develop a set of principles for climate engineering research.[25] While expressing caution about these technologies, particularly solar radiation management approaches, the reports called for a federal research initiative on climate geoengineering options.

There are also modest research programs in Europe. This includes the Implications and risks of engineering solar radiation to limit climate change (IMPLICC) project, a collaboration by five European universities to assess the potential effectiveness and risk of SRM climate engineering approaches with numerical earth system models;[26] the Stratospheric Particle Injection for Climate Engineering (SPICE) project in the United Kingdom, an aborted effort to conduct a field test on SRM approaches;[27] EuTRACE, the European

Transdisciplinary Assessment of Climate Engineering,[28] a consortium of fourteen institutions tasked with assessing the potential for deploying climate engineering technologies and policy options; and the Oxford Geoengineering Programme,[29] which advocates climate engineering research and stakeholder engagement.

The drumbeat for a fully funded research program for climate engineering may grow much louder should the parties to the UNFCCC fail in coming years to formulate a transformative long-term agreement to address greenhouse gas emissions. However, should this transpire, it could impose, as Maria Ivanova observes, "the most serious governance concern ... in the next couple of decades."[30] In the next section of this chapter, we outline the potential governance architecture for climate engineering should it come to be a reality on a New Earth.

Governing Climate Engineering: The Prospects within Existing Regimes

Climate engineering is a difficult emerging technology with which to wrestle. The upsides are enormous, but the risks run the gamut from intrusive (sulfate aerosol dispersal changing the color of the sky) to catastrophic (sulfate aerosol dispersal shutting down the South Asian monsoons). Besides its purportedly low cost, many proponents argue that one of climate engineering options' most attractive characteristics is that they could be deployed unilaterally. This is often contrasted with "the unprecedented international cooperation" required to effectuate mitigation of greenhouse gas emissions.[31] Unfortunately, this is also one of the most foreboding aspects of the emergence of geoengineering options, because deployment of SRM and CDR technologies could pose serious threats to the interests of many who could be denied a voice in a unilateral or limited multilateral decision-making process. For example, stratospheric sulfur injection approaches would almost invariably reduce rainfall in several vulnerable regions because evaporation is approximately twice as sensitive to sunlight as temperature. The consequent reductions in evaporation could substantially weaken Asian and African monsoons, potentially imperiling the food and water supplies of billions of people.[32]

Moreover, recent studies also indicate that climate engineering schemes that would enhance aerosol loads in the stratosphere could result in global annual mean decreases of the ozone column of 4.5 percent, more than the annual global mean decreases associated with ozone-depleting substances in the early part of this century. This could delay recovery of the ozone layer in the Antarctic by between thirty and seventy years.[33] This would likely have a disproportionate impact on populations in developing countries where medical care, including early diagnosis of disease, is often lacking.

Carbon dioxide removal schemes could also pose threats in a transboundary context or to the global commons. For example, ocean iron fertilization could potentially wreak havoc with ocean ecosystems by reducing surface nutrient inventories; imperiling productivity of downstream plankton communities;[34] inducing hypoxia (oxygen deprivation), which could imperil marine species;[35] and creating changes in the composition of phytoplankton communities that could adversely affect the populations of larger predators, including copepods, krill, salps, jellyfish, and other fish species.[36] Bioenergy capture and carbon sequestration options could substantially increase food prices for the poor, as they could divert substantial amounts of farmland or crops for biofuel production.[37] Moreover, already marginalized populations, including indigenous peoples, could be displaced in land grabs for feedstock.[38]

A failure to engage in a coordinated program of climate engineering research, should such a research program gather significant steam, could also result in a scenario in which a nation panics in the future and deploys a wholly untested technology, with potentially dire results. As John Virgoe notes, "Ignoring geoengineering today, and only considering it when all else has failed, is a recipe for bad, politics-led decision-making."[39]

Thus, it is critical that international governance mechanisms are put in place to ensure that any research on climate geoengineering that may ensue, as well as potential deployment, be structured in a way that protects the interests of the global community and particular populations and landscapes within it. In using the term *governance* in this context, we adopt the expansive definition of the Bipartisan Policy Center, which encompasses "the actions of government agencies, nation states and international institutions, but ... also includes formal and informal efforts by scientific organizations, non-governmental organizations and many other non-state actors and networks carrying out purposive acts of steering."[40]

A critical threshold question is determining the optimal forum, or forums, for situating such governance. We initially examine whether two international treaty regimes that have responded to ocean iron fertilization field research experiments, the Convention on Biological Diversity and the London Convention and its Protocol under the International Maritime Organization, are the appropriate venues for climate engineering governance.

At its annual meeting in 2009, the parties to the Convention on Biological Diversity adopted a resolution calling on the parties to not engage in ocean fertilization activities in the absence of "an adequate scientific basis on which to justify such activities," including risk assessment and transparent and effective control and regulatory mechanisms. An exception was carved out for small-scale scientific research studies in coastal waters, if justified for specific scientific purposes and without commercial purpose.[41] The parties essentially affirmed this position in two subsequent resolutions and expanded its scope to all climate engineering activities that may affect biodiversity. [42]

The CBD, however, would be ill equipped to serve as the primary forum to regulate climate engineering. Its remit is limited to threats to biodiversity, while many of the gravest threats posed by climate engineering are to humans. Moreover, the resolutions passed by the parties are not legally binding,[43] and there has been no movement to adopt a binding amendment, protocol, or annex to the convention to address climate engineering. Finally, one of the nations most likely to engage in climate engineering activities, the United States, is not a party to the treaty, and thus not subject to its mandates.

The other regime that has addressed climate engineering in the past few years is the Convention on the Prevention of Marine Pollution by Dumping of Wastes and Other Matter 1972 (London Convention) of the International Maritime Organization.[44] In 2008, the parties to the convention passed a resolution recognizing the treaty's jurisdiction over ocean fertilization activities and limiting such activities to "legitimate scientific research." The resolution also provided that scientific research proposals should be vetted on a case-by-case basis under an assessment framework to be developed by the Scientific Groups of the London Convention and its protocol.[45] In 2010, the parties adopted the Assessment Framework for Scientific Research.[46] Finally, in 2013, the parties adopted an amendment to the 1996 Protocol to the Convention, authorizing ocean fertilization activities under the convention only if they constitute "legitimate scientific research" taking into account any specific placement assessment framework. It also incorporated the Assessment Framework into an annex, and allowed for the London Protocol to consider, include, and regulate other marine geoengineering activities in the future.[47]

The London Convention, however, despite these actions, would also appear to be a problematic institution for climate engineering governance. First, it has only eighty-seven parties, limiting its legitimacy. This is in contrast to almost universal ratification of treaties such as the Convention on

Biological Diversity and the UN Framework Convention on Climate Change. Also, like the CBD, the convention suffers from the fact that its resolutions are not legally binding. Finally, the convention's focus on marine activities means that most contemplated geoengineering options would not fall under its regulatory purview. The marine geoengineering amendment to the London Protocol does legally bind its parties.. However, it has been ratified by only forty-five states to date, severely circumscribing its legitimacy, and again, the focus of the convention circumscribes the climate engineering options that could conceivably fall under its rubric.

International governance suitable to the potential deployment of large-scale climate engineering requires, then, a regime with broad reach and legitimacy. Additionally, any formal governance of climate engineering must be explicitly tied to efforts to reduce greenhouse gas emissions. This is because should a nation, or group of nations, choose to deploy an SRM approach, it would be critical to coordinate a scheduled reduction of emissions of sufficient rapidity to avoid the threat of a "termination" effect. The *termination effect* refers to the potential for a huge multidecadal pulse of warming should the use of an SRM scheme be terminated abruptly in the future due to technological failure or a decision by future policymakers (such as under threat of military retaliation by a nation that believes its interests are threatened). This would be a consequence of the buildup of carbon dioxide that had accrued in the atmosphere in the interim, with its suppressed warming effect, as well as the temporary suppression of climate-carbon feedbacks.[48]

The ramifications of the termination effect could be "catastrophic."[49] As one study recently concluded:

Should the engineered system later fail for technical or policy reasons, the downside is dramatic. .... The climate suppression has only been temporary, and the now CO_2-loaded atmosphere quickly bites back, leading to severe and rapid climate change with rates up to 20 times the current rate of warming of $\approx 0.2°C$ per decade.[50]

As a consequence, models suggest that temperatures could increase 6°C to 10°C in the winter in the Arctic region within thirty years of termination of the use of SRM technology, with northern landmasses seeing increases of 6°C in summer.[51] Moreover, temperatures could jump 7°C in the tropics in thirty years.[52] Projected temperature increases after termination would occur more rapidly than during one of the most extreme and abrupt global warming events in history, the Paleocene-Eocene thermal maximum.[53] It is beyond contention that climatic changes of this magnitude "could trigger unimaginable ecological effects."[54] To put this rate of temperature increase in perspective, a recent study concluded that even a warming rate of greater than 0.1°C per decade could threaten most major ecosystems and decrease their ability to adapt.[55] Should temperatures increase at a rate of 0.3°C per decade, only 30 percent of all affected ecosystems and only 17 percent of all affected forests would be able to adapt.[56] Moreover, temperature increases of this magnitude and rapidity would imperil many human institutions.[57]

Governing via the Existing Climate Change Regime

Ultimately we believe that the most appropriate venue for international oversight of climate engineering research and potential deployment would be the UNFCCC, the primary international instrument to address climate change. This should include assessment of the viability and impacts of response measures.[58] Moreover, the regime's legitimacy to address this issue globally is also enhanced by universal state ratification, with the exception of the Holy See.

Questions remain, however. One potentially serious barrier to tasking the UNFCCC with this role is its questionable jurisdictional authority over SRM climate engineering approaches. The text of the UNFCCC provides that its ultimate objective is "stabilization of greenhouse gas concentrations in the atmosphere at a level that would prevent dangerous anthropogenic interference with the climate system,"[59] primarily to be effectuated by "measures to mitigate climate change by addressing anthropogenic emissions by sources and removals by sinks of ... greenhouse gases."[60] John Virgoe contends that climate engineering approaches that don't seek to alter the composition of the atmosphere in terms of greenhouse gases would thus be outside the regulatory scope of the UNFCCC.[61] By its terms, this would preclude UNFCCC jurisdiction over all solar radiation management options because they don't seek to alter atmospheric concentrations of greenhouse gases, but rather the amount of incoming solar radiation.

We believe that this interpretation of the UNFCCC is too crabbed. Article 3(1) provides that the parties are to "protect the climate system for the benefit of present and future systems," with the term *climate system* defined as "the totality of the atmosphere, hydrosphere, biosphere and geosphere and their interactions."[62] Thus, to the extent that SRM approaches could profoundly affect precipitation patterns or the ozone layer, or more basically, alter heat distribution in the stratosphere, it would appear that the UNFCCC would have jurisdiction to address potential climatic threats posed by such technologies. Furthermore, Article 4(8) mandates that the parties "give full consideration" to the implementation of response measures to climate change on developing countries, which could clearly encompass climate engineering responses.

The UNFCCC regime does not directly engage in research, so one critical question would be how climate engineering research could be conducted under its rubric. We suggest that the UNFCCC has the legal authority to establish a coordinated transnational research program on climate engineering approaches. Article 4(1)(g) requires UNFCCC parties to "cooperate in scientific, technological, technical, socio-economic and other research ... related to the climate system." Furthermore, Article 5(a) provides for support and development of international and intergovernmental programs to facilitate such research.

The convention also authorizes an assessment process by the parties of any research that would grow out of such an initiative. Article 7 provides for the Conference of Parties to assess the effects of measures taken to address climate change and "to seek and utilize ... the services and cooperation of, and information provided by, competent international organizations and intergovernmental and non-governmental bodies." In conducting such assessments, the parties could also draw on the expertise of its Subsidiary Body for Scientific and Technological Advice,[63] which has established a Forum and Work Program on the Impact of the Implementation of Response Measures,[64] as well as the IPCC.

Every effort should be made to establish an international research program with broad representation of the world's scientific community. Potential forums for this program, in coordination with the UNFCCC, could include the Inter Academy Council of the world's scientific academic academies[65] or the World Climate Research Programme.[66] Such research should also be guided by the following principles:

1. *Transparency and public deliberation.* As Craik and Moore observe, "Transparency enables affected parties to understand their interests and effectively participate in case-by-case decisions."[67] Coordinators of research efforts should develop transparency protocols to maximize public access to pertinent information. These protocols should be based on the risk of any specific experiment as well as the risks that could be posed by deployment of the technology in question. Additionally, given the momentous implications of deploying geoengineering technologies in terms of both potential impacts and governance, every effort should be made to engender extensive public deliberation. This should include the use of deliberative

mechanisms such as citizen juries, deliberative mapping, and deliberative polling.[68]

2. *Impact assessments.* The UNFCCC provides for environmental impact assessment by its parties for measures to mitigate and adapt to climate change,[69] and thus should by extension mandate the same to potential climate engineering responses. Moreover, the International Court of Justice has held that there is an obligation under customary international law to conduct transboundary environmental impact assessments for any activity that may impose a risk of a significant adverse transboundary impact.[70] While mandates of environmental impact assessments usually do not result in halting projects, it often results in modification of projects in ways that may reduce their adverse impacts.[71] A good model for formulating such assessments would be the UN Convention on Environmental Impact Assessment in a Transboundary Context[72] (the Espoo Convention) and its associated Protocol on Strategic Environmental Assessment,[73] which could be applicable in the case of climate engineering deployment programs. Beyond the standard components of impact assessments, we would argue that climate engineering protocols should include a consideration of the implications of these technologies for human rights. The parties to the UNFCCC in their Copenhagen Long-Term Cooperative Action (LCA) negotiating text recognized that "parties should, in all climate change-related actions, fully respect human rights."[74] Some of the potential negative impacts of climate engineering technologies could have serious implications for human rights, including the right to life,[75] the right to health,[76], the right to food,[77] and the rights of indigenous people to enjoyment of land and natural resources.[78] The human rights obligations taken on by the parties in the Copenhagen LCA should be operationalized in climate engineering assessments by including a human rights assessment. This approach may help to ensure that the interests of the vulnerable, which might otherwise be overlooked in a strict cost-benefit analysis, are taken into account in the decision-making process.[79]

3. *Establishment of research thresholds.* Research initiatives should be limited initially to small-scale interventions, defined by strict criteria related to project scale and risk, employing metrics such as project area, duration, and potential system responses, such as potential changes in radiative forcing in the case of SRM approaches. Any escalation of research above such thresholds should require express approval by the parties to the UNFCCC.

4. *Coordination with other regimes.* The UNFCCC should seek to coordinate with other treaty bodies that have an interest in climate engineering

options because of their potential impacts. Beyond the Convention on Biological Diversity and the London Convention, this might include, for example, the Convention on the Conservation of Antarctic Living Resources in the context of ocean iron fertilization or the Vienna Convention for the Protection of the Ozone Layer. Every effort should be made, for example, to draw on the specialized expertise of these regimes in proposed research programs.

We are not so naive as to believe that these first steps toward a robust governance proposal would stop a powerful individual nation from proceeding with deployment of climate engineering technologies. However, efforts to create an international forum to scrutinize such options may, as Daniel Bodansky concludes, "prevent actors from making decisions that might have serious, even catastrophic consequences for others."[80]

Conclusion

The pressure to consider climate engineering is building. These pressures give rise to significant questions in our increasingly technology-saturated world. Indeed, comprehending the nature, meaning, and drivers of technological change must be considered one of the most pressing intellectual and political challenges of the New Earth. While there have been technologies for as long as there have been human societies, the technologies now possible are qualitatively different from any that we have seen before. We live in a time when information and communications technologies encircle the globe, driving forward and further extending the processes of globalization; when nuclear and nanotechnologies represent increasingly dramatic, sweeping incursions into the material world; and when, with biotechnology, the deep-seated human impulse toward technological wizardry has taken on new and remarkable proportions as we begin to tinker with the very makeup of life itself. Never before have technologies offered such power, along with such an excess of stark prospects.

There is talk now that there can be a "good" Anthropocene—that the arrival of the New Earth can usher in a new era of human flourishing. As recent debates between Andrew Revkin and Clive Hamilton demonstrate, this is difficult and contentious territory.[81] Our own view is that if a desire to produce a "good Anthropocene" leads to a kind of techno-infatuation—a belief that magical technologies will solve all of our problems—we are heading down a disastrous path. Global environmental politics scholar Paul Wapner has written of such efforts as part of a deep "will to mastery" that infuses much of the contemporary effort to comprehend and respond to a changing environmental condition.[82] Should the global community ultimately feel compelled to embrace climate engineering technologies, it should be done with a spirit of humility, acknowledging it not as triumph but rather a manifestation of our failure to control preceding technological excesses that now threaten catastrophic climate change. We must move toward a vision of a New Earth in which we seek to reconcile humankind's potential reach with the ecological limits intrinsic to our fragile planet.

Notes

1. Garreau, *Radical Evolution*.

2. Victor, "On the Regulation of Geoengineering."

3. Environmental Pollution Panel, "Restoring the Quality of Our Environment," 127.

4. United Nations Framework Convention on Climate Change, 31 I.L.M. 849.

5. Kyoto Protocol.

6. Climate Institute, "Moving Below Zero," 8.

7. International Energy Agency, *World Energy Outlook 2014*.

8. IPCC, *Climate Change 2014: Synthesis Report* 8 (2014).

9. IEA, *World Energy Outlook*, 2 (current emissions path "consistent with a long-term global average temperature increase of 3.6°C"); Rogelj et al., "Analysis of the Copenhagen Accord Pledges," 5 (pledges made by the Parties in the Copenhagen Accord at the Fifteenth Conference of the Parties may result in temperature of increase of 2.5°C to 4.2°C by 2100, with temperatures continuing to increase after this point).

10. Solomon et al., "Irreversible Climate Change Due to Carbon Dioxide Emissions."

11. See Simon Nicholson, "Reimagining Climate Engineering."

12. Crutzen, "Albedo Enhancement by Stratospheric Sulfur Injection," 214.

13. Scott, "International Law in the Anthropocene." More than 700 articles have been published on climate geoengineering in the science and social science literature, the vast majority since 2010.

14. Jha, "Obama Climate Adviser Open to Geo-Engineering to Tackle Global Warming."

15. US House of Representatives, *Geoengineering Parts I, II, and III.*

16. House of Commons Science and Technology Committee, *The Regulation of Geoengineering.*

17. Asilomar Conference Recommendations, *Conference Report.*

18. Bipartisan Policy Center, *Geoengineering.*

19. Solar Radiation Governance Initiative, http://www.srmgi.org/.

20. American Meteorological Society, "Geoengineering the Climate System."

21. Bracmort and Lattanzio, *Geoengineering: Governance and Technology Policy.*

22. Testimony by Frank Rusco before the House of Representatives Committee on Science and Technology, March 18, 2010 GAO-10-546T, www.gao.gov/assets/130/124271.pdf.

23. Committee on Geoengineering Climate, et al., Climate Intervention: Carbon Dioxide Removal and Reliable Sequestration (2015); Committee on Geoengineering Climate, et al., Climate Intervention: Reflecting Sunlight to Cool Earth (2015), http://nas-sites.org/americasclimatechoices/public-release-event-climate-intervention-reports/

24. National Academy of Sciences, "Geoengineering Climate."

25. Schiermeier, "Climate Tinkerers Thrash Out a Plan."

26. IMPLICC, "Implications and Risks of Engineering Solar Radiation."

27. http://www.spice.ac.uk.

28. http://www.eutrace.org. EuTRACE released a major report on climate geoengineering options in mid-2015, EuTRACE, "The European Transdisciplinary Assessment of Climate Engineering (EuTRACE) (Stefan Schäfer, et al., eds. 2015), http://www.iass-potsdam.de/sites/default/files/files/rz_150715_eutrace_digital.pdf

29. http://www.geoengineering.ox.ac.uk/.

30. Inman, "Planning for Plan B."

31. Barrett, "The Incredible Economics of Geoengineering," 49–50.

32. Burns, "Geoengineering the Climate."

33. Tilmes, Müller, and Salawitch, "The Sensitivity of Polar Ozone Depletion."

34. Cullen and Boyd, "Predicting and Verifying the Intended and Unintended Consequences of Large-Scale Ocean Iron Fertilization."

35. Rayfuse, Lawrence, and. Gjerde, "Ocean Fertilisation and Climate Change."

36. Abate and Greenlee, "Sowing Seeds Uncertain."

37. CBD Alliance, "Biofuels, Bioenergy, Biochar and the Technologies of the New Bioeconomy"; Azar, Johansson, and Mattsson, "Meeting Global Temperature Targets" (large-scale BECCS program could require one-third of global crop land).

38. Global Forest Coalition, *Stop the Destruction of Forests*.

39. Virgoe, "International Governance of a Possible Geoengineering Intervention to Combat Climate Change," 117.

40. Bipartisan Policy Center, *Task Force on Climate Remediation Research* 32 (2011), http://bipartisanpolicy.org/library/task-force-climate-remediation-research/.

41. Convention on Biological Diversity, *Ninth Meeting of the Conference of the Parties*.

42. Convention on Biological Diversity, *Tenth Meeting of the Conference of the Parties*; Convention on Biological Diversity, *Eleventh Meeting of the Conference of the Parties*.

43. Proelss, *Legal Opinion on the Legality of the LOHAFEX Marine Research Experiment*.

44. International Maritime Organization, Convention on the Prevention of Marine Pollution by Dumping of Wastes and other Matter, http://www.imo.org/en/About/Conventions/ListOfConventions/Pages/Convention-on-the-Prevention-of-Marine-Pollution-by-Dumping-of-Wastes-and-Other-Matter.aspx.

45. International Maritime Organization, London Convention, *Thirtieth Consultative Meeting*.

46. International Maritime Organization, London Convention, *Thirty-Second Consultative Meeting*. See also London Convention, *Assessment Framework for Scientific Research Involving Ocean Fertilization* (2010).

47. International Maritime Organization, London Convention, *Eighth Meeting of the Contracting Parties*.

48. Matthews and Caldeira, "Transient Climate-Carbon Simulations of Planetary Geoengineering."

49. Govindasamy et al., "Impact of Geoengineering Schemes on the Terrestrial Biosphere."

50. Brewer, "Evaluating a Technological Fix for Climate."

51. Brovkin et al., "Geoengineering Climate by Stratospheric Sulfur Injections."

52. Kintisch, "Scientists Say Continued Warming."

53. Ibid.

54. Ibid. See also Ross and Matthews, "Climate Engineering and the Risk of Rapid Climate Change" ("It seems likely that two decades of very high rates of warming would be sufficient to severely stress the adaptive capacity of many species and ecosystems, especially if preceded by some period of engineered climate stability").

55. Van Vliet and Leemans, "Rapid Species' Response to Changes in Climate."

56. Leemans and Eickhout, "Another Reason for Concern."

57. Kintisch, "Scientists Say Continued Warming," 1055.

58. UNFCCC, Article 4(1)(g)(h), Article 4(8).

59. Ibid., Article 4(1)(g)(h), Article 4(8) at Article 2.

60. Ibid., Article 4(1)(b).

61. Virgoe, *International Governance.*

62. United Nations Framework Convention on Climate Change, Article 1(3).

63. Ibid., Article 9(2)(a)(b).

64. UNFCCC, Subsidiary Body for Scientific and Technological Advice, FCCC/SB/2014/L.2.

65. InterAcademy Council, http://www.interacademycouncil.net/.

66. World Climate Research Programme, http://www.wcrp-climate.org/.

67. Craik and Moore, *Disclosure Based Governance for Climate Engineering Research, 2* .

68. Rowe and Frewer, "A Typology of Public Engagement Mechanisms."

69. United Nations Framework Convention on Climate Change, 31 I.L.M. 849.

70. *Pulp Mills on the River Uruguay (Argentina v. Uruguay) (Judgment).*

71. Knox, "The Myth and Reality of Transboundary Environmental Impact Assessment."

72. United Nations Convention on Environmental Impact Assessment in a Transboundary Context.

73. Protocol on Strategic Environmental Assessment to the Convention on Environmental Impact Assessment in a Transboundary Context.

74. UNFCCC, *Negotiating Text,* para. 8.

75. United Nations, Universal Declaration of Human Rights, Article 3; International Covenant on Civil and Political Rights Article 6.

76. United Nations, Universal Declaration of Human Rights, Article 25; International Covenant on Economic, Social and Cultural Rights, Article 12.

77. Ibid., Article 11.

78. United Nations, Office of the High Commissioner for Human Rights, *Mapping Human Rights Obligations.*

79. McInerney-Lankford, Darrow, and Rajamani, "Human Rights and Climate Change."

80. Bodansky, "The Who, What, and Wherefore of Geoengineering Governance," 541.

81. Revkin, "The Good, the Bad and the Anthropocene."

82. Wapner, *Living Through the End of Nature.*

Bibliography

Abate, Randall S., and Andrew B. Greenlee. "Sowing Seeds Uncertain: Ocean Iron Fertilization, Climate Change, and the International Environmental Law Framework." *Pace Environmental Law Review* 27 (2010): 555–98.

American Meteorological Society. "Geoengineering the Climate System," January 6, 2013. https://www.ametsoc.org/policy/2013geoengineeringclimate_amsstatement.html.

Asilomar Conference Recommendations on Principles for Research into Climate Engineering Techniques. *Conference Report.* 2010. http://www.climate.org/PDF/AsilomarConferenceReport.pdf.

Azar, Christian, Daniel J. A. Johansson, and Niclas Mattsson. "Meeting Global Temperature Targets: The Role of Bioenergy with Carbon Capture and Storage." *Environmental Research Letters* 8 (2013): 1–8.

Barrett, Scott. "The Incredible Economics of Geoengineering." *Environmental Resource Economics* 39, no. 1 (2009): 45–54.

Bipartisan Policy Center, Task Force on Climate Remediation Research. *Geoengineering: A National Strategic Plan for Research on the Potential Effectiveness, Feasibility, and Consequences of Climate Remediation Technologies.* 2011.

Bodansky, Daniel. "The Who, What, and Wherefore of Geoengineering Governance." *Climatic Change* 121 (2013): 539–51.

Bracmort, Kelsi, and Richard K. Lattanzio. *Geoengineering: Governance and Technology Policy.* Congressional Research Service R41371. 2013.

Brewer, Peter G. "Evaluating a Technological Fix for Climate." *Proceedings of the National Academy of Sciences of the United States of America* 104 (2007): 9915–16.

Brovkin, Victor, "Geoengineering Climate by Stratospheric Sulfur Injections: Earth System Vulnerability to Technological Failure." *Climatic Change* 92 (2009): 243–59.

Burns, William C. G. "Geoengineering the Climate: An Overview of Solar Radiation Management Options." *Tulsa Law Review* 462 (2012): 283–304.

CBD Alliance. "Biofuels, Bioenergy, Biochar and the Technologies of the New Bioeconomy: Are We Continuing to Fuel Biodiversity Loss?" 2012.

Climate Institute. "Moving below Zero: Understanding Bioenergy with Carbon Capture and Storage." 2014.

Convention on Biological Diversity. *Ninth Meeting of the Conference of the Parties, IX/16, Biodiversity and Climate Change* . 2009.

Convention on Biological Diversity. *Tenth Meeting of the Conference of the Parties, X/29, Marine and Coastal Biodiversity.* 2010.

Convention on Biological Diversity. *Eleventh Meeting of the Conference of the Parties, XI/20, Climate-Related Geoengineering.* 2011.

Craik, Neil, and Nigel Moore. *Disclosure Based Governance for Climate Engineering Research* CIGI papers 50. November 2014. http://www.cigionline.org/publications/disclosure-based-governance-climate-engineering-research

Crutzen, Paul J. "Albedo Enhancement by Stratospheric Sulfur Injections: A Contribution to Resolve a Policy Dilemma?" *Climatic Change* 77 (2006): 211–20.

Cullen, John J., and Philip W. Boyd. "Predicting and Verifying the Intended and Unintended Consequences of Large-Scale Ocean Iron Fertilization." *Marine Ecology Progress Series* 364 (2008): 295–301.

Environmental Pollution Panel, President's Science Advisory Committee. "Restoring the Quality of Our Environment." November 1965.

Garreau, Joel. *Radical Evolution: The Promise and Peril of Enhancing Our Minds, Our Bodies—and What It Means to Be Human.* New York: Doubleday, 2005.

Global Forest Coalition. *Stop the Destruction of Forests and Lands for Wood-Based Bioenergy* . http://globalforestcoalition.org/stop-the-destruction-of-forests-and-lands-for-wood-based-bio-energy-2.

Govindasamy, Bala, "Impact of Geoengineering Schemes on the Terrestrial Biosphere." *Geophysical Research Letters* 29, no. 2 (2002): 18-1–18-4.

US House of Representatives. Hearing before the Committee on Science and Technology, *Geoengineering Parts I, II, and III* . 2010.

UK House of Commons. Science and Technology Committee. *The Regulation of Geoengineering.* Fifth Report of the Session 2009–10. 2009.

IMPLICC. *Implications and Risks of Engineering Solar Radiation to Limit Climate Change.* http://implicc.zmaw.de/Home.551.0.html.

Inman, Mason. "Planning for Plan B." *Nature Reports Climate Change*, December 17, 2009. <http://www.nature.com/climate/2010/1001/full/climate.2010.135.html.

International Energy Agency. *World Energy Outlook 2014* . 2014.

International Covenant on Civil and Political Rights (1966), 999 U.N.T.S. 171, 6 I.L.M. 368.

International Maritime Organization. *Convention on the Prevention of Marine Pollution by Dumping of Wastes and Other Matter* http://www.imo.org/OurWork/Environment/LCLP/Pages/default.aspx.

International Maritime Organization. London Convention. "Thirtieth Consultative Meeting of the Contracting Parties to the London Convention and the Third Meeting of the Contracting Parties to the London Protocol, Resolution LC–LP.1 (2008) on the Regulation of Ocean Fertilization." 2008.

International Maritime Organization. London Convention. "Thirty-Second Consultative Meeting of the Contracting Parties to the London Convention and the Fifth Meeting of the Contracting Parties to the London Protocol, Resolution LC–LP.2(2010) on the Assessment Framework for Scientific Research Involving Ocean Fertilization." 2010.

International Maritime Organization. London Convention. "Eighth Meeting of the Contracting Parties to the 1996 Protocol to the Convention on the Prevention of Marine Pollution by Dumping of Wastes and Other Matter 1997, Annex 4, Resolution LP.4(8) on the Amendment to the London Protocol to Regulate the Placement of Matter for Ocean Fertilization and Other Marine Geoengineering Activities." 1997.

Jha, Alok. "Obama Climate Adviser Open to Geo-Engineering to Tackle Global Warming." *Guardian*, April 8, 2009. http://www.theguardian.com/environment/2009/apr/08/geo-engineering-john-holdren.

Kintisch, Eli. "Scientists Say Continued Warming Warrants Closer Look at Drastic Fixes." *Science* 318 (2007): 1054–1055.

Knox, John H. "The Myth and Reality of Transboundary Environmental Impact Assessment." *American Journal of International Law* 96 (2002): 291–319.

Kyoto Protocol to the United Nations Framework Convention on Climate Change. FCCC/CP/1997/L.7/Add. 1, 37 I.L.M. 22. December 10, 1997.

Leemans, Rik, and Bas Eickhout. "Another Reason for Concern: Regional and Global Impacts on Ecosystems for Different Levels of Climate Change." *Global Environmental Change* 14 (2004): 219–228.

Matthews, H. Damon, and Ken Caldeira. "Transient Climate-Carbon Simulations of Planetary Geoengineering." *Proceedings of the National Academy of Sciences of the United States of America* 104 (2007): 9949–9954.

McInerney-Lankford, Siobhan, Mac Darrow, and Lavanya Rajamani. "Human Rights and Climate Change." World Bank study 61308. 2011.

National Academy of Sciences. "Geoengineering Climate: Technical Evaluation and Discussion of Impacts." https://www8.nationalacademies.org/cp/projectview.aspx?key=49540.

Nicholson, Simon, "Reimagining Climate Engineering: The Politics of Tinkering with the Sky," in Hilal Elver and Paul Wapner, eds., *Reimagining Climate Change*, New York: Routledge, forthcoming.

Proelss, Alexander. *Legal Opinion on the Legality of the LOHAFEX Marine Research Experiment under International Law* , 2009.

"Protocol on Strategic Environmental Assessment to the Convention on Environmental Impact Assessment in a Transboundary Context." UN document. ECE/MP.EIA/2003/2. May 21, 2003.

Pulp Mills on the River Uruguay (Argentina v. Uruguay) (Judgment). ICL Report 60, para. 224. 2010.

Rayfuse, Rosemary, Mark G. Lawrence, and Kristina M. Gjerde. "Ocean Fertilisation and Climate Change: The Need to Regulate Emerging High Seas Uses." *International Journal of Marine and Coastal Law* 23 (2008): 297–326.

Revkin, Andrew C. "The Good, the Bad and the Anthropocene." *Dot Earth*, July 7, 2014. http://dotearth.blogs.nytimes.com/2014/07/07/the-good-the-bad-and-the-anthropocene/?_r=0.

Rogelj, Joeri, "Analysis of the Copenhagen Accord Pledges and Its Global Climatic Impacts: A Snapshot of Dissonant Ambitions." *Environmental Research Letters* 5, no. 3 (2010): 1–9.

Ross, Andrew, and H. Damon Matthews. "Climate Engineering and the Risk of Rapid Climate Change." *Environmental Research Letters* 4 (4) (2009): 1–6.

Rowe, Gene, and Lynn J. Frewer. "A Typology of Public Engagement Mechanisms." *Science, Technology & Human Values* 30 (2) (2005): 251–290.

Schiermeier, Quirin. "Climate Tinkerers Thrash Out a Plan." *Nature*, December 2, 2014. http://www.nature.com/news/climate-tinkerers-thrash-out-a-plan-1.16470.

Scott, Karen N. "International Law in the Anthropocene: Responding to the Geoengineering Challenge." *Michigan Journal of International Law* 34 (2013): 309–58.

Solomon, Susan L., Gian-Kasper Plattner, Reto Knutti, and Pierre Friedlingstein. "Irreversible Climate Change Due to Carbon Dioxide Emissions." *Proceedings of the National Academy of Sciences of the United States of America* 106 (2009): 1704–1709.

Tilmes, Rolf Müller, and Ross Salawitch. "The Sensitivity of Polar Ozone Depletion to Proposed Geoengineering Schemes." *Science* 320 (2008): 1201–1204.

United Nations. "Convention on Environmental Impact Assessment in a Transboundary Context." 30 I.L.M. 800. 1991.

United Nations Framework Convention on Climate Change. 31 I.L.M. 849. May 9, 1992.

United Nations. Framework Convention on Climate Change. *Negotiating Text.* FCCC/AWGLCA/2009/8. 2009.

United Nations. Framework Convention on Climate Change, Subsidiary Body for Scientific and Technological Advice, FCCC/SB/2014/L.2. Forum and Work Program on the Impact of the Implementation of Response Measures. 2014.

United Nations. Office of the High Commissioner for Human Rights. *Mapping Human Rights Obligations Relating to the Enjoyment of a Safe, Clean, Health and Sustainable Environment, Individual Report on the International Covenant on Economic, Social and Cultural Rights.* December 2013.

Universal Declaration of Human Rights. G.A. Res. 217A, U.N. GAOR, 3d Sess., 67th plen. mtg., U.N. Doc. A/810 (1948), Art. 3;

van Vliet, Arnold, and Rik Leemans. "Rapid Species' Response to Changes in Climate Require Stringent Climate Protection Targets." In *Avoiding Dangerous Climate Change*, edited by Hans Joachim Schellnhuber, 135–41. Cambridge: Cambridge University Press, 2006.

Victor, David G. "On the Regulation of Geoengineering." *Oxford Review of Economic Policy* 24 (2) (2008): 1–15.

Virgoe, John. "International Governance of a Possible Geoengineering Intervention to Combat Climate Change." *Climatic Change* 95 (2009): 103–19.

Wapner, Paul. *Living through the End of Nature: The Future of American Environmentalism.* Cambridge, MA: MIT Press, 2010.

Narrative frames are, as Paul Wapner states elegantly in chapter 15, "broadly shared understandings that provide an account of reality." Human beings are crafters of tales. We make sense of the world by filtering our sensory experiences through complex layers of concepts, metaphors, and story-lines. Such filters can at times appear entrenched and intransigent. For instance, for much of human history it was widely understood across a variety of places and societies that it was fit and proper for some human beings to own other human beings. Slavery was never simply some brute economic arrangement derived from some immutable natural law. Power-ful narrative frames, instead, made it appear a universal truth—a truth that broached no alternative—until, that is, an alternative became visible in an antislavery counternarrative and in a social and political movement that emerged to make that counternarrative real in the lived experiences of peoples everywhere.

Paul Wapner makes clear that environmentalism is itself a counternarra-tive. It is a narrative that runs counter to a dominant storyline of endless, unfettered economic growth and ever-advancing human domination and rule over the workings of the world. He shows, using a history of the West-ern environmentalist counternarrative and an analysis of the modern cli-mate justice movement, that working within a counternarrative is at once perilous and enlivening. "What is it like," he asks, "to live at the margins of public discourse?" Wapner's keen analysis suggests that a life spent on the margins has much to offer not just to the world but also to the individuals who come together to act under the umbrella of the environmental movement.

Peter Dauvergne's complementary chapter that follows zooms in on the hotly contested environmental narrative surrounding sustainability. *Sustainability* is a term that has received much academic treatment. There are countless articles, and there have been and will continue to be an endless string of classroom conversations, surrounding the question of what is or is not "sustainable." Dauvergne moves beyond this broad debate to examine the contestation between multinational business and environmentalists working to capture and define the powerful sustainability narrative.

Dauvergne illuminates a multiyear effort by big corporations to take control of the sustainability agenda. He distinguishes a "corporate sustainability," focused on production efficiencies and business-friendly aspirational goals, from a "New Earth sustainability," focused on human interdependence and development of resilience in the face of increasing ecosystemic instability. Dauvergne urges environmentalists and scholars of global environmental politics to fight to win back the sustainability narrative as part of charting the course to a new, more prosperous future.

The production of new and more effective narrative frames, or the struggle to regain control of older narratives, is an essential element of life on a New Earth. Narratives are powerful tools in defining interests and action and can set the course for policy and identity. Although developing counternarratives, such as "New Earth sustainability," is not straightforward, Wapner and Dauvergne argue persuasively that there is great value, of many kinds, to be found in the struggle.

Framing Questions Posed to the Authors in Section 8

- As the global resource base shrinks, sinks fill, and landscapes degrade, how will humanity live together?
- Will people embrace a survivalist mentality and try to wall themselves off from others in an attempt to flourish and survive? Or is it possible that new cooperative sensibilities will emerge, informed by ethical traditions, in which our humanity will be particularly expressed?
- What will be the major areas of struggle as the world experiences increasing environmental harm?

15   Living at the Margins

Paul Wapner

Narrative frames are broadly shared understandings that provide an account of reality. They connect events and instill meaning to make the world legible. Environmentalism has long been a counter-narrative that arose in opposition to and has long remained in the shadow of an ascending set of understandings that have grown and continue to deepen across societies. This more dominant narrative advances industrialization, consumerism, unrestrained economic growth, and a whole set of values that prize human capabilities to colonize and remake the world. Over the decades and even centuries, environmentalism has worked to stay relevant and offer an alternative discourse from the sidelines. At times, it has been extraordinarily efficacious in questioning the dominant storyline but, over its lifetime, it has done little more than put a dent in the leading narrative's armor. Environmentalism remains a subsidiary voice in contemporary society.

What is it like to inhabit the margins of contemporary life? How does environmentalism persist and flourish muffled under the roar of its prominent competitor? What is the fate of a counter-narrative?

~ ~ ~

The first wave of environmentalism as a social movement arose during the Industrial Revolution. For centuries, humanity's presence on Earth was fairly limited as people relied mainly on manual labor as the central form of energy. Starting in the late eighteenth and early nineteenth centuries, societies harnessed fossil fuels in large quantities and replaced manual labor with steam-powered manufacturing and locomotion. Humans suddenly found themselves able to travel distances in shorter amounts of time, pull resources from the far corners of the globe, and churn out products at speeds and in quantities undreamed of by their predecessors. The Industrial Revolution plugged humanity into sources of energy that translated into immense power to reformat landscapes, reorder social relations, and alter even widespread subjective understandings. The Industrial Revolution, in other words, ushered in a new material and ideational reality that forever changed life on Earth.

At the heart of this shift was a renewed belief in human ingenuity, technological prowess, and human entitlement. Coming off the heels of the broader scientific revolution that gave birth to modernity, industrialization represented the Enlightenment on steroids. Suddenly, scientific investigation saw no limits, and engineering efforts were electrified, as it were, as humans began to take over and control expanding areas of land—bringing far-flung regions under agricultural cultivation and pushing the boundaries of human habitation. It was as if the Industrial Revolution unleashed a pent-up capability of inquiry and an urge to exploit everything in humanity's grasp. Humanity now had the means to imprint itself everywhere, and it wasted no time in doing so.

Along with these elements, notions of growth, promise, and possibility infused human affairs. Industrialization suggested that people could continue harnessing the Earth's treasures seemingly indefinitely, turning them into resources and exploiting them as sinks. The only constraints were the imagination, pace of technological change, and available capital. Industrialization deepened a more ancient view that humanity is the exceptional species—not tied to nature's imperatives—and thus free to alter the Earth as it sees fit. In other words, anthropocentrism, which many equate with the Judeo-Christian tradition (but which clearly predates the tradition and exists beyond the Western world), found material and ideational fuel during the Industrial Revolution. Humanity is not simply one species among many, but a significant cut above and increasingly master of the many. Prometheus came unbound. The Industrial Revolution, marked by a new more pervasive and seemingly inexhaustible fire, created a new Atlantis. Finally, humanity could realize an ancient aspiration to live independent of nature's constraints, and exercise its innate abilities to shape and control the world.

Industrialism's successes were just short of miraculous. Railroads, steam-powered ships, manufacturing plants, and so forth began dotting and then crisscrossing the earth. Innovations in health, industrial design, engineering, and production processes took off with no end in sight. For those in the center of industrialization, human life grew safer and more predictable, and the scourge of poverty for many became something from which one could actually escape.

Of course, all was not good. Industrialism brought its own blights and hazards. Smokestacks and air pollution appeared in an increasing number of cities, and the iron horse spliced rural landscapes and made the "hills echo with its snort like thunder, shaking the earth with his feet, and breathing fire and smoke from his nostrils," as Thoreau put it.[1] Manufacturing poured growing amounts of waste into waterways, and society's mounting appetite increased deforestation across the globe. People's sense of time and place also changed as the pace of life quickened and capitalism's incessant call for greater profit and material colonization commodified living. Economic incentives dug underneath people's skin and moved them to see their lives as appendages to a larger financial machine that made its own demands and flattened life into an endless grasping for more and more material things.

Environmentalism arose as a critique of these changes. Proto-environmentalists like William Wordsworth and John Ruskin lamented industrialization's encroachments on the countryside and sought to preserve the quality of village life unplugged from industrialism's insatiability. Others, like William Morris, Edmund Carpenter, and Octavia Hill, objected to the inhuman working conditions required by early industrialization, the bleak scenes of polluting factories, and the eroding moral fiber that industrialism frayed as it multiplied wants and pitted individuals against each other in an economic race toward greater production. Thoreau and Emerson joined this chorus as they worried about the colonization of humanity's inner life amid the din and velocity of industrialization.

From a different corner, scientists emerged who cautioned against a rapacious grab on resources and warned of ecological limits. George Perkins Marsh, Dietrich Brandis, and Alexander Humboldt called for more efficient resource use to protect stocks and decrease waste. As early voices in the budding conservation movement, they advocated for sustainable yields, rational land use policies, and scientific management of soil, water, wildlife, and fisheries. To them, industrialism threatened to outdo itself: it was pitted to gobble up the very foundations on which it depended. Scientific conservation was one attempt to stem industrialism's tide.

Finally, the first wave of the environmentalist critique included advocates for wilderness. Various writers and activists feared that industrialism's fingers would extend to the far reaches of the Earth—into the deepest forests, steepest mountains, pristine deserts—taming the unbidden quality of wildlands and remote environments, turning every place and sphere under the influence if not dominance of human presence. Most prominent in this strain of thought was John Muir, who wrote of the sheer beauty of wilderness areas and how being away from so-called civilized life provided a necessary reprieve from a world increasingly "nerve-shaken" and tired by the exigencies of industrial production.

Together, these affective and technical responses to industrialization accreted into a more coherent criticism that posed an alternative voice to the ideology of growth, progress, productivism, and human mastery. This counternarrative, by necessity, emerged at the interstices of industrialization. It was as if the voice of history had spoken, and those in dissent could express themselves only in the nooks and crannies of an expanding and ascending worldview.

~ ~ ~

Over the decades, environmentalism deepened and expanded its critique and developed a more coherent counternarrative. Part of this had to do with the increasing reach and depth of industrialization and its later manifestations. Mass consumerism, skyrocketing population, suburbanization, widespread use of toxics, and a wholesale embrace of human ingenuity troubled those like Aldo Leopold, Rachel Carson, Paul Ehrlich, and Barry Commoner, and sparked the emergence of organizations that denounced an ever-increasing colonization of the life-world and decried widespread instances of environmental degradation and harm. This expression grew as the scale and magnitude of ecological threats magnified. What were once circumscribed cases of pollution, resource scarcity, and ecosystem deterioration became global problems. Ozone depletion, loss of biological diversity, and climate change, for instance, became representative of environmental intensification and signaled a shift in scope and concern. The environmental movement raised its voice in the name of planetary fragility. It worried, organized, lobbied, and mobilized on behalf of environmental precaution. The system, birthed with the Industrial Revolution, was out of control. It was, in today's language, unsustainable. Unchecked, it simply could not go on. There were "limits to growth," thresholds of ecological stability, boundaries of overshoot. Moreover, there were moral reasons for sticking up for the voiceless other creatures and the politically powerless whose quality of life was being undermined by rapacious grabs on resources and the unconscionable release of poisons in certain communities and underdeveloped regions of the world. The environmental movement took up the cause of those living "downstream" and argued against the injustice being meted out on humans and nonhumans alike. Environmentalists, in other words, were the organized voices of caution. They saw many of the benefits of hyperindustrialization, but also its dark side, and they stayed up nights worrying about environmental harm and injustice, and, in the extreme, ecological collapse.

~ ~ ~

No matter how urgent or rational the movement's messages have been, environmentalists have always been underdogs, seemingly on the wrong side of history. Few people who have enjoyed the comforts, economic benefits, and entertainments of modern society wish to question the foundations on which the system depends. There is simply too much material and cultural momentum to doubt, in a sustained manner, the engines of growth, technological capability, human ingenuity, and the sense of confidence that goes along with contemporary societies. Environmentalists have been the Cassandras of the world—the ancient Greek goddess blessed with the gift of insight and prophecy, but cursed that her warnings would fall on deaf ears. Indeed, many have long looked at environmentalists as a sorry lot—haranguing the powers that be in the service of some Elysium that never existed and does not seem particularly attractive, or at least keeping their hands on the brakes of society's accelerating forward motion. In such a context, environmentalism has had to work at the margins—at best ingratiating itself into the halls of political power, but more consistently shouting to have its voice heard. Pegged as espousing an apocalyptic sensibility, misanthropy, or simply a fearful precautionary mentality, the movement has had its work cut out for it trying to convince the rest of society to care about and adopt aggressive and effective policies in the service of environmental protection.

To be sure, environmentalism has not always been a lone wolf. Over the past couple of decades or so, it has become seemingly mainstream. Green parties have emerged in certain countries, environmentalism has become chic in particular quarters, and no one—not even the most unsustainable industries or stubborn countries—espouses anti-environmentalism as a platform. Indeed, everyone today, at least rhetorically, claims to be an environmentalist. Everyone says they care about air, water and soil quality, the well-being of the victims of environmental harm, and the fate of innumerable species being sacrificed at the helm of contemporary practices. Peter Dauvergne in chapter 16 underlines such mainstreaming by showing that even corporations—those at the forefront of capitalist expansion and drivers of consumerism—cloak themselves in the banner of environmentalism and even partner with environmental organizations. They do so, he tells us, not necessarily because they subscribe to environmentalist values— although some might—but because they recognize the widespread appeal of environmentalism and use it to gain greater market access. Put differently, they take advantage of the mainstreaming of environmentalism to sell more products. When environmentalism becomes a route to capitalist expansion, it is clear that environmentalists are not isolated in their criticisms and concerns.

But the mainstreaming of environmentalism goes only so far. As Dauvergne so insightfully reveals, the alliance between corporations and environmentalist organizations has a dark side. Partnerships may, for instance, encourage corporations to reduce waste, use more sustainable materials, and otherwise lead to efficiencies in manufacturing, but they also enable corporations to sell more stuff and, taken in the aggregate, this materially overrides incremental corporate efficiencies. Furthermore, the partnerships encourage non-governmental organizations to temper the cutting edge of their critiques, especially criticisms aimed at the social and ecological consequences of economic growth in general and corporate practices in particular. After all, it is impolite, if not financially unwise, to bite the hand that feeds you.[2]

Corporate environmentalism reveals an even broader dynamic at work in the so-called greening of societies. This has to do with the relative power of competing narratives. Dauvergne explains how corporations have designed their own notion of environmentalism—what he calls "corporate sustainability." Corporate sustainability is about sustaining profits, not advancing principles of equity, ecological integrity, and justice. Corporations invoke these principles only as instruments of market penetration, not as ends in themselves. Corporate sustainability enables corporations to co-opt the counter-hegemonic narrative at the core of contemporary environmentalism—what Dauvergne refers to as "new Earth sustainability." It allows them to claim that they, like everyone else, care about the Earth and its resources, and so there is no need to question, let alone criticize, corporate practices. In fact, those who truly care about environmentalism should join forces with corporate bodies to usher in a more sustainable world.

The corporate co-optation of environmentalism widens the power gap between the hegemonic and counter-narratives. It explains why environmentalists may win a victory here or there but continue to lose the wider battle. Environmentalists simply cannot compete against the broader, more entrenched modernist view that subscribes to an end-of-history faith in economic growth, progress, capitalism, technological optimism, and a sense that society can always bumble through. Environmentalism's core critique, then, gets buried even deeper against a storyline of corporate environmentalism, and environmentalists must work that much harder to articulate and advance their aims. Given the narrative differentials, environmentalism is like a battery next to a nuclear power plant. It has cultural and political power, but not nearly as much as the moneyed interests that thrive on capitalist expansion and human hubris and have worked to saturate the public with a blind optimism that the "system" is working, and working well. Call it false consciousness or genuine insight, but most people these days throughout the world do not worry about environmental problems to the degree or way environmentalists wish. Most publics around the world are tone-deaf to environmentalist pleas. Yes, they may pay lip-service to such concerns, but when it comes to how they live their lives, which political issues they most advance, and how they spend their money, environmentalism is a distant animator. Despite its exclamations, its messages sound like whispers amid the roar of contemporary life.

Nowhere is this dynamic more obvious than in climate politics. The science of climate change has been settled for over a decade. The signs of climate change abound in erratic weather, melting ice caps, thawing permafrost, more intense storms, longer growing seasons, droughts, and the like. Furthermore, most people agree that anthropogenic climate change is a reality. But much of this understanding shifts when it comes to doing anything about it. Many flock to climate skepticism not because they do not believe in climate change but because they do not like the prescriptions required to address it. Too many people object to more governmental action in their lives or perceive that climate legislation will undermine economic growth, and thus they reject climate change out of hand. Others may not go so far but nevertheless stop short of advocating for aggressive climate action out of a sense of helplessness, political apathy or distraction, or simply not wanting to be bothered. Still others are bothered but lack the tools—or believe they lack the tools—to work with others on behalf of climate protection in a way that would make a meaningful difference.

One sees this last explanation at the international level. Governments signed the United Nations Framework Convention on Climate Change in 1992. They agreed to the Kyoto Protocol in 1997, which required them to reduce their greenhouse gas emissions roughly 5 percent below 1990 levels by 2012. Despite all the clamoring and emergency calls from environmentalists, the 2012 deadline came and went with little fanfare, and countries are now grasping at straws to create a post-Kyoto agreement that will have any promise of curbing climate change. Part of this involves agreeing not to let global average temperatures exceed a 2°C rise over pre-industrial levels. Yet the latest Intergovernmental Panel on Climate Change report claims that without dramatic action, the world will blow through that threshold in a matter of a couple of decades.[3] And, of course, no dramatic action is on the horizon. The world is too busy with other issues or too inured to environmentalist appeals. Yes, environmentalism may have made inroads in mainstream culture and politics, but it is still a marginalized voice. It lacks political heft to move legislation in international bodies, economic might to significantly shift corporate behavior, or even the cultural power to effect widespread lifestyle change. Cassandra continues to call out her warnings into the night while everyone else is sleeping.

~ ~ ~

What is it like to live at the margins of public discourse? How can environmentalists persist under the weight of a distracted world materially committed to long-range ecological degradation, punishing environmental injustice, and large-scale harm? In what ways can environmentalists act in a counterhegemonic fashion knowing full well that their efforts will always fail to meet their deep-seated objectives? How can environmentalists keep voicing a counter-narrative in the face of mounting evidence of irrelevance?

Activist Bill McKibben works to give climate change a face. Climate change is, by any measure, abstract. It has to do with invisible gases migrating through invisible air to trap invisible heat, with the consequence of global baking. How do you bring this to public consciousness? As mentioned, the science is there: almost every peer-reviewed study confirms that the buildup of greenhouse gases (GHGs) traps heat from escaping the Earth's inner atmosphere and that humans play a central part in the process. But science does not seem to be enough. Politics is not simply about facts translating into policies—the so-called linear model—but power working to shape widespread thought and behavior, and this has to do fundamentally with narrative frames. As Larson explains, "frames trump facts."[4] (Narrative frames, remember, are not simply statements of facts or even accounts of particular events, but broad understandings that explain various phenomena and render an interpretation that provides meaning.) McKibben has worked for decades trying to shift the dominant narrative about environmental protection and sees climate change, given its global scope and devastating consequences, as the core environmental concern.

McKibben, along with students at Middlebury College, created 350.org to build a movement focused primarily on climate change. The name 350. org stands for 350 parts per million (ppm) of carbon, the limit above which many scientists believe is unsafe. 350.org has been McKibben's way to draw attention to and mobilize on behalf of climate protection.

350.org undertakes many campaigns. One of its most prominent is opposition to the Keystone XL pipeline, which aimed to bring tar sands or, more accurately, a form of petroleum known as bitumen, from Alberta, Canada to Texas and then refine it for export. 350.org chose to target the pipeline because it threatened to accelerate tar sands excavation on boreal forests prized by native peoples and lead to an increase in carbon emissions as the petroleum is mined, transported, and eventually burned to create energy. More generally, the XL pipeline represented a deepening commitment to fossil-fueled energy at a time when the world must reverse course if it is to avoid further and more intense negative consequenceed from climate change. Finally, the pipeline would have crossed international boundaries and thus represented a focus for international awareness and action. The XL pipeline, in other words, held tremendous symbolism for articulating concerns about climate change.

The decision to authorize the pipeline rested with President Obama. More specifically, the State Department had to sign off on any international enterprise that might compromise US national security, and the Department of State had to forward a recommendation to Obama. In November 2015, Obama rejected the pipeline. This was a surprise to many political pundits and other observers. In fact, it was partly a surprise to McKibben who, for years, assumed 350.org was fighting an uphill battle.

In his most recent book, *Oil and Honey*, and out on the stump before Obama rejected the pipeline, McKibben was honest about the movement's prospect for stopping the pipeline. He acknowledged that the conventional wisdom was that the pipeline would be approved. But this did not stop McKibben's action. As he put it, Obama may approve the XL, "but not without a fight."[5]

Not without a fight. This is one way to wage a counter-narrative battle. In fact, it may be a key strategy for all oppositional counter-movements. Against overwhelming odds, the best one can often do is put up a fight and see what happens. You may go home with your tail between your legs, but other outcomes are possible, including learning how to live with defeat.

Let's say that the pipeline was approved. Would this have been a defeat? Would it have been the end of 350.org's campaign? Would the battle be over? On some level, yes: 350.org mobilized partly on behalf of rejecting the pipeline as a way to curb carbon dioxide emissions; if the pipeline had been approved, the organization and wider movement would have certainly suffered a significant loss. But one can still ask: Would that have ended 350.org's effort?

Movements always make specific demands and devise particular strategies and tactics to advance their efforts. The civil rights movement, for instance, carried out hundreds of protests and boycotts, worked to change voting laws in particular states, and sought desegregation in particular schools. Over the decades, it lost many battles. Still it persisted. Its goals were not tied to a particular action or campaign. It sought to deracialize American society, and while some parts of the movement retreated and others got more radical, the movement as a whole would lick its newest wounds and get back in the fight. Like the climate movement today, the civil rights movement was not going to let racism continue without a fight.

Eventually, as we all know, the fight proved triumphant in some of the most important ways. The US federal government passed the Civil Rights Act and the Voting Rights Act, and blacks were granted equal legal status. But the victories of the movement highlight the complicated nature of staging an anti-hegemonic effort. Few today question the achievements of the civil rights movement, but we can still ask about the movement's success. Has racism disappeared? Are blacks and whites equal either in society at large or even in the eyes of the law? Today, blacks outnumber whites in prison seventeen to one. There are close to 900,000 black men in prisons throughout the United States.[6] In terms of professions, whites overwhelmingly hold positions of power and authority.[7] In fact, point to any sector of social life and the scourge of racism appears. (Indeed, skin color is the primary predictor of environmental harm in the United States and around the rest of the world.[8]) This is not to belittle the achievements of the civil rights movement but to underline the complexities of measuring movement outcomes. Putting up a fight is simply that. It involves not accommodating oneself to the status quo and the dominant narrative. It entails resistance. The important thing to remember is that although one is fighting an uphill battle, the outcome is never assured or even really defined. The battle to rid society of racism continues and, sadly, will continue well beyond the foreseeable future. But no one could have predicted what putting up a fight would look like and the significant gains that emerged. Likewise, no one can say definitely what the defeats meant in the light of civil rights history.

This speaks to a critical point about countering dominant narratives. There are no definitive thresholds for success or defeat. A few years ago, the world community agreed that global average temperatures should not exceed 2°C. Above 2°C, we face planetary baking. But what really does that number mean? What does it mean to the victims of Hurricane Katrina, the thousands of Indians who perished in rains and floods in summer 2013, or the thousands who died from Typhoon Haiyan in the Philippines? If we keep these people in mind, the battle against climate change is already over. The movement lost. It is time to go home and rid itself of the fantasy of ever turning things around. Yet it refuses to do so. In the same way, 350.org refuses to call it quits even though carbon concentrations exceed the organization's own estimate of a climate catastrophe threshold (350 ppm). Put another way, when it comes to waging a counter-hegemonic narrative battle, putting up a fight is an open-ended strategy. It is open-ended because the principles that animate movements are not extinguished in the heat of a strategic defeat. Sometimes they can even grow in significance. Moreover, resistance is open-ended because, as Richard Falk, scholar and fellow contributor to this book, often remarks, "We are not smart enough to predict social movement outcomes." Few foretold the emergence of the Egyptian opposition movement under Mubarak. For decades, the Egyptian regime was monolithic, governing through both force and cultural and economic hegemony. That Mubarak was forced out of power is a testament to the possibility of unlikely outcomes. (It must be mentioned that although the movement was eventually co-opted and its democratic aspirations squashed by the post-Mubarak military regime, this does not negate the promise of resistance. Egypt is living through a new [troubling] chapter in its long history; few have the foresight to predict what will come next. The ongoing struggles in Egypt are like the ongoing struggles of all counter-narrative movements, including environmentalism.) Despite Fukuyama's proclamation, history has not ended. Dominant discourses are not forever codified. We simply do not know how political conditions will develop.

Putting up a fight is relevant not simply because it unhinges the hegemonic narrative and creates a sliver of hope for change, but also because it generates and expands social criticism. Social criticism is the age-old practice of public complaint. One can think of it as the intellectual rationale behind much movement politics. This helps us when we think about the fate of counter-narratives insofar as social criticism persists even when it is clear that it can never turn the tables on dominant discourses. As Michael Walzer writes,

Success as the world measures it is not the measure of social criticism. The critic is measured by the scars his listeners and readers bear, by the conflicts he forces them to live through, not only in the present but also in the future, and by the memories those conflicts leave behind. He doesn't succeed by winning people over—for sometimes it just isn't possible to do that—but by sustaining the argument.[9]

Sustaining the critical argument may be little consolation when the many destructive forces of society are hurtling forward in unjust and environmentally tragic ways. But neither is it insignificant. As Martin Buber points out, even if criticism is "misunderstood, misinterpreted, misused … its sting will rankle."[10] In such a situation, all is not fine—the master narrative continues to operate—but neither is all hopeless. Voices of conscience have spoken, and the tapestry of social life is thus no longer the same. Speaking out, leveling criticism, expressing moral outrage—all of which are vehicles of social movements—alter the ethical landscape, sowing doubt and thus piquing conscience. Sometimes this is the only thing counter-hegemonic efforts can effectuate. It does not dismantle a master narrative; it simply wounds it. But wounds are more than injuries. They can also be opportunities for reflection, awakening, and living a different kind of life.

~ ~ ~

So far I have been discussing how a counter-narrative can influence the "other"—those who could be called maintainers of the status quo. There is another measure of counter-narrative politics, however, that deserves its own treatment. This has to do with what operating at the margins does to an activist. How does fighting an uphill battle affect the actor? What is the experience of aligning oneself with a counter-hegemonic effort? Environmentalism is and will continue to be a minority movement. How does working on behalf of a more sustainable, although unlikely, world affect the activist?

"Full effort is full victory," Gandhi once remarked. He was drawing attention to the distinction between endeavor and goal attainment and saying that the former is more important. This may seem strange given the stakes involved in public affairs. It certainly sounds odd in environmental struggles where environmentalism is not trying to alter people's ideas or senses of the self per se but advance environmental well-being and social justice. Writers Jensen, McBay, and Keith highlight this when they ask of environmentalists, "Do we want to feel better or do we want to be effective?"[11] Jensen et al. ask it as a critique of nonradical strategies that advocate for lifestyle change, green consumerism, government lobbying, and corporate partnering. To them, these kinds of strategies may give one satisfaction, but they do not make a whit of a difference when it comes to environmental protection. Effort is important but only because it leads to outcomes. Short of this effect, effort is an exercise in narcissism. Environmentalist David Brower made a similar point when he declared, "Polite conservationists leave no mark save the scars upon the Earth that could have been prevented had they stood their ground."[12] To Brower, standing one's ground finds meaning with its success. It is measured by the scars on the Earth that were prevented, not an inner sense of commitment.

But what about effort itself? Does it have a place in counter-narrative environmental politics beyond consolation? Does Gandhi's comment have relevance for environmentalism?

Political theorist Hannah Arendt observed that when we act in the public realm, our efforts almost never realize their exact intentions because we insert ourselves into a world of others who interpret, respond to, and otherwise interact with our attempts in ways that scramble our imagined goals. (To Arendt, this is not a bad thing since it explains the emergence of novelty and makes possible genuine freedom.) This is the predicament of environmental action. Many campaigns try to stop specific instances of environmental harm, or advance particular sustainability practices, or, at the grander level, work to dismantle the ideologies of the modernist narrative. But, let's face it: they never do. Yes, they may gain partial victory, but it is the rare environmental campaign that actually wins; few campaigns get to declare victory. The movement is, after all, an oppositional one.

But by virtue that the movement continues year after year, decade after decade, suggests that something else is happening as well. Like other social justice, poverty alleviation, peace, or human rights efforts, environmentalism also feeds those who participate, and this should not be lost in our evaluation of life at the margins.

Imagine you live in a society that is fundamentally at odds with your deepest aspirations and values. What do you do? How do you live your life? You could simply give in and find some type of accommodation. Indeed, many environmentalists would say that too many people do this and that it accounts for the high degree of environmental harm. But for some of us, this would never do. We would find our lives inauthentic and false. We would experience ourselves as divided selves, paying lip-service and participating in reproducing the status quo, on the one hand, and secretly wishing for a different reality, on the other.

Another option is to resist: to cultivate thoughts and sensibilities that support one's values and to act in ways that publicly try to bring about a different set of affairs. Such resistance may very well be futile. But this does not take away from the impulse and reasons for engaging in it. Sometimes, and on some deep level, one may have no choice. Life lived outside resistance may feel too inauthentic and enervating. This is the way most environmentalists may feel and, I would imagine, most other compatriots of counter-narrative movements.

Climate change, mass extinction, freshwater scarcity, pervasive toxic poisoning, and so forth constitute the great challenges of our time. To be sure, they are folded into and are a consequence of contemporary culture and practice, but they nevertheless represent some of the most immediate, profound dilemmas on the horizon. Many environmentalists would say that they have little choice but to confront these issues. With knowledge comes responsibility, and many environmentalists cannot, in good conscience, turn away in ignorance. For decades, Greenpeace has experimented with different ways of not diverting our eyes. It has perfected publicly the strategy of bearing witness—a practice that involves trying to change what it can but, short of this, not allow injustices and harm to persist without being seen and, one might say, suffered through. Importantly, Greenpeace tries to make bearing witness a public enterprise as it uses various media to send out images and descriptions of particular injustices. When it does so, it knows that it will not stop, for instance, whaling, toxic dumping, drilling for petroleum, and so on. But stopping such atrocities is not the only point. For Greenpeace and others, bearing witness is simply what is called for. To turn away would be not simply cowardice but also damaging to the self. The self would be diminished since it would pretend that affairs were otherwise, and thus one would be complicit in such injustice. Many environmentalists through the decades have refused to experience this.

The fear of diminishment is not simply about guilt or even responsibility. Many environmentalists feel passionate about righting environmental wrongs and working on behalf of those on the receiving end of environmental harm and injustice. It is as if they find their juice in life by being of service to environmental well-being. One can dismiss this as "normal" excitement as we each find our vocation in life. But it seems to be more than this. Like other efforts on behalf of justice and the enhancement of life, environmental activism is about building a meaningful life where meaning derives from addressing the civilizational challenges of our time. Theologian Frederick Buechner says that a "vocation is where our greatest passion meets the world's greatest need."[13] Working for environmental protection enables many people to experience a calling and invest themselves in something that provides deep satisfaction (even if it excludes great joy). Environmentalists who are cultivating and foisting a counter-narrative onto the world get to experience this. To be sure, this does not make them any better than anyone else, and environmentalists, as personalities, enjoy no more virtues than others. But that environmental work offers the possibility of a vocation goes a long way toward explaining what it is like to live at the margins of political life.

The idea of vocation speaks to another interior dimension of counter-narrative politics. In positioning oneself against the status quo, one implicitly lives at the interface between current conditions and a vision for how they could be better. Occupying this space is never easy, as it creates an uncomfortable tension between the experience of the way things are at present and how they could be. When one sees environmental work as a vocation, this tension grows in depth but also challenges one to come to term with it. It challenges one to navigate their sadness about current affairs and their aspirational excitement about a more attractive future. Many, to be sure, fail to wade through the tension and find themselves either corrosively cynical at the inability to create new conditions or naively starry eyed with the dream of a different world. Working on behalf of a counter-narrative offers the opportunity to live in a more productive relationship to the tension. In the best cases, it invites one to learn how to stay committed to social change and buoyant in the face of stark realities, and yet not become negatively disgusted with present conditions. Put differently, advancing counter-narratives allows one to know what is and what should be, and to love both. This may sound trite, almost Hallmarkish, but it captures what many would say is at the heart of wisdom.

~ ~ ~

The world operates, as Navroz Dubash points out in chapter 13, according to narratives. Over the past three centuries or so, a modernist narrative has emerged and seeped into the pores, muscles, and bones of contemporary life. During its ascendancy, environmentalism emerged to counter the dominant narrative's excesses. Doing so has always been difficult. It is like working against gravity. But it has also been inescapable. Too many environmentalists look out into the world and see things that are unacceptable and do real harm to life.

In this chapter, I have reflected on what it means to live at the margins of collective life and wage the counter-narrative of environmentalism. I hope these reflections show that while environmentalism will probably always fight an uphill battle, there is much to recommend being in the trenches. As poet Theodore Roethke puts it, "In a dark time/the eye begins to see."[14]

Notes

1. Thoreau, *Walden*, 125.

2. Along with Dauvergne's contribution to this book, chapter 16, see Dauvergne and LaBaron, *Protest, Inc.*

3. IPCC, "Climate Change 2013."

4. Larson, *Metaphors for Environmental Sustainability*, 16.

5. McKibben, *Oil and Honey*, 220.

6. Mauer and King, "Uneven Justice."

7. Mintz and Krymkowski, "The Ethnic, Race, and Gender Gaps in Workplace Authority."

8. Robert Bullard, *Dumping in Dixie*.

9. Walzer, *The Company of Critics*, 79.

10. Buber, *Israel and the World*, 112.

11. Jensen, McBay, and Keith, *Deep Green Resistance*, 25.

12. Quoted in Whiteside, *Divided Natures*, 31.

13. Quoted in Palmer, *Let Your Life Speak*, 16.

14. Roethke, "In Dark Time."

Bibliography

Buber, Martin. *Israel and the World: Essays in Time of Crisis*. New York: Schocken Books, 1963.

Bullard, Robert. *Dumping in Dixie: Race, Class, and Environmental Quality*. Boulder, CO: Westview Press, 2000.

Dauvergne, Peter, and Genevieve LaBaron. *Protest, Inc.: The Corporatization of Activism*. Cambridge: Polity Press, 2014.

IPCC. "Climate Change 2013: The Physical Science Basis. Summary for Policymakers. Working Group I Contribution to the Fifth Assessment Report of the IPCC." https://www.ipcc.ch/pdf/assessment-report/ar5/wg1/WGIAR5_SPM_brochure_en.pdf.

Jensen, Derrick, Aric McBay, and Lierre Keith. *Deep Green Resistance: Strategy to Save the Planet*. New York: Seven Stories Press, 2011.

Larson, Brendon. *Metaphors for Environmental Sustainability: Redefining Our Relationship with Nature*. New Haven, CT: Yale University Press, 2011.

Mauer, Marc, and Ryan S. King. "Uneven Justice: State Rates of Incarceration by Race and Ethnicity." Washington, DC: Sentencing Project, 2007. http://www.sentencingproject.org/doc/publications/rd_stateratesofincbyraceandethnicity.pdf.

McKibben, Bill. *Oil and Honey: The Education of an Unlikely Activist.* New York: St. Martin's Griffin, 2014.

Mintz, Beth, and Daniel H. Krymkowski. "The Ethnic, Race, and Gender Gaps in Workplace Authority: Changes over Time in the United States." *Sociological Quarterly* 51 (2010): 20–45.

Palmer, Parker. *Let Your Life Speak: Listening for the Voice of Vocation.* San Francisco: Jossey-Bass, 2000.

Roethke, Theodore. "In Dark Time." In *The Collected Poems by Theodore Roethke.* New York: Doubleday, 1961.

Thoreau, Henry David. *Walden.* New Haven, CT: Yale University Press, 2006.

Walzer, Michael. *The Company of Critics: Social Criticism and Political Commitment in the Twentieth Century.* New York: Basic Books, 2002.

Whiteside, Kerry. H. *Divided Natures: French Contributions to Political Ecology.* Cambridge, MA: MIT Press, 2002.

16 The Sustainability Story: Exposing Truths, Half-Truths, and Illusions

Peter Dauvergne

Multinational business has tried to control environmentalism since the movement began to emerge as a global force in the 1960s. Lobbyists have worked the world's capitals to network with bureaucrats and buy off politicians. Industry scientists have published findings to reassure consumers and governments of the safety of products. Corporate lawyers have silenced whistle-blowers and sued government agencies. And corporate PR divisions have glossed over environmental disasters with feel-good annual reports and slick advertising.

The past decade, however, has seen big business going much further to control the sustainability debate. The world's biggest firms are now claiming to be sustainability leaders, promising to go beyond government regulations and reaching out to partner with nongovernmental organizations (NGOs). In doing so, as this chapter reviews, multinational corporations are rewriting the narrative of sustainability, turning what was once a powerful critical discourse of environmentalism into a strategy to expand business (sales, profits, and stores) as well as gain more control over suppliers worldwide. For these firms, sustainability is defined as improving the efficiency and competiveness of business in a globalizing world economy of increasing scarcity, ever-higher risks, and long supply chains.

Some environmentalists, seeing sustainability losing its original meaning, are giving up on the concept. This is a mistake. The narrative of sustainability is too valuable to surrender to business. When infused with principles of ecology, equity, and social justice, as I argue in this chapter, it has the capacity to offer a realistic frame to assess today's crisis on the New Earth, as well as a way to imagine a better future: absolutely necessary, as Simon Nicholson and Sikina Jinnah emphasize in the introduction to this book, for fashioning more effective responses to rising scarcity, overflowing sinks, and degrading landscapes. Struggling against the narrative of corporate sustainability will not be easy. The promises and claims are alluring. Most governments are devolving authority to firms, and just about every international NGO is now partnering with multinational business to finance projects, cobrand products, and fundraise for causes. Yet it is still possible to regain the integrity of the narrative of sustainability as a strong voice within the counternarrative of environmentalism. Global environmental politics scholars, I further contend in this chapter, are especially well placed to unmask the half-truths and illusions of corporate sustainability.

Global environmental politics scholarship offers insights into when, how, and why corporations and states subvert and rewrite critical environmental narratives. The global and interdisciplinary range of global environmental political analysis also helps to reveal the full scale, depth, and complexity of the global environmental crisis. For these reasons, global environmental politics scholars can play a particularly valuable role in weighing evidence, debunking corporate rhetoric, and revealing what's really going on. Doing so, however, will require global environmental politics scholars to retain a sharp, critical edge. Not only is it necessary to contest corporate sustainability and the claims of corporate social responsibility, but global environmental politics scholars must also interrogate NGOs that are collaborating with (and taking money from) multinational oil companies, brand manufacturers, and big-box retailers. Past global environmental politics scholarship already provides a base of knowledge to take on this task, revealing the broad moderating tendencies within environmentalism itself as states crack down on civil disobedience, NGOs face pressures to pay staff and finance projects, the liberal economic order assimilates counternarratives, and capitalism and consumerism deepen. But more research and more action are necessary.

Environmentalism remains a powerful counternarrative, as Paul Wapner insightfully reveals in chapter 15. The value of "living at the margins"—of choosing less consumptive lifestyles, of questioning the limits of economic growth, of challenging the ideology of neoliberalism—is not necessarily about one day overthrowing the capitalist world order but in setting examples, bearing witness, and provoking reforms. The "fight" itself, as Wapner tells us, is doing a great deal of good, and environmentalists should not let charges of impracticality or romanticism or hypocrisy force a retreat—or, worse, resignation. Giving up on the concept of sustainability and instead promoting an ecological idea like resilience or stewardship might seem tempting. Yet as Wapner helps us to see, much of the power of the counternarrative of environmentalism comes from *not* retreating and cowering in the face of the gale force narrative of ever-more economic growth, prosperity, and technological progress. Besides, if a concept like resilience or stewardship was to ever gain the global presence and influence of the concept of sustainability, corporations would surely work just as hard to capture it for advertising and business purposes.

To wrest back the sustainability narrative as a story about the crisis of the Anthropocene epoch, global environmental politics scholars need to expose the illusions of corporate sustainability and NGO-corporate partnerships in front of a world audience. For this reason, global environmental politics scholars need to avoid falling prey to disciplinary jargon, now so common in academia, as well as overwrought writing, now so common in popular media. They will need to defend global sustainability as a narrative frame able to diagnose the ills of the New Earth, yet one that is still able to help citizens and consumers imagine a future where humanity is living together with far more equality, justice, and ecological integrity.

The Narrative of Global Sustainability

Narrative frames shape how people see the world, and why they act—or don't. Narratives will always crisscross and contradict each other, including, among many others, religious, patriotic, scientific, technocratic, and xenophobic frames. The world is simply too diverse and constantly evolving for even a single environmental narrative to ever emerge. This chapter is not meant to survey the many nuances and intricacies of the sustainability debate.[1] Instead, it limits itself to reviewing what most of the authors of *New Earth Politics* would see as sustainability.

For them, sustainability is not a condition that the Earth will one day reach but rather an ever-adapting politics to limit ecological damage, social injustice, and economic instability. Moving toward sustainability will require fundamental guiding values and principles—of balance, precaution, justice, intergenerational equity, respect for nature—so those now on Earth do not irreparably harm present or future life, in all its forms.

This sustainability narrative, which I call "New Earth sustainability" to distinguish it from "corporate sustainability," assumes high interdependence of socioeconomic and environmental systems with feedback loops and tipping points within and across each system. These systems are inherently resilient; still, vulnerability and instability do rise as degradation accrues and pressures grow. Effective solutions must therefore take account of the complexity and fluidity of these systems—as well as the need to respond before damage becomes irreversible. Acting locally is necessary for global sustainability. But international action to prioritize the Earth system (which includes humans) is equally, if not more, essential. A state of global unsustainability is far easier to identify than New Earth sustainability. Symptoms of unsustainability include rapid deforestation, dying oceans, mass extinctions, historic levels of chemicals and poisons in waterways and animal life, and unprecedented climate change.

The New Earth is an age of unsustainability. Acknowledging this, and looking through a New Earth sustainability frame, brings to the fore the need to think in geological time, both far into the past and far into the future. It points to the historical and ongoing destruction of ecosystems and cultures, especially in postcolonial states in the global South. It emphasizes the inequity of trade and corporate investment, highlighting the disproportionate gains of billionaire entrepreneurs, corrupt rulers, and ruthless dictators. And it connects the globalization of production to the depletion of natural resources and the exploitation of the poor.

New Earth sustainability as a frame further helps reveal the ecological and social shadows of consumption. It demonstrates how global supply chains tend to shift the environmental and social consequences of consumer goods into ecosystems and onto peoples with less power in the world economy. It shows the ways municipal and national policies in the global North end up exporting waste and pollution. It brings forth how risks and harms can accumulate across time and space and why precaution when introducing new industrial processes or consumer products is so essential in a globalizing world. It exposes the consequences of eating fast food, owning a smartphone, driving an SUV, wearing designer clothes, shopping at Walmart, vacationing overseas, or flying to a conference. And it reveals why solutions like recycling or ecolabels or ecoefficiency are not going to solve global unsustainability—and indeed could make matters worse—unless the ultimate goal is consuming less and differently.[2]

Told in this way, global environmental politics students can find the narrative frame of New Earth sustainability disheartening, even depressing. But despair does not define this narrative. The way I think about New Earth sustainability assumes the future is one of hope: of the possibility of moving toward a global politics of sustainability and a new ethic for everyday living.

Defined thus, sustainability as a way of understanding the world is ambitious. As with ideas like justice or liberty, however, this leaves it more vulnerable to capture by powerful interests than if it was a precise and measurable goal.

Corporate Sustainability

The past decade has seen multinational corporations striving to increase their influence and control over the sustainability narrative. The companies claiming to be sustainability leaders are the Who's Who of big-brand business. Costco and Walmart. Coca-Cola and Pepsi. KFC and McDonald's. Nestlé and Unilever. Nike and Adidas. Johnson & Johnson and Procter & Gamble. Mars and Cadbury. Danone and Kraft. These companies are financing NGO projects and volunteering to self-regulate as governments look to cut expenses and as international environmental negotiations stall. And their "aspirational" goals are like nothing before: 100 percent recycling; zero waste to landfill; 100 percent sustainable sourcing; 100 percent carbon neutrality; 100 percent water neutrality; zero deforestation; 100 percent renewable energy; zero toxic discharges. The CEOs are not shy about trumpeting to the world the value of corporate sustainability. "We are not perfect," Walmart CEO Doug McMillon told the Aspen Ideas Festival in 2012, "but we are a force for good, and things are better because we are here."

At first glance this might all sound promising, even enticing—and, as mentioned, just about every international activist and advocacy organization is now partnering with multinational corporations. On some measures corporate sustainability is doing some good. By renovating buildings and greening technologies, these companies are increasing the efficiency of energy and resource use. More efficient packaging is reducing product weights, per product emissions, and transport costs. And recycling and waste recovery is rising. New sourcing guidelines are even helping brand manufacturers and big-box retailers to avoid "controversial" supplies, such as "conflict minerals" and "deforestation crops" (e.g., oil palm, soy, and beef from Indonesia and Brazil). Corporate sustainability is certainly helping big business to produce more with less. And manufacturing and retailing each product is using less energy, plastic, wood, and water, as well as wasting less and emitting fewer greenhouse gases.[3]

But the goal of these companies is not sustainability of the planet. All gains are going straight back into generating more sales and more profits and more stores. And total environmental pressures are rising as discount consumerism spreads and cheap and disposable products proliferate.[4] Sustainability for these companies is about competing and expanding in the world economy. And it is about gaining competitive advantages, enhancing business value, and sustaining market share.[5]

The main goals of corporate sustainability are saving money and reducing costs. Companies like Walmart are aiming to offer discount prices to consumers to drive small and medium-sized firms out of business. They are trying to better manage risks, appease critics, and protect brand reputations. And they are drawing on the sustainability narrative to brand products and capture emerging markets. "The opportunity," Nike's website explains, "is greater than ever for sustainability principles and practices to deliver business returns and become a driver of growth."

Through sustainability codes of conduct, certification programs, and audits, multinational corporations are striving to gain more control within global supply chains. Doing so is providing many business advantages. Generally more opportunities exist to improve efficiencies—and thus lower costs and prices—within supply chains than within home operations. Management advice and new technologies can quickly multiply savings, especially for a company such as Walmart with more than 100,000 suppliers worldwide. Managing supply chains also enhances the capacity of brand manufacturers to secure high-quality inputs (increasingly important as scarcity rises in the age of unsustainability).

For these companies, sustainability is never about selling fewer disposable products or reducing consumption. Nor is it about avoiding thresholds or respecting the need for extreme precaution when introducing new elements into complex systems. Measures of success are not planetary stability or human welfare but rather the company's bottom line.[6]

Given the goals of corporate sustainability, one might expect the world's biggest environmental NGOs (ENGOs) to contest how corporations are reimagining the sustainability narrative. But just the opposite is happening.

Intoxicated: Partners in Cobranding and Cause Marketing

Uniting the contributors to *New Earth Politics* is the belief that the Earth is in crisis. Most agree that this crisis is escalating and that humanity is "on a hinge of history,"[7] facing the prospect of cataclysmic instability unless we act now. Corporate sustainability is helping to hide this crisis from the public. Even more worrying, so are increasingly moderate and conformist NGOs. Grassroots environmentalism still retains much radicalism, with activists, indigenous groups, and communities demanding controls on trade, corporations, and greed. Yet ENGOs like WWF, the Environmental Defense Fund, the Nature Conservancy, and the Sierra Club are increasingly embracing markets and trade as solutions. In doing so, these groups are making the environmental movement more accepting of capitalism, with more and more people who describe themselves as "environmentalists" accepting of international political norms and willing to work with (and within) mainstream institutions.[8]

Back in the 1960s and 1970s, environmentalists were far more likely to campaign for structural change to the world order. Calls for a world government and an end to sovereignty were common. So were appeals for a new international economic order and localization of economic affairs. So were demands for more equality and justice for exploited peoples. So were calls for population controls, limits on economic growth, and a lowering of worldwide consumption. And so were demands to respect indigenous knowledge and empower communities in the global South. Even in the 1980s and 1990s, antiglobalization activists were still calling for an end to exploitative trade and lending, as well as new rules to control rapacious investors and self-interested donors.

Today's NGO buzz, however, is about the value of corporate partnerships, cobranding, and cause marketing.[9] More and more nongovernmental programs and projects fit into, or at least do little to challenge, the increasing dominance of a market liberal worldview within both domestic and international politics. This worldview rejects the idea of a New Earth. Problems do exist, but market liberals argue that declaring a "global environmental crisis" exaggerates and misleads. For them, science and technology, human ingenuity, and economic growth are all improving life on Earth—and globalization is spreading the benefits. For more moderate market liberals, national regulations and international treaties are sometimes necessary, and at times this may require some restrictions and some measure of precaution. The most effective course of action for market liberals, however, is to allow markets to correct inefficiencies, let firms compete without policy distortions, support business efforts to export clean technologies, and allow voluntary corporate responsibility to do its magic.[10]

Among ENGOs, WWF is a leader in applauding voluntary corporate responsibility, calling its approach "cause marketing partnerships." Its freshwater partnership with Coca-Cola, which began in 2007, is now set to run until at least 2020: what on its website Coca-Cola declares is a "transformational partnership." Coke and WWF also maintain a partnership for

Arctic conservation; in one deal, Coke even put polar bears on its iconic Coke can for a month in 2011. In 2014 Coke was matching donations to WWF Arctic work of up to $1 million—with WWF putting the Coca-Cola logo on its website and praising the company for its "generosity." Financially, the US branch of WWF has been prospering with its focus on cause marketing partnerships, with revenues up more than 25 percent from 2008 to 2013.[11]

WWF is not media shy when explaining why it is partnering with big business. Jason Clay, senior vice president in charge of "market transformation" at the US branch of WWF, gave a 2010 TED Talk entitled, "How Big Brands Can Help Save Biodiversity." WWF is especially enthusiastic about its partnership with Coca-Cola. "Coke," the past president of WWF Canada told journalist Simon Houpt in 2011, "is literally more important, when it comes to sustainability, than the United Nations."[12]

WWF is courting many other big brands as well. The NGO is direct in how its partnerships work: "License the panda logo and WWF name," its worldwildlife.org website pitches to companies "to secure revenue and to build brand awareness." When raising "$1 million or more," WWF now offers companies the "honor" of becoming a "Million Dollar Panda." Besides Coca-Cola, Gap is one such company, donating a portion of sales a few weekends each year. Bank of America and Avon are also Million Dollar Pandas, as is Domtar, one of the world's biggest pulp and paper producers, which WWF describes on its website as a "sustainable paper company," having now "committed to responsible fiber sourcing for all of its wood-based products."

Confused Citizens and Consumers

International NGOs such as Greenpeace continue to campaign against corporate malfeasance. And tens of thousands of local NGOs continue to oppose whaling, logging, and mining; sue polluters and developers; and fight for indigenous and community rights. Yet even Greenpeace is partnering with Unilever, Coca-Cola, and Pepsi to market "natural refrigerants." And the website of Greenpeace USA now reassuringly declares, "Corporations can be extraordinarily dynamic, powerful and swift allies."

As ENGOs cobrand products and partner with big business, branches of the same international NGO can end up defining sustainability in quite different, and even contradictory, ways. For the majority of grassroots environmentalists, sustainability still requires far-reaching change and immediate action. Yet as partnerships deepen and NGOs become tangled in webs of corporate fundraising schemes, more and more NGOs across the world are accepting, or at least not openly criticizing, the narrative of corporate sustainability.

NGO praise of big business sustainability is further confusing citizens and consumers. Already consumers are facing a barrage of fair trade labels and ecocertification promises. Deciding what to buy, and especially what not to buy, is becoming more, not less, confusing as NGOs slip into the corporate net. And for citizens deciding what to protest—and what to acquiesce to—it's becoming harder, not easier. What partnerships between NGOs and corporations claim to achieve can be very hard to evaluate for average citizens. The WWF-Coke partnership on water sustainability, for example, claims (among many other successes) to have averted 128 million liters of yearly runoff from polluting Thailand's Chi River and to have cleaned up more than 100 billion liters of water flowing annually into Australia's Great Barrier Reef.[13]

The claims of corporate sustainability can seem impressive to even the most discerning NGO, government, or consumer. Take the claims of Walmart. The company has set three aspirational sustainability goals: to generate "zero waste," use "100 percent renewable energy," and only "sell products that sustain people and the environment." According to Walmart, the company is already recycling far more, conserving vast tracts of land, and renovating its stores to use less energy and water. It further claims that it is reducing food waste and donating excess food to homeless shelters and food banks; requiring fair trade certification and ecolabeling; sourcing more sustainably produced products (e.g., palm oil and beef); and supporting small farmers and local communities.

Walmart is making many precise claims of progress. Across all of its retail units, Walmart says it has cut greenhouse gas emissions by nearly 13 percent from 2005 to 2011. Compared to 2005, the company claims that greener technologies have made its fleet of delivery trucks nearly 70 percent more efficient. By just packaging its shoes differently, Walmart says it cut 400,000 pounds of waste and used 2.4 million gallons less water in the first ten months of 2011. One Walmart Supercenter in New Mexico, the company calculates, was able in 2011 to reduce its solid waste going to landfill by 96.5 percent. That year Walmart says it cut its landfill waste by over 50 percent across its outlets in Brazil, with ten stores reaching 90 percent or higher. In 2012 alone, the company says it eliminated more than 3 billion plastic bags from its stores.

Walmart further claims that as of 2012, independent and qualified third-party inspectors had certified more than three-quarters of its seafood suppliers—meeting at a minimum the standards of the Marine Stewardship Council and Best Aquaculture Practices. Walmart Supercenters and Sam's Clubs are stocking fair trade sugar products, fair trade coffee, and fair trade bananas, selling, for example, more than 1.6 million boxes of Fair Trade Certified bananas since 2007. In addition, Walmart claims it has put in place training and purchasing policies to help rural communities, estimating that in 2011 alone, it managed to increase "locally sourced produce" by 97 percent across its US stores.[14]

Of course, Walmart is telling its sustainability story in the best possible light. But this is not simple greenwash. What makes Walmart's story so confusing for consumers and activists is that most of its claims are basically "true." What makes the narrative so dangerous for sustainability of the Earth, however, is that what Walmart is calling "progress" hides the bigger story of growing sales, expanding corporate power, rising inequality, and mounting global environmental pressures. Walmart's sales in 1979 were around $1 billion; in fiscal year 2015 (ending January 31) revenues exceeded $485 billion. In fiscal year 2015 Walmart was once again the world's biggest company in terms of revenue, generating over $50 billion more than third-place finisher Royal Dutch Shell and over $100 billion more than fifth-place finisher Exxon Mobil. From 2011 to 2015, Walmart turned over three times more revenue than Apple, six times more than Microsoft, and seventeen times more than McDonald's.[15] Worldwide, since 2000 only Royal Dutch Shell and ExxonMobil have managed to turn over more annual revenue, and in most years Walmart has ranked first on Fortune's Global 500.

Walmart is continuing to expand rapidly in countries such as China. Worldwide, Walmart has some 2.2 million employees and over 11,000 stores. The company does not question the sustainability of selling more cheap plastic toys. Or water bottles. Or disposable diapers. Indeed, the genius of Walmart founder Sam Walton was to always aim for more sales rather than just profits, building more and bigger stores, and offering the lowest possible prices to bankrupt local retailers (as well as kindle demand for cheap stuff). The very notion of ecological sustainability is antithetical to the business model of Walmart.

On the surface, then, the promises and claims of brand sellers like Coca-Cola and big-box stores like Walmart can seem enticing to policymakers and environmentalists. A closer look at motives and goals, however, raises many questions about the actual value of what companies label as "sustainability gains." The focus of global environmental politics makes the subfield especially well placed to reveal to citizens and consumers what's rhetoric—and what's worthy—in this increasingly confusing sustainability story.

The Power of Global Environmental Politics

One day the globalizing world could well implode into protectionist states and survivalist camps. Yet at least in the near future, this would seem unlikely. *Homo sapiens* is a highly adaptive and resilient species, a main reason that humans now dominate all other species. Nonetheless, whatever we do, a storm of global change over the next half-century would seem to be on the way as the global North and global South collapse into one world culture of hyperconsumerism. How much damage this will cause is an open question.

Global environmental politics scholars can help to mitigate damage by revealing the dangers of turning sustainability into a tool of economic growth rather than deploying it as a brake on capitalism. And they can help by confronting the increasing acquiescence of multinational NGOs to big business sustainability as well as the tendency of governments since the 1980s to define sustainability as "sustainable development," which, defined as "meet[ing] the needs of the present without compromising the ability of future generations to meet their own needs," is too accommodating of global capitalism and the status quo to ever allow for New Earth sustainability.[16]

Increasingly, both corporations and governments are treating sustainable development and sustainability as if these concepts are synonyms. Yet sustainable development is fundamentally a compromise between development and environment advocates. In practice, it is still primarily aiming to maximize economic growth, with an eye toward trying to retain future growth opportunities. New Earth sustainability, however, rests on the idea of environmental, social, and economic balance, where principles of equity, ecological integrity, and justice are incontestable priorities. Sustainable development does little to question the world's growing inequality, or the thirteen-fold increase in the number of billionaires from the mid-1980s to 2015.[17] As an organizing and narrative frame, sustainable development does encourage states and firms to try to grow more efficiently (including more efficient use of natural resources) and with less outright and short-term ecological damage. But the concept does little to challenge overconsumption or wasteful consumption, and arguably it encourages more per capita consumption without caring what is being consumed. In contrast, New Earth sustainability aims for a fairer and more just world economy, as well as more equitable consumption, and less consumption overall, especially of nondurable and environmentally destructive products.

Cynics and anarchists, however, are not going to steer us toward New Earth sustainability. Nor are apologists and boosters of global capitalism. We need realistic optimism, creative thinking, and bold ideas—characteristics of the best global environmental politics scholars.[18] But global environmental politics scholarship as a whole will need to sharpen its tools and more forcefully challenge corporate sustainability and state-defined sustainable development. This is especially vital as the environmental movement becomes more restrained and conciliatory, as more and more activists reinforce, rather than struggle to transform, the world order.

The academy is well placed to offer balanced and accurate knowledge. Most academics do not need to worry about profits, or climbing organizational hierarchies, or even job security after tenure. Yet turgid writing across the academy is now so common that many academics have come to believe that bad writing is a sign of expertise and nuanced thinking.[19] Far too often academic writing is full of jargon, with vague ideas and awkward sentences, developing "theory" about nothing while the planet burns. Achieving real change on the New Earth requires global environmental politics scholars to speak to the world.

At the same time, global environmental politics students and scholars should remain wary of popular and Internet writing. Google now draws Wikipedia to the top of most searches, a source of knowledge replete with errors and plagiarism. Wikipedia says it requires sourcing, yet only rarely does an expert verify the quality and accuracy of the sources, and even then anyone can change an entry at any time. What kind of knowledge is that? Equally worrying, most popular books look nothing like past environmental best-sellers such as Rachel Carson's *Silent Spring* or E. F. Schumacher's *Small Is Beautiful*.[20] Most of today's best-sellers do away with subtlety and complexity. And such books will never gain the power of a *Silent Spring* to oppose corporate rhetoric and advertising.

Conclusion

The world needs the academy to challenge the ignorance and recalcitrance now stalling action on the New Earth. This theme recurs across the chapters of *New Earth Politics*, with Wapner's analysis in chapter 15 of the power of environmentalism as a counternarrative bringing this point home especially well. Scholars in this busy, busy world of avalanching information need to write clearly, challenge political and corporate narratives, and demand action. We should not think in terms of one day "winning" a debate, but instead, as Wapner says, see the struggle itself as innately valuable—not just politically and socially but also personally. Above all else, however, we must pursue truth and knowledge, as those in the academy have a duty to expose the lies and tricks of business and politics.

Global environmental politics students and teachers can play a lead role by challenging the narrative of big business as a sustainability leader, exposing corporate social responsibility as a strategy to increase profits, enhance control, and nurture businesses. Global environmental politics scholars should acknowledge the increasing per unit efficiency of making, transporting, retailing, and recycling consumer goods. But they also need to contest the narrative that corporate sustainability is slowing the escalating crisis on the New Earth. On a planetary scale, corporate sustainability can even make matters worse as firms invest environmental gains in advertising and marketing, stimulating more consumption of everything from Coca-Cola to Pampers: a message global environmental politics scholars need to relay in particular to the NGOs and consumers fooled by the slight-of-hand of corporate sustainability.

Finally, global environmental politics scholars, as part of sustaining the power of environmentalism as a counternarrative, can help to recapture the narrative of sustainability as a critical yet inspirational way forward. Ironically, big business would seem vulnerable to this strategy having infused the word *sustainability* into brands, reputations, and risk management. Done well, New Earth sustainability could offer a way of imagining a future where new political, economic, and ethical traditions could emerge to allow humanity to live together in peace and prosperity without any symptoms of global unsustainability.

Notes

1. For some sense of the different ways to understand sustainability, see Harrison, *Sustainable Capitalism and the Pursuit of Well-Being*; Thiele, *Sustainability*; Nemetz, *Business and the Sustainability Challenge*; Blowfield, *Business and Sustainability*; Lipschutz, "The Sustainability Debate"; Edwards, *Thriving beyond Sustainability*; Leach, Scoones, and Stirling, *Dynamic Sustainabilities*; Dresner, *The Principles of*

Sustainability; Princen, *The Logic of Sufficiency*; Princen, *Treading Softly*; Princen, "A Sustainability Ethic."

2. Dauvergne, *The Shadows of Consumption*; Dauvergne, "The Problem of Consumption"; Princen, Maniates, and Conca, eds., *Confronting Consumption*.

3. Laszlo and Zhexembayeva, *Embedded Sustainability*; Cramer and Karabell, *Sustainable Excellence*; Werbach, *Strategy for Sustainability*; Esty and Winston, *Green to Gold*.

4. Lichtenstein, *The Retail Revolution*; Shell, *Cheap*; Mitchell, *Big-Box Swindle*.

5. Dauvergne and Lister, "Big Brand Sustainability"; Porter and Kramer, "Strategy and Society"; Porter and Kramer, "Creating Shared Value"; Bhattacharyra, Sen, and Korschun, *Leveraging Corporate Responsibility*; Lister, *Corporate Social Responsibility*; Lubin and Esty, "The Sustainability Imperative."

6. For this argument in full, see Dauvergne and Lister, "The Power of Big Box Retail"; Dauvergne and Lister, "Big Brand Sustainability"; Dauvergne and Lister, *Eco-Business*.

7. Head, *On a Hinge of History*.

8. Dauvergne and LeBaron, *Protest Inc.*; Bernstein, *The Compromise of Liberal Environmentalism*.

9. Dauvergne and LeBaron, *Protest Inc.*; Kapoor, *Celebrity Humanitarianism*; Richey and Ponte, *Brand Aid*.

10. Clapp and Dauvergne, *Paths to a Green World*.

11. Stokstad, "Major Conservation Group Guts Science Team."

12. Simon Houpt, "Beyond the Bottle."

13. WWF and Coca-Cola, *A Transformative Partnership to Conserve Water*.

14. See Walmart's website: www.corporate.walmart.com.

15. Calculated from Fortune 500 and Global 500 data at http://fortune.com/rankings.

16. World Commission on Environment and Development, *Our Common Future*.

17. See Piketty, *Capital in the Twenty-First Century*; Harvey, *Seventeen Contradictions and the End of Capitalism*; Robbins, *Global Problems and the Culture of Capitalism*. The increase in the number of billionaires is calculated from the Forbes (www.forbes.com) annual list of billionaires.

18. See, for instance, Nicholson and Wapner, eds., *Global Environmental Politics*; Litfin, *Ecovillages*; Speth, *America the Possible*; Speth, *The Bridge at the Edge of the World*; Wapner, *Living through the End of Nature*; Wapner, "Sacrifice in an Age of

Comfort"; Wapner, "Horizontal Politics"; Maniates and Meyer, *The Environmental Politics of Sacrifice*; Princen, *Treading Softly*; Princen, *The Logic of Sufficiency*.

19. Sword, *Stylish Academic Writing*.

20. Carson, *Silent Spring*; Schumacher, *Small Is Beautiful*.

Bibliography

Bernstein, Steven. *The Compromise of Liberal Environmentalism*. New York: Columbia University Press, 2001.

Bhattacharyra, C. B., Sankar Sen, and Daniel Korschun. *Leveraging Corporate Responsibility: The Stakeholder Route to Maximizing Business and Social Value*. Cambridge: Cambridge University Press, 2011.

Blowfield, Michael. *Business and Sustainability*. Oxford: Oxford University Press, 2013.

Carson, Rachel. *Silent Spring*. Boston: Houghton Mifflin, 1962.

Clapp, Jennifer, and Peter Dauvergne. *Paths to a Green World: The Political Economy of the Global Environment*, 2nd ed. Cambridge, MA: MIT Press, 2011.

Cramer, Aron, and Z. Karabell. *Sustainable Excellence: The Future of Business in a Fast-Changing World*. New York: Rodale, 2010.

Dauvergne, Peter. "The Problem of Consumption." *Global Environmental Politics* 10, no. 2 (2010): 1–10.

Dauvergne, Peter. *The Shadows of Consumption: Consequences for the Global Environment*. Cambridge, MA: MIT Press, 2008.

Dauvergne, Peter, and Genevieve LeBaron. *Protest Inc.: The Corporatization of Activism*. Cambridge: Polity Press, 2014.

Dauvergne, Peter, and Jane Lister. "Big Brand Sustainability: Governance Prospects and Environmental Limits." *Global Environmental Change* 22, no. 1 (2012): 36–45.

Dauvergne, Peter, and Jane Lister. *Eco-Business: A Big-Brand Takeover of Sustainability*. Cambridge, MA: MIT Press, 2013.

Dauvergne, Peter, and Jane Lister. "The Power of Big Box Retail in Global Environmental Governance: Bringing Commodity Chains Back into IR." *Millennium: Journal of International Relations* 39 (2010): 145–60.

Dresner, Simon. *The Principles of Sustainability*, 2nd ed. London: Earthscan, 2008.

Edwards, Andrés R. *Thriving beyond Sustainability: Pathways to a Resilient Society*. Gabriola Island, BC: New Society Publishers, 2010.

Esty, Daniel, and Andrew Winston. *Green to Gold*. New Haven, CT: Yale University Press, 2006.

Harrison, Neil E. *Sustainable Capitalism and the Pursuit of Well-Being*. New York: Routledge, 2014.

Harvey, David. *Seventeen Contradictions and the End of Capitalism*. Oxford: Oxford University Press, 2014.

Head, Ivan. *On a Hinge of History: The Mutual Vulnerability of South and North*. Toronto: University of Toronto Press, 1991.

Houpt, Simon. "Beyond the Bottle: Coke Trumpets Its Green Initiatives." *Globe and Mail*, January 13, 2011, B6.

Kapoor, Ilan. *Celebrity Humanitarianism: The Ideology of Global Charity*. New York: Routledge, 2013.

Laszlo, Chris, and Nadya Zhexembayeva. *Embedded Sustainability: The Next Big Competitive Advantage*. Sheffield, UK: Greenleaf, 2011.

Leach, Melissa, Ian Scoones, and Andy Stirling. *Dynamic Sustainabilities: Technology, Environment, Social Justice*. New York: Earthscan, 2010.

Lichtenstein, Nelson. *The Retail Revolution: How Wal-Mart Created a Brave New World of Business*. New York: Metropolitan Books, 2009.

Lipschutz, Ronnie D. "The Sustainability Debate: *Déjà Vu* All Over Again?" In *Handbook of Global Environmental Politics*, 2nd ed., edited by Peter Dauvergne, 480–91. Cheltenham, UK: Edward Elgar, 2012.

Lister, Jane. *Corporate Social Responsibility and the State: International Approaches to Forest Co-Regulation*. Vancouver: UBC Press, 2011.

Litfin, Karen T. *Ecovillages: Lessons for Sustainable Communities*. Cambridge: Polity Press, 2013.

Lubin, David, and Daniel Esty. "The Sustainability Imperative." *Harvard Business Review* 88 (May 2010): 42–50.

Maniates, Michael, and John M. Meyer. *The Environmental Politics of Sacrifice*. Cambridge, MA: MIT Press, 2010.

Mitchell, Stacy. *Big-Box Swindle*. Boston: Beacon Press, 2006.

Nemetz, Peter N. *Business and the Sustainability Challenge: An Integrated Perspective*. New York: Routledge, 2013.

Nicholson, Simon, and Paul Wapner, eds. *Global Environmental Politics: From Person to Planet*. Boulder, CO: Paradigm, 2014.

Piketty, Thomas. *Capital in the Twenty-First Century*. Cambridge, MA: Belknap Press, 2014.

Porter, Michael, and Mark Kramer. "Strategy and Society: The Link between Competitive Advantage and Corporate Social Responsibility." *Harvard Business Review* 84 (December 2006): 78–92.

Princen, Thomas. A Sustainability Ethic. In *Handbook of Global Environmental Politics*. 2nd ed., edited by Peter Dauvergne. 466–479. Cheltenham, UK: Edward Elgar, 2012.

Princen, Thomas. *Treading Softly: Paths to Ecological Order*. Cambridge, MA: MIT Press, 2010.

Princen, Thomas, Michael Maniates, and Ken Conca, eds. *Confronting Consumption*. Cambridge, MA: MIT Press, 2002.

Princen, Thomas. *The Logic of Sufficiency*. Cambridge, MA: MIT Press, 2005.

Richey, Lisa Ann, and Stefano Ponte. *Brand Aid: Shopping Well to Save the World*. Minneapolis: University of Minnesota Press, 2011.

Robbins, Richard H. *Global Problems and the Culture of Capitalism*, 6th ed. New York: Pearson, 2013.

Schumacher, E. F. *Small Is Beautiful: Economics as If People Mattered*. New York: Harper and Row, 1973.

Shell, Ellen Ruppel. *Cheap: The High Cost of Discount Culture*. New York: Penguin, 2009.

Speth, James Gustave. *America the Possible: Manifesto for a New Economy*. New Haven, CT: Yale University Press, 2013.

Speth, James Gustave. *The Bridge at the Edge of the World*. New Haven, CT: Yale University Press, 2008.

Stokstad, Erik. "Major Conservation Group Guts Science Team in Strategy Shift." *Science* 343 (March 7, 2014): 1069.

Sword, Helen. *Stylish Academic Writing*. Cambridge, MA: Harvard University Press, 2012.

Thiele, Leslie Paul. *Sustainability*. Cambridge: Polity Press, 2013.

Wapner, Paul. "Horizontal Politics: Transnational Environmental Activism and Global Cultural Change." *Global Environmental Politics* 2, no. 2 (2002): 37–62.

Wapner, Paul. *Living through the End of Nature: The Future of American Environmentalism*. Cambridge, MA: MIT Press, 2010.

Wapner, Paul. "Sacrifice in an Age of Comfort." In *The Environmental Politics of Sacrifice*, edited by Michael Maniates and John M. Meyer, 33–59. Cambridge, MA: MIT Press, 2010.

Werbach, Adam. *Strategy for Sustainability: A Business Manifesto*. Cambridge, MA: Harvard Business Press, 2009.

World Commission on Environment and Development. *Our Common Future*. Oxford: Oxford University Press, 1987.

WWF and Coca-Cola. *A Transformative Partnership to Conserve Water: Annual Review 2012*. WWF and The Coca-Cola Company, 2013.

Epilogue

Politics for a New Earth: Governing in the "Anthropocene"

Frank Biermann

The chapters in this book offer a fascinating, highly varied picture of the rapid transformation of our world. One irrefutable conclusion emerges: today we are living on a "New Earth." In a variety of research communities, this "New Earth" has found its own terminology. Starting in 2000,[1] scholars, journalists, politicians, and activists began to refer to the current state of our fundamentally transformed planet as the Anthropocene, a term introduced to mark a new epoch in planetary history, separating it from previous epochs such as the Holocene, which refers to the last 12,000 years before the present.[2] The neologism *Anthropocene* combines the two key elements that mark our "New Earth": the Greek suffix *-cene* (new), denoting the novelty of this epoch in planetary history, and the Greek word for our species (*anthropos)*, which has evolved into the dominant factor transforming our planet.

The Anthropocene differs from the earlier Holocene in clearly distinct ways.[3] To name a few examples, atmospheric concentrations of carbon dioxide and other greenhouse gases are now significantly higher than in the Holocene, resulting in myriad measurable changes in Earth system parameters, such as sea-level rise, ocean acidification, glacier melt, and more erratic weather patterns. Species diversity in the Anthropocene is much lower, with a strong trend toward continued depletion. Sedimentation processes have changed, and numerous natural systems have been altered, from river runoff to entire coastal zones. The terrestrial landscape is fundamentally transformed, now placing roughly 40 percent of all land area of our planet directly under human control, with the main purpose being human use. Numerous new substances have been introduced into the planetary system, from plastics to persistent organic pollutants, genetically modified organisms, and new types of radioactive substances. Human infrastructures have altered the face of our planet, from roads and railroad tracks to the vast concrete jungles of our modern urban settlements. In short, no planetary system, no part of the globe has not been fundamentally transformed over the last hundreds of years—and in some ways even over the last thousands of years, when humans started to kill off large parts of terrestrial megafauna and transform the planet by wildfires, agriculture, and the domestication of animals. Given this dominant planetary role of our species, our New Earth has in the Anthropocene aptly found its new scientific title: as a distinct, new, and unprecedented epoch in planetary history.

Understanding our time in terms of such a fundamentally new epoch in planetary history helps to emphasize new issues, interconnections, and interdependencies. Most of these have been outside the more restricted focus of the traditional notion of environmental policy as it has emerged since the 1960s and 1970s.

For example, an Anthropocene lens helps to understand the multiple ways through which global transformations of land use patterns or water cycles are interrelated with a variety of socioecological systems and socioeconomic processes, be it climate change, population growth and migration, changes in food consumption patterns (e.g., toward more meat-based diets), market incentives, or changing trade flows (see Ken Conca's overview in chapter 1). The preservation of local fisheries, for instance, is as much affected by ocean acidification as by global markets and consumption patterns. Traditional notions of environmental policy fall short in capturing this complexity, as Daniel Deudney and Elizabeth Mendenhall show in chapter 2.

Moreover, new technologies and novel sociotechnical systems that mark the Anthropocene generate entirely new challenges that go beyond traditional environmental policies.[4] Such challenges include the emergence of genetic modification;[5] domestication of fish species in aquaculture; synthetic biology and nanotechnology; up to possible further intrusions in the genetic makeup of species, including new possibilities of "deextinction" of species for which DNA traces still exist. New challenges also arise from novel technologies to actively "manage" Earth systems, such as solar radiation management or ocean fertilization to remove carbon dioxide from the atmosphere. Many of these new technologies pose unprecedented challenges for international politics, given that unilateral development and deployment is technically often feasible. For instance, a major highly polluting country may decide that because of its inability to reduce fossil fuel emissions, it should begin a massive program of ocean fertilization to increase carbon dioxide uptake. What institutional constraints and decision-making processes exist for other countries to prevent such attempts at actively modifying and managing key planetary systems?

An Anthropocene lens also helps to break down artificial barriers between mitigation and adaptation in environmental policy. Politics in the Anthropocene goes beyond mitigating human interference within an external environment that is conceived of as being outside the human sphere. Instead, an Anthropocene lens emphasizes an integrated perspective of evolving social-ecological systems that require not only active management of human influences, but also the adaptation of human societies to inescapable changes. The governance of such societal adaptation processes, from local to global levels, poses formidable challenges for policy. Of course, adaptation to changes in Earth systems has been a key challenge for humans since time memorial. But the scope of the challenge in the Anthropocene has increased by orders of magnitude. For example, about half of humanity today lives in complex urban settlements, with the trend moving toward 70 percent of people living in cities in a few decades. Of these megacities, many lie in coastal zones; overall, about 50 percent of all humans live today along often very vulnerable low-lying coastlines. Sea-level rise and more severe storm surges, likely consequences of climate change, put large sections of humanity at existential risk, requiring complex adaptation programs. These programs must start locally, but they will also need to rely on support, coordination, and guidance through global governance arrangements. In extreme cases, adapting to global warming might even require the slow but steady relocation of entire populations, ranging from the low-lying deltas of major rivers to small island nations in the Pacific.[6]

In sum, the emergence of the Anthropocene changes the context for both politics and political science.[7] The traditional notion of environmental policy, as it emerged in the 1960s, has helped shape human understanding and political responses for the past fifty years. Yet it has focused merely on the natural surroundings of the human person and human settlements and on the prevention of pollution and ecosystem degradation. The increased novel understanding of the magnitude of human influences, along with more advanced knowledge of the possible scales of impacts and degree of risks that these influences bring with them, thus requires new approaches, as also argued by Deudney and Mendenhall in their chapter. In the Anthropocene, the notion of an "environment" loses its significance and is replaced by a holistic understanding of

socioecological systems from local, place-based systems toward an integrated view of the planetary system that encompasses humans and
nonhuman elements. Traditional notions of "nature conservation"
become less relevant on a "New Earth," where there is no nature left that
is not shaped, harmed, managed, modified, or controlled by humans.[8]
Politics in the Anthropocene, on our "New Earth," cannot be business as
usual, but requires fundamentally new visions and paradigms.[9] *Environmental policy* has been an appropriate term for the policies and institutions
of the 1970s and 1980s, but it falls short in describing the multifarious
changes and interlinkages of our "New Earth." An alternative paradigm
that more aptly describes the new focus of political institutions and policies—which need to care for the stability of life-maintaining functions of
the entire planetary system—is hence "Earth system" governance, emphasizing the challenging new agenda that lies ahead.

I sketch five elements of where change in political analysis as well as
political practice is most urgently needed within the larger context of planetary stewardship, effective Earth system governance, and the political
challenges of navigating the New Earth.

Revisioning Institutional Architectures for the Anthropocene

First, the more sophisticated understanding of our common epoch as the
Anthropocene poses new questions regarding the overall institutional
architecture of politics, which go beyond what has traditionally been analyzed within the realm of environmental policy.

Importantly, modern politics still follows the principle of independent
nation-states, represented by national governments as the sole arbiter of
their destiny. Yet this system, inherited from the nineteenth century, masks
fundamental conflicts in human societies, such as between the millions of
city dwellers, with their myriad teleconnections with other urban areas
outside their own countries, and the many rural communities, which are
often disadvantaged in terms of income, provision of clean water or electricity, health services, education, and so forth. Economic globalization
and global capitalism have also created new contradictions between a
global middle class and a global class of impoverished people, which often
cuts across traditional lines of national jurisdictions and outdated understandings of North and South. But how can global political conflicts
between urban and rural, rich and poor, cutting across national boundaries, be best represented in political analysis and political practice? Are
global alliances of megacities, for example, part of a solution, or would

strengthening such alliances as governance mechanisms reinforce the global dominance of the urban class vis-à-vis the rural hinterland?[10] What is the role of newly emerging global superpowers that are often still, in political practice as much as in political theory, seen as part of a less relevant "Third World" or a group of developing countries, while their real power already extends far into the political capitals, financial centers, and corporate boardrooms of the traditional, self-declared "First World"? Regardless of the high per capita consumption levels in Europe and North America, the future of humanity in the Anthropocene will be ensured only if global agreements are negotiated that account for transformed global constellations of political and economic power, notably in Asia and Latin America, which increasingly marginalize the traditional political centers of the nineteenth and twentieth century (very insightful here are Joyeeta Gupta's chapter 11, Judith Shapiro's chapter 12, and Kate O'Neill's chapter 7). These are just some examples of the fundamental political questions posed by our "New Earth."

An Anthropocene lens also requires a new look at the policy domains that we are studying and the traditional sectoral organization of politics, inasmuch as it creates new objects of concern that cut across traditional lines of governance and might require an entirely new view on the organization of public policy at local and global levels. The global and national regulation of energy, for example, might require urgent reform, calling among others for novel institutions that are able to work toward multiple objectives at the same time, as Navroz Dubash laid out convincingly in chapter 13. As another example, the integrated understanding of planetary systems now places special emphasis on the nitrogen cycle, which is, however, so far only indirectly addressed in political debates and institutions. To put it provocatively, do we need at some point national ministries of nitrogen or a global organization for monitoring and managing nitrogen? Ocean acidification, as a third example, becomes a central area of concern, with complex links that range from global warming, as the main causal factor, to local fisheries in poor regions that are likely to be negatively affected by increasing acidification of our seas.[11] This global problem is, again, only indirectly addressed in international and national policies, from energy policy to fishery management, yet without a holistic understanding of the scale and dynamics of the problem. Geoengineering, from solar radiation management to ocean fertilization, is a fourth illustration of a typical Anthropocene problem that will call for novel institutions and governance approaches, especially given that many geoengineering options are technically possible through unilateral action by (larger) countries without cooperation or consultation with others (see the extensive discussion in chapter 14 by Wil Burns and Simon Nicholson).

The New Normativity in the Anthropocene

Importantly, our New Earth also requires new normative debates and discourses. As compared to earlier epochs in planetary history, the Anthropocene signals the inescapable dominance of the human species. Human societies are no longer reacting to environmental changes and pressures. We are essentially shaping and reshaping our planet. This insight creates fundamentally new normative problems. How on earth do we want our planet?

As an illustration, we can consider the management of the Oostvaardersplassen, a nature reserve in the Netherlands. This area of 56 square kilometers is entirely artificial, created on land that was reclaimed in a former bay area in the 1950s and 1960s within the new Dutch province Flevoland, itself in its entirety created on reclaimed land. Within this nature reserve, which is largely closed off to human visitors, numerous animals and plants have settled, and others have been introduced by park managers. More than one thousand wild horses and numerous deer now roam in the area, all of which are considered under Dutch law as "wild" animals, with the consequence that management, and especially feeding during the winter period, is forbidden. In some harsh winters, about a third of the grazers do not survive, with their cadavers not being removed, given the legal definition of a "wild area." This situation has led to vivid national debates about the management of this artificial wilderness on reclaimed land, involving hunting associations (which want to open the area up for hunters), nature conservationists (with different views on the "right" species composition), animal welfare campaigners (arguing for by-feeding of starving grazers), ecologists, and a variety of representatives of the surrounding, heavily urbanized human population, including campaigns by concerned school children who sought to protect the "wild" horses. In 2005, the question became an issue in the national parliament, which convened the International Committee on the Management of Large Herbivores in the Oostvaardersplassen to offer policy advice and a resolution of the key obstacles. This example is admittedly extreme, given the special situation of the Netherlands (according to the old adagio that "God has created the Earth except for Holland—this was done by the

Dutch"). On the other hand, the normative conflicts around the Oost-vaardersplassen are emblematic for the entire Anthropocene. There is essentially no "nature" left that remains unaffected by human interference, and that hence is not managed in some way by human agents. Large parts of the terrestrial surface of the planet have been transformed for human use. Fish stocks are depleted across the planet, with new trends of domestication of fish in globally spread aquacultures. Remaining "wild" parts of the land surface exist only at the mercy of human will, protected by human institutions, and often administered by specialized bureaucracies. In many regions, all remaining "wild" megafauna is registered, monitored, and managed by complex political institutions for "wildlife management."

Yet the current quest for managing and shaping "nature" goes beyond confined "nature reserves." Discourses similar to the ones concerning the Dutch Oostvaardersplassen are beginning to emerge even at the global level. For example, almost all governments have agreed in the framework of the UN climate convention on limiting global warming to a maximum value of 2°C above the assumed values of around 1780. In other words, governments have decided on a temperature target for our planet, an unprecedented feat for international diplomacy. This "2 degree target" exemplifies the normative complexities that are so characteristic of the Anthropocene. The target is informed by science, no doubt. But in the end it is also political, for the planet has no clear-cut tipping points or "temperature switches," at least not within the confines of human understanding. The 2 degree target is no environmental policy goal in the traditional understanding but the outcome of global conflicts of power, with far-reaching equity implications given the high risks that the target brings for small island nations and poor people in low-lying developing countries, to name just a few affected groups whose livelihood has been put at additional risk by this international acceptance of a substantially warmer planet. On the other hand, many experts believe that politically, the 2 degree target is too demanding and thus not realistic given the slow pace of policy development. In this way, the target might even appear as symbolic policy, with little chance of realistic implementation. A "temperature target for planet earth" might have sounded absurd forty years ago, when governments met for the 1972 Stockholm Conference on the Human Environment. Today, such discourses are part and parcel of our New Earth, and the changed context heralded by the advent of the Anthropocene, with its needs for effective Earth system governance.

And the 2 degree climate target is just one example. For instance, the often heated debate on "planetary boundaries," kicked off in 2009 by an influential *Nature* article by a group of (largely) Northern academics,[12] has driven such debates to new degrees of sophistication, now adding discussions on Earth system boundaries in domains as diverse as land use, freshwater, chemical pollution, and biodiversity depletion. The underlying logic of the planetary boundaries approach is that there are boundary conditions in the planetary systems that could, if violated, switch the system, or some of its parts, into new equilibria. Proponents of such planetary boundaries suggest that such thresholds, or "tipping points," in the Earth system can be identified by science, and to some extent even quantified. Critics contest, however, that many key processes in the system have no global threshold values that lead to systematic changes, that the science is too uncertain to establish such threshold values, and that the identification of many of such boundaries is an inherently political process under the guise of (Northern) science. Examples for such controversies are boundaries in the domains of freshwater depletion, land use, and biodiversity depletion.[13] As a consequence of such controversies, the notion of planetary boundaries, while supported by many leading scientists and science organizations, did not find its way into the final declaration of the 2012 UN Conference on Sustainable Development, held in Rio de Janeiro. This debate shows the complex challenges of modern Earth system governance where science and politics are inherently intertwined, national and global processes are integrated, and the normative underpinnings of political science are elevated from personal values to the core of the analysis (see also chapter 8 by Maria Ivanova).

Political Studies within Earth System Science

The Anthropocene is not only a major challenge for political decision making. It is also a major challenge for political science and the traditional field of environmental studies.

First, an integrated understanding of socioecological systems, from local to global levels, requires new efforts to integrate various social science disciplines, as O'Neill argues in chapter 7. Understanding the societal components of socioecological systems requires cooperation and integration of different directions of scientific inquiry. What is needed is a holistic understanding of the psychological and anthropological foundations of human actions, along with the sociological analysis of our societies, in-depth study of modern complex capitalist economies, improved understanding of key processes in governance and political steering, detailed understanding of the functioning of national and international law, and the philosophical scrutiny of the normative basis for Earth system governance in different countries. In all this, different levels of governance need to be better integrated, combining studies of local governance with a holistic understanding of their global interdependencies and teleconnections.

Second, social scientists need to more actively engage with the broader communities of Earth system scientists, including integrated fields such as land science or food system research. How to feed another 2 billion additional humans in the future, along with the 842 million people who currently lack sufficient nutrition, is one of the foremost challenges for scholars of the Anthropocene; it cannot be sufficiently addressed without integrated insights from development studies, economics, political science, ecology, agricultural science, climatology, and other areas. The challenge of integrating social and natural sciences is partially methodological, given that most natural sciences build on computer-based analysis, quantification, scenario studies, and, when it comes to analysis of human influences, methodological reductionism. Political science has to find ways to contribute to such integrated research programs by adding vital insights on decision making, distributive conflicts, regulatory effectiveness, and power relations, among other key aspects. Political science is also much needed for the critique of current integrated research programs that are often oblivious to key political questions relating to power, equity, democracy, and legitimacy. The analysis of land, for example, as a coupled social-ecological system, is hardly complete without a sophisticated understanding of power conflicts around land use, the distributive effects of variant systems of property and use rights, the legitimacy and effectiveness of local and regional land management, and the political analysis of global trade flows or novel dynamics of global land grabs by rich and powerful countries to ensure sufficient future food production for their own populations.

In sum, global change research and the emerging field of integrated Earth system science require a sophisticated perspective from an interdisciplinary Earth system governance research program that cuts across social science disciplines and levels of analysis. This requires an increased openness from the more natural science–oriented research traditions, to engage with social science perspectives and accept and critically interrogate the political nature of global change science. But it also requires the willingness of political scientists to leave their ivory towers of university departments and to cross disciplinary boundaries, with a view toward generating novel insights into the key societal problems of the Anthropocene, from food and water to coastal zone management and integrated land system science. Protective ghettos of social scientists—such as the annual conventions of the International Studies Association, with their almost exclusive attendance by disciplinary political scientists—need to embrace the challenge of bridging disciplinary divides and seeking a holistic understanding of the Anthropocene.

From Disciplinary Science to Transdisciplinary Knowledge Generation

But we need to go beyond breaking down barriers and boundaries between our disciplines. We also need to seek new alliances between political science and political practice. Again, this requires university-based political scientists to move beyond their protected academic spaces, reclusive academic journals, and esoteric theoretical debates. Political scientists must become more willing to engage in public debate and provide answers to the pressing societal problems of our time, even if our knowledge and understanding is uncertain or inconclusive. At the same time, university scientists need to better engage with, and integrate, nonscientific knowledge and information in their analysis. While attending typical political science conferences in North America and Europe, one is easily reminded of the beautiful dialogue from Bertolt Brecht's *Turandot or The Congress of Whitewashers*, when the teacher asks his student, Si Fu, to name the key questions of philosophy. Si Fu answered, "Are things outside of us, for themselves, also without us, or are the things within us, for ourselves, not without us?" When the teacher further inquired about which opinion was correct, Si Fu responded that no verdict has been reached yet, adding that the congress that was to yield the final verdict took place—as it has done for the past two hundred years—in the monastery Mi Sang on the banks of the Yellow River. The concrete question posed to delegates was: Is the Yellow River real, or does it exist only in our heads? However, during the congress, there was a snow-melt in the mountains that led the Yellow River to rise above its banks and sweep away the monastery Mi Sang and all congress participants. Thus concluded Si Fu, "The proof that the things are outside of us, for themselves, also without us, therefore, has not been furnished." Also today the glaciers are melting as they did near the monastery Mi Sang in this lovely play, and, equally aloof, our philosophers and political scientists often seem to be in the panels of our political science congresses, developing—as Peter Dauvergne notes in chapter 16—"theory about nothing while the planet burns."

The central role of (often novel) normative questions in the Anthropocene calls not only for better integration with policy communities; it might also pose new and possibly difficult questions for university scholars. Even their personal lives and leadership might be questioned (and surely is by many of their students). One can safely assume that many OECD-based Anthropocene scholars belong with their families to the "overconsumers" that Conca identifies in chapter 1. But to what extent do scholars need to walk the talk? In an ideal world, university professors function as thought leaders, thought provokers, critics, and cocreators of our leading normative discourses and paradigmatic understandings. Ideally university professors would also be thought multipliers, as teachers and writers who influence the next generations of university-educated politicians, bureaucrats, journalists, activists, and, not least, the next generation of university professors.

What does this responsibility require from academics in the Anthropocene? Richard Falk offers in chapter 4 an inspiring narrative of engaged citizenship and engaged scholarship (see also Karen Litfin's chapter 5). Yet there might be reason to doubt whether such engaged scholarship in modern academia is the norm rather than an admirable exception. Instead, in many ways, the discipline of political science seems to veer away from a more political role. The production of academic papers seems to have become more relevant than the production of novel insights into how to solve the key challenges of the Anthropocene. Citation scores by Thomson Reuters beat societal relevance and impact. Academic congresses, such as the annual meetings of the International Studies Association, are organized in ways that ensure that hardly any practitioner would feel inclined and welcome to participate and learn from the key insights that disciplinary science might have generated.

Last but not least, as Liftin also showed, our university communities need to critically reflect on our own practices. What to do with the consumption levels of our own community, individually but also in our professional practices? Halving the number of conferences? Having conferences on global issues also in other parts of the globe? Engaging with students not only in debates on the most effective international politics and abstract notions of global justice, but also opening up discussions about the "good life" among ourselves (see also Conca, chapter 1)? Erik Assadourian's proposal in chapter 10 of an "ecophilosophical missionary movement" that should replace today's "light green environmentalism" might sound far-fetched for many of us, as might Falk's self-description in chapter 4 of a "citizen pilgrim." Yet undoubtedly such discussions about the political, social, and personal roles of scholars of the Anthropocene will become more prominent in the years ahead.

From Incrementalism toward Transformative Thinking

Finally, the contribution of political science in the Anthropocene is not only to provide novel insights into the functioning of political systems. Equally important is its role in envisioning alternative futures that can protect and enrich the lives of all people while maintaining the life-supporting functions of our planet. What is needed, in particular, are transformative ideas that are based on sound evidence and theoretical understanding, but also help to point to new modes of governance, as Falk argues in chapter 4. The nineteenth and twentieth centuries were marked by the transformation of national political systems in many industrialized and newly industrializing countries, including strong public institutions, adherence to democratic principles, and powerful mechanisms for ensuring the protection of the less powerful and the poor. Today in the Anthropocene epoch, a novel challenge is to create effective systems of Earth system governance that range from local to global, but that especially address the "Anthropocene governance gap" (as Oran Young has coined the term) in the cooperation and coordination of more than 190 states.

Effective Earth system governance is unlikely to emerge unless it can draw on successful intergovernmental institutions (see also chapter 11 by Gupta).[14] In the same way in which the limited state of the nineteenth century has over time expanded to cover a wide range of societal problems and human concerns, the intergovernmental institutional architecture will now have to be revised to allow for stronger governance at Earth system level and more effective, but also more equitable, planetary stewardship.[15] The existing core set of institutions has evolved around, and follows the basic principles of, the United Nations, an institutional model that was designed seventy years ago at an entirely different state of socioecological integration, before the "great acceleration"[16] that has essentially shaped our New Earth (see also Conca's chapter 1). Other institutions have evolved outside the UN system, such as the Group of 20 major economies, public-private partnerships, and numerous novel types of private governance at the global level, such as the Forest Stewardship Council and the many transnational organizations that have followed this institutional innovation.[17] Yet as recent research has shown, it remains doubtful whether nonstate institutions and organizations can really fill the Anthropocene governance gap that the failing intergovernmental system leaves behind.[18]

Instead, leadership by national governments and intergovernmental organizations still seems pivotal in setting up the much-needed global and regional institutions for effective Earth system governance. But the precise contours of such leadership and the resulting mechanisms of governance that can facilitate pathways into a "good Anthropocene" remain vague, and open for debate. There is urgent need for more research in these questions within larger global study programs that combine natural and social sciences, along with the humanities and health, legal, and engineering professions. It is unlikely, however, that national political elites at the state level, who have heavily invested in the status quo, will take on the challenge of societal transformation without a strong groundswell of local action and rebellion (e.g., chapter 9 by Peter Jacques, chapter 6 by Michael Maniates, and chapter 15 by Paul Wapner). This is where the call for engaged citizenship and rebellious social movements intertwines with the quest for stronger political institutions through which governments can implement the change agendas that are needed, not the least with a view toward curbing the vast power of major multinational corporations and the financial markets (see also Dauvergne's chapter 16).[19]

For traditional political science, including its now fairly established subfield of global environmental politics, this requires an additional step change toward a new openness for interaction between science and policy, interdisciplinary and transdisciplinary research, and the continuous quest for novel, radical thought leadership that leaves behind the comfort zones of methodological restraint, academic straitjackets, and national and middle-class parochialism (see also Falk's chapter 4 and Maniates's chapter 6). This does not mean that the only role for political science is to generate grand designs and revolutionary visioning—equally important, as Oran Young convincingly argues in chapter 3, is a reasoned diagnostic approach that goes beyond simple panaceas that are likely to be in most cases misleading or even dangerous. However, if the only effective solution to resolving the challenges of the Anthropocene is, as Falk argues in chapter 4, a revolution of human consciousness, it is fair to assume that the academic study of political systems and processes cannot remain unaffected by such transformative needs.

Conclusion

It is important to see the Anthropocene *sine ira et studio*, with realistic, sober analyses and expectations that veer away from fatalistic doom, on the one hand, and naive techno-optimism and political megalomania, on the other.

Surely the Anthropocene is one of the most dangerous times for our species, given its characteristics of high scientific uncertainty, myriad still largely unknown system interactions, complex teleconnections, and an ever increasing vulnerability of human settlements and socioeconomic systems to Earth system transformations. Yet we should also not characterize the Anthropocene only in terms of catastrophe and cataclysm. Let us not underestimate human ingenuity, with a realistic view of the civilizing progress that our species has achieved since the times of ubiquitous witch hunts, genocide, slavery, and all-out war that marked most of earlier human history. And in any case, there is no way back. The New Earth is here, and a return to the Holocene is no option. It is up to our generation to consciously embark on a political and ethical discourse on how best to navigate the Anthropocene, with a view toward effective, equitable, and legitimate systems of Earth system governance that range from local politics to planetary-scale institutions and governance.

Notes

1. Crutzen and Stoermer. 2000. "The 'Anthropocene.'"

2. Jan Zalasiewicz et al., "The Anthropocene"; Steffen et al., "The Anthropocene."

3. Overviews in Steffen et al. *Global Change and the Earth System.*

4. Galaz, *Global Environmental Governance, Technology and Politics.*

5. See Gupta, "When Global Is Local."

6. Biermann and Boas, "Preparing for a Warmer World."

7. See in more detail Biermann, *Earth System Governance.*

8. Wapner, "The Changing Nature of Nature."

9. See in more detail Biermann, *Earth System Governance.*

10. See, for example, Bulkeley and Schroeder, "Beyond State/Non-state Divides."

11. Biermann et al., "Down to Earth."

12. Rockström et al., "A Safe Operating Space for Humanity."

13. Galaz et al., "Planetary Boundaries"; Biermann, "Planetary Boundaries and Earth System Governance."

14. See also Biermann et al., "Navigating the Anthropocene."

15. See in more detail Biermann, *Earth System Governance.*

16. Steffen et al., "The Trajectory of the Anthropocene."

17. Mert, *Environmental Governance through Transnational Partnerships*; Pattberg, *Private Institutions and Global Governance*; Pattberg et al., eds., *Public-Private Partnerships for Sustainable Development*.

18. Kalfagianni and Pattberg, "Fishing in Muddy Waters."

19. See also Dauvergne and Lister, *Eco-Business*.

Bibliography

Biermann, Frank. *Earth System Governance: World Politics in the Anthropocene*. Cambridge, MA: MIT Press, 2014.

Biermann, Frank. "Planetary Boundaries and Earth System Governance: Exploring the Links." *Ecological Economics* 81 (2012): 4–9.

Biermann, Frank, Kenneth Abbott, Steinar Andresen, Karin Bäckstrand, Steven Bernstein, Michele M. Betsill, Harriet Bulkeley, et al. "Navigating the Anthropocene: Improving Earth System Governance." *Science* 335, no. 6074 (2012): 1306–1307.

Biermann, Frank, Xuemei Bai, Ninad Bondre, Wendy Broadgate, Chen-Tung Arthur Chen, Pauline Dube, Jan Willem Erisman, Marion Glaser, Sandra van der Hel, Maria Carmen Lemos, Sybil Seitzinger, and Karen C. Seto. "Down to Earth: Contextualizing the Anthropocene." *Global Environmental Change: Human and Policy Dimensions* (forthcoming).

Biermann, Frank, and Ingrid Boas. "Preparing for a Warmer World: Towards a Global Governance System to Protect Climate Refugees." *Global Environmental Politics* 10, no. 1 (2010): 60–88.

Bulkeley, Harriet, and Heike Schroeder. "Beyond State/Non-state Divides: Global Cities and the Governing of Climate Change." *European Journal of International Relations* 18 (2011): 743–66.

Crutzen, Paul J. "The Anthropocene: Geology of Mankind." *Nature* 415 (2002): 23.

Crutzen, Paul J., and Eugene F. Stoermer. "The 'Anthropocene.'" *IGBP Newsletter* 41 (2000): 17–18.

Dauvergne, Peter, and Jane Lister. *Eco-Business: A Big-Brand Takeover of Sustainability*. Cambridge, MA: MIT Press, 2013.

Galaz, Victor. *Global Environmental Governance, Technology and Politics: The Anthropocene Gap*. Cheltenham: Edgar Elgar, 2014.

Galaz, Victor, Frank Biermann, Beatrice Crona, Derk Loorbach, Carl Folke, Per Olsson, Måns Nilsson, Jeremy Allouche, Åsa Persson, and Gunilla Reischl. "Planetary

Boundaries: Exploring the Challenges for Global Environmental Governance." *Current Opinion in Environmental Sustainability* 4, no. 1 (2012): 80–87.

Gupta, Aarti. "When Global Is Local: Negotiating Safe Use of Biotechnology." In *Earthly Politics: Local and Global in Environmental Governance*, edited by Sheila Jasanoff and Marybeth Long, 127–48. Cambridge, MA: MIT Press, 2004.

Kalfagianni, Agni, and Philipp Pattberg. "Fishing in Muddy Waters: Exploring the Conditions for Effective Governance of Fisheries and Aquaculture." *Marine Policy* 38 (2013): 124–32.

Mert, Ayşem. *Environmental Governance through Transnational Partnerships: A Discourse Theoretical Study*. Cheltenham: Edward Elgar, 2014.

Pattberg, Philipp. *Private Institutions and Global Governance: The New Politics of Environmental Sustainability*. Cheltenham: Edward Elgar, 2007.

Pattberg, Philipp, Frank Biermann, Sander Chan, and Ayşem Mert, eds. *Public-Private Partnerships for Sustainable Development: Emergence, Influence, and Legitimacy*. Cheltenham, UK: Edward Elgar, 2012.

Rockström, Johan, Will Steffen, Kevin Noone, Åsa Persson, F. Stuart Chapin, Eric F. Lambin, Timothy M. Lenton, et al. "A Safe Operating Space for Humanity." *Nature* 461 (2009): 472–75.

Steffen, Will, Angelina Sanderson, Peter D. Tyson, Jill Jäger, Pamela A. Matson, Berrien Moore III, Frank Oldfield, Katherine Richardson, Hans-Joachim Schellnhuber, B. L. Turner II, and Robert J. Wasson. 2004. *Global Change and the Earth System: A Planet under Pressure*. New York: Springer.

Steffen, Will, Wendy Broadgate, Lisa Deutsch, Owen Gaffney, and C. Ludwig. "The Trajectory of the Anthropocene: The Great Acceleration." *Anthropocene Review* (2015). doi:10.1177/2053019614564785

Steffen, Will, Jacques Grinevald, Paul Crutzen, and John McNeill. "The Anthropocene: Conceptual and Historical Perspectives." *Philosophical Transactions of the Royal Society A* 369 (2011): 842–67.

Wapner, Paul. "The Changing Nature of Nature: Environmental Politics in the Anthropocene." *Global Environmental Politics* 14, no. 4 (2014): 36–54.

Zalasiewicz, Jan, Mark Williams, Alan Haywood, and Michael Ellis. "The Anthropocene: A New Epoch of Geological Time?" *Philosophical Transactions of the Royal Society A* 369 (2011): 835–41.

Contributors

Erik Assadourian is a Senior Fellow at the Worldwatch Institute, and has directed four State of the World reports, including *State of the World 2013: Is Sustainability Still Possible?* Over his 14 years with Worldwatch, he has researched many sustainability trends, including consumerism, corporate responsibility, degrowth, cultural change, ecological ethics, and sustainable communities.

Frank Biermann is Professor of Global Sustainability Governance with the Copernicus Institute of Sustainable Development at Utrecht University, The Netherlands, and visiting professor of Earth System Governance at Lund University, Sweden. He also chairs the Earth System Governance Project, a global transdisciplinary research network. Biermann specializes in the study of global environmental politics, with emphasis on climate negotiations, UN reform, global adaptation governance, public-private governance mechanisms, the role of science, and North-South relations. Among other honors, he has won a Societal Impact Award for his "path-breaking research on global environmental policy." His most recent book is *Earth System Governance: World Politics in the Anthropocene* (MIT Press 2014).

Wil Burns is Co-Director of the Forum for Climate Engineering Assessment in the School of International Service at American University. Formerly, he served as Director of the Energy Policy & Climate program at Johns Hopkins University. He holds a Ph.D. in International Environmental Law from the University of Wales-Cardiff School of Law.

Ken Conca is a Professor of International Relations in the School of International Service at American University. His teaching and research focus on global environmental governance; environment, conflict, and peacebuilding; water politics and policy; and the United Nations. He is the author/editor of several books on these and related topics, including

Governing Water, Confronting Consumption, Environmental Peacemaking, and the widely used teaching anthology *Green Planet Blues*. His most recent book is *An Unfinished Foundation: The United Nations and Global Environmental Governance* (Oxford University Press, 2015).

Peter Dauvergne is a Professor of International Relations at the University of British Columbia. His research interests include the environmental politics of social movements, corporations, and consumption. Recent books include *The Shadows of Consumption* (2008), *Paths to a Green World* (2nd ed., 2011, with J. Clapp), *Timber* (2011, with J. Lister), *Eco-Business* (2013, with J. Lister), and *Protest Inc.* (2014, with G. LeBaron).

Daniel Deudney is an Associate Professor of Political Science at Johns Hopkins University. He has written extensively on IR theory and global issues, notably nuclear weapons, the environment, and outer space. His book, *Bounding Power: Republican Security Theory from the Polis to the Global Village* (Princeton, 2007) received the Book of the Decade Award from the International Studies Association.

Navroz K. Dubash is a Senior Fellow at the Centre for Policy Research in Delhi, India, and coordinator of the Climate Initiative. His research and policy interests include climate change policy and governance at subnational, national and international scales, the political economy of energy and water, the emergence of the regulatory state in the developing world and the role of civil society in global environmental governance. His current research focuses on governance mechanisms to operationalize "co-benefits" in the context of national climate policy.

Richard Falk is Albert G. Milbank Professor of International Law and Practice Emeritus, at Princeton University and currently Research Fellow, at the Orfalea Center of Global Studies, UCSB. He was UN Special Rapporteur for Occupied Palestine, 2008-2014. For the last several years he has been Director of the project on Climate Change, Human Rights, and the Future of Democracy. In 1972 he published *This Endangered Planet: Prospects and Proposals for Human Survival*. His most recent books are *Humanitarian Intervention and Legitimacy Wars* (2014), *Palestine: The Legitimacy of Hope* (2015), and *Chaos & Counterrevolution: After the Arab Spring* (2015). Since 2008 he has been annually nominated for the Nobel Peace Prize.

Joyeeta Gupta is Professor of Environment and Development in the Global South at the Amsterdam Institute for Social Science Research of the University of Amsterdam and is also Professor at the UNESCO-IHE Institute for

Water Education in Delft. She is editor-in-chief of the journal *International Environmental Agreements: Politics, Law and Economics.*

Maria Ivanova is an international relations and environmental policy scholar specializing in governance and sustainability. Her research focuses on international environmental institutions and their performance, environmental sustainability, and the science-policy interface. She is Associate Professor of Global Governance at the John W. McCormack Graduate School of Policy and Global Studies at the University of Massachusetts Boston where she also co-directs the Center for Governance and Sustainability. She serves on the UN Secretary-General's Scientific Advisory Board.

Peter J. Jacques directs the Political Ecology Lab and teaches global environmental politics at the University of Central Florida. His most recent book is *Sustainability: The Basics* (Routledge, 2015).

Sikina Jinnah is an Assistant Professor of International Relations at American University's School of International Service. Her first book, *Post-Treaty Politics: Secretariat Influence in Global Environmental Governance* (MIT Press, 2014), won the International Studies Association's 2016 Harold and Margaret Sprout Award for best book in international environmental affairs. Her research has also been published in several scholarly journals, including: *Global Environmental Politics, The Journal of Environment and Development, Environmental Research Letters, Berkeley Journal of International Law Publicist, Georgetown International Environmental Law Review,* and *Science.*

Karen T. Litfin has been on the Political Science and Environmental Studies faculty at the University of Washington since 1991. Her books include *Ozone Discourses: Science and Politics in Global Environmental Cooperation* (Columbia University Press, 1994) and *The Greening of Sovereignty* (MIT Press, 1998). In her research and teaching, she endeavors to integrate the cognitive, emotive, and practical dimensions of sustainability. That commitment led her to write a book about her travels to ecovillages around the world: *Ecovillages: Lessons for Sustainable Community* (Polity Press, 2014.)

Michael F. Maniates is Professor of Social Science and Head of Studies of Environmental Studies at Yale-NUS College in Singapore. His research focuses on sustainable consumption, framings of power and politics in contemporary environmentalism, and the dynamics of undergraduate environmental-studies education. Many know his work from *Confronting Consumption* (MIT Press, 2002), and *The Environmental Politics of Sacrifice* (MIT Press, 2010).

Elizabeth Mendenhall is a graduate student of Political Science at Johns Hopkins University, and is currently writing a dissertation on the politics of international governance in the global commons, including the ocean, atmosphere, outer space, and the electromagnetic spectrum. She has also written on contemporary Arctic politics.

Simon Nicholson is Assistant Professor and Director of the Global Environmental Politics program in the School of International Service at American University. His work centers on global environmental governance, global food politics, and the politics of emerging technologies, with a focus most recently on climate engineering. He is co-editor, with Paul Wapner, of *Global Environmental Politics: From Person to Planet* (Routledge, 2015).

Kate O'Neill is Associate Professor in the Department of Environmental Science, Policy and Management at UC Berkeley and co-editor of the MIT Press journal *Global Environmental Politics*. She is author of *Waste Trading Among Rich Nations: Building a New Theory of Environmental Regulation* (MIT Press, 2000) and *The Environment and International Relations* (Cambridge University Press, 2009, currently in preparation for 2nd edition).

Judith Shapiro directs the Natural Resources and Sustainable Development Dual MA program at American University's School of International Service. She is the author of numerous books on China, including *Mao's War against Nature* (Cambridge, 2001) and *China's Environmental Challenges* (Polity, 2012, Second Edition 2016).

Paul Wapner is Professor of Global Environmental Politics in the School of International Service at American University. His research focuses on environmental ethics, climate suffering, global environmental activism, and contemplative environmentalism. His books include *Living through the End of Nature: The Future of American Environmentalism*, and *Environmental Activism and World Civic Politics*.

Oran R. Young is Professor Emeritus at the Bren School of Environmental Science and Management at the University of California (Santa Barbara). He works on theoretical issues pertaining to governance as a social function as well as applied issues relating to climate change, the oceans, and the polar regions. His current research focuses on governing complex systems. He is a long-time member of the global change research community and has played numerous roles in strengthening the dialogue between science and policy with regard to policy issues.

Index